Sex in Revolution

Sex in Revolution

Gender, Politics, and Power
in Modern Mexico

Edited by

JOCELYN OLCOTT,

MARY KAY VAUGHAN,

AND GABRIELA CANO

Foreword by

CARLOS MONSIVÁIS

Duke University Press   Durham & London   2006

© 2006 Duke University Press
All rights reserved
Printed in the United States of America on acid-free paper ∞
Designed by Katy Clove
Typeset in Adobe Garamond by Keystone Typesetting, Inc.
Library of Congress Cataloging-in-Publication Data
appear on the last printed page of this book.

Frontispiece: Guillermo Kahlo, "Frida poses in men's clothing with family, 1927."
Photo, courtesy of Colección Isolda Pinedo Kahlo.

Contents

Acknowledgments

This volume came out of a conference, "*Las Olvidadas*: Gender and Women's History in Postrevolutionary Mexico," held at Yale University in May 2001. We are extremely grateful for the institutional support for that event and this volume provided by Gil Joseph and Beatriz Reifkohl, the Yale Center for Latin American and Iberian Studies, the Yale Center for International and Area Studies, the William and Flora Hewlett Foundation, the Andrew W. Mellon Foundation, and the Edward J. and Dorothy Clarke Kempf Fund.

The discussions at that conference and the papers that emerged from it (some of which have been or are being published elsewhere) all benefited from intense engagement among presenters, commentators, and participants. In particular, we would like to thank Susan Besse, Katherine Bliss, Sarah Buck, Elizabeth Dore, Rob Buffington, Elaine Carey, Deborah Cohen, Matthew Gutmann, Kristin Harper, Elizabeth Hutchison, Tom Klubock, Rachel Kram, Sonya Michel, Stephanie Mitchell, Carmen Ramos, Marta Rocha, Karen Rosemblatt, Jeffrey Rubin, Nicole Sanders, Eileen Suárez-Findlay, Ageeth Sluis, Heidi Tinsman, Ann Varley, and Peter Winn.

Paul Liffman and Tanya Huntington provided translation assistance for the essays originally written in Spanish.

Finally, we express our deepest thanks to Duke University Press Senior Editor Valerie Millholland for her unwavering support of and patience with this volume, as with so many others related to Latin America. We are also grateful to Miriam Angress, Mark Mastromarino, Katie Courtland,

and Erin Hathaway of the press for their diligent work and to the three anonymous readers who carefully reviewed the manuscript and offered thoughtful, constructive suggestions.

ACKNOWLEDGMENTS

Foreword

When Gender Can't Be Seen amid the Symbols:

Women and the Mexican Revolution

CARLOS MONSIVÁIS

M ary Kay Vaughan, Jocelyn Olcott, and Gabriela Cano have com-
piled a series of essays (investigations, thematic incursions) on
women, gender, and the Mexican Revolution. This anthology touches on
a wide range of themes: female colonels in the revolution, machismo
applied with scissor snips in Mexico City, the cinematographic treatment
of indigenous women, divorce in conservative circles, women's education,
the construction of new families, labor-union life, rationalized sex, activism among women in Catholic and rural organizations, and sexism in the
Popular Front. Despite the variety, the book offers a complex, coherent
panorama, energetically distancing itself from generalizations. It is well
known that God, the devil, and attentive readers are in the details.

The Beginning before the Beginning:
Feminists from the Start

A welcome was extended to feminism by way of ridicule and hostility and,
what's more, it came relatively late. The society created by the 1857 Constitution and 1860 Reform Laws rendered inadmissible any female participation outside the "holy zone" (the bedroom, the kitchen, household

chores, Mass, the confessional). This, despite the fact that women had been demanding civil rights since 1821, demands invigorated by the liberal cause. But the social gaze did not take them into account, instead erasing and silencing them. There were exceptions. Toward the end of the nineteenth century, for example, a prophet of sorts mixed mystic hallucinations with radical disturbances: Teresa Urrea, the Saint of Cabora, proclaimed her visions (a medium not recognized in mass communications at that time), acquired disciples, and became a symbol of resistance against injustice. In 1896, Heriberto Frías narrated the uprising in her name carried out by the people of Tomochic, Chihuahua, and the tragic suppression that ensued.

During the nineteenth century and beyond in Mexico City, the country's most free or least intolerant space, groups emerged that passionately upheld the rights of "woman" in the singular (defending the species, but not its members). The members of such groups attended trade-union meetings, participated in strikes—not as leaders but as indispensable activists (who else would feed the strikers?)—and joined the anarchosyndicalist Mexican Liberal Party (Partido Liberal Mexicano, or PLM). Their presence turned out to be inconceivable outside this environment. Patriarchal zeal and its transmutation into a code of reflexes conditioned by families ("A woman who speaks Latin neither marries nor ends well," "An independent woman does not attend Mass") sanctified women's backwardness.[1] During the second half of the nineteenth century, the vast majority of women had no access to education or the public sphere, and because of this, and in pursuit of secularization, Juárez liberals backed certain changes. Thanks to one point in the government program of 1861, women selectively and gradually entered universities, and in the provinces, teacher-training schools were founded "for young ladies." The writer Laureana Wright de Kleinhaus, yearning to expand female spaces and convinced of the emancipatory impulse of education, established Mexico's first "gender" magazine, *Violets of Anáhuac* (*Violetas de Anáhuac*, 1884–87), which, amid a multitude of poems and moralist reflections, demanded women's suffrage and equality for the sexes.

Significant events also took place in the field of labor. The Social Chapter (La Social) sent two women as representatives to the 1876 session of the General Workers' Congress of the Mexican Republic (Congreso General Obrero de la República Mexicana). During the general assembly, according to John M. Hart, the socialist Juan de Mata Rivera opposed female intervention in public affairs and convinced La Social that sending women delegates to the congress set a risky precedent. José Muñúzuri, editor of *The Son of Labor* (*El hijo del trabajo*), persuaded the assembly

CARLOS MONSIVÁIS

otherwise, and for the first time in the history of the Mexican workers' movement, women participated in a national organization.[2]

Inspired by their fathers and brothers, led by exceptional women and men, hundreds of militants embarked on a cultural and political battle that allowed neither machismo nor the Catholic Church. In 1901, for example, the ladies of Cuicatlán, Oaxaca, proclaimed to the ladies of Zitácuaro, "The Mexican woman, who up until now has been the instrument of clumsy passions and an insurmountable obstacle to the violent development of progress due to the effects of the cancerous virus hypocritically spread by religious fanaticism, must rise up like the heroic Boer women who repelled the invaders, united and resolved to combat clericalism as the most cunning and fearsome enemy of our honor, our conscience, our family, and our fatherland."[3] Thus, at the dawn of feminism in Mexico, anticlericalism was fundamental to the feminist perspective, but it escaped society's notice because women's proposals were neither heard nor read.

Feminists also strongly opposed Porfirio Díaz, the autocratic president of Mexico from 1876 to 1880 and 1884 to 1910. Carmen Serdán of Puebla, a member of a family of anarchists and the most eloquent symbol of female anti-Díaz crusaders, died in combat on 20 November 1910, the mythical day at the beginning of the Mexican Revolution on which the populace participated in an armed uprising against the Díaz government. The known revolutionary women were generally middle- and upper-class señoras and señoritas who founded antigovernment clubs and—with no social voice at all—discussed alternatives to the dictatorship. Women from the popular social strata suffered multifaceted violence, which may explain their scant participation in mobilizations; furthermore, their lack of social and labor mobility made them susceptible to disinformation, which was the beginning and end of their depoliticization. In 1904 the first feminist group formed—the Society for the Protection of Women (its very name sanctifying prejudice)—and published the magazine *Mexican Woman* (*La mujer mexicana*) to explain its purpose. The Cosmos International Feminist Society formed soon thereafter, and in 1906, a group called Women Admirers of Juárez demanded legal rights, specifically the right to vote.

The most lucid and combative militants were the anarchosyndicalists of the PLM. In 1895 Juana Gutiérrez de Mendoza, daughter and wife of railroad workers, began her career as a revolutionary agitator and feminist theorist. As a colonel in the Zapatista army, she confronted Emiliano Zapata in an attempt to prevent soldiers' abuse of women. She instilled life into the notion of women's rights by exercising them boldly and with the help of her *compañeros*. As the anarchist Praxedis G. Guerrero stated in November 1910, "Freedom frightens those who do not understand it and those who have made their medium the degradation and misery of others; therefore, the emancipation of women encounters one hundred opponents for each man who defends it or works toward it."[4]

According to the anthropologist Marta Lamas, despite hints of feminist organization, the majority of feminists in the early 1900s did not demand gender rights, preferring to adhere to the ideals of those who initiated in 1910 or 1911 what would later be called the Mexican Revolution: "Already during the Revolution itself, women's participation was intense, not only in terms of traditional supportive tasks (nursing, delivering messages and spying, printing flyers and proclamations, sewing uniforms and flags, distributing weapons, and providing meals, laundering, and other personal services) but also in command of troops, coordinating some major military operations and participating in some high commands of the armed movement (several of them achieving the rank of colonel). During the Revolution, an unavoidable issue was putting a stop to the soldiers' vandalism and protecting women and children."[5] A select few attained positions of leadership, as did Elvia Carrillo Puerto, the sister of a great radical leader, Felipe Carrillo Puerto.

"Corpse, Benito Juárez's. The rest are just dead bodies"

What was "the Mexican Revolution"?[6] A succession and intertwining of stages, factions, and military leaders. The rudimentary ideas and complex arguments that spawned military episodes, extremely cruel massacres, conspiracies, tumultuous violations, sacrifices, deeds, betrayals, accords and discords between different social classes. The Mexican Revolution has been unified in order to be understood as a whole (a trap that facilitates the assimilation of history and the creation of institutions) and has been characterized however the regime pleases, which prohibits understanding its complexity. Yet, even within the realm of generalities, one thing is notorious: women (the gender, the groups, and the enormously dynamic individuals) mean very little in political and social terms and practically nothing when set before the deity of those times: History, an exclusively masculine territory. According to patriarchal doctrine, neither power nor violence nor indubitable valor nor historic lucidity are women's issues. Therefore, in the historical recovery of women's roles in the armed struggle and in institutional life, a common error is to situate women's conduct as if the moment were excessively influenced through their presence in the social consciousness. Although women's participation in the revolution may have been influential in many ways, patriarchy is nothing if not an endless strategy of concealment. During the revolutionary stage from 1910 to 1940 or 1950, to extend the term "Mexican Revolution," women were seen in an ahistoric light; they existed on the margin of the optics of political and social prestige and barely managed to join in "everyday rumor," the rhythm that, because it was secondary, did not form part of History.

The Army of Brave Young Girls Who Followed Them

The female emblem of the revolution is the *soldadera*, or less frequently, the *coronela*, a subject addressed in this collection by Gabriela Cano. The figure of the soldadera forms part of the picturesque quality ascribed to the revolution and corresponds to a capacity for wonder that the factious struggle maintained as a mental-health strategy. Thus, for example, in *Mexico, Insane Asylum* (*México manicomio*) Salvador Quevedo y Zubieta described the arrival of Victoriano Huerta's conquering army in the capitol, an arrival contemplated by the entire city.

> The "column" deteriorated into a string of armed wanderers. Plenty of ammunition, of course; a surplus of cartridges to make up for the lack of uniforms. Up to three magazine belts stuck to raw cotton cloth, two of them crossed over the chest like swordbelts, another tightened at the waist. Cartridge belts completely covered the women, militarized with impressive ranks: corporals, sergeants, lieutenants. . . . Many of them on horseback, with great, wide-brimmed straw hats, lashing at the flanks with blows from their bare heels; some of them on foot, carrying their rifles and brats; others on carts, flowing into the Zócalo via Cinco de Mayo Avenue, burdened with sleeping and cooking gear. There they paraded in gypsy-like fashion, the *metates* [grinding stones] of the division.[7]

The women: the ones who brandished rifles and metates, helpmates in war and kitchen patrol. More than through literature, their protagonism stems from the fact that they set in relief the presence of the *soldados*. That is what really draws attention, the world of the *adelitas*, the *valentinas*, the *marietas*. And their triumphant song is "La Adelita."

On top of a rugged mountain chain a regiment was found camping,	En lo alto de una abrupta serranía acampado se encontraba un regimiento,
and a young girl who courageously followed them,	y una moza que valiente los seguía
crazy in love with the sergeant.	locamente enamorada del sargento.

Foreword

Adelita was popular with the troops,	Popular entre la tropa era Adelita,
the woman the sergeant idolized,	la mujer que el sargento idolatraba,
aside from brave, she was pretty	que además de ser valiente era bonita
and even the colonels respected her.	y hasta el mismo coronel la
	respetaba.
And it was heard that he said,	Y se oía que decía.
the one who loved her so:	aquel que tanto la quería:
if Adelita were to run off with another	si Adelita se fuera con otro
I would follow by land and by sea,	la seguiría por tierra y por mar,
if by sea, on a battleship,	si por mar en un buque de guerra,
if by land, on a military train.	si por tierra en un tren militar.

"La Adelita" is a great classic text (melody included) of daily life in the army. At the center is a heroine, a desirable woman who is recognized in combat, uplifted by the community, and adored by a military man who no longer lets fly with "mine or nobody's," accepting that by all military means available he will seek out the ungrateful woman, either seducing her or appealing to her coquetry and her desire for respectability.

If Adelita wanted to be my girl,	Si Adelita quisiera ser mi novia,
and if Adelita were my bride,	y si Adelita fuera mi mujer,
I would buy her a silk dress	le compraría un vestido de seda
to take her dancing at headquarters.	para llevarla a bailar al cuartel.

There are thousands or tens of thousands of rumors regarding Adelita's true identity, and for a long while no self-respecting Mexican man or woman lacked a personal or family testimony about her ("She was a lady who lived across from my mother's house . . ."). But these are anecdotes. What is definitive is the way a song can evoke an ambience of love and loss, becoming the emblematic seal of daily life in the revolution.

One night when the guard returned	Una noche en que la escolta regresaba
carrying the sergeant among its ranks,	conduciendo entre sus filas al sargento,
a prayer was heard in the camp	por la voz de una mujer que sollozaba
from the voice of a sobbing woman.	la plegaria se escuchó en el campamento.
Upon hearing her, the sergeant, fearful	Al oírla el sargento temeroso
of losing his beloved forever,	de perder para siempre a su adorada,

CARLOS MONSIVÁIS

hiding his emotions under his collar	ocultando su emoción bajo el embozo
sang to his beloved	a su amada le cantó de esta manera.
and he who loved her so	aquel que tanto la quería
was heard to say:	y se oía que decía:
If I should die on the campaign	Y si acaso yo muero en campaña
and my body should be buried,	y mi cadáver lo van a sepultar,
Adelita, I beg you by God,	Adelita, por Dios te lo ruego
weep for me with your eyes.	que con tus ojos me vayas a llorar.

To the amorous, sexual and bellicose functions of the soldadera, another indispensable purpose must be added: the primordial condition of indebtedness on the part of the survivor who carries memories from the battlefields, of the companion who bears witness to an honorable death, as consigned (in a manner of speaking) through the song "La Valentina."

Valentina, Valentina,	Valentina, Valentina,
I surrender at your feet:	rendido estoy a tus pies,
if they are to kill me tomorrow	si me han de matar mañana
let me be killed in one blow.	que me maten de una vez.

Revolutionary narrative and a deluge of eyewitness accounts humanize the female combatants of highest military rank because of their renunciation of the "feminine condition." Only once they are "masculinized" do they fulfill the requisites of military life. This is depicted most notoriously in *Angustias, the Dark-Skinned Woman* (*La negra Angustias*), Francisco Rojas González's 1944 novel about a female colonel who is victorious in leading the troops but defeated by love. Once the struggle is over, Angustias is dissolved, transformed once again into a submissive shadow who carries meals to her man, a construction worker. The "redemption" of femininity is also achieved through crime, as witnessed by Nellie Campobello's magnificent vignette in *Cartridge: Stories of the Struggle in Northern Mexico* (1931).

Nacha Ceniceros

Near Chihuahua, at station X, a big encampment of Villa's forces. All is quiet and Nacha is crying. She was in love with a young colonel named Gallardo, from Durango. She was a coronela and had a pistol and wore braids. She cried as she listened to the advice of an old soldadera. She began to clean her pistol in her tent and was quite distracted when a shot went off.

In another tent, Gallardo was sitting next to a table; he was chatting with a woman; the shot misfired by Nacha in her tent hit Gallardo in the head and he fell down dead.

"They've killed little Gallardo, my General."

Horrified, Villa said, "Shoot him."

"It was a woman, General."

"Shoot her."

"Nacha Ceniceros."

"Shoot her."

She cried for her beloved, she put her arms over her face, her black braids hanging down when the volley hit her.

She made a pretty picture, indelible for all those watching the firing squad. Today, an anthill stands where they say she is buried.[8]

Soldaderas were not romantic figures, and in "The Soldadera in the Mexican Revolution: War and Men's Illusions," Elizabeth Salas warned against idealization.[9] The soldaderas' lives were opposed to romantic notions. They went to war because "their men" were there, because they were recruited by force. They walked while men rode, or they perched on the rooftops of trains while men journeyed inside boxcars. They accompanied the armies in charge of supplying provisions and food. They gathered the wounded and buried the dead. They manufactured crosses with stones or maguey cactus thorns. And they fought in the countryside with energy and fearlessness, as exemplified by Petra Herrera, a Maderista combatant who, dressed and rebaptized as "Pedro," dynamited bridges and led dangerous missions; after her boldness in the capture of Torreón in 1911, she earned the rank of a *corrido* (popular ballad).

The brave Petra Herrera	La valiente Petra Herrera
threw herself into combat	al combate se lanzó
always being the first,	siendo siempre la primera
it was she who opened fire	ella el fuego comenzó.

The soldaderas suffered rape, rejection, and victimization to such a degree that in 1925, Secretary of Defense General Joaquín Amaro called them "the main cause of vice, diseases, crime, and disorder" and ordered them expelled from barracks.[10] Most of them came from poverty and misery and lived with discrimination and without rights. They were indigenous and mestiza, born in villages and small towns. Nevertheless, their contributions were ample, as captured in photographs (kept in the Casasola Archives), wherein they gaze on their men or prepare to descend from trains, seeming amazed by the miracle of traveling from one town to the next. They were the force that the makers of History ignore in order to avoid complications.

"Oh, that's great! I finally got rid of that pest!"

Violence brought with it more "relative" morality, similar to that of the dictatorship ruled by the governing class and hacienda owners (in the unlikely event that these were not one and the same), but already pervading the entire social spectrum.[11] During the first long stage of the revolution, culminating in the Maximato, the era of Plutarco Elías Calles (1929–34), literature ruled the collective imaginary, then the product of legends, echoes of public opinion, and testimonial narratives. Here the role of women was ghostly, only occasionally being presented in the foreground, as in the most read revolutionary narrative, *The Underdogs* (*Los de abajo* [1915]). The author, Mariano Azuela, a doctor who participated in the Villa movement, went into exile in El Paso, Texas, horrified by the barbarity. There he wrote his masterpiece, which includes two female characters: Camila, virtuous, noble, and in love with an opportunist cad; and La Pintada, or Painted Woman, a novelty in terms of her temperament and unlimited greed, opposed to any habitual meekness or resignation. She gets her men, belts out her opinions, and commits murder not so much out of jealousy as much as to better defend her property rights. The tragedy occurs within minutes. Demetrio, the leader of the unit, tells La Pintada that she will no longer accompany them.

> "You're not coming with us anymore."
>
> "What?!" she gasped.
>
> "You can stay here or go wherever you damn well please, but not with us."
>
> "What are you saying?" she exclaimed in astonishment. "You mean, you're getting rid of me? Ha, ha, ha. . . . Well, what the . . . What kind of man are you if you believe that woman's gossip . . . !"
>
> And Pintada proceeded to insult Camila, Demetrio, Luis Cervantes, and anyone else who came to mind with such energy and originality that the soldiers heard insults and profanity they'd never even imagined.
>
> Demetrio waited a long time patiently; she showed no sign of stopping, and he said to a soldier quite calmly,
>
> "Throw this drunken woman out."
>
> "Güero Margarito, love of my life! Come and defend me from these . . . ! Come on, Güero dear. . . . Come show them you're a real man, and they're nothing but sons of a . . . !"
>
> And she gesticulated, kicked, and shouted.[12]

Incapable of withstanding humiliation and what she considers to be deprivation, La Pintada stabs Camila to death. Demetrio immediately orders that she be killed, then relents and lets her go because—it is implied —a woman is never responsible for her destiny. But La Pintada's character was a warning: without attracting notice, the traditional mentality of women from different sectors, already opposed to the most atrocious forms of feudal oppression, had begun to break apart. Those who were ready to fight and die fighting and those who studied and read about rights rejected customs of submission. Thus, in 1913, for example, women arrested for their opposition to the Victoriano Huerta dictatorship established in prison the Daughters of Cuauhtémoc (Las Hijas de Cuauhtémoc), an organization of revolutionary struggle demanding women's rights.

The Divorce Law of 1914 was of great significance (if women can separate from men, autonomy is already conceivable). And thanks to the exceptional interest of the socialist governor of Yucatán, General Salvador Alvarado, feminism appeared almost formally in 1915, when he announced the First Feminist Congress (Primer Congreso Feminista) in Mérida. Despite the "lyric" overtones of the texts read at that gathering (almost as if such language were demanded from "the women"), many of the proposals were highly critical of sex discrimination. The congress discussed the anti-feminine prejudices of Mexican society and spread the democratic and socialist ideals proclaimed by Alvarado's government.

In 1917 the new constitution of the republic did not concede to women the right to vote and be elected; the national project outlined therein excluded them from exercising citizenship and, by omission or commission, denied their aptitude to govern, declaring them to be social and political "minors." They were too weak, their thinking too elementary, and they couldn't neglect the home given that from the dawning of independent Mexico or of the national tradition, femininity had been confined to "the domestic." (As Saint Teresa said, "The Lord walks among the stewpots.") Institutions created on and against the individual excluded women from the nation-state. Because they were absent from civil structures, their role in visible development continued to be more or less symbolic even after 1953, when President Adolfo Ruiz Cortines, trusting in the alliance of the Institutional Revolutionary Party (Partido Revolucionario Institucional, or PRI) with the Catholic hierarchy, granted women the right to vote. A more realistic insertion occurred once women's presence in the production apparatus became impossible to ignore; albeit still overshadowed by distrust of their capacities and by the governing cabal's intention to manipulate them, their presence was already marked by the irreversible nature of the advance.

CARLOS MONSIVÁIS

Women on the Right

Conservative women, the guardians of tradition and "eternal values," have been studied insufficiently. During the nineteenth and twentieth centuries, traditionalists were the animating force on the right and the emotional shelter of the far right, as is apparent in *The Edge of the Storm* (*Al filo del agua*) by Agustín Yáñez, written in 1945 and published in 1947. The chapter "Preparatory Act" offers eloquent images of a town (a religious culture) where femininity is spectral, transformed into an appendage of religious devotion and household slavery: "Village of black-robed women. At night, at the first stir of dawn, throughout the long course of the morning, in the heat of the noonday sun, in the evening light—strong, radiant, colorless, long-suffering—old women, matrons, maidens in the bloom of youth, young girls; they may be seen on the church steps, in the deserted streets, inside the shops, and glimpsed through a few, the very few, furtively open doors."[13]

The novel is called *The Edge of the Storm* because it takes place in 1908 or 1909, just before the revolutionary storm and during the final stages of the "golden age" of clerical control through religious organizations.

> The pious activities of old and young, of men and women, find expression in many societies. But the two most important are the Association of the Good Death and the Daughters of Mary. The Daughters of Mary, to a great extent, in fact almost exclusively, shape the character of the village, exercising a rigid discipline over dress, movements, speech, thoughts, and feelings of the young girls, bringing them up in a conventional existence that turns the village itself into a kind of convent. Any girl reaching the age of fifteen without belonging to the Association of the black dress and blue ribbon with its silver medal, the black dress with the high neck, long sleeves and skirt reaching the ankles, is regarded with grave disapproval. In this Association, all vie with one another in jealous vigilance, and expulsion from it constitutes a scandalous blot on the reputation that follows one through life.
>
> There is a strong segregation of the sexes. In church, the Gospel side is reserved for men, and the devout female sex occupies the Epistle side. It is not considered proper for men and women, even when related, to stand chatting in the street or doorway, not even for a moment. When a meeting occurs, brief greetings are exchanged, all the briefer if the man or woman is alone; but this rarely happens, especially if the woman is unmarried, since then she is always accompanied by another woman.[14]

Society under the dictatorship was ill prepared for the emergence of women, be they soldaderas or union members, coronelas or suffragettes;

and the Catholic clergy and the right considered any feminine liberty to be monstrous. However, the Cristero War (1926–29), instigated by an army created at the behest of Catholic fundamentalism, brought to the surface the bellicose will of traditionalist women capable of rashness, fury, sacrifice, and decisive extermination. But their loyalty and devotion were not worth much: conservatism pushed them to one side and treated them like "one of the herd." They were not heroines; they were churchgoers who did not fear death so much as excommunication. The only attempt to mythologize them came from liberal novelist Jesús Goytortúa Sánchez in *Pensativa* (1944), whose protagonist is a fervent believer and a Cristero general.

> "Chacha," Cornelio said to me, "here is the *generala*."
> You cannot imagine how I felt. There she was, our saint, the invincible one, our Joan of Arc, the one who makes the government soldiers tremble. How brave and fearless the *generala* was!
> "Was she handsome?" I asked Chacha.
> "She was ugly," Basilio exclaimed. "Violent."
> "She looked beautiful to me," Genoveva clarified. "To me, there has never been such a beautiful woman as she."
> "Not even Pensativa?" I demanded.
> Not even Pensativa. This one possessed a mystic, saintly beauty. She was Joan of Arc, she was the defender of the Fatherland and the Faith, the emissary of God sent to conquer the persecutors of freedom of speech. I did not dare embrace her, and I kissed her hands.[15]

The revolution confirmed the fragility of provincial middle-class women, not only because of the conditions of war but because they were raised to delight in the subjugation that protected them. They were perhaps servile and decorative—they would have put it differently but quite acutely—but they did not understand the reality beyond their walls. The revolution—known to them as the Uprising, a whirlwind of passions of the soil—devastated them, and the only opposition they possessed was the shield of their beliefs. Celia Herrera described this cultivated fragility in her testimonial text "Life in Parral: Dreaded nightmare" (La vida en Parral: Tenebrosa pesadilla), which related the experience of women and girls who took refuge for weeks in 1916 in the home of a woman they had never met.

> There, our room was a great gallery in which we fit everyone's beds. We even had space to set up an altar of sorts, before which we would pray for hours and hours, every afternoon; we would pray five or fifteen Rosaries; the *triduum* to

the Sacred Heart of Jesus in the morning of the first day, at midday on the second, and in the afternoon of the third; major litanies, prayers for blessed souls, the Magnificat, the Three Necessities . . . and since even in our "hide-out" news reached us that this person or that had been imprisoned, when we were finished with our prayers we would add an Our Father for Mrs. Julia Baca de López, . . . another for Mr. Alejandro Ricaud . . . , etc.

Miss Meléndez was the principal of the public school I attended. This remained closed for long periods, for months. Classes were interrupted many times by frequent alarms that often turned out to be false. Some woman would arrive at the school looking for her daughters: "Miss, I've come for my daughters because there's a lot of alarm; they say that they're coming . . . everyone has already started stocking up on provisions . . . they are already closing the shops . . . please, Miss, now, let my darlings come with me. . . ."

I would say this to her without being able to control a strong trembling in my entire body, with pale lips, with anxiety, with such a horrified stare that the teachers themselves were infected. Once the other schoolgirls realized they would start in, "Miss, miss, the mother of so-and-so already came . . . I think there's an alarm . . . let me go home, I live far away. . . ." And instantly, as if by electricity, the news would spread across the entire school and the crying would begin, the tears would come down in torrents, the eldest would look for their little sisters, and some of us would escape by climbing out of windows, or we would trample each other on the stairs, or we would jump down them in a single leap . . . and all our supplies would be scattered because in the rush, no one would carefully put her things away. And in the midst of these histrionics the voice of Miss Meléndez would scarcely be heard saying, "Calm down, girls, calm down."[16]

In the revolutionary narrative that spans Mariano Azuelo's *Andrés Pérez, Maderista* (1911) and Elena Garro's *Recollections of Things to Come* (*Los recuerdos del porvenir* [1963]), the role of women is generally predictable and circular. In *Recollections of Things to Come*, Garro describes the mood during those years from a man's perspective: "Unhappiness, like physical pain, fills the minutes. . . . To disperse those petrified days all I had was the ineffectual illusion of violence, and cruelty was practiced furiously on the women, stray dogs, and Indians. We lived within a quiet time and the people, like actors in a tragedy, were caught in that arrested moment. It was in vain that they performed acts that were more and more bloody. We had abolished time."[17]

The right and the clergy did not take women, "Servants of the Lord," into account, but the "abolition of time," or if one prefers, the exclusion of History in the sense of State and society, did not impede the devotion of these determined women, who were prepared to confront the power of the State and were as courageous as they were ruthless. One would look in vain for any mention of women in right-wing associations and groups, whose ideologies equated full humanity with virility; women were conceded only the talents of reproduction, of raising and nourishing the species. That, and that they unreservedly comply with the strict norms of life ordained by dogma, the guide of the nation and of conduct: "Catholicism," according to Sinarquista leader Salvador Abascal, "is the father and essence of Mexico, but as for men, Hernán Cortés is the founding father of our land."[18]

The history within the reach of women who formed part of a right wing that declared itself counterrevolutionary was a history corrupted by the abolition of theocracy, its ideal form of government. More specifically, the far right considered the nineteenth-century liberal reform to be the cause of death of the Mexican nation. Thus, Benito Juárez was the devil incarnate to them, a "traitor to our nationality." (When well-born ladies from the provinces—a very combative species when their values were challenged—got up to go to the bathroom, they said, "I am going to visit Juárez.")

Women on the right accepted without hesitation decrees such as the "Ten Norms of Sinarquista Life," a continuation of parochial teachings: "1) Deny yourself what is easy and comfortable in life. . . . 3) Do not expect recompense or gratification. 4) Guard all your passions if you truly want to save Mexico. . . . 8) You must have a deep faith in victory. Understand that this struggle cannot be defeated and that blood and suffering will give us victory."[19]

Once political defeat became inevitable, women on the right concentrated their efforts on practicing religious teachings and promoting censorship.

The Emergence of Feminism

In 1919, the Mexican Feminist Council (Consejo Feminista Mexicano) was established "for the political, economic, or social emancipation of woman." It promoted mutual aid and published a biweekly magazine, *Woman* (*La mujer*). In 1920, a congress of female workers and peasants convened, and in 1923 the First National Feminist Congress (Primer Congreso Nacional Feminista) met in Mexico City with 110 delegates and feminist claims: the right to vote, a nondiscriminatory sexual morality, child care, public dining halls, coeducation for young women, and protection for domestic workers. Perhaps as a result of the First National Feminist Congress, the governor of San Luis Potosí soon conceded the right to vote, and in 1924 the governor of Chiapas followed his example.

During the 1920s, the federal government and the majority of regional governments wanted to balance the not-so-relative liberalization of customs with an exaltation of the civic and moral "virtues" of Woman. Mother's Day, a commercial celebration that had become a deep-rooted tradition by 1922, was speedily established. The consequences of the Great War (the First World War) and the Mexican Revolution were endless, and feminism, albeit to a small degree, was assisted by the modernity of an already Americanized society as well as by the demand for development. In 1926 Guadalupe Zúñiga de González became the first woman judge in the juvenile court, and in 1929 Palma Guillén was sent to Colombia and to Denmark as Mexico's first female ambassador. The anachronism of the Civil Code (passed in 1884) was so evident that in 1928 Calles's administration ordered a new one. Thus, before attaining equality in politics, women gained equality before the law.

Public school teachers merit a chapter of their own. Courageously and selflessly defending causes that benefited the people and women (what was then called mystique), tens of thousands of women carried out literacy training and political work from 1920 to 1940. They were promoters, activists for parties and groups. They were martyrs of homicidal "piety" among the mobs of Cristeros and Sinarquistas, as well as victims in the 1930s of fanatical right-wing and clerical opposition to the unsuccessful and bombastic radical project of socialist education and to the necessary project of sexual education. The boldness of these teachers fueled educational secularization—so vital to the nation given that laicism is the gateway to modernity. The Catholic Church unreservedly defended religious education in public schools. Given that teachers were a determining factor in rural schools and cultural missions, many paid for their enthusiasm with beatings, rapes, and murders. *El Machete*, a Communist Party organ, narrated a typical case that occurred in Rita, a town in the municipality of Tacámbaro, Michoacán, where María Salud Morales was killed by fanatics: "The teacher Morales has set an example of integrity and sacrifice. Upon her arrival there, she noted the opposition of a group of fanatics who attempted to scare her off. The teacher, aware of the danger she was in, refused to leave her post; however, she did procure a pistol. . . . On the 16th, they assaulted the teacher inside the school, and, surprising her while she was unarmed, they beat her to death with sticks and stones."[20]

These militants (and martyrs) were feminists in the full sense of the word: workers, educators, and political activists who combined their demands with professional duties. The teacher Hélice Medina tells what took place in the town of Tenabo, Campeche, in April 1937:

> In Tenabo the teachers were expelled with the threat of stripping the women. The municipal president Luciano Muñoz and local police assaulted them with machete blows and bullets. They had to leave on foot to reach Hecelchakan at three in the morning and seek the protection of Pacheco Torres. But the would-be attackers wanted vengeance because they couldn't get their hands on the teachers, so they took their pleasure with the unhappy women of the Sole Front for Women's Rights [Frente Único pro Derechos de la Mujer, FUPDM] and its president, Matilde Cen. She was stripped and beaten as they paraded her through the streets of Tenabo. Is this civilization?[21]

The "Proletarian" Revolution and Its Factory of New Men

The feminists from the 1920s and 1930s were vehement veterans. In defending and promoting their rights, they drew on their persistence (the nerve!) and not much more. The majority belonged or were close to the Communist Party, and their fervor helped them bear the machismo of comrades who saw in women only adelitas, faithful companions unfit for leadership. They were valiant, imaginative, literally willing to hand over their lives, but, according to the high command, this was not reason enough to grant their autonomy. Militant women were barred from important positions and maneuvered into political corners. Their drive and ideas were quashed. In her autobiography, *Benita*, the militant Benita Galeana refers to her experience as a rural woman, cabaret performer, and agitator rejected by her own party's stubbornness.

> As for me, I had managed to pull myself away from the cabaret and to awaken my revolutionary conscience. . . . And it wasn't because the Party bothered itself much to educate its members. On the contrary, I criticize how it ignores the men and women who fight for it. They don't take much time to educate people. I use myself as an example of that. I saw that the most capable and intelligent comrades were those who treated their *compañeras* the worst, scornfully, and without taking the time to educate, betraying the female comrades with other women, just like any petit-bourgeois, yet they were the first to say, "She's a whore!" when a woman found another man.[22]

Because of sectarianism and an esprit that would have liked to have been Bolshevik, the left was opposed to the Mexican Revolution because it was "democratic-bourgeois" and because it oppressed the masses. They were partly right. But they forgot about achievements in education, communication, health, and workers' rights, and failed to take into account social mobility, no matter how selective it was. The left challenged Calles, supported Lázaro Cárdenas, failed to consolidate their strengths, and never seriously considered the participation of their female comrades.

In 1931 the First National Congress of Women Workers and Peasants took place. In 1933 and 1934 the two follow-up congresses convened. Even during his presidential campaign, General Cárdenas encouraged women's organizing. The feminine sector of the National Revolutionary Party (Partido Nacional Revolucionario, or PNR) was organized in 1934, and the Sole Front for Women's Rights, which at its peak boasted 50,000 affiliates, was founded in 1935. Due to its Stalinist internal structure, the PNR ignored or segregated women's groups, and once incorporated into the PNR party structure (between 1938 and 1940), the FUPDM literally disappeared, converted into the "feminine sector," an innocuous letterhead. The feminine sector produced deputies, senators, high officials, and mayors who received their fraction of power under one condition: gratitude toward the men who had awarded them their public existence.

In 1937, President Cárdenas sent a bill to the Chamber of Deputies granting women the right to vote, but it was defeated despite the approval and recommendation of the president of the republic. Politicians argued that the women's vote would strengthen the right due to the clergy's control over their consciences.

In 1940, two confederations were formed: the National Feminine Committee (Comité Nacional Femenino), which supported the presidential candidacy of Manuel Ávila Camacho, and the National Feminine Alliance (Alianza Nacional Feminina), composed of feminine secretariats of the workers' and campesinos' central offices, the Confederation of Popular Organizations (Confederación de Organizaciones Populares), and labor-union federations, including the Confederación de Trabajadores de México (CTM), Confederación Nacional Campesina (CNC), Confederación General de Trabajadores (CGT), Federación de Sindicatos de Trabajadores del Estado (FSTE), and Sindicato Nacional de Trabajadores de la Educación (SNTE). After Mexico entered World War II in 1942, the FUPDM became the Coordinating Committee of Women in Defense of the Fatherland (Comité Coordinador de Mujeres para la Defensa de la Patria). The end of the war brought the establishment of the National Coalition of Women (Bloque Nacional de Mujeres), which became the National Union of Women (Unión Nacional de Mujeres), an organization that typically never called itself feminist, claiming its autonomy from the state and, incapable of mobilization, limiting itself to honor guards in public acts and to a handful of "lyrical" radical speeches with anti-imperialist exhortations utterly lacking in feminist demands. The union abhorred all birth-control projects and was affiliated with a political machine of Stalinist origins: the Women's International Democratic Federation (Federación Internacional de Mujeres Democráticas).

Women "officially" entered public life once the old feminist movement evaporated and radical demands were concealed. In 1953, under President Ruiz Cortines, the previous draft of the constitutional article was amended giving adult female and male citizens the right to vote and be elected. Within an official environment, women's organizations were merely decorative support for the PRI, and few independent groups survived. Any criticism of women's post-revolutionary condition was buried under layers of integrationist demagoguery, and women's contributions through paid labor and the productive apparatus went unrecognized. Mexican capitalism completely ignored feminist demands, and the social, religious, and cultural discourses overvalued and mythologized the traditional roles of mother and housewife (whatever "house" may have meant). This authorized the exploitation of women: much work was temporary, and women were paid lower (apprenticeship) salaries, received no training, and were assigned "double shifts."

The revolution was a historic change. However, by the 1940s the impetus of traditionalist women had faded. They retained the fervor of censorship, but not much else.

"Marieta, don't flirt / because men are just no good, / they promise many gifts / and what they give are only blows"

In her research, Julia Tuñón analyzes female gender representation, particularly of indigenous women, in movies directed by Emilio "El Indio" Fernández.[23] Two films, *María Candelaria* and *Maclovia*, set in the "time out of time" before the revolution, exhibit both the energy and the weaknesses of a vision that ranges from vivid imagery (with the grand aesthetic quality of Gabriel Figueroa's cinematography and the beauty of the leading actors: Dolores del Río, María Félix, Pedro Armendáriz) to stereotypes and the confinement of clichés regarding nation and race. Nonetheless, Mexican film production dedicated to the revolution's racial and social causes and to its armed struggle constructed visions of collective imaginary about the movement with greater credibility than that of books, personal experiences, or textbook History.

CARLOS MONSIVÁIS

With the exception of *The Underdogs* (*Los de abajo*) and Martín Luis Guzmán's books *The Eagle and the Serpent* (*El águila y la serpiente*) and *The Shadow of the Caudillo* (*La sombra del caudillo*), the images that dominate the collective imagination of the revolution come from cinema and songs, in sequences that depict, for example, charging troops and dying heroes, Pancho Villa as either the popular conscience or the unwitting liberator of the people (take your pick!), or the soldadera's apotheosis into a Venus in cartridge belts (María Félix in a series of fantasies about the armed struggle). The lesson, so to speak, was quite clear: the revolution was a man's affair and women formed the decorative background for drawn-out confrontations that resulted in a nation of men with an attached reserve of women.

But the realm of spectacles, the liveliest during the dead times of combat, did demand the presence of women, divas, cabaret stars, chorus girls, the artifices of corridos and "ultra-Mexican" songs. During the revolution, frivolous or music-hall theater was the calling card of a light-hearted and fascinating capital city that transformed the revolutionaries' mentality. Within this environment, its symbol was a singer of couplets and songs with double-entendre lyrics: María Conesa, also known as La Gatita Blanca (the White Kitten), a cabaret star who started in the theater in the early twentieth century and became a symbol of impunity in the hour of the ruthless revolutionaries. In effect, only her status permitted her, once she finished singing, to descend among the audience, enter General Pancho Villa's box, and, with a knife, cut the buttons from his uniform.[24] Only she had license to mock the triumphant army in the presence of enthusiastic generals.

My father was a glorious soldier,	Fue mi padre un glorioso soldado,
who made general by the time he was thirty	que a los treinta llegó a general,
because he was there on May Fifth	pues estuvo en el Cinco de Mayo
and knew how to repel invasions.	e invasiones supo rechazar.
But on the other hand I've got a son	Pero en cambio me ha salido un hijo,
who day before yesterday was just a corporal,	que anteayer era cabo nomás,
he doesn't know the smell of gunpowder	no conoce el olor de la pólvora
and now he tells me he's a general.	y me sale con que es general.
In my time, everyone sang	En mis tiempos todos entonaban
our anthem with great devotion:	nuestro himno con gran devoción:
to think, oh dear fatherland, that the heavens	piensa oh patria querida que el cielo
gave you a general in every son.	en cada hijo te dio un general.[25]

Foreword

The adoration of the people and María Consesa's deep convictions ("Clowns and divas are authorized to tell the truth") are among the facts that highlight women's importance during the revolutionary period. They were not emblems of the nation but rather of the modernity contributed by frivolity, coquettishness, sensuality, and the desire to laugh at solemnity that arises from the cemeteries and formations of political and economic power.

Notes

1. These were both popular sayings in Mexico: "Mujer que sabe latín, ni tiene marido ni tiene buen fin" and "Mujer que se independiza no asiste a misa."
2. Hart 1978, 73–74.
3. Quintero Figueroa 1977, 481.
4. Armando Bartra 1977, 203.
5. Marta Lamas, personal communication, 12 February 2004.
6. The section head is from a popular saying: "Cadáver, el de Benito Juárez, los demás son muertitos."
7. Quevedo y Zubieta 1927, 47.
8. Campobello 1931, 35–36.
9. Salas 1994, 93–105.
10. Herrera-Sobek 1990, 93; Lieuwen 1968, 94, as cited by Salas 1994, 101.
11. The quotation in this section's heading is from Margarito the Fair referring to La Pintada in Azuela 2002.
12. Azuela 2002, 119–20.
13. Yáñez 1963, 3.
14. Ibid., 12–13.
15. Goytortúa Sánchez 1969, 88.
16. Celia Herrera 1985, 85–86.
17. Garro 1969, 58.
18. *Mañana*, 20 May 1944, as cited by Campbell 1976, 99.
19. *El Sinarquista*, 3 October 1940, as cited by Campbell 1976, 99.
20. Raby 1974, 150–51.
21. Ibid., 223.
22. Galeana 1994, 130.
23. The heading of this section is a song from the decade of 1910: "Marieta, no seas coqueta / porque los hombres son muy malos, / prometen muchos regalos / y lo que dan son puros palos."
24. Enrique Alonso 1987, 99.
25. Translator's note: The final verse plays on the lyrics of the Mexican national anthem, which state that the heavens gave the fatherland a soldier in every son.

Introduction

Pancho Villa, the Daughters of Mary, and the Modern Woman: Gender in the Long Mexican Revolution

MARY KAY VAUGHAN

The Mexican Revolution of 1910 was the first social revolution of the twentieth century, part of a much broader conflagration that devastated Europe in internecine warfare and, from the peripheries of Russia, China, India, Egypt, and Mexico, challenged empires, landlords, and capitalists. Yet Mexican events are best understood in the context of the rapidly urbanizing Latin American nations Argentina, Chile, and Brazil, where emerging middle and working classes confronted oligarchic power linked to the exportation of primary products and the importation of metropolitan ideas and fashions. Only in Mexico did this political challenge explode in social upheaval. Sclerotic oligarchs failed to negotiate a peaceful transition from the long reign of Porfirio Díaz (1876–1910) to a more inclusive regime. The pent-up frustrations and rebellious traditions of a marginalized peasantry fueled the energies, talents, and visions of ambitious middle-class men. Imbued with the modernizing ideals of North American progressivism, such men also benefited in critical moments from U.S. military and political support. Peasant rebellions further opened opportunity to the nascent working class to organize and press demands. While the civil war that tore the country apart from 1910 to 1920 cost upward of a million lives, it also produced the Western Hemisphere's most progressive legal blueprint. The Constitution of 1917 promised land reform to the peasantry; protection, welfare, and organizing rights to the working class; national control over natural resources; and liberation from Catholic control over hearts, minds, and bodies.[1]

In Mexico, in contrast to other Latin American countries, the Revolution destroyed the oligarchic state. Thus, earlier than elsewhere, Mexican middle-class actors could control—indeed, create—a new state that would incorporate peasants, workers, and middle classes while asserting more national direction over the economy. Given the level of social and military mobilization, state consolidation was fitful and tumultuous in the 1920s, not least because politicians both encouraged and sought to control popular militancy. The confluence of populist organization, political centralization, and social activism meant that in the 1930s, when the collapse of export markets fostered populist regimes in Latin America, the Cárdenas government was the most radical in levels of mobilization, social reform, and economic nationalism. It also institutionalized the Popular Front as the Mexican Revolutionary Party (Partido Revolucionario Mexicano or PRM, formerly the PNR and later the PRI), a single, official party that included organized workers, peasants, middle classes, and women, and facilitated control over them as Mexico embarked on bourgeois-led industrialization. In contrast to developments in other Latin American countries, the PRI marginalized the military from politics without abandoning authoritarianism, state violence, or repression.[2]

As Carlos Monsiváis vividly writes in his preface, art, literature, and cinema remembered women in the revolution as witnesses of male valor, objects of their affections, and nuisances in the march toward modernity. The historiography of the revolution eliminated them entirely from the drama. As Monsiváis notes, the patriarchal imagination hides and obscures. Yet were one to adopt the very terms of the orthodox narrative and place it in comparative context, one would acknowledge that while women did not win the national vote until 1953, they made important gains in civil and social rights earlier than in other Latin American countries. Between 1914 and 1931, the winning Constitutionalists legalized divorce. Married women gained custodial rights over their children on a par with men. They could own and manage property and participate in legal suits and contracts. Paternity legislation allowed fathers to legitimize children born out of wedlock, and mothers and children to pursue such legitimization. Labor legislation recognized women as workers and provided them with the legal armor to combat the stain of prostitution attached to poor women who worked outside the home.[3]

MARY KAY VAUGHAN

Skeptics (until recently, the majority of Mexican historians) derided the act of exploring Mexican women's history as one of feminine romantic willfulness: the search for small groups of insignificant actors in obscure places. On the contrary, the act of uncovering women's voices and defining gendered spaces and practices has not so much been one of voluntarism as it has been the ongoing discovery of new languages with which to read accepted texts and processes. While these increasingly inform studies of the Mexican Revolution in general, they have also emerged over the past twenty years in the transnational development of women's and gender historiography.[4] The latter has revealed gendered states, economies, and marketplaces that were remarkably similar across the large cities and nations of the Euro-Atlantic world from the late nineteenth century through the mid-twentieth. In the last quarter of the nineteenth century, intense market development and improvement in communications and transportation fostered urbanization and industrialization, culminating in twentieth-century Fordism, or the proliferation of industrial production for mass consumption. In Latin America, the emergence of primary extractive export economies delayed heavy industrialization until the mid-twentieth century. Nonetheless, in Latin America as elsewhere, the increasing use of technology in industry and the rise of trade unionism marginalized women from many industries that had employed them in large numbers in the late nineteenth century. Complementing this marginalization was the rationalization of domesticity, that is, the focus of state, marketplace, and social professionals on the female-directed organization of the household responsible for the reproduction of healthy, loyal, and productive subjects.[5] The nineteenth-century political state built around an abstract male voter and property owner became the twentieth-century biopolitical state that partnered with women in the nurturing of healthy bodies for purposes of defense and production.

While a good portion of emerging consumption was oriented toward the home, consumer culture was above all one of public spectatorship, built around the enjoyment of cheap pleasures found in new urban spaces—department stores, parks, dance halls and theaters, photography and radio studios, post offices, trams, and spacious boulevards. The products sold ranged from hats to postcards, records, and celluloid images. This was not so much a feminine phenomenon, as intellectuals and artists often defined it, as it was an arena through which women moved noticeably into public space as performers, spectators, and consumers, complementing their growing presence as workers, students, and political actors. As Monsiváis suggests with reference to the popular diva, María Conesa

(La Gatita Blanca), the growing presence of women was subversive and threatening because it was irreversible. It was part of the emergence of mass society and politics.[6]

To date, the historiography of the Mexican Revolution has been excessively hermetic. Reifying this national event has removed it from transnational context. One contribution of this volume and of women's and gender history is to show how local experiences shape and become shaped by broadly shared processes. Take the *soldaderas*, those thousands of women who went to the revolution as cooks, nurses, lovers, mothers, spies, scavengers, undertakers, soldiers, and commanders. As women, they represented a uniquely modern force. They had been born of a premodern condition: many came from rural areas, and in the armies, they substituted for the sex-segregated modern quartermaster's corps, the nursing and medical units that had yet to be organized. Yet, the soldaderas rode the waves of a migration that had been under way from the late nineteenth century, spurred by railways, new communication media, the capitalization of the countryside, urbanization, and cheap pleasures. As Monsiváis has written elsewhere, the Mexican Revolution, for all its violence, violation, and destruction, was an erotic mobilization of enormous proportions.[7] In no other military conflagration of modern times did such a huge cross-class contingent of women participate. They cooked, gave birth, buried the men and each other. Pancho Villa romanced and shot them; countless others raped and abandoned them. But the women also sang and danced—not just the traditional *corrido* or *jarabe* but the waltz and the fox trot before moving on to *danzón* and the shimmy.

Take the Yaqui Indian girl Dominga Ramírez. Rescued from semislavery on a Yucatán plantation by a Yaqui officer in the Constitutionalist forces who attached himself to her mother, Dominga had the time of her life traveling across the country, dressing up in high heels and new frocks, applying makeup, and kicking up her heels to the latest dance.[8] She was part of a transnational movement, counterpart of the charity girls who worked by day in New York garment factories and enjoyed the dance halls at night, poor sister to Louise Bryant, Mabel Dodge Luhan, and Emma Goldman in their bohemian circles of free love, art, and revolutionary politics in Greenwich Village and Provincetown. The soldaderas heralded a more open, mobile, and experimental womanhood. They were the forerunners of the *chicas modernas* (modern girls) who popped up all over Mexico City in the 1920s, sporting bobbed haircuts and short, flowing dresses. If the chicas shed their corsets, the soldaderas never wore them. In one of her first portraits, Frida Kahlo paints herself as Adelita. No campfire lass in long homespun petticoats, Kahlo sits as an urban Adelita in a strapless evening gown. Above her head is a portrait of Pancho Villa in a suit and tie. Flanking him on one side is a folkloric rendition of peasant soldiers sitting atop a boxcar strumming their guitars. On the other side is an abstract Cubist landscape painting. In the foreground, a nightclub entertainer is poised to play his piano.

The revolution was not just an attack on property, social hierarchy, and exclusion; it assaulted Victorian morality and rules of sexual repression and brought women into public space in unprecedented ways. Threatened artists and intellectuals turned women into traditional archetypes they could control. They could get away with it because, as Monsiváis points out, the voracious machismo of war all but eclipsed a nascent feminist movement. Just as the novelist Mariano Azuela turned his female characters Camila and La Pintada into the familiar binary of virgin and whore, Diego Rivera painted the nation in patriarchal narrative relying on another tired trope: women represented fertility and nature; men were the rational conquerors of nature, the makers of politics, science, technology, and finished goods. But Azuela wrote much about women, and Diego Rivera painted them everywhere—as corn mothers, flower vendors, gaunt wives of suffering workers, school teachers, and even, in the case of Frida Kahlo, as a red-shirted revolutionary (albeit handing out rifles to men). The presence of women was undeniable. They were a de facto part of the national project.

As Temma Kaplan notes in her conclusion to this volume, practices of challenging patriarchy became endemic in the revolution and its aftermath. Herein are the stories of those who seized the opportunities opened by the conflagration and its confluence with transnational trends. Gabriela Cano introduces Amelia/Amelio Robles, who began life on a ranch in the rugged mountain state of Guerrero, where she loved to work with horses. Not even the ferociously repressed and repressive Daughters of Mary could knock the boy out of Amelia. She joined the revolution for the excitement of battle, dressing and fighting as a man. In contrast to many of her fellow cross-dressers who took up arms and commanded troops, she never reclaimed womanhood. Amelio guarded his male identity with a pistol, a reminder that both violence and intolerance accompanied the eroticization and democratization of national culture. He also used modern spectator culture to fashion his identity: in front of the camera in the photographer's studio, he posed in his tailored suit as a sophisticated man about town, in one hand a cigarette, in the other a pistol.

Thousands of other women whose stories are told here claimed what they thought were their revolutionary rights. The coffee-bean sorters of Veracruz (Heather Fowler-Salamini), the knitwear workers of Puebla

(Susan Gauss), the textile- and tortilla-industry workers of Guadalajara (María Teresa Fernández-Aceves) organized into unions. In Yucatán, hundreds of abused or abandoned wives went to court to take advantage of the divorce laws passed by the radical governors Salvador Alvarado and Felipe Carrillo Puerto (Stephanie Smith). In Mexico City and Veracruz, workingwomen—housewives, vendors, factory workers, prostitutes—sustained long and vociferous strikes against high rent.[9] Even Catholic women, who dressed in black and shut down Guadalajara in a massive boycott, fought for their rights to worship as they pleased (Kristina Boylan). In Mexico City, as Patience Schell reports, young women flocked to vocational schools to learn trades and encountered teachers like Dolores Angela Castillo Lara, who reportedly told her students that it was better to be divorced three times than put up with a husband's humiliations. She allegedly went on to talk about the need for companionate marriage and birth control.

Such effervescence met fierce opposition—not the least from some students and their families. In their moral indignation, they found plenty of support. The well-heeled women of the Damas Católicas (Catholic Ladies) campaigned not only against divorce and birth control but also against the "pornography" of cinema and against the nude, female, brown flesh Rivera and José Clemente Orozco painted in their first murals in the National Preparatory School (Escuela Nacional Preparatoria). Through the spring and summer of 1924 the Mexican City press railed against the *pelona*—the chica moderna who bobbed her hair, raised her skirt, and exposed her arms and legs to take up dancing and sports. As Anne Rubenstein recounts, medical and preparatory school students pilloried these female students who had invaded their privileged male space. They grabbed two of them, dragged them into the showers, and shaved their heads. Preparatory students inflicted similar humiliation on pelonas from a nearby vocational school. As Rubenstein and Schell suggest, this was also a class and racial issue. The vocational schools often attracted dark-complected working girls. Many were refugees escaping revolutionary violence and dearth. In pursuit of economic opportunities and often less constrained than middle-class and upper-class girls by Victorian mores, many may have had more freedom to enjoy the pleasures of the chica moderna. Aspirants to middle-class status via education, they threatened class as well as gender boundaries.

Unable to fit the chica moderna into its gender repertoire, the capital press denounced the pelonas: they hailed from the United States like the dreadful sounds of jazz, like the women agitators devoid of "tender sentiments," like the fashionable women of Wall Street and the Jewish quarters, like vaudeville actresses and movie stars.[10] With specific reference to robust North American female athletes, an alarmed woman journalist wrote that there was no place in Mexico for this "third sex" that would surely ruin the "race."[11] Priests and Damas Católicas agreed and threatened to block the bobbed-haired women from entering churches.

Around the same time, conservatives, bristling with Catholic moral indignation that barely hid their fear of losing their properties, overthrew and assassinated Yucatán's radical governor Felipe Carrillo Puerto. Not that his government had proven to be as committed to championing women's rights as he claimed. Not for Amelia Azarcoya Medina and many women like her. As Stephanie Smith relates, Azarcoya Medina sued for divorce from her abusive husband, but his political influence and the court's connivance sank her case. The judge ignored her testimony and ordered her children to live with their father. She was cast out of the conjugal home, alone and penniless, while her husband occupied it with their children and his mistress. After the initial upsurge of women's divorce filings, women backed away, discouraged by the reality of unsympathetic officials and lawyers, the fear of social shame, and lack of alternatives. Husbands frequently used the law to restore their personal honor, besmirched by their wives' desertion and airing of dirty laundry. They deployed the new rhetoric of romantic love to toss off an unwanted wife for an attractive mistress.

Thriving machismo took its toll on the modern woman. Antonieta Rivas Mercado, a Louise Bryant to the mediocre artist Manuel Rodríguez Lozano and to the cultural *empresario* José Vasconcelos, committed suicide in Notre Dame Cathedral. Graciela Amador, wife of muralist and communist David Alfaro Siqueiros, thrived as a labor organizer, journalist, and poet until he left her; abandoned, she fell into a depression from which she never recovered.[12] Frida Kahlo subordinated her life to Diego Rivera and painted her suffering. Today, Kahlo's rendering of that suffering on canvas may be a source of gratifying emotional identification in an era of relative female autonomy, but one cannot forget Kahlo's turmoil: her broken body and anguished mind caught between the cult of motherhood and a man who claimed women's brains were his favorite meal.

In the 1920s, the Mexican state was a chaotic, multiauthored work in progress. It was built on the backs of regional governments like that of Felipe Carrillo Puerto in Yucatán, José Guadalupe Zuno in Jalisco, Adalberto Tejeda in Veracruz, and Adrián Castrejón in Guerrero, all actors in these essays, all builders of populist, clientelist regimes that resembled the political machines of U.S. cities. But the national government was also in competition with those state governments and resolved to subordinate and incorporate them in part by imitating their political model and in part by centralizing regionally based armies more loyal to their commanders than to the nation. Thus, the bureaucratization of the military, associated with the brutal elimination of women and nonrecognition of their service, formed part of the long processes of centralization and demilitarization.

Broadly speaking, the central government could no more tolerate unbridled male sexual license and gun madness than it could advocate free love for women. But neither could it endorse the rigid traditionalism defended by Catholic women in black. Stabilization and development required the modernization of patriarchy. That did not mean an end to male privilege or female subordination, but it did imply the empowerment of women, particularly in their domestic roles as promoters of the health and education of the family. In part for this reason and to accomplish the goal, the state became a refuge and support for organized and de facto feminists. They entered public service not only as teachers in a rapidly expanding school system but also as nurses, hygienists, juvenile justice and social workers, and gymnasts and athletic directors. Much has been written about them.[13] In this collection, in addition to Schell's examination of vocational-school programs in rational domesticity, Ann Blum looks at social workers in charge of child adoption in the new Ministry of Public Assistance (Secretaría de Asistencia Pública). She examines adoption's slow, uneven, but ultimately effective transformation from being a mechanism for acquiring cheap labor to being one that promoted the formation of affective families. A series of laws and their implementation through new institutions suggested a new valuing of childhood as a life stage to be nurtured, protected, studied, and rationalized. These initiatives created new status and entitlement for women as mothers, a democratizing category that cut across class lines.

Feminists also joined the state as labor inspectors and sought government protection as organizers. That is the story Fernández-Aceves tells about Guadalajara's Círculo Feminista del Oriente (CFO), led by textile worker and labor inspector María Díaz and school teacher Guadalupe Martínez and encouraged by Governor Guadalupe Zuno, who saw the secular organization of women workers as a means of offsetting women's participation in Catholic mobilizations against government anticlericalism. Taking as their models Rosa Luxemburg, Alexandra Kollantai, and the martyrs of Haymarket Square, and demanding women's rights to jobs, education, and political and civil equality, CFO women fought to unionize the tortilla industry. Although they were exhilarated in struggle, their experience turned bittersweet as women lost their skilled jobs to men.

MARY KAY VAUGHAN

This traditionally female industry masculinized as it mechanized. In the bloody, drawn-out, internecine conflicts sparked by competing male unionists, the women learned the values of loyalty, discipline, and respect as they subordinated themselves to a union patriarch who became the head of the state branch of the official, national workers' confederation within the official political party. Similarly, Gauss describes how male-dominated textile unions in Puebla campaigned to keep women in the home where, as mothers, they would strengthen the "race" and the "Patria." As Kaplan writes in her conclusion, working-class men entered a pact with the state, exchanging their organizational power and independence for economic benefits and their right to private control over women and children.

But the stories Veracruz coffee-bean sorters told to Fowler-Salamini complicate this picture. To be sure, the sorters held the labor-intensive menial jobs men were willing to leave them. Nonetheless, in their own view, theirs was a successful struggle for dignity and honor. As they told their life stories, they recalled how elites and priests denigrated them as dark-skinned prostitutes given to brawling like men in the streets over union issues. To the contrary, they argued that they had struggled for their rights as workers and labored hard to support their families and their children's education. These women, once isolated in rural households, had developed new feminine cultures of solidarity and interest working together on the factory floor, going to dance halls, movies, union meetings, and demonstrations. Together they talked about family, romance, and health as well as union politics and worker rights. Indeed, some worked part-time as prostitutes, but female worker identity and bonding emerged stronger than notions of sexual purity. Despite the fact that the union was male-dominated and privileging, the experience propelled the coffee sorters into practices and discourses that transformed their sense of themselves. Further, despite the anti-Catholicism of their trade union and cruel rhetoric of their priests, they built their solidarity in part around the pilgrimages they organized in honor of the Virgin of Guadalupe.

Social rights won out over political rights in this emerging environment of controlled politics. President Cárdenas encouraged the Sole Front for Women's Rights (FUPDM) to press for the vote, then abandoned the cause out of concern that Catholic women would elect the opposition candidate in the 1940 elections. As Jocelyn Olcott notes in her analysis of the FUPDM, radical and progressive women mobilized not just for the vote but for a series of benefits they hoped to obtain from the state: child care, education, school breakfasts, public health and sanitation, labor protection, corn mills, sewing machines, and low-cost food. Olcott suggests that social rights were more important than the vote both to the most radical women (members of Communist Party cadres) and to women of the popular classes who found their material needs most effectively addressed through focused political mobilizations and patronage networks. A particular style of Mexican politics emerged as other alternatives faded (effective, multiparty electoral democracy, independent unionism, or socialist revolution). A radical discourse of female rights evolved into one of maternalism, as secular feminists submitted to the discipline of the emerging hegemonic party. Maternalism became the discourse and practice for an active female citizenship in dialogue with a paternalistic state. If social benefits were more readily provided to male heads of households as unionized workers or land-reform recipients, the benefits were intended for children for whom women were the primary caretakers and the aggressive defenders. Monsiváis is right: the post-1940 reification of motherhood was exaggerated and overdrawn, but it was also a dignifying, empowering space for Mexican women, including thousands of single mothers.

By contrast, for organized Catholic women, civil rights—and sometimes political rights—trumped social rights. As Boylan reports, they consistently struggled against state assaults on the right to worship, assembly, and educational choice. Their mobilizations were always larger than those of the government-allied feminists; their organizations, as Kaplan suggests, often seemed to offer more protection than those of the state or of the left. In the 1930s they forced state governments to reopen the churches. In 1933–1934 they successfully defeated a government proposal for sex education. As Monsiváis notes, they continued after 1940 to act as an organized brake on the liberalization of social and sexual behavior promoted by the ever-expanding transnational mass media and consumer culture. They also led in struggles for freedom of education and after 1968, many of their daughters and sons would join the far more radical social movements inspired by the Second Vatican Council and liberation theology. Examined in this volume by Lynn Stephen, these movements no longer defended the faith but embraced it to struggle for equality and social justice.

The Mexican revolutionary intelligentsia took pride in the nationalist ideology of *mestizaje* that celebrated racial mixture and tolerance in contrast to white racial exclusivism in the United States. Historians and anthropologists have noted how this unifying ideology masked persistent racist attitudes and behaviors in Mexico.[14] The essays in this volume bring such attitudes and behaviors to light. The entry of new transnational cultural media and consumerism accessible to large numbers

MARY KAY VAUGHAN

of people tilted the meaning and process of mestizaje in Mexico toward the urban, modern, and white (despite the popularity of Afro-American music) and created new distances between the modern urban cosmopolitan and rural/indigenous worlds. As Rubenstein notes, commercial beauty culture spawned by film, radio, department stores, and advertising brought a new denigration or negative assessment of the indigenous woman's "barrel-shaped body." In her analysis of Emilio Fernández's films Julia Tuñón notes an iconography repeated in revolutionary art, literature, scholarship, and tourism. Indigenous Mexico represents the authentic, primordial Mexico. In a linear narrative, it is (like woman) the nation's foundation, but not its history or progress. The latter are white, urban, European, and male. Indigenous culture was feminized in Fernández's cinema and other aesthetic genres as primitive, sentimental, and natural, as immobile, passive, and unchanging. Modernity, rationality, progress, technology, and historical agency, defined as the conquest of nature— these were masculine. Just ask Diego Rivera, or a fellow from Puebla who worked in a textile factory.

The image of Mexican rural society as immobile, passive, and unchanging dominated the Mexican media after 1940, obscuring its ongoing dynamism. Although the essays in this volume are focused primarily on urban women, Stephen offers an illuminating essay on rural women's organizing since the 1970s. As she notes, it owes much to the Revolution's legacies in rural women's education, their mobilization around household and community issues, and their participation as family members in land reform. From 1940, the very survival of peasant agriculture depended increasingly on women, and, thus, as Stephen argues, it was not strange to find women present in radical organizations, Catholic and Marxist, that mobilized in defense of campesino and indigenous communities from the 1970s. Second-wave feminism, originally embraced by urban middle-class women who had participated in the student protests of 1968, helped to create in these and proliferating urban social movements a new feminist agenda that placed questions of sexual assault, violence against women, and reproductive control on a par with women's concerns for housing, food, land, healthcare, and working conditions.

These social movements coincided in the 1980s with the advent of neoliberalism and the collapse of the welfare state that forced women into the workforce and out of the home in unprecedented numbers. While these processes battered the already teetering model of the patriarchal household, they did not weaken the principle of women's responsibility for family welfare. But the ensuing mobilization of women around such issues as water, food, housing, and health took place within a distinct political environment. Women were no longer pleading with an authoritarian state to give them justice, but demanding a more egalitarian, democratic order and their human rights as citizens. The new feminism reached its most resonant articulation where least expected—out of what Diego Rivera and Emilio Fernández had called the primordial, unchanging, irrational feminine. Out of the jungles of Chiapas in January 1994 came armies of Mayan peoples. Women marched in the vanguard, fully integrated and calling for equality in home, community, organizations, and national law. Today the Zapatista Army of National Liberation (EZLN) is a weaker force than it was a decade ago, and patriarchy has by no means disappeared from Mexico. Still, as Kaplan comments, the images of Mexican women as suffering mothers and bereaved witnesses, as objects of male desire, and as obstacles to modernity have receded: the Mexican woman as activist mobilized in pursuit of her human rights has taken center stage.

Notes

1. The historiography of the Mexican Revolution is enormous. The general reader might wish to start with summary, analytical essays such as Hart 2000 and Knight 1985.
2. The historiography of Mexican post-revolutionary state formation is also vast. For a summary of events, policies, and processes see Benjamin 2000. For bibliography and historiographical shifts see Joseph and Nugent 1994a, 1994b, and Vaughan 1999.
3. Soto 1990, 57–58; Porter 2003.
4. The new studies of the Mexican Revolution opened with Joseph and Nugent (1994a, 1994b).
5. Historiography of the rationalization of domesticity is likewise enormous. See, among others, De Grazia 1992 (1–17, 99–110).
6. On cheap pleasures see Peiss 1987 and Enstad 1999. On gender and consumer culture see essays in De Grazia 1996.
7. Monsiváis 1997, 166–95.
8. Kelley 1978, 162–72.
9. Lear 1998, 75–78; Lear 2001, 300–315, 355–58; Wood 1998, 102–6.
10. Serrano 1924, 9, as cited by Anne Rubenstein, "The War on Las Pelonas" in this volume.
11. Santín de Fontoura 1924, 38, as cited by Anne Rubenstein, "The War on Las Pelonas" in this volume.
12. Cueva Tazzer n.d., 16–62.
13. See, among others, Bliss 2001, Cano 1991b, Cano 1993, Macías 1982, Soto 1990, E. Tuñón Pablos 1992, J. Tuñón 1999, Vaughan 1977, 1990, 1997, 2000.
14. For important treatments of race and ethnicity in the Mexican Revolution see, among others, Knight 1990; C. Lomnitz 2001 (103–4, 231–56); Bonfil Batalla 1996.

PART ONE

Embodying Revolutionary Culture

Unconcealable Realities of Desire

Amelio Robles's (Transgender) Masculinity

in the Mexican Revolution

GABRIELA CANO

O ne can almost see it: a smile of satisfaction spreading across Amelio
Robles's face as he looks at the studio portrait in which he poses like
a dandy: dark suit, white shirt, tie, wide-brimmed black hat, leather
shoes, and a white handkerchief peeking out of the breast pocket.[1] Standing with a cigarette in one hand and the other placed prominently over his
revolver as if to draw attention to the weapon holstered in his belt. The
formal elements of the photograph—composition, even lighting, ambience and, above all, the contained and serene pose of the subject at the
center of the scenery—largely conform to studio portrait conventions
in which those who were photographed wore their finest outfits and
posed with decorum. The photo was taken around 1915 in one of many
photographic studios that flourished in cities and towns across the nation
during the first decades of the twentieth century, when technological
simplification and falling costs made it possible to satisfy the growing
demand for portraits.[2]

Studio portraits sought to establish the social identity of individuals
being photographed by following the prevailing code of etiquette. Posing
with a lit cigarette suggested a cosmopolitan attitude, while the prominently exhibited pistol, modern substitute for the saber and the weapon

1. Portrait of Amelio Robles,
circa 1915. Courtesy of Instituto
Nacional de Antropología e
Historia, Archivo Casasola,
63944.

of choice for dueling at the turn of the century, symbolized the subject's virility. The masculinity of the pose, gesture, and mode of dress are perfectly credible. No one would guess that the dandy in the portrait had once been a young lady.

The radical and permanent transgendering of a young rural woman from the state of Guerrero occurred during the Mexican Revolution. Amelio Robles—previously, Amelia Robles—joined an uprising taking place across southern Mexico under the agrarian banner of Emiliano Zapata and forged a masculine identity within the rough environs of war. His link to the Zapatista movement was not ideological, but emerged instead from a passion for the intensity of war, so full of dangers and strong emotions. Once the armed struggle had ended, Amelio Robles continued to live as a man, maintaining this masculinity for the rest of his life, in public and in private activity, even through old age and infirmity.

The pistol and cigarette in the image were not props from the photographic studio, but Robles's personal belongings. His masculine appearance expressed his sense of being a man; it was not a momentary pose for the camera as was, for example, the one adopted by Frida Kahlo, who dressed in a man's suit for the family portraits taken by her father in 1926.[3]

GABRIELA CANO

Kahlo's was a playful, somewhat irreverent gesture, perhaps following international fashion *à la garçon*. Kahlo did not attempt to be taken for a man, but Robles did and achieved that goal most effectively.

Amelio Robles's masculinization should also be distinguished from strategic transvestitism—the adoption of male dress in order to pass as a man—to which some women resorted during wartime to protect themselves from the sexual violence that intensifies during armed conflicts, to gain access to military commands prohibited to women, or simply to fight as soldiers and not as *soldaderas*, that is, without the social gender restrictions that usually burden women in combat. During the nineteenth-century nationalist wars and afterward in the Mexican Revolution, soldaderas were in charge of supplying the troops and caring for the sick and wounded. At times, they acted as messengers and participated in the smuggling of weapons and goods, but only in exceptional cases did they take up arms.

Although it is not possible to determine the frequency of transvestitism in the Mexican Revolution, there are various reports of women, like María de la Luz Barrera or Angel/Angela Jiménez, who adopted male identities during the war but later returned to wearing women's clothing and performing female roles in society as mothers and wives.[4] Not Amelio Robles. His radical change in gender and sexual identity was not simply due to a pragmatic desire to enjoy the social advantages of men, but rather the product of a deeper, more vital desire to radically transform the female identity assigned to him at birth in order to make himself masculine in every aspect of life.

Amelio Robles made the transition from an imposed feminine identity to a desired masculinity: he felt like a man, acted like a man, and constructed a male appearance. Little is known about his sexuality, but reports suggest that he sustained romantic relationships with feminine women and that he once courted a schoolmate as her beau; these were erotic relationships inscribed within a heterosexual logic in which Amelio Robles performed the masculine role.[5] Amelio Robles could be described as a butch lesbian or a tomboy, but current terminology regarding gender and sexual identity would more appropriately locate him as a transgendered male, a subject who adopts the physical appearance, the behavior, and the gender role culturally assigned to the opposite sex. Lesbian sexual identity, on the other hand, is defined as an erotic inclination toward people of the same sex, which does not necessarily imply a desire to transgender: to change gender identity, physical appearance, or sexual anatomy. The term *lesbianism* is not synonymous with masculinization, of course, but neither does it exclude masculine identification. Nevertheless, identifying categories are flexible categories rather than hermetically sealed spaces. During her transition stage, Amelia Robles could very well be characterized as a butch lesbian who later became a transgendered male person.

Transgendered identities vary in degree and endurance, and Amelio Robles stood at one end of the spectrum, where the individual feels a deep dissatisfaction with her gender and sexual anatomy and wants to change her appearance and body. Today, certain sexual characteristics can be transformed through surgical procedures and hormone therapy. Such medical treatment has been available in institutions in the United States and Europe since the mid-twentieth century, when the term *transsexual* was coined to refer to people who received treatments that transformed their sexual anatomy. *Transsexual*, however, is inadequate to describe Robles given that his case involved neither surgery nor hormone changes. However, his dissatisfaction with his identity, physical appearance, and feminine anatomy was perhaps as strong as that experienced by those inclined to subject themselves to medical intervention so that their bodies might resemble to some degree their subjective configurations.[6]

In the early twentieth century, without surgical intervention or hormones, Amelio Robles constructed a masculine body image and social identity with the cultural resources available to him in an isolated rural area of Mexico. He dexterously manipulated those cultural resources: pose or gender performance; a visual body culture inaugurated by studio photography; and a modern press that, avid for sensationalist news items, took an interest in the story of the Zapatista revolutionary and legitimized him. Amelio Robles's masculinization was established mainly through a gender performance.[7] The poses, gestures, and attitudes involved in this daily performance were complemented by a carefully selected wardrobe featuring the pants, shirts, jackets, and hats common in rural environments. He chose shirts with large chest pockets that concealed his small breasts. Studio photography was central to the establishment and acceptance of this masculine appearance. Photographic portraits transformed visual body culture and made it possible for common people to fix their desired physical images in lasting prints, something that until then had been done only through the portraits afforded to a few. Manufactured with the camera as intermediary, the desired body and social identity could be forever preserved in a photographic portrait and shown as often as one liked. Each time the portrait was viewed by oneself or someone else, the body image and the identity created by the photograph was confirmed.[8]

This legitimizing effect was accentuated in the event, however unlikely, that a studio portrait was reproduced in the press, as with the photograph

GABRIELA CANO

2. Amelio Robles (right) with Guadalupe Barrón in Iguala, Guerrero, 1976.
Photo by Marcelo González Bustos.

that illustrated a news item on Robles published in *El Universal*, the Mexico City newspaper with the highest national circulation in the 1920s.[9] Although it would reveal the secret of his sexual identity—an ill-kept secret, widely known in the local community—the newspaper multiplied by the thousands the visual credentials his image conveyed: an elegant man who, albeit not particularly distinguished, displayed an uninhibited demeanor and boundless self-confidence. The photo's publication amounted to a proclamation of Robles's virility in the town plaza, a virility exemplified in his face, pose, and wardrobe, and accentuated by the exhibition of a firearm.

Amelio Robles's masculinity was "a cultural declaration of the body and a political act" that troubled the social assignation of gender and heterosexual norms.[10] His transgendering questioned the naturalness attributed to the feminine and the masculine, and subverted the ingrained notion of gender identity as an immediate and unavoidable consequence of anatomy that neatly defined men and women into social groups with immutable qualities. Transgendering processes interrogate (and sometimes reify) the fixed categories of man and woman. Such categories are often considered transparent and unchanging realities, which doesn't take into ac-

Unconcealable Realities of Desire

count their plasticity, a plasticity that becomes evident in light of gender transitions such as Amelio Robles's, one of the few processes of its kind to have been documented in the history of Latin America.[11]

Historiography dedicated to the armed stage of the Mexican Revolution has focused mainly on the ideological, political, and military aspects of the struggle; daily life in the trenches, the details of day-to-day existence of armies, has been studied very little. Amelio Robles's masculinization did not take place overnight, but rather was a gradual process that began during the forced displacement and social disorder of wartime. In combat, manners and reserves were abandoned, creating certain spaces of tolerance that allowed Robles to begin to reconstruct himself as a man and enjoy relative acceptance among comrades-in-arms, who admired his courage and capacity as a *guerrillero*. On the battlefield, the constant threat of death amid the destruction of war also fortified a gender ideology embedded in nationalist narrative, identifying masculinity with traits of courage and personal daring as well as patriotic attitudes and nationalist, revolutionary ideologies. As time passed, the stereotype of the courageous revolutionary became an iconic image in both popular culture and the nationalist discourse of the post-revolutionary state.[12]

Colonel Robles embodied the ideal of the macho revolutionary soldier: courageous and daring, capable of responding to aggression immediately and violently, and skilled in handling arms and horses. His romantic relationships with women conformed to conventional models and reproduced the gender polarity of feminine and masculine roles. In a Polaroid snapshot, Amelio Robles, dressed in worn clothing and with a red kerchief around his neck, appears beside Guadalupe Barrón, one of the women with whom he maintained a relationship and whose feminine presence accentuates Robles's virility, as does his own posture, which is as self-assured as it was in more youthful portraits. Both Amelio and Guadalupe exhibit the rigid body language typical of photographic studio conventions, in stark contrast to the spontaneous gestures that portable cameras, increasingly accessible during the second half of the twentieth century, attempted to capture. The couple dominates the image, barely permitting a glimpse of the hat worn by a third person—probably Soreniano Delgado Vázquez, also a Zapatista colonel—who peeks out from behind Amelio and Guadalupe.

Interest in Amelio Robles's story goes beyond its particulars: his figure can be seen as a site of debate, a dispute around the definition and meaning of gender, of masculinity and femininity, framed in the discourse of post-revolutionary Mexican nationalism. There existed three different and, at times, contrasting perceptions of Amelio Robles: (1) that of his army comrades, who admired his precise emulation of a masculinity understood as a display of strength and violence; (2) the sensationalist gaze that, finding solace in the exhibition of his eccentricity, also legitimized his transgression; and (3) the normalizing and homophobic perspective that erased transgendering by applying essentialist gender categories. To understand perceptions of Amelio Robles, one must begin with the social identity and the masculine body image that Amelio Robles constructed for himself through pose, gesture, and wardrobe, as well as his skillful handling of studio photography and media attention.

Amelio Robles's masculine body image was supported by identifying documents that accredited his membership in various social and political organizations, including credentials that recognized him as an affiliate of the Socialist Party of Guerrero (Partido Socialista de Guerrero, 1934), a delegate of the Central League of Agrarian Communities in Xochipala, Guerrero (Liga Central de Comunidades Agrarias, 1945), an affiliate of the National Confederation of Veterans of the Revolution (Confederación Nacional de Veteranos de la Revolución, 1948), and as a member of the Ranchers' Association of Zumpango del Río (Asociación Ganadera de Zumpango del Río, 1956 and 1958). The credentials' identifying photographs confirm Robles's masculinity, whose name and signature always figure as male.[13]

Perhaps the greatest evidence of the effectiveness of his masculine appearance is the medical certificate required for admission to the Confederation of Veterans of the Revolution. Issued in 1948 by Doctor Pedro González Peña at his Mexico City clinic, the certificate attested to Robles's good health, age, and the scars from six bullet wounds on different parts of his body, including one in the thigh and another in the armpit—all without alluding to his sexual anatomy.[14] The medical investigation required by the Confederation of Veterans of the Revolution was not a thorough examination but rather a prerequisite intended to certify any war wounds, considered irrefutable proof of valor on the field of battle. Even so, there was no reason for the doctor to doubt Robles's masculinity: his reserved attitude, gesture, wardrobe and body movements—"the gait of an old soldier"—were those of a nearly sixty-year-old man from the countryside who must have modestly revealed certain body parts to show the doctor the bullet wounds he carried so proudly. On other occasions, Robles did not hesitate to show a scar on his leg to lend realism as he narrated his wartime exploits.[15]

The Ministry of National Defense (Secretaría de Defensa Nacional, or SDN) legitimated Amelio Robles's masculine identity by decorating him in 1974 as a *veterano* of the revolution, not as a *veterana*, an honor bestowed on over three hundred women for their services in the revolutionary cause.[16] The recognition of the country's highest military officials must have provided Amelio Robles with enormous satisfaction, although the SDN did not corroborate the rank of colonel that he claimed in the Zapatista army, which is generally recognized not as a professional military body, but rather as a "people in arms" composed of rebel groups of men gathered around their leaders with no systematic procedures for promotion. Robles did not receive a military pension.[17]

Amelio Robles demanded recognition as a man, both in public and in private. A neighbor recalled, "I never addressed him as señora or madam, I always used Mr. Robles, because he would take out his pistol if anyone called him a woman or lady."[18] Although exaggerated, this statement illustrates the ways in which Robles insisted on recognition of his social identity as a man. His family accepted Amelio's masculinity as a given fact; his grandnieces addressed him as uncle or grandfather and learned his sexual identity only after they became adults, since the subject of his queerness was never raised at home. Only on exceptional occasions, when the bonds of homosocial trust among friends were reinforced by alcoholic beverages, did an older, weakened Robles allow some of those in his inner circle to address him in the feminine as "my *coronela*."[19]

Amelio Robles adopted forms of masculinity particular to his rural environment, a cultural code that included daring courage and constant shows of force. These characteristics, in later years, led him to initiate violent personal conflicts that killed more than one person. Like many men, Amelio frequently indulged in alcoholic excesses; he was authoritarian; he was a womanizer, cursed, and was rarely disposed to account for his actions among family members, not even during the periods of illness that marked a lengthy old age. Amelio Robles, a macho among machos, took the stereotype of masculinity that prevailed at his rung of the social ladder to an extreme. Paradoxically, his peculiar creation and re-creation of masculine values unsettled the naturalness with which they were recognized as virile attributes. The paradox was that Amelio Robles's successful gender transition simultaneously subverted and reinforced normative heterosexuality and the stereotypical masculinity it re-created.

Amelia the Girl

According to the civil registry, Amelia Robles was born in 1889 in Xochipala, Guerrero. The birth certificate leaves no room for doubt: the baby presented to the commissary by her mother and father was a girl. In keeping with the Catholic saint's calendar, her parents gave her the middle name Malaquías, but at home they called her by her first name, Amelia.[20] She came from a family of ranchers, a social class of midsized landowners who were the main political actors of the Mexican Revolution in Guerrero.[21] On her family's ranch, Amelia learned to handle weapons and horses, which did not keep her from also becoming a member of the Daughters of María, a Catholic congregation dedicated to refining young women's spiritual education. As a daughter dedicated to domestic family tasks who had not yet joined the guerrilla fighters (a neighbor remembers her working in a family restaurant, or *fonda*, that offered food to revolutionaries passing through the zone), Amelia wanted to study medicine, a masculine professional aspiration shared by Juan Andreu Almazán, for whom Robles professed great admiration, having met him through the Zapatista movement.[22]

As a guerrilla fighter, Amelia discovered, in her words, "the sensation of being completely free," something she had not experienced while living as a woman in a town that she could generally leave only on foot. In the town, young Amelia's prowess at arms and horses earned admiration as a good spectacle, whereas among the troops these same talents were essential and highly valued in guerrillero Robles.[23]

Robles's Zapatista stage lasted for five or six years, from 1912 or 1913 until about 1918, a period in which he participated in numerous calls to arms; his connection to Zapatismo was not so much ideological as elemental, resulting from a taste for guerrilla life, much freer than that of the town and with the added intensity of constant danger. When reminiscing about revolutionary times, Robles referred little to agrarianism and social radicalism; he delighted in tales of daily life on the battlefield, where loyalty to military leaders, personal achievements, and rivalries provided daily sustenance.

Like many other Zapatistas from the region, Robles recognized Venustiano Carranza's government around 1918 and eventually became a soldier of the Mexican Army. He supported the Aguaprieta rebellion, which rendered Álvaro Obregón the victorious military leader of the revolution.[24] More important, Robles fought against Adolfo de la Huerta's rebels under the leadership of former Zapatista Adrián Castrejón, who would be appointed governor of Guerrero in 1928. The victories of Castrejón's men against the delahuertistas also consolidated the bonds of friendship and homosocial solidarity among Robles, his officer, and his comrades-at-arms. These ties, forged in combat, contributed in a significant way to the official recognition of Robles's masculine self. Aware of Robles's peculiar identity, Castrejón was instrumental in organizing an interview with Miguel Gil for the newspaper *El Universal*, and in later years his authority as

Unconcealable Realities of Desire

governor was essential to Robles's incorporation into Castrejonista organizations such as the Socialist Party of Guerrero and the League of Agrarian Communities, both of which provided Robles with political influence in his town. Amelio Robles also benefited from the political weight of another comrade, Rodolfo López de Nava Baltierra, who as governor of Morelos was happy to give him a certificate of revolutionary merit and recommend his admission into the Mexican Legion of Honor of the SDN, an achievement also shared by others among Robles's associates.[25]

Classification as a revolutionary veteran required providing the SDN with a series of letters of recommendation and proofs of merit with the specific goal of obtaining authorization of the interested party's request. These endorsements conformed with criteria established by the Mexican Legion of Honor without necessarily establishing incontrovertible proof of events that had taken place decades earlier and whose details had most likely been forgotten.[26] Given that it was commonplace to adjust merit and service records to reflect military reports provided by superior officers, it must have seemed equally reasonable to Robles to change the sex registered on his birth certificate so that his main document of identity would conform to his appearance and internal sensation of being a man. His personal file in military archives includes an apocryphal civil-registry act that certifies the birth of a boy, Amelio Malaquías Robles Ávila. Except for the baby's name and sex, all other data coincides with the original birth certificate found in the corresponding civil-registry book.[27] Convinced of his masculinity and enjoying the political protection of a network of social relations in the region, Amelio Robles must have harbored no doubts regarding the advisability of presenting apocryphal documentation to enjoy the designation as a veterano—not a veterana—of the revolution.

Unconcealable Realities

During the armed movement, sexual violence that especially affected the female population increased in direct proportion to revolutionary violence. At the same time, for some individuals the revolution also opened up possibilities of self-determination that previously had remained beyond reach. The war caused geographic displacement and "shook the foundations of respectability and good manners."[28] What Carlos Monsiváis refers to as a "temporary demolition of modesty" ensued, making "the realities of desire unconcealable," at least within certain exceptional spaces of tolerance such as the one that allowed Amelio Robles to enjoy relative acceptance, spaces that had no equivalent in urban areas or towns as far as we know. One perceives only the visibility gained by a few conspicuous homosexuals in Mexico City during the 1920s: artists and intellectuals like Salvador Novo or Roberto Montenegro, two of those whom the painter Antonio "El Corzo" Ruiz caricaturized as effeminate.[29]

Tolerance toward marginalized sexualities was not the norm in the Zapatista movement. Manuel Palafox, of Puebla, one of the main intellectuals of Zapatismo, was repeatedly discredited because of his homosexual inclinations. Maurilio Mejía, a guerrillero leader and nephew of the Zapata brothers, Emiliano and Eufemio, categorically dismissed Palafox: "a poor devil of the wrong sex such as yourself cannot be called a friend to those of us who are real men."[30] Male homosexuality drew extreme condemnation because it was perceived as being effeminate and a rejection of masculinity, which was identified with revolutionary convictions and displays of patriotism; its rejection was therefore considered a betrayal of fundamental nationalist values. Robles's transgendering, on the other hand, enjoyed relative tolerance precisely because it exaggerated the masculine values exalted by the civil war.

This does not mean, however, that tolerance toward Amelio Robles was simple or universal. By the end of the revolutionary movement, Amelio chose to settle in Iguala in order to avoid hostilities in his hometown, Xochipala, where he owned family property, although he did return home years later. According to some accounts, Amelio Robles was assaulted by a group of men who wanted to reveal the secret of his anatomy, and in self-defense he killed of two of his aggressors, costing him a jail sentence that he served in Chilpancingo. This imprisonment is rumored to have inflicted the additional humiliation, as Amelio was held in women's facilities.[31] Whether true or not, this anecdote expresses the anxiety, often translated into buried or open aggression, that Amelio provoked by questioning cultural gender classifications. His identity was the butt of many jokes, more or less crass, even among those who offered him their protection, like Castrejón or López de Nava. Both military men adopted an ambiguous position toward Amelio, given that they officially certified his masculinity while referring in private to "the *coronela* Amelia Robles."[32]

Amelio Robles's transgender performance was not limited to his political and military activities. In intimate circles, Robles also behaved like a man and enacted a masculinity consistent with twentieth-century Mexican rural society. He sustained romantic relationships with several women; with Ángela Torres he even adopted a daughter who, as an adult, preferred to distance herself from Amelio. Ángela Torres came from Apipilco, a nearby town, where Robles resided in 1934, and was perhaps the "schoolmate" on whom he had showered attention.[33] Amelio Robles's masculine appearance, as suggested in the photograph that shows him posing beside Guadalupe Barón (with whom he also shared a sentimental bond), remained within a polar opposition of male and female physical appearances.

Likewise, Robles's masculinity implied a division of the functions socially assigned to men and women within rural environments. As a typical rural man, Amelio never took on the domestic tasks he must have learned in his youth, when he was raised as a small-town Catholic lady while also becoming an expert shot, rider, and horseman. As an old man, once infirmity had limited his mobility, Amelio often received visits from Angelita Torres, who traveled regularly from Apipilco, bringing all the necessary utensils to cook for Amelio while visiting him in Xochipala. This anecdote is highly reminiscent of the popular image of the "Adelita," a female soldier who would follow her "Juan" with children and household goods in tow, re-creating a rustic but homelike environment despite the adversities of the battlefield.

Disputed Gender

The press turned Robles into a local celebrity, thus contributing to the legitimacy of his transgendering process. Amelio Robles attracted Miguel Gil, a reporter from *El Universal*, and fascinated Gertrude Duby, a Swiss journalist exiled in Mexico who had fought fascism in several European countries. Also, in revolutionary times, Robles was photographed anonymously and his image included in the *Graphic History of the Mexican Revolution* edited by the famous family of photographers, the Casasolas.[34]

During the 1920s, the front page of *El Universal* was dedicated mainly to political information. However, it also frequently included sensationalist news items, crime stories, tragedies, or extraordinary events, written in a colloquial style intended to elicit visceral reactions of horror or pity among potential readers in what is now a standard commercial strategy of the modern press. In April 1927, other news briefs with attention-grabbing headlines were printed: "Gertrude Ederle, the Little Frog Woman Who Swam across the English Channel" or "The Secret of a Woman who is One Hundred and Forty-Three Years Old."[35]

However, the prominent publication of news regarding Amelio Robles was due not only to sensationalist elements in his story but also to his record during the revolution. A decade after the passage of the 1917 Constitution, memories of the revolutionary process were still fresh, and the public was interested in the testimony of both participants and witnesses. During April and May of 1927, for example, *El Universal* published two vignettes by Martín Luis Guzmán that would later form part of the canonical novel *El águila y la serpiente* (*The Eagle and the Serpent*). The newspaper also carried an interview by Miguel Gil with Carmen Serdán of Puebla, an emblematic figure of the revolution.

It is likely that Miguel Gil composed the item on Amelia Robles deliberately for publication around 10 April 1927, the anniversary of Emiliano Zapata's death. From the start of the Álvaro Obregón administration (1920–24), which supported agrarian distribution and named several Zapatistas as cabinet members, the anniversary was an occasion for local organizations and the government to promote the image of the leader from Morelos as a symbol of dispossessed peasants. Yet by 1927, the administration of Plutarco Elías Calles (1924–28) was abandoning support for agrarian redistribution. In keeping with this position, *Excélsior* only briefly mentioned the local ceremonies organized in Cuautla, the heartland of Zapatismo. *El Universal* reported nothing on the ceremonies and a few days after the 10 April anniversary published Gil's article on Robles.[36]

Miguel Gil's article offers a visual description of Amelio Robles that highlights significant details. Following Joseph Pulitzer's globally influential recommendations for effective news writing, Miguel Gil establishes a vivid portrait of Robles and avoids conceptually touching on the subject of his gender identity while leaving a lasting impression in the following aside: "When he rolls up his pants leg to show me the bullet scar left on his leg I notice that he's wearing men's stockings and garters. A tiny detail, but a detail nonetheless!"[37] The visual portrait is meant to prove that Amelio Robles "is not the slightest bit feminine." Nothing suggests womanhood "in the air of his laugh or the look in his eyes; not in the way he stands, or the way he expresses himself, or in the ring of his voice." His body image, face, gestures, tone of voice, and personality traits are those of a man. The manly nature of his body movement and gestures are also evident in his style of dress: "The way he sports the coat and pants, the hat tilted slightly to the left and worn with elegance, is nothing if not a sign of masculinity."[38]

Although Gil does not use the term *sexual inversion*, his vision of Amelio Robles draws on this broad concept from nineteenth-century sexology, which embraced diverse homosexual and transgender identities —all of which continue to be categorized as sexual inversion. Sexology enjoyed popularity in the mass media of Great Britain and the United States during the 1920s, attaining a certain degree of resonance in Mexico. In keeping with sexological discourse, Gil sees Robles as a masculine spirit trapped in a feminine "body wrapping": "La Coronela is a man, nonetheless, he was born a woman."[39]

Gil's voyeuristic curiosity about Amelio is undeniable, but the journalist does not see Robles as a specimen from a freak show but rather regards him with admiration, as a "superb character for a novel."[40] Nor does he evince any sarcasm, moral condemnation, or commiseration, attitudes that appear in a news item on Robles published decades later by the sensationalist newspaper *Alerta!*[41] Amelio Robles may have preferred that *El Universal* present him simply and plainly as a brave revolutionary without referring to him as a woman; however, he may also have felt flattered to see his photograph displayed on the front page of the Mexico City newspaper. He saved the clipping from *El Universal* throughout his life, along with other personal photographs and souvenirs. Although *El Universal* portrayed him as an eccentric, Amelio Robles took advantage of the celebrity that the newspaper offered him not as someone who was socially marginal but as someone fully integrated in his social and family circles.

While Gil tolerated Robles's masculinization, he showed no sympathy whatsoever for homosexuals. The reporter expressed his evident condemnation and sarcasm in an article about effeminate, transvestite homosexuals wearing flashy makeup who were imprisoned in the Federal District penitentiary.[42] The journalist followed the same guidelines governing sensationalist treatment of transgressive gender identities that the penny press applied to the emblematic mass arrest of forty-one homosexuals in 1901, referring to "the neuters" as "incongruent, incomprehensible beings . . . who are neither women nor men."[43] With their poses and gestures, the prisoners parodied a caricatured femininity by means of an affected pose or a counterfeit gesture that threatened heterosexual gender norms. On another occasion, while writing about the Islas Marías penitentiary, Gil referred to homosexuals as "half-men," but softened his condemnatory tone with a compassionate attitude by encouraging reflection "on the great injustice of Nature."[44] Gil's views of homosexual prisoners clarifies his tolerance towards Robles, whose masculinity seemed acceptable to him because it was an exceptional case that had no followers and that exalted the values of machismo. On the other hand, "the neuters" from jail and their peers circulating on the city streets flaunted an effeminacy that was not quite as exceptional, drawing the maximum penalty from a society in which the values of an allegedly invincible masculinity prevailed.

The Essentialist Turn

In time, recognition of Amelio Robles's transgender condition gradually disappeared, and someone who had achieved acceptance during his lifetime as a man in social and family circles and even by the country's highest military authority ended up, in the 1980s, as a symbol of "the revolutionary woman." This conceptualization was imposed as the result of an understandable eagerness to provide an appraisal of the achievements and rights of women, dismissing both the effective masculinization of Robles and the fact that the SDN had recognized him as a revolutionary veteran and that everyone addressed him as a man. The village dandy who proudly bore arms, confidently flaunted a virile body, and boasted of his machismo and courage in the Zapatista war and as a soldier in the service of the Mexican Army was commemorated by an elementary school in his hometown named after "Coronela Amelia Robles."

The censorship of Amelio Robles's masculinity within the social memory of the discourse that restored "women" to the Mexican Revolution became evident when the Amelia Robles Museum-House opened its doors in 1989, five years after his death, under the influence of the recently inaugurated Secretariat of Women of the State of Guerrero (Secretaría de la Mujer del Estado de Guerrero) and with the collaboration of the Robles family.[45] Two purposes converged in the museum. On one hand, it commemorated the contributions of women whose actions were perpetually relegated to a secondary role in the official history that generally features military heroes. On the other, it commemorated local history, conventionally subordinated to a centralist perspective that valued the meaning of regional historic processes solely from the standpoint of nation-state formation.

The erasure of Amelio Robles's transgender identity resulted from an understandable and necessary eagerness to recognize what should have been obvious: that women are historical subjects, capable of making significant contributions to civic life and all aspects of history.[46] However, such restorative efforts attribute fixed qualities to the categories of woman and man and, therefore, recognize neither the elasticity of gender constructions nor marginalized expressions of desire. This heteronormative conceptualization carries implicit attitudes of phobia and condemnation of gay, transgender, and transsexual identities.

The paradoxes of this essentialist conceptualization of gender can be appreciated through Gertrude Duby, an exile in Mexico during the Second World War who visited Robles in his town in the early 1940s as part of a project to document firsthand the participation of Zapatista women in the Mexican Revolution. Just over twenty years after the end of the armed conflict, records of revolutionary participation among women were scarce if not nonexistent, as indicated by Matilde Rodríguez Cabo, activist in the Sole Front for Women's Rights (Frente Único Pro Derechos de la Mujer).[47]

A militant in the socialist movement opposing fascism in Europe, Gertrude Duby imagined Mexico as a land of social revolution, rural traditions, and ancient cultures, an idealized vision shared by many other foreigners who visited Mexico, intrigued by the country's possibilities of social emancipation, which appeared to be canceled in the Old World. Through French ethnographer Jacques Soustelle, Duby learned of Emiliano Zapata, "the only revolutionary leader who understood the situation of the peasantry in the Mexican Revolution."[48] Shortly after her arrival in Mexico, Duby outpaced Soustelle in her idealization of Miliano, as he was known, becoming convinced that the leader from Morelos emulated the socialist aims of the Russian Revolution.[49]

The Zapatista women's recollections of the "war against the landholders" of Morelos allowed Duby to forget, for a time, the European war. Armed with a secondhand camera, Gertrude Duby took photographs of a dozen female participants in the Zapatista movement, whom she interviewed over the course of several months. She was moved by the revolutionaries' stories of sacrifice and struggle, but Amelio Robles made the strongest impression on her. Attracted by his "legendary figure," Duby traveled to Guerrero more than once, took several photographs of Robles, and wrote a chronicle of his life, which remained unpublished. A regular writer in the European socialist press, Gertrude Duby had experience in editorial political journalism, but the texts on the Zapatista women were literary chronicles that rejected sensationalism and aspired to a timeless value.

During her first visit, Gertrude Duby spent the night and part of the morning in Amelio Robles's home. She asked questions about his participation in the revolution, addressing the Zapatista at all times as a male, as everyone else did. However, both her field notes and the final version of her chronicle refer to Robles in the feminine: "La Coronela Amelia Robles will forgive me for treating her as a woman; she honors the female sex with her courage, intelligence, and industriousness."[50]

According to Gertrude Duby, Amelio Robles's masculinity was not the expression of an authentic subjectivity and physical identity resulting from a powerful, intimate desire, but rather a pragmatic resource used to confront the social restrictions weighing down on the female sex. "During a century in which women are relegated to second-class status because of their sex and in which their capacities are considered worthless," she wrote, "in a town far from the highway, it is my understanding that la Coronela Amelia Robles lives, works, and serves her people by dressing as a man and acting like one." From Duby's perspective, Robles represented an emancipatory ideal in which men and women shared public respon-

3. Amelio Robles and Esteban Estrada, circa 1942.
Photo by Gertrude Duby Blom. Courtesy of Na Bolom Museum.

sibilities and women did not dedicate themselves exclusively to the home. Instead, they participated in social life in an egalitarian utopia, a vision that had inspired Duby's militant efforts as far back as her leadership of the feminine section of the Swiss Social Democratic Party in the early 1920s. The utopia of equality between men and women had been the subject of an article published during those years in the Swiss newspaper *Frauenrecht*.[51]

A photograph featuring Amelio Robles and Esteban Estrada makes it impossible to completely deny Amelio Robles's masculinity, given that his pose and appearance are as virile as his companion's. Confronted by the obvious, Duby described "men's clothing, short hair, the will to be treated as a man" and recognized that Estrada and Robles spoke "man to man" about land-related issues. However, Duby also encountered features that undermined the masculinity of Robles's appearance: "Her hair is very short, slightly gray already, a high forehead, a fine profile, clear and very lively eyes, and a mouth of surprising energy. Her voice is strong, but melodious and not masculine; her skin is fine and very white; her movements are somewhat brusque and very determined." The narrative

Unconcealable Realities of Desire

4. Gertrude Duby, Amelio Robles, and an unidentified woman, circa 1942.
Photo by anonymous. Courtesy of Na Bolom Museum.

included details regarding the domestic surroundings and hospitality offered by Amelio Robles, but Duby went beyond by discovering stereotypical feminine and even maternal characteristics in the hospitality and protective, warm attitude of "la coronela Robles" toward visitors: "Despite the late hour, we were served an excellent dinner with genuine hospitality; later in a bed prepared for me with very white sheets and warm, soft blankets, I spent the night in perfect rest." The person described by Duby does not seem to be the same one whom Miguel Gil saw as "not the slightest bit feminine."[52] Duby's desire was to find in revolutionary and indigenous Mexico a local figure who would incarnate her own ideals of revolution, social justice, and egalitarian emancipation for women.

Like many other authors who sought visibility for women's participation in historical processes, Duby attributes a coherence and a unique meaning to the activity of women who participated in the Zapatista revolutionary faction. She does not consider that the armed movement might have held diverse meanings for its protagonists, both men and women, or recognize that despite its destructive momentum, the war may also have made possible the expression of unconcealable realities of desire, including Amelio Robles's marginalized and silenced desire to become a man. He certainly would not have forgiven Duby for "treating her as a woman."

Gertrude Duby's gaze contributes something more than a foreign perspective, disillusioned with the European war, seeking an Eden of social revolution and feminist emancipation in indigenous Mexico. It is a homophobic perspective that also, inspired by the first and second waves of feminism, seeks to vindicate women through the commemorative local discourse of the revolution in Guerrero. Therefore, the most arduous battle fought by Colonel Robles was not out in the open and did not smell of gunpowder, nor did it require bearing the agrarian ideological arms of the Mexican Revolution. It was a cultural battle, a slow and silent struggle, whose great victory was to become a man by denying a female physical anatomy. Amelio Robles sculpted the body he desired for himself and lived as a man for seventy of his ninety-four long years. For seven decades, during which he acted and felt like a man, he sustained a masculine presentation and behavior. Bedecked in military uniform, suit and tie, or simply peasant-style trousers and wool jacket, Amelio displayed a body whose virility most people recognized. When he died, rumor held that in his final moments, Amelio Robles requested that he be buried dressed as a woman, thus denying the masculinity he had sustained in life, occasionally at gunpoint. This purported eagerness to normalize his masculine identity prevailed in the tombstone motto found in the Xochipala, Guerrero, cemetery—"Here lie the remains of *la coronela zapatista*"—contradicting the intimate joy of Amelio Robles: to feel, present, and know himself as a man.

People of transgender identity like Amelio Robles are sometimes seen as positive symbols of transgression; at other times, their gender and physical aspect are perceived as unauthentic manifestations that are ridiculous or even grotesque, reinforcing the conservative stereotypes of masculine and feminine.[53] However, Amelio Robles's transgendering should be seen as neither an optimistic reaffirmation nor a refutation of gender ideology to judge positively or negatively. Rather, it is a manner—as legitimate as any other—to articulate an individual way of being and feeling through the cultural resources at hand and within contemporary cultural debates regarding the masculine and feminine. Interwoven with social conflicts, this process exposes tensions between rural and urban environments, the transnational circulation of cultural representations, and the construction of memories regarding the Mexican Revolution.

Notes

1. Amelio Robles's successful transgendering makes it necessary to use both masculine and feminine pronouns when writing about this person. "He" and "his" are used to refer to Amelio Robles during the long period of his life when his masculine identity was widely recognized. In Spanish the grammatical gender is indicated by the "o" ending, rendering the name masculine: Amelio. On the other hand, the pronouns "she" and "her" are used to refer to Robles in early life, when she lived as woman. During childhood and early youth, Robles's first name was Amelia, ending with an "a," which in Spanish indicates the feminine. Similarly, the feminine pronouns and proper name were used in discourses that feminize Robles's identity and deny his masculinity.

2. Monsiváis 2002, 178–221.

3. Herrera, Taymor, and Hayek 2002, 33; Stellweg 1992, 102–3.

4. Salas 1994.

5. Miguel Gil, "Amelia Robles una mujer del estado de Guerrero que puso su libertad y su vida al servicio de la Revolución en el Sur," *El Universal*, 14 April 1927, 1, 8.

6. Meyerowitz 2002, 5, 9–10.

7. Butler 1999, vii–xxvi.

8. Lalvani 1996, 68–69.

9. Gil, "Amelia Robles," 1, 8; Lepidus 1928, 77.

10. Molloy 1998, 141–60.

11. The nun Catalina de Erauso, or Alférez, was a well-known figure in colonial history of Latin America. Erauso took on a masculine identity and appearance on enlisting as a soldier in the service of the Spanish Empire during the seventeenth century but recognized her feminine identity toward the end of her life—the narrative voice in her memoirs is a female one—unlike Amelio Robles, who died without renouncing his masculinity or recognizing himself as a woman (Erauso 1996).

12. O'Malley 1986, 136–37.

13. AHTF, Instituto Nacional de Antropología e Historia, file no. GRO-06.

14. AHTF, Instituto Nacional de Antropología e Historia, file no. GRO-06, medical certificate, 4 March 1948.

15. Gil, "Amelia Robles," 8.

16. AHSDN, Cancelados, Amelio Robles and Mendieta Alatorre, 1961, 112–22.

17. AHTF, Instituto Nacional de Antropología e Historia, file no. GRO-06.

18. Eduardo Albarrán Orozco, "Nadie podía decirle mujer al *Güero* Robles porque sacaba su pistola," *La Jornada del Sur*, 21 June 1999, 12.

19. Guadalupe Robles, taped interview by author, 18 January 1999; Gabriel Heredia, taped interview by author, 18 September 2002, Xochipala, Guerrero.

20. Civil registry of Zumpango del Río, Guerrero, book of certificates of birth, adoption, recognition, and arrogation for the year 1890, Act 160, sheets 59 and 60,

4 November 1889. On 3 November, Catholics commemorate the martyr Malaquías, according to *Calendario más antiguo de Galván* 2002 (141).

21. Jacobs 1982.

22. AHTF, Instituto Nacional de Antropología e Historia, file no. GRO-06, Gil, 1927.

23. AHTF, Instituto Nacional de Antropología e Historia, file no. GRO-06, Gil, 1927.

24. APGD, Museo Na Bolom, M/1987, 1945.

25. AHTF, Instituto Nacional de Antropología e Historia, file no. GRO-06. Rodolfo López Nava de Baltierra, Francisco Mendoza Palma, Estaban Estrada, and Ignacio Nava de Catalán issued certificates of merit in favor of Amelio Robles between 1956 and 1958.

26. Decree creating the Mexican Legion of Honor, *Diario Oficial*, 1949, 5; AHTF, Instituto Nacional de Antropología e Historia, file no. GRO-06, letter from Amelio Robles to Juan Andreu Almazán, 16 February 1953.

27. AHSDN, Cancelados, Amelio Robles Ávila file, birth certificate, 8 April 1957.

28. Monsiváis 1984, 159–77.

29. Ibid.; Monsiváis 1998, 23.

30. Womack 1968, 306, 314; Brunk 1995, 328.

31. Fernando Gaitán, "La mujer coronel cuenta su vida," *Alerta!* 25 February 1978, 5.

32. Gil 1927, and López de Nava Camarena 1995, 101–22.

33. AHTF, Instituto Nacional de Antropología e Historia, file no. GRO-06, Gil, 1927.

34. Casasola 1973, 759.

35. "Gertrude Ederle, la pequeña mujercita rana que cruzó a nado el canal de la Mancha," *El Universal* 3 April 1927, 1, 8; "El secreto de una anciana que tiene ciento cuarenta y tres años de edad," *El Universal*, 27 April 1927, 1, 3.

36. O'Malley 1986, 49–54.

37. Silvestre 1997, 34.

38. Gil, "Amelia Robles," 1.

39. Prosser 1998, 116–51; Gil, "Amelia Robles," 8.

40. Gil, "Amelia Robles," 8.

41. Gaitán, "La mujer coronela," *Alerta!* February 1978, 5.

42. Gil 1933, 8, 9, 15.

43. Irwin, McCaughan, and Nasser.

44. Gil 1938, 187.

45. Vega 1999, 35.

46. The essentialist perspective on Amelia Robles that I criticize here also underlies a brief article of mine (Cano 1988a, 22–24), which marked the initial recovery of Robles's figure in the commemorative discourse of women in the history of Guerrero and was followed by others that shared the same essentialist vision: Turok 1988, 41–44; Enríquez 1998, 41–43; Olga Cárdenas 2000, 309–19. Eltit 1991 and Cano 1999 (25–34) distance themselves from this perspective.

47. Rodríguez Cabo 1937, 20.

48. Soustelle 1976, 39.

49. Duby 1942, 27; APGD, Museo Na Bolom, M/1987, 1945.

50. Duby 1945.
51. Pappe 1994, 27.
52. AHTF, Instituto Nacional de Antropología e Historia, file no. GRO-06, Gil, 1927.
53. Meyerowitz 2002, 11–15.

GABRIELA CANO

The War on "Las Pelonas"

Modern Women and Their Enemies, Mexico City, 1924

ANNE RUBENSTEIN

Se acabaron las pelonas
Se acabó la diversión
la que quiera ser pelona pagará contribución

In the summer of 1924, Mexico still trembled on the edge of revolution-ary conflict, as it had for many years.[1] The Sonoran elite had not yet consolidated their hold on the national government: the possibility of armed struggle for power remained open. Nor did the government yet control much of the country with any certainty. But in Mexico City—at least if the magazines and newspapers of the day can be trusted—a truly important battle was being fought that summer: the debate over the length of women's hair had escalated to the point where men brawled in the streets and violently attacked women.

This was a global conflict, or nearly so. A fashion for short, blunt haircuts ("bobs") had followed the international spread of silent cinema. Given its connections to the movies, getting such a haircut represented a commitment to "the modern" and a break with "tradition" anywhere a woman tried it—though which of the multiple and complicated mean-ings of those terms were intended depended on whose hair was cut. In the English-speaking world, women who made such gestures of affiliation with all that was up-to-date were known as New Women, or flappers, a reference to their loose, relatively short dresses which supposedly flapped in the wind. But in Mexico, such women called themselves *las pelonas,* the short-haired women, and that is what their enemies called them, too. Their short hair, more than anything else, inspired violence from their male peers.

The Vogue for Athletic Women

In the spring and summer of 1924 masculinized self-presentations by Mexico City women met with a great deal of rhetorical resistance, even before the physical violence began. The vogue for short hair and athletic bodies for women caused a kind of border panic because it had come from outside Mexico and because it was spreading beyond the small group of elite women who had already adopted it. Opposition to the style was cast in terms of defending national or racial purity. The first signs of trouble appeared at the newsstands of Mexico City in April 1924, as magazines and newspapers suddenly took up the question of las pelonas, with dozens of articles describing them in either critical or joking terms. One of the most popular magazines in the country, *Revista de Revistas,* devoted an entire issue to them.[2] As the debate intensified, the Mexico City press tended to depict las pelonas condescendingly, characterizing them as women attempting to follow imported trends. But other tensions lay beneath such nationalist objections to the pelona style: the debate was not only about the distinction between the national and the international but also about race and class divisions.

Indeed, a new and radically different idea of feminine beauty had taken hold in urban Mexico, as it had in Europe and the United States, and by 1924 relatively poor and dark-skinned young women had begun to experiment with it. While the modern image was reflected in fashion—flapper dresses, short hair, and new cosmetics, shoes, and undergarments—the change was not limited to material goods that could be purchased at salons, boutiques, and department stores. It also encompassed a new ideal for women's bodies and women's ways of moving, what Ageeth Sluis has called "the Deco Body": long, thin limbs and torsos, short hair, and vigorous (but graceful) physicality.[3] Beginning sometime around 1920, a rage for female athleticism, or at least for images of female athleticism, shaped the pictures ordinary Mexicans encountered, if not the activities they pursued.

Relatively few Mexican women actually participated in athletic activities (except for dancing) in the 1920s, but *images* of women in vigorous motion were omnipresent and influential. True, masses of young people, male and female, had been mobilized in demonstrations of nationalist fervor through group gymnastics—in Mexico City hundreds of students and teachers engaged in such displays during at least five inaugural ceremonies for the new Estadio Nacional that took place in the spring and summer of 1924—and many more were learning folk dances, volleyball, and basketball through the missionary efforts of the new, revolutionary Ministry of Education. But imagery of women athletes tended to represent members of a rarified elite: the country-club set. The First Lady herself, who often appeared in flapper dresses and cloche hats, belonged to this category. Describing another (more or less) First Lady, Plutarco Elías Calles's daughter Hortensia, who became his formal escort upon the death of her mother, Sara Sefchovich writes, "She was a dynamic youth, who exemplified the changing lifestyles of women who belonged to the comfortable classes: dressed in the fashions of the twenties, with loose clothes, liberated now from rigid corsets, adorned with long necklaces and with hair cut short . . . playing tennis dressed in white and driving her deluxe automobiles."[4] Upper-class women from the United States who lived in Mexico at the time helped popularize such fashions; for example, in a well-publicized debutante ball for Mexico City's "American colony," seven of the nine young women pictured in newspaper coverage of the 1924 event had bobbed hair.[5] Although there could not have been many such elite, athletic young women in Mexico City, they were pictured everywhere: architectural decorations and murals, silent films imported from Europe and the United States, newspaper and periodical advertisements, movies, cartoons, comic books, illustrations in textbooks and advice manuals, fashion magazines, matchbook covers, burlesque theater and other public spectacles, and both the women's pages and the sports sections of newspapers.[6]

Such pictures reflected changing ideals of femininity. "Fashion gave way to comfort," according to Julia Tuñón, and at last "women who were thin, agile, and athletic could consider themselves beautiful too."[7] But this was not at all a rebellion against fashion; rather, it was sweeping change in the clothing, accessories, and "look" that high society accepted as fashionable. The chic clothing of the 1920s, which minimized breasts and hips while it exaggerated the length of arms and legs, announced this new look for women. After almost a century of argument and agitation, the international dress-reform movement had triumphed: elite women abandoned corsets and heavy, ankle-length skirts in favor of clothing that enabled them to move easily, breathe deeply, and participate in active sports. Newspapers and other media celebrated female stars of the day—Isadora Duncan, for instance, who was much admired in Mexico's print media, or the president's daughter described in the passage above—precisely because of their physical ease and grace.[8] Indeed, journalists frequently linked lightweight, flowing clothing and physical exercise; one magazine article, for example, exhorted female readers to "never make use of corsets, because gym classes and elastic-waist skirts are enough to give you a lovely body."[9]

All the changes in fashion added up to an idealization of lean, androgynous, youthful women in vigorous motion. In pursuit of this ideal, advice books and magazines for women published between 1920 and 1940—in North America, South America, and Europe; in Spanish, French, German, and English—almost always suggested daily exercise, ranging from sit-ups to hurling "Indian clubs." (Often such advice sounded vaguely political: one such book proclaimed that "no other remedy remains—if we are not to fall into the morbidities of decadence—than to return to . . . Nature, above all in that which touches on hygiene and sport.")[10] The boyish look of the healthy, active New Woman, flapper, or pelona remained one of a range of possibilities for female self-presentation in Mexico at least through the end of World War II.

The new fashion spread across Mexico rapidly, but unevenly, beginning around 1920. It arrived first at places where women had the greatest access to recently imported media: silent films, fashion magazines, and dress patterns. So the image of the pelona appeared in Mexico City, port cities like Veracruz, and cities at the border with the United States before it entered the rest of the country. In those places the new fashion was supposed to be reserved, at first, for unmarried young women of the upper classes. For instance, in 1925 elite society in Mérida decreed that "it was terrible for a married woman to have short hair," though bobs were in vogue for unmarried young women and hair was kept short on children of both sexes. But in 1926 "lots of [elite] married women had their tresses cut, and nobody had anything to say about it."[11] In rural Yucatán and small-town Morelos through at least 1928, young women kept their hair long in back even when they trimmed it in front.[12] A visitor to Mexico City as late as 1928 was so startled to see an older middle-class acquaintance's short hair that he noted it in his journal: "Her hair is bobbed."[13] But in photographs taken in Mexico City after 1920, upper-class girls and women attending tennis tournaments or country-club dances were far more likely than not to have short hair, and almost no women photographed playing tennis or golf had long hair.[14] Some young women even received encouragement from their parents to take this bold step, as one Mexico City woman was to remember some decades later: "I cut off my braids. My mother said okay. My parents agreed that it wasn't anything harmful or dangerous, just a new fashion. Fashion is the least predictable thing in the world. My father didn't get involved with [the question of] my braids. It was my mother who said: 'Nobody wears braids any more, why are you still wearing them?'"[15]

But the plethora of images of athletic women in mass media and high art reflected a reality beyond shifting fashions in dress and hairstyle. Elite Mexican women were busily engaged in the sporting life in the 1920s and 1930s. Many of them played tennis, while some participated in other athletic activities.[16] Some continued riding bicycles, as upper-class young women had been doing since the turn of the century.[17] Photographs taken in the 1920s show well-to-do women engaged in golf, diving, swimming, various forms of equitation, and fencing. Some Mexican women even tried mountain climbing: in 1921, female adventurers made single-day ascents of Popocateptl.[18] And for women of all classes and practically all ages there was dancing.

Ordinary Mexican women, without access to elite pastimes, encountered the new vogue for female athleticism in other ways. They saw athletic women depicted in magazines, newspapers, and silent films, where they always seemed both desirable and up-to-date. (A male clerk summed up the meanings implicit in these descriptions when he responded to a Mexico City newspaper's survey of opinions about the pelona style: "It is very clean, very hygienic, and very well suited for these modern times.")[19] Ordinary women also encountered the new female athleticism through the state, especially through their recruitment into various programs and projects of the Ministry of Education. People drew connections among state-sponsored events—for instance the training of hundreds of young women as gym teachers in Mexico City's new school especially dedicated to that purpose—and the wider trend toward "modern" mobilizations of women's bodies in the arts and spectator sports, and the new fashions which some young city women were adopting. Thus, in 1924, criticism of fashionable young women could be, by extension, criticism of the political project with which they had associated themselves.

Trying to Resign from *La Raza Cósmica*: Critiques of Las Pelonas

In July 1924, a newspaper advertisement for a silent movie from the United States, presented in Mexico as *Mujeres modernas* (*Modern Women*), connected the image of international modernity with the idea of changing gender roles and relations when it described the global danger posed by New York society women: "Our era . . . of ascendant progress in civilization, has brought with it the unbinding of women in every sense: physically, morally, socially, psychologically, and materially. Today the woman is not what she was . . . the weak being who, from the stone age until the beginnings of this century, has not had a voice nor a vote, nor a will of her own. Women grow more powerful every day. . . . The vogue for bobbed hair, hygienic and aesthetic, has spread to every corner of the world."[20] Similarly, from 1923 to 1925, when Mexico City periodicals printed reviews of movies made in France, England, and the United States, they frequently described the leading actress—Theda Bara, Constance Talmadge, Clara Bow, or Laura La Plante—as a flapper, and the term was never intended as unmixed praise.[21] And reviewers assumed that Mexican "señoritas would go to the cinema to witness the defense of or the attack on this new mode of feminine hairdo."[22]

Thus, opposition to the vogue for flapper clothes, short hair, and athletic female bodies could be cast in terms of defending national or racial purity, which the cultural critic Salvador Novo did almost fifty years later. "The thick hair inherited from la Malinche," he wrote, was a special source of national pride, which in turn explained why "las pelonas called more attention to themselves [in Mexico] than they did in other nations, and were the objects of mockery."[23] That is, a woman who cut her hair could be seen as trying to resign from *la raza cósmica*. Similarly, in 1924 a woman journalist worried, "Today we admire the strength, agility, and health of foreign races, obtained through exercise . . . [but] in Anglo-Saxon countries, an excess of sporting activity by women is creating a third sex, known as the neuter sex; this, in place of benefiting the race, will tend to destroy it. This will happen due to the abuse that the weaker sex has made of some sports in the crazy rage to masculinize itself."[24] The criticism of new ways of moving and dressing as foreign was implicit in a slang term for one style of bobbed hair: women with especially short hair were called "rapados a la Boston."[25] Defenders of the vogue for athletic women—perhaps undiplomatically—also emphasized its racialized aspects and the challenge it posed to Mexican nationalism. For instance, the artist Angel Zárraga (who was then living in Paris and painting a series of heroic portraits and murals of male and female athletes) told an interviewer from a Mexico City magazine that he made a picture of women playing soccer "to counteract . . . the impulse our race has toward morbidity. . . . That deliberate effort at perfecting ourselves, submitting the body to gymnastic practice, will serve us well in Mexico where dreamers are so abundant."[26]

Racialized explanations for opposition to women's haircuts moved easily from national pride to uglier sentiments. Another magazine article published in 1924 offered this history of the trend for short hair: "In our times, women of every nation have cut off their braids . . . to follow a style set by the girls of a nation whose women lack tender sentiments and agitate for change. . . . Three years ago in New York City this [trend] started among the fashionable women of Wall Street, and especially those of the Jewish neighborhoods, arriving instantly among the actresses of vaudeville and some from the cinema too who appeared with their hair done à la 'Bob.' "[27] Humorists, too, expressed anxiety over the possibility of this trend spreading into the nation and outside its appropriate social and racial location. The magazine *La Dama Católica* parodied an article supposedly taken from a French periodical called *Pages Medicales et Parisiennes*. *La Dama Católica*'s version suggested that the healthiest "modern sports for women" would be "those ancient ones which one cannot fear overdoing": mopping, sweeping, and washing clothes.[28] This joke relied on the assumption that the masculinization of Mexican women was caused by the prestige of foreign ideas about health, sport, and gender. Perhaps the end point of the process through which the media conflated pelona style, sport, and the exotic came in July 1924, when the weekly magazine *Jueves de Excélsior* jokingly ascribed the vogue for short hair to women's yearning for more free time in which to play "the Asian game of Mah Jong": "No woman . . . wants to waste a minute in which she could be engrossed in the play of the 'dragons,' 'winds,' and other exotic figures."[29]

Sometimes, however, jokes and complaints about las pelonas implied that they had made themselves sexually unavailable or unattractive to men. Several journalists, a poet, and the advertisement for *Mujeres modernas* all mentioned the German philosopher Schopenhauer's dictum that a real woman was long of hair and short of thoughts—with the implication that short-haired women were likely to lack feminine charm in other ways, as well.[30] Self-declared opponents of the new style warned "ugly girls (and ugly old women)" not to be "tricked" by pretty pelonas into bobbing their own hair.[31] In other words, only women whose value on the marriage market was high had enough social capital to risk some of it by bobbing their hair.

The androgynous pelona style threatened to erase the visual differences between the sexes, and Mexican media sometimes wrote as if the new style also threatened to erase the visual markers of racial difference. One newspaper cartoon, again from the summer of 1924, showed an aged woman whose body type and dress suggested that she was an Indian; throwing off her rebozo to reveal a short, blonde haircut, she explained that she had "made herself chic!"[32] The cartoon's humor (and anxiety) arose from the woman's incongruous age, social class, and (especially) race. Another cartoon from the same newspaper, published a week later, depicted two housepainters observing a female passerby leaving a beauty parlor: "Just like our old brushes," one observed, "so little hair and so much paint [makeup]!"[33] The tension underlying this joke lay in how an upper-class woman had made herself the object of comment for working men—her new hairstyle brushed away the barriers between classes. Similarly, the Sunday supplement of the Mexico City newspaper *Excélsior* ran a photograph of three women getting their hair cut in a barber shop—a very male space—with a caption which referred to the "various *criollitas* [little white girls] waiting their turn," tempering the shock of androgyny in the image with language that stabilized the subjects' race and class.[34]

Defenders of las pelonas tended to accept this view. A woman who referred to herself as "pelona y todo" in an interview with a newspaper conceded that not all women had "the right to cut their hair"; those who were too ugly, too thin or too fat, too old, not healthy enough, or "one of those barrel-shaped girls so representative of our race" should keep their hair long.[35] So the idea of *raza*, or race, was key to both sides of this argument: neither opponents nor defenders of las pelonas wanted women who appeared too Indian ("barrel-shaped") or too poor to adopt this new style. Both sides—at least, both sides among the group of people whose views on the topic appeared in Mexico City periodicals—were complicit in a bargain in which newly permeable boundaries between genders were traded off for increased rigidity in the barriers between races.

But a *corrido*, or folk ballad, of the day drew a very different picture of las pelonas. It mocked them as "sitting at their window / waiting for Pancho Villa / so that he would give them a sister"—in other words, they were his concubines.[36] The ballad thus suggested that the pelonas resembled the beautiful young women whom everyone understood to have been Pancho Villa's many wives: mestiza and from poor or working-class backgrounds, apparently sexually available, closely associated with the revolution, and both participants in and examples of feminine modernity. The tension between these two ways of thinking about las pelonas, either as white, elite young women participating in an international fashion trend or as poorer and darker-skinned young women participating in the revolution, helps explain some of the confusion and anger that led to physical violence against real-life pelonas in the summer of 1924.

ANNE RUBENSTEIN

The War against Las Pelonas

The arguments against las pelonas soon moved beyond rhetoric. Some of the real-life consequences of these words were relatively minor, as when immigration officials turned away a group of women tourists attempting to enter from Brownsville, Texas, because they were wearing "knickers." A consular official explained to journalists that "previously many women had entered in such attire and had conducted themselves not in a manner in accord with the dignity of decent Mexican families."[37] But in Mexico City in the summer of 1924, things went further.[38] Sixty years later, a woman who had been a young, short-haired student herself at the time remembered it as follows.

> When short hair came into fashion, it even led to fights between [preparatory school students]. . . . Those of us who had cut our hair produced a moral panic among the boys. They did not tolerate it. There were fights . . . because a girl who had been passing by the School of Medicine—in those days in the Plaza de Santo Domingo—was taken away by the boys to be punished. They hit her or maltreated her. And this infuriated [students from another school]. They felt bad, well, who knows what they felt? It was a historical episode, something very expressive of what a man wanted to find in a woman. I think that there were many very serious differences between us, but one of the most notable, the most objective, was hair, long hair.[39]

Although her account does not agree in every detail with newspaper reports printed at the time, the speaker's remarkably close recall of these events more than half a century later suggested how important and upsetting they were.

The rhetorical war in the newspapers and magazines of the day began in April but had escalated by late June to the point where most newspapers mentioned the topic every day. In mid-July the church weighed in on the question. The archbishop of Mexico City gave a long interview in which he threatened to take steps against "women who forget decency, natural modesty, and elementary decorum in attire" similar to those that had been taken by the archbishop of Milan, Italy, two weeks earlier: banning women with short hair from the local cathedral.[40] (That the archbishop of Mexico City turned immediately from this subject to his complaints against the revolutionary state may indicate how closely connected las pelonas were to the revolutionary government, at least in the archbishop's imagination, or it may simply suggest that both topics mattered to the cleric and the journalist who interviewed him.) A few days later the same newspaper reported on a "meeting of Catholic ladies" in

Brussels which had denounced the new fashions for women, insisting that they were especially ill-suited for churchgoing. The congress of Catholic women declared, "In a Christian fashion one may deduce that there will be immorality where there is immodesty, and one may affirm that the churches are not cinemas or dance halls."[41] In reprinting this section of the declaration, the newspaper spacialized the issue of las pelonas in two ways: first, it drew attention to the transnational dimensions of the new fashion and of opposition to it; second, it juxtaposed two types of urban space, the church and the theater, as stages for different types of public enactments of femininity. In Mexico City, other urban spaces—the public schools, the streets, government offices, and a train—soon offered a new kind of stage to this drama.

At the same time as the archbishop was airing his views, an afternoon tabloid printed a very long account of a meeting of anti-pelona activists. The story in *El Universal Gráfico* was so lurid that it lacked the slightest plausibility, as its second sentence made obvious by assuring readers that "this has nothing to do with a reporter's fantasy, but is a real fact." The account probably does not describe what really happened as much as it conveys what editors thought they could get away with; thus, it can point to what readers at the time—with expectations raised by the rhetorical war over female modernity in the newspapers, by popular songs, and by cinema—believed *might be happening*. The article details a meeting of "a strange grouping of students and workers" to plan "direct action" against "our modern 'flappers' which will begin this very day. Five young girls have been selected to suffer the exemplary punishment . . . of having their heads shaved in public." The reporter claimed to have learned of this by eavesdropping on a "heated discussion" in a train from Mexico City to an unnamed small town. He followed the young men he had been listening to off the train, through the town, and to "an old farmhouse" where, "hidden behind a tree," he observed more debate among a larger group of "men whose faces were obscured and bodies partly covered" by large, pointed hats and loose robes. As the leader explained to the reporter once he had been discovered, the members of this group were arguing about how best "to impose punishment on whatever woman does not repudiate this Yankee style." In case readers missed the reference, the article help-fully reminded them of the recent "case of Señor Mercader . . . who had perished due to the activities of the famous gang, the Ku Klux Klan. At the time nobody placed any faith in our information and even now there are persons who believe the whole story was made up by the editors of this newspaper." But, the article reiterated, violence really would be visited on pelonas who did not "abstain from going out on the street until their hair grew long again"—and the attacks would begin very soon, perhaps the next day.[42]

Of course, this tale of the defense of female purity owes very little to facts about the Ku Klux Klan and its activities against Mexicans resident in the United States, and almost everything to the movie that established the myth of the Klan, D. W. Griffith's *The Birth of a Nation*. If the anti-*pelona* men quoted in the article did exist, they and the reporter would have seen this film very recently: although produced in Hollywood in 1915, the silent film premiered in Mexico City 9 October 1923 and played in second- and third-run movie houses in the city for months afterward.[43] There are some bizarre aspects to this analogy between the story detailed in the newspaper article and the plot of *The Birth of a Nation*. In the film, African American men threatened the virtue of white American women, who were defended by white American men; in the newspaper story, young Mexican women threatened their own virtue, and had to be pro-tected from themselves by young Mexican men. But the plot of *The Birth of a Nation* must have seemed to fit a conservative vision of Mexico's situation in the early 1920s. The movie tells of heroic male interventions in the aftermath of a civil war. These interventions are, according to the logic of the film's plot, justified during a period in which political chaos (summed up in the movie's stunning representation of President Lincoln's assassination) and newly permeable boundaries between the races (figured in the movie as the threat of sex between white women and black men) menace the peaceful, patriarchal home. *El Universal Gráfico* may or may not have gotten its facts right about the particular meeting it described, or invented, in this article. Yet the article did reveal some important truths about the underlying tensions and conflicts that would soon result in physical violence against young women in Mexico City.

To express the growing sense that something bad was going to happen soon to las pelonas, even more respectable newspapers than *El Universal Gráfico* probably fabricated certain stories. By the middle of July 1924, Mexico City's dailies certainly contained some unlikely reports. *El Univer-sal*, for instance, wrote about a group of pelonas living in the upper-class neighborhood of Tacubaya who announced that they planned to form a "Pro-Pelonas Club" that would "be just like a union, with the goal of supporting this hygienic and modern style, which in no way offends against morality and proper behavior."[44] This report was, at least in part, a joke—the "Pro-Pelonas Club" never reappeared in the media—but, again, it responded to an intangible but widely felt sense of menace. And two weeks after *El Universal* printed this article, something did happen.

At 8:30 in the evening, Monday, 21 July 1924, a group of preparatory school students grabbed a young woman with bobbed hair from the entryway to her school, the Escuela Nocturna Doctor Balmis. (As a student of this new vocational night school, she would most likely have been mestiza and working-class: a perfect representative of the kind of "quasi-flapper" disdained even by the elite ·pelonas.)[45] The preparatory school students took her to another location where they shaved her head, then released her—a crime small enough that at least one major daily paper, *El Universal*, did not bother to cover it. But the following evening the anti-pelona forces made their actions much more public. Around seven o'clock, at the brand-new campus of the Mexico City Medical School, a group of male students—both first-year medical students and students of the nearby National Preparatory School—gathered in front of the school gates, where they made loud, insulting comments to any short-haired woman in their vicinity and applauded passers-by with long hair. Young women studying at the medical school had to be escorted out of the building by older male classmates. The younger students who were part of this mob started throwing water as well as insults at any pelona they saw and making feints at them with scissors and razors. Finally they dragged two unlucky young women inside the medical school, forced them into the building's new showers to be "washed," and shaved their heads. This event was large and public enough to draw a crowd, which was eventually joined by the police and a Cruz Blanca ambulance in which the young women were borne away.

Various groups responded quickly, almost always in support of las pelonas or, at least, in opposition to violent attacks on young women. The first reactions came from some of those who were directly involved: the students and the newspapers. The male medical students who had defended their female peers visited newspaper offices, complaining about the scandalous behavior of their younger male colleagues. Female medical students and female students at the preparatory school wrote to the newspapers explaining that the majority of their male colleagues made them welcome, even though the schools had only recently begun admitting women. The "modernity" of the whole affair entranced commentators: one report noted that *El Universal* had been kept informed of the news by "more than fifty persons who used the telephone to contact us." Yet the papers also editorialized against "an attack which dishonors the city," as one headline put it, while they reported on the negative responses of other interested parties.[46]

Some responses seemed opportunistic. Reinforcing the connection between silent film and the pelona identity, one chain of Mexico City cinemas took out an ad denouncing the attacks and promising that "las peloncitas" would be "very much at home and completely secure" in their theaters.[47] The most important Mexico City theater went further: five days after the attacks began, el Teatro Iris announced two special shows, a matinee and an evening performance, to which only women would be admitted. The centerpiece of the show was a speech by the director of the theater, the famous diva Esperanza Iris, titled "The Right to Have Short Hair, Dedicated especially to Las Pelonas." (El Teatro Iris thriftily repeated the entire program the following weekend for a mixed-gender audience, and Esperanza Iris was still lecturing her audiences on the subject when she toured Colombia in 1928.)[48] Meanwhile, the municipal government, which already had a special police patrol assigned to movie houses and theaters in the city, stepped up surveillance of these locales "with the object of impeding any barbarian who would attempt such an indescribable crime."[49]

Political actors of several types also entered the argument. The industrial workers' union, CROM (Confederación Regional Obrera Mexicana) had its representative tell reporters that the workers were opposed to attacks on las pelonas, adding, "Now we are certain that any worker is more correct in his behavior and better knows how to respect a lady than any student does."[50] The spokesman for the National Agrarian Commission sent a telegram to the governor of the Federal District (essentially, the unelected mayor of Mexico City) complaining that the female employees of the commission feared similar "outrages" and demanding that the government act to protect them.[51] The Ministry of Education (SEP) announced that if it caught the students who had committed the assaults, they would be expelled.

At the same time, some students acted to assure the public and the state that they could police themselves. Male students from the School of Medicine formed a "Pro-Pelona Committee" in opposition to their classmates who had attacked the pelonas, while cadets from the Military College and the School of Aviation proclaimed their intention to join patrols that would guard pelonas at other schools, including the Medical School. This, in turn, led to confrontation between the male students of the different schools three days after the second attack. In an atmosphere of great excitement and tension, young men from the School of Aviation and Military College marched to the Medical School, where students from other schools had gathered in support of male students. Reporters had gathered to watch, along with a number of members of the army, who were in uniform and armed. (Newspaper reports are unclear about whether someone in authority had sent them there in an official capacity or whether they went simply out of curiosity or solidarity with the cadets.)

Shouted taunts between the two groups of students seemed to be on the verge of turning into physical confrontation when the soldiers began ordering the entire crowd to disperse. Finally, one soldier fired his gun into the air, nonetheless mildly wounding a student, and this convinced everyone else to leave.

The next day, another group of young men in Tampico attacked two short-haired women who had been sunbathing at Miramar beach, but the women managed to swim away while the boys were arrested and briefly jailed. Meanwhile, presumably under some pressure from the authorities, leaders of the two groups of Mexico City students met privately and agreed to a public reconciliation. Thus, the "question of honor" was resolved among the young men, without a word from the women over whom they had quarreled.[52] Indeed, at least temporarily, las pelonas disappeared from the story.

A Question of Honor

As magazines recounted the whole story in subsequent weeks and months, public disavowal of the attacks on las pelonas took on a more joking, relaxed tone. Journalists focused once again on who the short-haired women were and whether or not they were sexually attractive. Commentary on the young men who had attacked them shifted quickly to a register of amused comprehension. A typical magazine article combined mild scolding of the attackers—"Everyone has the right to follow universal fashions, however ridiculous they are, and nobody should mind if their neighbor puts on the most absurd things. . . . That is, actually, one of the great triumphs of civilization"—with explicit approval of them: "One can understand this student gesture against some of the exaggerations into which we slip by imitating the styles of other places. There are short-haired types who ought to be banned from the city streets . . . who deserve to be locked up and fed nothing but bread and water until they allow their hair to return to the simple and plain style of their nation. These tonsured types . . . who have all the habits of present-day Yankees, now I do believe that they require direct action. Those [women] really should be bathed and given prosthetic braids."[53] Who were these young men, that their public attacks on women could be so easily understood and forgiven? What about las pelonas inspired their violence?

The position of all the groups of students—las pelonas, their attackers, and their defenders—in relation to the post-revolutionary state was critical. To begin with, all were students. As a great deal of historical research has shown, education in all its aspects was formed by the post-revolutionary state's efforts to build the nation and legitimize itself. Who was able to learn or teach what, and the locations and conditions in which they did so, were product and project of the state's ideological and pragmatic interests. And the experience of education was profoundly gendered.[54] Although newly available educational opportunities benefited both young men and women in Mexico City, women had more to gain. For women other than those who belonged to the very highest strata of the elite, education was a gift of the beneficent new government, whether they were attending recently gender-integrated institutions such as the National Preparatory School, recently created vocational schools, or recently expanded and improved schools such as the Normal School. As they adopted the pelona style, ordinary young Mexico City women were claiming two different identities: they were embodying the glamorous look of local society women and international celebrities, but at the same time they were associating themselves with the revolution and its gendered educational projects.

Young men who were privileged and powerful enough to attended such important, longstanding institutions as the National Preparatory School and the Military College had little to gain and much to lose by these changes in the national system of higher education. Such young men might have felt called on to defend these institutions and their positions within the political life of the nation. (Among the student leaders who spoke for groups on the side of the pelonas were young members of the Ávila Camacho and the Cosío Villegas families, which gives some indication of the schools' important role in the formation of the nation's military, political, and intellectual leadership.) Both those who attacked the pelonas and those who defended them used their status and the traditions of their institutions to shape and give meaning to their words and actions. Throwing water and violently shaving the heads of the unwilling were longstanding habits of students at most of the schools involved, usually practiced by older students against new students and understood as an act of initiation. When first-year students turned these practices against female students of other schools or went to the campuses of other preparatory schools in order to engage in these practices, they inverted their meanings in a refusal of school tradition. At the same time, the shaved heads, as well as being an ancient gesture of shaming and social ostracism, also implied "modern" hygienic practices, as in the treatment of prisoners or of people suffering from lice. In doing so, the young men who attacked las pelonas positioned themselves as the agents of (revolutionary) moder-

The War on Las Pelonas

nity and their victims as the subjects of modernization. (Recognizing this, las pelonas responded by claiming their hairstyle as "more hygienic" than long hair.)[55]

The military cadets who defended las pelonas, on the other hand, wielded a different discourse. Instead of acting from within the intellectual framework of modernizing social hygiene and repudiation of tradition, the military cadets adopted the paternalist stance of the new Mexican government. The post-revolutionary regime in 1924 was just beginning its efforts at inserting all Mexicans into a "Revolutionary Family" with itself as the patriarchal head of household.[56] The young male defenders of las pelonas cast themselves as representatives of the head of household; hence they became responsible for "their pelonas" as the newspapers put it, in "a question of honor."[57]

Both groups of young men—attackers and defenders—can best be understood as trying to fit las pelonas back into a subordinate position within a new reality. (This new reality was not limited to the political and economic changes created by the revolution; it also included cultural change encouraged by movies, radio, cheap periodicals, and changing fashions.) Las pelonas had challenged this subordination, both in the national imagination and in their real lives in the classrooms they shared with male students. These attacks did not put an end to their challenges to gender hierarchy, but it did shift the terms on which they fought.

Embodying Revolution (Las Pelonas Strike Back)

The student attacks and the cultural climate which enabled them to happen pushed las pelonas to stop claiming to belong to a "global revolution" in fashion spread by international media.[58] Instead, they protected themselves from physical danger, and improved their opportunities, by strengthening their cultural and political affiliations with the state. Rather than trying to resign from la raza cósmica, they came to embody the revolution.

To understand the terrain to which las pelonas moved, consider another series of events occupying the newspapers in the spring and summer of 1924: the inaugural celebrations of the National Stadium. These ceremonies—grander versions of the inaugural festivities with which the SEP celebrated the opening of public schools in the capital—began even before construction was entirely finished, so that (as newspaper ads explained) ticket sales could finance completion of the building. Such mass performances of "rhythmic gymnastics," to use the English-language term, have nearly vanished from public memory, and they have received little attention from cultural historians or other scholars.[59] But at that time they were important and popular alternatives to spending leisure time attending church or going to the movies—the other pastimes available on the Sunday afternoons during which such events were held.

The new stadium's modernist architecture earned little admiration. "From the beginning, in 1924, it was the target of abundant joking due to its unpleasant looks," Eduardo Flores Clair wrote, which added to the "general suspicion" that the edifice would find its most frequent use in "political ritual, that is, mass meetings, state-sponsored demonstrations, and political rallies."[60] (This rumor proved true: by 1932, the head of the physical education department was forced to plead with SEP administrators for even occasional use of the stadium for track-and-field events, rather than for "festivales . . . del departmento del Gobierno.")[61] But if the stadium lacked public approval, that only would have increased Secretary Vasconcelos's interest in emphasizing its importance. Thus the Ministry of Education organized not one, but three grand patriotic festivals to inaugurate the National Stadium.

Most of the women involved in these spectacles—choreographers, organizers, dancers, athletes, and Red Cross nurses—conformed to the flapper mode. Some had not cut their hair, but tucked it away under caps or cloche hats. Although such was not Secretary Vasconcelos's intention, these festivals and similar occasions became opportunities for women employed by the state to display themselves en masse as both pelonas and representatives of the revolution. Thus, newspaper coverage of these events tended to show women in gym clothes or pseudo-Greek togas, all cut more or less on the model of the flapper dress. Such events also demonstrated, probably inadvertently, the vast numbers of young women who had found a place for themselves within the SEP. The program for the third of the three inaugural events, for instance, included a mixed chorus of a thousand voices singing pieces by Beethoven, Delibes, and Wagner; an "Egyptian Dance" performed by female students from the school of physical education; and baton-twirling by a group of 200 female gym teachers.

Newspaper coverage pointed out that the crowd in the cheap seats responded enthusiastically to all "the different numbers on the program," which the reporter claimed to be "a proof of the intellectual betterment of the people."[62] Spectacle organizers seem to have believed that large numbers of performers would, in themselves, attract audiences: one of the advertisements for the National Stadium inauguration was headlined "800 GYMNASTS/300 DANCERS/1,000-VOICE CHORUS."[63] Members of the audience shared the experience of being in a dense, somewhat disorderly

The War on Las Pelonas

crowd while watching a highly organized (but almost as tightly packed) group of nearly the same size, and this seems to have been the most memorable—perhaps the most meaningful?—part of the experience. The SEP certainly took great care to have as many participants as possible in the parades, demonstrations, rallies and mass spectacles it organized, requiring teachers to attend, if not join in or organize, such group displays. The SEP used whatever means it had to reward participation. The *Boletín de la Secretaría de Educación Pública* printed detailed accounts of "Festivales al aire libre" in most of its early issues.[64] Teachers responsible for the organization of such small festivals or the choreography of portions of larger ones like the National Stadium inaugurations were excused from giving classes, sometimes for weeks.[65] Teachers who led students in successful performances during patriotic festivals received fulsome letters of congratulations from their supervisors, which went into their permanent files.[66] The SEP also punished teachers who failed to attend or participate in patriotic festivals (which often took place on national holidays when teachers might not otherwise have been working). School officials had to distribute written orders requiring attendance, take roll at the events themselves, and write memoranda to their own heads of section explaining any absences.[67] Special inspectors visited gym classes regularly to make sure that teachers were preparing students properly for their roles in such events. In sum, a system of surveillance, reward, and punishment helped the SEP make these patriotic spectacles what they were.

All this might suggest that viewing or participating in these spectacles was a dreary business, engaged in only by those who had no choice. But other evidence shows that large numbers of people attended events such as the inauguration of the National Stadium eagerly and enjoyed what they saw. The first inauguration ceremony filled every seat in the stadium, according to newspaper accounts, at ticket prices ranging from two pesos for a seat on the shady side to fifty centavos for general admission— roughly the same price as a theater ticket and slightly more than a first-run movie theater seat. People waited in long lines to enter the stadium, with women holding parasols to ward off the sun and policemen standing by to enforce order. The two subsequent inaugural ceremonies were not quite as popular: photographs of the stadium show perhaps half the seats empty. Nevertheless, someone did steal or counterfeit a large bloc of tickets for the third inaugural ceremony, which suggested that the criminal assumed that the tickets could be sold easily enough to make the crime worth the trouble.[68] These were popular events, and their popularity was their point: the people who collaborated in producing them hoped to create a new kind of spectacle and a new form of civic ritual, displacing both cinema and church.

Through events like these, athletic women claimed the New Woman as their own, and they made a healthy Mexican revolutionary out of her, even as other sectors of the revolutionary state insisted that the proper way for women to contribute to the revolution was as good mothers (Gabriela Mistral's *Lecturas para mujeres* best illustrates this tendency). As the athletic, energetic, and short-haired New Woman retreated from her public affiliation with transnational media culture, she sought protection within the new revolutionary state by entering the new schools as a student, teacher, or administrator. During and after the days in which the new stadium was inaugurated, las pelonas found other ways to continue self-fashioning and self-presentation by working within the SEP. They elided the terms of art and physical education, much as they had blended sports with fashion in their self-presentations as pelonas. Thus the Ministry of Education made "physical culture" a part of its fine arts division during its 1921 organizational phase, while schools taught gymnastics, sports, games, and dance as a single subject from the beginning of primary school through the end of normal school.[69] (Rhythmic gymnastics remained part of the public school curriculum, at least for little girls, through the 1960s.)[70] School inspectors checked physical education teachers to see how well they taught dance, how much revolutionary zeal they displayed, and how well their students worked together in forming gymnastic tableaux; in rural schools, visiting inspectors were often greeted with special pageants, which included demonstrations of dance by "las señoritas profesoras" and their students, exhibitions of students' skills in basketball or track and field, and declamations of patriotic sentiment written by well-trained pupils.[71] Women teachers made rhythmic gymnastics and folk dance central to the patriotic mobilization that was supposed to take place within the new urban public schools.[72] The SEP sent piano accompanists (almost all women) from school to school in Mexico City to help.[73] Sports and the arts blended together—especially as practiced by women—and enlisted themselves in the project of building the new, revolutionary (female) Mexican citizen. This was partly a matter of the state marshaling all possible resources for its project, partly a question of genuine belief and enthusiasm on the part of participants, but also partly a reflection of ambitious women's ability to make use of the state.

This does not mean that the Mexican flapper lived happily ever after. Short hair on women remained a troublesome image to many Mexicans, inspiring a *lotería* card that elided the pelona figure with the image of death. More than twenty-five years later, *El Universal Gráfico* sent a reporter out to ask random passers-by what Mexico's worst problems were, and one of them complained that "short hair on women . . . makes it possible to confuse them with men."[74] Women's haircuts continued to inspire controversy until they were replaced in the public imagination by the question of men's hair—specifically, long hair worn by male university students—in the late 1960s. And the memory of the 1924 attacks on las pelonas lingered, at least in the minds of university women, longer still. High schools, colleges, and universities remained a site of gender conflict. As late as the 1980s, at least one women's athletic team at Universidad Nacional Autónoma de México (UNAM) called itself Las Pelonas in memory of the women who were attacked in 1924.[75] And as newspaper articles and magazine stories from the summer of 1924 suggest, at the time and well into the future las pelonas remained easy to mock and to trivialize, if not to physically abuse. Yet it is also true that by taking advantage of the new opportunities the post-revolutionary state opened up for them, las pelonas made their way in the world at least partially on their own terms. A limited victory, but a real one.

Notes

Research for this article was funded through the Social Science and Humanities Research Council of Canada. Thanks, too, to fellow panelists and audience members at the first Conference on Mexican Women's and Gender History, and the 2003 Reunión de Historiadores Mexicanos, Estadounidenses y Canadienses for especially lively and helpful discussions of this topic. Although all the readers and editors of this volume aided greatly in clarifying the argument here, I am especially grateful to Gabriela Cano for her scholarly solidarity and sense of humor; without her help, this article could not have been written at all. Translations throughout are by the author unless otherwise indicated.

1. "The pelonas are finished / The fun is done / She who wants to be a pelona / Will have to pay her dues." Thanks to Carlos Monsiváis, who remembered this rhyme from his youth, and to Gabriela Cano, who passed on the citation.

2. *Revista de Revistas* 15, no. 733 (25 May 1924).

3. Sluis 2005.

4. Sefchovich 1999, 225.

5. "Prominent Society Women and Debutantes of the American Colony," *El Universal*, 4 July 1924, sec. 3, p. 3.

6. For images of female athletes in commercial imagery, high art, and architecture see the exhibit catalogue *Art Déco* (1997, 25–30 and throughout). For athletic women in murals, see the frontispiece to "Decoración de la Sala de Conferencias en la antigua iglesia de San Pedro y San Pablo," *Boletín de la Secretaría de Educa-*

ción Pública 1:2 (1922); also see Angel Zárraga's murals for the Mexican embassy in Paris, as reproduced in *Angel Zárraga* 1990. For athletes on matchbox covers see *Mexicana* 1998.

7. J. Tuñón 1987, 167.

8. On grace in motion see, for example, the Sunday-supplement cover story "La Gimnasia Armónica," *Excélsior*, 8 May 1922, sec. rotograbado, p. 1. On Isadora Duncan's reception in Latin America see Blair 1987 (261–68).

9. Alvarez 1920, 6.

10. García Martí n.d., 170. Thanks to Eric Zolov for the reference.

11. Asael T. Hansen, "S-T-Y-L-E-S—1–9-2–0–1–9-3–3," unpublished field notes on Mérida, folder 24, box 47, Robert Redfield Papers, Special Collections, Regenstein Library, University of Chicago.

12. Asael T. Hansen, "Miss Blackburn. Styles," unpublished field notes on Mérida, folder 25, box 11, Robert Redfield Papers, Special Collections, Regenstein Library, University of Chicago; Margaret Park Redfield, journal entry for 24 January 1928, folder 17, box 3, Margaret Park Redfield Papers, Special Collections, University of Chicago.

13. Frederick Starr, journal entry, 15 July 1928, notebook 56, box 21, Frederick Starr Papers, Special Collections, Regenstein Library, University of Chicago.

14. This refers to thousands of photographic negatives from this era, mostly taken at country clubs but some from other sporting events (AGN, Fototeca, Enrique Díaz collection, boxes 14–17 and elsewhere).

15. Guadalupe Zúñiga de González, quoted in Cano and Radkau 1989 (34).

16. Evidence for this in the 1920–1930 period can be found in newspaper coverage of country-club tennis tournaments and other sporting events, particularly in the sports sections of *Excélsior* and *El Universal*, as well as in photographs from the Díaz collection (AGN, Fototeca, Enrique Díaz collection, boxes 14–17 and elsewhere).

17. Beezley 1987, 50–51.

18. Frederick Starr, journal entry, 7 September 1921, notebook 53, box 21, Frederick Starr Papers, Special Collections, Regenstein Library, University of Chicago. Starr's informant, Carmen Tancerrado, joined an expedition led by the painter and muralist Dr. Atl (Gerardo Murrillo), which left the base camp at two in the morning, she complained, in order to make the sixteen-hour round trip. She appears to have had little respect for Dr. Atl: she told Starr that the artist's book on Popocateptl was "not scientific and exact." William Beezley writes that mountaineering, including climbing Popo, was of no interest to Mexicans before the 1922 founding of the Explorers' Club; the expeditions led by Dr. Atl appear to have been more a nationalist expression than a gesture toward adventure or fitness (1987, 40–41).

19. "El reporter preguntón," *Excélsior*, 12 July 1924, p. 5.

20. Advertisement for *Mujeres modernas* (*El Universal*, 9 July 1924, sec. 1, p. 5). The same advertisement appeared six more times in the subsequent ten days. What was this movie? The advertisement contained no imagery, merely this somewhat inflammatory text. It lists "Corinne Griffite," surely a misspelling of Corinne

Griffith (a huge star of the day), as the film's lead actress. But the usually reliable Internet Movie Data Base (http://us.imdb.com/) does not mention Griffith's participation in any such film, although she did star in a 1922 melodrama about high-society life titled *Divorce Coupons*—perhaps these advertisements refer to some version of that film?

21. See the reviews reprinted in Garrido 1997 (402–4, 410–12, 415, 418–20, 456).

22. "Celuloide" [Jaime Torres Bodet], review of *Pelona* in *Revista de Revista*, 29 November 1925, cited in Garrido 1997 (451).

23. Novo 1972, 31.

24. Santín de Fontoura 1924, 38.

25. Sorando 1924, 6; also "Por cada pelona que sea rapada se cortará el pelo a una trenzuda," *El Universal Gráfico*, 23 July 1924, sec. 2, p. 1.

26. Frías 1924, 22.

27. Serrano 1924, 9.

28. "Deportes femeninos modernos," *La Dama Católica*, 1 August 1924, p. 25. Thanks to Patience Schell for this citation.

29. "De la excentricidad mundial" 1924, 13.

30. For instance, Jacobo Dalevuelta, "Las pelonas dispuestas a defenderse con energía," *El Universal*, 22 July 1924, sec. 2, p. 1; "Las Pelonas" 1924, 6; Serrano 1924, 9.

31. "Por cada pelona que sea rapada se cortará el pelo a una trenzuda," *El Universal*, 23 July 1924, sec. 2, p. 1.

32. Cartoon, *El Universal*, 12 July 1924, sec. 1, p. 5.

33. Cartoon, *El Universal*, 15 July 1924, sec. 1, p. 5.

34. "También en nuestro medio," *Excélsior*, 1 June 1924, sec. rotograbado, p. 2.

35. Jacobo Dalevuelta, "Las pelonas dispuestas a defenderse con energía," *El Universal*, 22 July 1924, sec. 2, p. 1.

36. D. P., "Las tres pelonas," in Kuri-Aldana and Mendoza Martínez 1987 (402). Thanks to Gabriela Cano for this reference.

37. "Mexican Officials Kick on Women in Knickers," *El Universal*, 14 July 1924, English news section.

38. The following account of these events is based on coverage in the Mexico City newspapers *El Universal*, *El Universal Gráfico*, and *Excélsior* and the magazines *Jueves de Excélsior* and *Revista de Revistas*, 1 April—15 August 1924, except where otherwise noted.

39. Guadalupe Zúñiga de González, quoted in Cano and Radkau 1989 (33–34).

40. "Interesantes declaraciones del arzobispo de México," *El Universal Gráfico* 12 July 1924, p. 2.

41. "La moral y la moda," *El Universal Gráfico*, 15 July 1924, p. 3.

42. "¿Se trata de ejercer la acción directa contra las pelonas?" *El Universal Gráfico*, 16 July 1924, p. 8.

43. See Amador and Ayala Blanco 1999, 186.

44. "En tacubaya se formará un Club Pro-Pelonas," *El Universal*, 10 July 1924, sec. 1, p. 11. The phrase was "moralidad y buenas costumbres."

45. "Los enemigos de las pelonas hacen su víctima," *El Universal Gráfico*, 22 July 1924, p. 7.

ANNE RUBENSTEIN

46. "Por cada pelona," *El Universal*, 23 July 1924, sec. 2, p. 7; "Una Cuestión de Honor que deshonra la cuidad," *El Universal*, 25 July 1924, 3.

47. "Como y en donde estarán seguras las pelonas" [advertisement], *Excélsior*, 24 July 1924, p. 7

48. "Teatro Iris hoy Sábado 26" [advertisement], *Excélsior*, 26 July 1924, p. 8; "Hoy Sábado se repetirá la función femenina en el Iris" [advertisement], *Excélsior*, 2 August 1924, p. 11; AHDF, Fondo Esperanza Iris, program, expediente 14, caja 101. Unfortunately, no documentation remains of what Esperanza Iris said in these lectures.

49. "Una protesta de la Sociedad de Alumnos," *Excélsior*, 23 July 1924, sec. 2., p. 1.

50. Ibid.

51. Ibid.

52. "Se solucionó la 'cuestión de honor' entre cadetes y estudiantes de medicina," *El Universal*, 27 July 1924, sec. 2, p. 1.

53. Sorando 1924, 6.

54. See, for example, Bantjes 1998; Becker 1995; Gonzalba Aizpuru 1998; Loyo 1997; Rockwell 1994; Vaughan 1982; Vaughan 1997.

55. "La opinión de ellas," *El Universal*, 22 July 1924, sec. 2, p. 1.

56. For a discussion of the concept of the "revolutionary family" see Zolov 1999 (1–8).

57. "Los cadetes del Colegio Militar lanzan un reto a los estudiantes de medicina," *El Universal*, 25 July 1924, sec. 2, p. 1.

58. Jacobo Dalevuelta, "Las Pelonas dispuestas a defenderse con energía," *El Universal*, 22 July 1924, sec. 2, p. 1.

59. There are exceptions. See, for instance, Lorey 2001, 233–48; Flores Clair 1991–92, 163–69; Vaughan 1982, 239–66; Gallo 2005, 201–26.

60. Flores Clair 1991–92, 168.

61. Memorandum, Jefe de la Sección de Educación Física to Subsecretario del Departmento de Bellas Artes, 6 May 1932, expediente 4, caja 44, ramo Subsecretaría de Educación Pública.

62. "El festival artístico de ayer en el Estadio Nacional resultó muy brillante y concurrido," *El Universal*, 14 July 1924, sec. 2, p. 7.

63. Advertisement, *El Universal*, 13 July 1924, sec. 2, p. 8.

64. See, for instance, *Boletin de la Secretaría de Educación Pública* 1, no. 2 (n.d. [1922?]): 207–10.

65. See, for instance, José Gorostiza to Judith Cabrera, 12 September 1932, expediente 3995bis/2, tomo 9114, fondo Bellas Artes, Subsecretaría de Educación Pública.

66. For instance, José Martínez Ceballos to Emilio Alcazar, 18 September 1928, expediente 1, tomo 9504, fondo Bellas Artes, Subsecretaría de Educación Pública.

67. For example, see Adalberto G. Moreno al Jefe del Depto. de Bellas Artes, 29 November 1934, expediente 13, tomo 3958, fondo Bellas Artes, Subsecretaría de Educación Pública.

68. Advertisements for tickets to the event warned customers not to buy the "missing" tickets (see advertisement, *El Universal*, 13 July 1924, sec. 2, p. 8).

69. "Anteproyecto para la organización," expediente 1049, caja 9512, ramo Bellas Artes, Subsecretaría de Educación Pública.

70. Blanca de Lizaur, personal communication, 2 August 1999.

71. Frederick Starr, journal entry, 19 August 1928, notebook 57, box 21, Frederick Starr Papers, Special Collections, Regenstein Library, University of Chicago.

72. See, for instance, the life history of the dance teacher and athletic coach Alura Flores (Cano and Radkau 1989).

73. For the inspection forms of physical-education teachers and teaching schedules of piano accompanists see the personnel files in caja 9504 and caja 9114, ramo Bellas Artes, Subsecretaría de Educación Pública.

74. Antonio Ortiz, "En la calle se Dice," *El Universal Gráfico*, 11 January 1950, p. 16.

75. Verenice Naranja, personal communication, 12 July 2001.

ANNE RUBENSTEIN

Femininity, "Indigenismo," and Nation
Film Representation by Emilio
"El Indio" Fernández

JULIA TUÑÓN

Emilio Fernández was one of the great directors from the so-called golden age of Mexican cinema.[1] He was nicknamed "El Indio" because his mother was Kickapoo.[2] Identifying himself with indigenous Mexicans, he felt himself an outcast.[3] While his movies were closely linked to the official nationalist project, they also expressed his own obsessions, which did not always coincide with state ideology. His stereotypical images of Mexico and all things Mexican—images in which women and indigenous peoples are fundamental—were viewed around the world.

Although Fernández filmed all forty-one of his motion pictures between 1941 and 1978, his ideals regarding many themes, such as *indigenismo*, derive from the 1920s and 1930s. During the 1940s, he established a prototype repeated with slight variations and expressed through the themes of his movies, his theories, and his artistic expression. His films do not express a homogenous block of ideas but rather a field of force among ideas, motion pictures, and social practices. His stories outwardly display the ideology of post-revolutionary government, but in their mimesis and diegetic incongruities, filmic "*lapsus*" (as Marc Ferro would say) seep through that reveal shades of meaning within his thought—contradictions, ambiguities, incoherencies.[4]

One central cultural theme in Mexico during the 1940s dealt with nation-building and the search for Mexican identity, which official policies attempted to sustain through indigenous culture despite common practices of contempt and racism toward living Indians. Emilio Fernández clearly promoted opinions coinciding with post-revolutionary nationalist projects, such as the exaltation of patriotism, agrarianism, secular positions regarding religion, indigenismo, and the need for education. He conveyed them through love stories and displayed them adorned with panoramic beauty and pre-Hispanic and colonial works of art. He preferred to set his stories in rural environments. Yet, despite his role as an agent of official ideology, one would be mistaken to consider his filmic stories as univocal; on the contrary, he often criticized existing injustices, albeit in an oblique fashion.

Fernández had his own filmic style, fed by classic Hollywood cinema, especially that of John Ford, and also by the Russian Sergei M. Eisenstein, from whom he discovered "the struggle and freedom through social justice."[5] El Indio attempted to build a nationalist project through film, and his works join those of other greats in what is known as the Mexican School of Cinema.[6] Despite their peculiarities, his films form part of Mexican institutional cinema.[7]

According to Fernández, indigenous people form the most delicate, pure, and beautiful part of society. Through his images, he transported the indigenous from the periphery toward the center and endowed them with a symbolic prominence. *María Candelaria* (1943) received at the 1946 Cannes Film Festival an award that, at the time, was commemorative rather than competitive. From that point on, his films gained appreciation in the Old World and his characters took on iconic dimensions, bathed in their own light. Considered paradigms of quality and beauty, his films were exported around the world. His stereotypical indigenous people became a widely accepted cultural symbol that seemed to reference the "true and authentic Mexico," which coincided with the interest in primitivism in vogue among Europeans who admired the innocence and ferocity of peoples marginalized by civilization.[8]

Fernández's gaze toward Indians combined interestingly with his perception of women. Although the director boasted of his machismo, one look at the titles of his movies demonstrates women's centrality to them as well as to his construction of the nation, where women have a significant role as Mexico's emblem and sustenance. "Women are the soul of a people, the inspiration, everything, no?"[9]

The Problem of the Indian in El Indio

Fernández was a director with ideas of his own, but he also expressed the context in which he lived. During his filmmaking years, Mexico savored post-revolutionary peace and crossed into modernity while conserving and/or adapting many pre-revolutionary ideas and practices. One of Fernández's main themes of conflict refers to Indians. As specific, historic beings they do not seem to fit in comfortably within the abstract concept of "the indigenous" that was rhetorically considered the symbolic foundation of Mexican nationality. In those years, the age-old distinction between the contemporary Indian, seen as a hindrance to modernity, and the pre-Colombian Indian, endowed with heroism and dignity, was clear. Despite explicit valorization of the indigenous, Indians had occupied an inferior position in the social hierarchy since the sixteenth century. The only options open to them were adaptation to the dominant culture, which implied losing their own characteristics, or marginalization, wherein they would remain apart from the advantages of development.

During the 1940s, the debate over the definition of indigenous persisted: were they indigenous by race, culture, and/or language? Rodolfo Stavenhagen studied the most common analytical perspectives based on concepts of culture, social class, community, ethnicity, and internal colonialism (exploitation) and observed that each one of these perspectives called for a different approach.[10] However, for each perspective, culture "provides identity and distinction to a human group and strengthens social bonds."[11] For Mexican Indians, the category "ethnicity," which implies a definition of cultural rather than racial (biological) or social characteristics, was useful. In fact, those Indians who assimilated into national culture eventually considered themselves mestizos regardless of their racial characteristics.

Indigenous culture is expressed largely through language, but also through the importance attributed to the use value (versus exchange value) of natural resources; forms of land tenure; the value ascribed to animals; social, political, and labor organization; the practice of medicine and hygiene; and concepts of loyalty and identity. At a time when cultural difference was perceived as inimical to the national modernizing project, aboriginal cultures were seen as unchanging, endowed with an essential, ontological nature that blocks their development.[12] Associated with passivity, atavism, and magical thinking, Indians have, in short, been stereotyped as a beautiful but savage group of human beings.

In 1950, Luis Villoro defined indigenismo, understood as "a configuration of theoretical conceptions and processes of consciousness that, throughout the ages, have manifested that which is indigenous."[13] He synthesized ideas prevailing during Fernández's time, noting that the indigenous appear always as a reality that is revealed but never revealing: they are named by the European, by the *criollo*, and by the mestizo, but they never assume the role of judge before those who describe them. Thus, they appear as an object to be illuminated from the vantage point of concerns and needs that are foreign to them. Their function is to symbolize the hidden, incomprehensible side of Mexican identity.[14] "That which is Western symbolizes the reflexive light; that which is indigenous, the deep, dark, unknowable magma that the light attempts to illuminate. The indigenous is symbolic of the part of the spirit that escapes our rationalization and refuses to be illuminated."[15] The Indian, then, is the other that contradicts and is configured in opposition to Western thinking. According to Villoro, indigenismo is a basic reference in the construction of Mexicanness, proceeding from negation to recovery to integration with the national. He addresses diverse and often polemical ideas, but in the main agrees with Marie Chantal Barre that the indigenous gradually lose the character of their origins in order to transform themselves into an ideology at the service of the state and "yet another resource for maintaining and replicating exploitation and oppression."[16] She adds, "*Indigenista* policy appears as a mixture of liberalism, nationalism, and internal colonialism that . . . can take on progressive . . . or reactionary characteristics."[17]

The issue of integration was particularly important in the twentieth century because it was vital to fulfilling the revolutionary ideal. The theme of integration appeared in El Indio's films, as it coincided with some of his personal obsessions. When Fernández made his films, indigenismo was a vibrant ideology in which he enthusiastically participated. As he sought to recover his own aesthetic, favoring new artistic expressions, the romantic desire to discover a Mexican essence or nature became his obsession. As Carlos Monsiváis wrote, "Perhaps there is grandiloquence, but there is no demagoguery. . . . [T]he indigenous *is* the national."[18] Emilio Fernández emulated this sentiment and represented it in cinematographic language, enthusiastically appreciating the culture without perceiving the contradictions that seeped into his films.

Mexican cinema was undergoing an unprecedented boom. The ideas and culture of Fernández's time, including its contradictions and tensions, were expressed in his films, which was why he was able to create a special bond with his public. Jorge Ayala Blanco has noted that in these films the indigenous presence is quite scant if one takes into account that nearly 10 percent of the population belonged to one of these ethnicities and that over half were mestizo.[19] Fernández's infrequent indigenous figures tend to be extras or scenery, lacking psychological complexity or the ability to take action: either they are good-natured characters who provide comic relief because they speak Spanish poorly and do not understand technological advances, or they are enigmatic Indians who seem impenetrable and blend into the background. Either way, one witnesses in Fernández's films the most hackneyed stereotypes. Nevertheless, ideas transmitted via representations and stereotypes forcefully expressed meaning. Such filmic representations exposed the generalized notion of that era that indigenous groups were social throwbacks, jeopardizing the very modernity to which Mexico aspired, and thus contradicting another dimension of indigenismo: the idea of assimilating them into modernity through education and other social policies.

The first films to touch on the *indigenista* theme were silent movies. With the advent of "talkies," new standards of representation were set by *Janitzio* (Carlos Navarro, 1934), the first film starring Emilio Fernández. By the 1940s, Fernández dominated the theme. In his movies, it was not always clear who were Indians and who were peasants, probably due to the influence of Cardenismo (1934–40), a populist movement in which the concept of "Indian" became for a short time synonymous with exploitation rather than ethnicity. However, in some films Fernández does provide an explicit indication of culture, highlighting forms of dress, mentality, customs, and even language, with the indigenous appearing as "the other" of the established order. The movies in which his protagonists were clearly Indian were *María Candelaria* (known in the United States as *Portrait of Maria*), *La perla* (1945), *Maclovia* (1948), and *Paloma Herida* (1962). In others, the indigenous presence consists of extras, as in *Río Escondido* (1948), or else their characters are not explicitly Indian but rather poor mestizos or assimilated Indians, as in *Pueblerina* (1948).

Emilio Fernández emphatically declared his appreciation of the indigenous world, turning his gaze toward it in order to elevate it: he made it beautiful, possessing a certain honor, dogged by suffering that absolved it of any evil: "I want to dramatize their lives through my work in order to touch and raise the awareness of the wretched governments that marginalize our true race [la verdadera raza nuestra]. . . . It is our race and they are the victims."[20] Beautiful but defeated victims: yet in his films, features of the Indian as a social throwback creep in.

His model of indigenismo is suggested in *María Candelaria*. An initial scene shows the continuity between pre-Hispanic culture and living Indians, with Fernández repeating the technique Eisenstein used in the rushes for *¡Qué Viva México!* (1930–32), in which pre-Colombian sculptures alternate with living, dispassionate faces, revealing the similarities between their physical characteristics and suggesting the preeminence of the past in the present, the force of an "eternal" culture. The influence of Robert Flaherty and his ethnographic cinema is also clear, as is that of F. W. Murnau in *Taboo* (1930), with regard to the protagonists' association with "the noble savage" persecuted by Westerners.

In Fernández's construction of the indigenous, not only do story and plotline count but cinematic language does as well. For example, the solemnity and rigidity of the faces are reflected in the movements of the camera itself, which are very slow or even fixed: in *La perla* only the wind moving the clothes of Indians as they watch the sea reveal that this is cinema and not a projection of still photography. The figures are more like sculptures than human beings and convey a permanence beyond social change. The soundtrack also influences the stereotype. Indians often appear in silence, attentive to natural sounds. Speech is not their strength: their characters' lines are always sparing and enigmatic.

Moreover, Fernández's depiction of the masses insists on a rigid concept of the indigenous, since crowds are presented as a block, as part of a collective devoid of individuality, moving atavistically without any opinions of their own, like a machine. This is evident in the groups carrying torches that advance menacingly in *María Candelaria* or *Maclovia*. In *Río Escondido* the priest has the bells rung for the Indians to line up and receive their vaccinations; the villagers are surprised by their docility and liken them to sheep. A great many of Fernández's stories narrate the conflicts of heroes who attempt to live their own lives amid this homogenous and overwhelming group that is the collective.

Although Fernández emulates Eisenstein in the use of natural actors, he positions them always in the background, leaving the leading roles to famous celebrities and stars. Secondary actors conform the masses, while audiences identify with the heroes, whose faces they recognize. The scholar Aurelio de los Reyes finds that indigenista nationalism blends with cosmopolitan nationalism, which in turn is based on glamorization.[21]

Fernández stereotypes his Indians, transforming them into an ideal, a symbol of purity and dignity despite their defeat. They are all equal and form part of nature, of that landscape of impassioned beauty known as Mexico. The cultural differences of indigenous groups are homogenized by an undifferentiated use of scenery, costumes, music, and rites to narrate the films. It seems that being photogenic is more important than ethnographic precision. Fernández plays close attention to customs: one sees dances, pilgrimages, the blessing of animals on Corpus Christi day in *María Candelaria* and on the Day of the Dead in Pátzcuaro in *Maclovia*. Although this is folklore for tourists, it does provide an account of the protagonists' rituals and devotions. One sees the respect paid by Lorenzo Rafael (the leading man in *María Candelaria*) in honoring the rites of a healing woman, but one also sees him pray in front of the church.

A hallmark of his plots is a tension between tradition and modernity that goes beyond the theme commonplace in contemporary cinema. Fernández refers to two conceptions of a nation not yet integrated and in perpetual conflict. In one conception is an essential, eternal, centripetal Mexico that communicates only through symbols and symptoms, a Mexico of cyclic time and inescapable destiny, of natural disposition: the indigenous Mexico.[22] Above this conception, without penetrating, modifying, or suppressing it, is modern Mexico, made up of individuals who make their own history and face social and political conflicts. Civilization attempts to impose itself over elemental Mexico, and the two worlds interact, blend, and repel each other. Dominating and resisting, they work together and then grow apart. Their heroes are trapped within this struggle. Fernández explicitly endorses the official discourse of indigenismo and attempts to modify the order of things, but among the lines and images he equates the indigenous with nature and the Western with culture.

His films were successful in European festivals, but their acceptance among the national cultural elite was problematic. Before *María Candelaria* received any awards, painter Diego Rivera ranted, "This conceited guy . . . may be a success beyond our borders, where our reality is unknown [but] the film is rubbish, a terrible attack against the reality of our Indians."[23] Emilio Azcárraga, boss of movie exhibition circuits, also felt the film was pessimistic and would be unsuccessful. Only after it received an award at Cannes did it come to be considered a national treasure. Thus, the foreign gaze assigned a value to the film and transformed it into a banner of the nation.

Women and Indians: The Necessary Other

Since the late nineteenth century, women's social participation had increased; however, the standard of conduct for women remained conservative. Women's conditioning was strict: they represented the nation. Mexican women had to be docile, pretty, chaste, and hardworking in order to act as an emblem of the fatherland, a notion that held firm throughout the twentieth century. Woman, as a dark continent (as Freud put it), had to forgo her own projects in order to symbolically fulfill her function of alterity. The representation of women in established Mexican cinema expressed this cliché. Women were the other for men: the feminine was constructed in opposition to the masculine and formed an abstract entity, "Woman," an entity that suppressed the social characteristics of actual women and likened them to a biological species. Yet, for the purpose of narrating cinematic stories, this "Essential and Eternal Woman" was disassociated through a series of stereotypes, with the figures of Eve or Mary being the most evident.[24]

El Indio takes his own stand in this regard, albeit supported by the binary system guiding Western mentality: the values and characteristics assigned to men and women are exclusive and specific, and the masculine hierarchy is superior. Women are associated with nature, while men represent a culture with the ability to go out and hunt. Although common to Western thinking, the concept of nature in Fernández is overwhelming and rooted in mythical thinking. His couples represent the original dyad, the original complementarity that human beings tirelessly seek, and his tragedies narrate his protagonists' successive failures to achieve this completion. His images stereotypically express a series of fundamental archetypes, such as those that place nature in opposition to culture.[25]

The coincidence between feminine and indigenous figures is noteworthy, as the latter also fulfills the function of the other. In the mid-twentieth century difference meant otherness. Throughout Mexican history, women and Indians were the most closely watched and judged social groups, and on the grounds of their difference, whether biological or cultural, their conduct was structured and supervised.

The stereotype of the Indian describes him as a submissive, timid, weak, subordinated being who is tied to the earth and to nature, with an atavistic and irrational mentality due to his intellectual weakness and his identification with nature. The same attributes are ascribed to women because of their reproductive function: they embody the other, opposite manly reason and activity. Indigenous women thus appear as doubly oppressed figures; in fact, they present an ideal metaphor for both the feminine and the indigenous conditions. In Fernández's cinema they are both.

In an attempt to characterize the psychology of Mexicans based on their history, Santiago Ramírez, points out that since the years of the conquest "women have been devalued to the extent they are gradually identified with the indigenous. Men have been overvalued to the extent that they are identified with the conqueror, dominant and prevailing."[26] He goes on to say that masculine-feminine parity associated with the active-passive principle acquires "significant and dramatic aspects."[27] Ramírez concludes that, for the Mexican, "the indigenous and the feminine have been converted into an unconscious equation."[28] Such seems clear to a director who constructs women, "making them feminine, demanding from them morality, a vibe, a certain pride, and naturally a certain dignity, right? But I want to have them always as faithful dogs, obedient to man and man ready to die in defense and honor of his woman . . . and [for] the construction of a family."[29] For Emilio Fernández, women are nature, not only nourishing but also the realm of fate and destiny, a ferocious, over-whelming, and devouring nature that absorbs human beings. Men, on the other hand, are culture: it is therefore ideal that men order and command, while women follow and obey.[30]

The indigenous woman is perhaps the best-known feminine figure in Fernández's cinema, with María Candelaria (Dolores del Rio) as the para-digm. Fernández considers indigenous women to be the most virtuous, because they assume their role in nature more naturally. In his films they distinguish themselves by preserving tradition, the home, and ties to the land as well as by their instinctive character and their abnegation in the face of suffering.

Despite Fernández's explicit discourse of indigenismo, he likens the feminine to the indigenous while the masculine is associated with the mestizo or the criollo. Indigenous men are very handsome and dignified but incapable of fulfilling their prescribed function of naming, acting on, and imposing themselves on nature. Indian women are doubly women, while Indian men are feminized. This, according to Emilio Fernández, who prides himself on his machismo, positions Indians on an inferior level and apparently contradicts his own most forceful assertions.

In *Paloma Herida*, Danilo Zeta (Emilio Fernández) arrives in a Gua-temalan village to exploit the Indians and corrupt their customs one by one, killing all those who oppose him and raping the women. The film is a critique of false progress, to such a degree that in a cabaret called La dolce vitta, the Indians learn to dance the twist. In one important sequence Zeta announces his new order to the invaded town: during a slow, lengthy scene, the image of a row of indigenous men's naked legs and huaraches-shod feet alternates with the image of the pants-sheathed legs of the row of women facing them. The shot opens up to reveal the Indians with woolen wraps and headdresses and the prostitutes, mestizas, chewing gum and watching indifferently as the mestizo master shouts out orders, brandish-ing his pistol and promising them to the Indians in exchange for the latter's docility. The crux of the image is Danilo Zeta, in the center of the frame, imposing order that, while unjust and brutal, is order nonetheless. The Indians are dressed in a type of skirt, the so-called *enredo*, and the women wear trousers: they are the agents of a false progress that breaks the natural order of the sexes, an original Eden in harmony with nature where all was fun and games. The Indians will not be able to transcend their submission: they are shown drunk, fighting among themselves, and beating their wives, who abandon them. The protagonist, Paloma (Patricia Conde), will be the one who, in her character as nature, kills the villain.

Just as women bring life, they also bring death. Paloma appears in a beach town one day, quiet and sad, dressed in white with a black shawl, determined to kill her rapist. She is in jail and refuses to speak: the muteness of the indigenous woman is absolute, and she tells her story—that is, the plot of the film—only when they threaten to take away her son. She kills Zeta, but the evil had already been done: the muteness in which she prides herself can only exist once "progress" has suppressed her true voice, leaving none in its place. The indigenous is defeated, leaving the women voiceless and the men feminized. Paradise has been shattered.

The Films

María Candelaria exemplifies Fernández's indigenista theme. The script was written on thirteen napkins by the director himself as a birthday present to Dolores del Rio, who played the protagonist, and was inspired by the plot of *Janitzio*, in which del Rio starred in 1934. (*Janitzio* was also the basis for *Maclovia*.) *Janitzio* narrates the ill-fated love of a couple driven from Eden because of the imbroglios caused by a white man, with whom Eréndira, the female lead, has sexual relations in order to save her betrothed from prison. She is considered a traitor to her culture and her people, and her punishment is to be stoned to death. Joanne Hershfield argues that through the indigenista theme *Janitzio* reasserts the Malinche myth.[31] This theme was also critical for Emilio Fernández: tragic love would become his recurring plotline.

In the initial scripts for *María Candelaria*, the film is called *Xochimilco* and tells a much simpler story than the final version. The protagonist, María del Refugio, is loved and appreciated in her town, but her betrothed has a jealous temperament and rejects outsiders. The theme tells of the difficulties of integration and the tension between two Mexicos. The definitive script incorporated the element of the town's hatred for the newly baptized character of María Candelaria, moderating the boy's jealous temperament and dramatizing the situation of the protagonist, her marginalization and weakness, making her kindness more noteworthy and her sacrifice more absurd.

María Candelaria establishes itself from the outset as a banner for nationality. Its publicity declared, "Impregnated with the utmost femininity, profoundly racial in character and most distinctive to us, this film, *Xochimilco*, will become a Mexican emblem on screens around the Spanish-speaking world," because the actors "did not disdain dressing in the modest costumes of our indigenous peoples nor to talk as they do, eat as they eat, work as they work and, finally, suffer as they suffer." Thus, the film was considered not only "an artistic endeavor [but also a] patriotic one."[32]

María Candelaria tells the story of a girl rejected by her community because her mother was a prostitute: a woman who was lynched by the villagers, as María Candelaria will be. The scenery consists of the canals and floating gardens, or *chinampas*, of Xochimilco, where she grows flowers and her betrothed, Lorenzo Rafael, cultivates vegetables. José de la Colina notes the omnipresence of this funereal landscape from the first moments of the film, thus foreshadowing the ending.[33] The central theme that structures indigenous life is death: death is its destiny.

The adversity confronted by the couple reaches a climax when María Candelaria falls ill from malaria and Lorenzo Rafael calls on a healing woman, a painter who seeks María Candelaria to paint her portrait, and a doctor. In the film, the artist is meant to be Diego Rivera, who emphatically declares that he wants to paint Mexico and that María Candelaria is "the face of Mexico itself! . . . A pureblood Indian . . . with the beauty of the ancient princesses who eventually subdued the conquerors." Lorenzo Rafael cannot acquire the government-supplied quinine, since Don Damián, the mestizo shopkeeper who controls the medicine's distribution, harasses María Candelaria over an outstanding debt. Lorenzo Rafael enters Don Damián's store at night to steal the medicine and, as an afterthought, takes a dress for María Candelaria to wear in their wedding; for this Lorenzo is sent to prison. María Candelaria turns to the painter for help and agrees to allow him to reproduce her face. When she refuses to pose nude, he completes her figure with the body of another model. Indigenous feminine beauty is the symbol of Mexico, but the canvas cannot be completed without the nude body of a woman. In keeping with pictorial conventions, the face represents the soul ("The face of Mexico itself!"), but the painter needed more: he needed a sexed feminine body. Through the mishaps of the melodrama, the canvas is viewed by all eyes in the town, and María Candelaria ends up being chased and stoned to death, fulfilling an inescapable destiny. Her response continues to be a denial. "I have done nothing wrong," she repeats again and again, as if her conduct were the cause of her misfortune: her murderers are her own impassioned people. Lorenzo Rafael takes her in a funeral ceremony aboard a canoe through the canals of Xochimilco along which they usually strolled.

Femininity, Indigenismo, *and Nation*

María Candelaria symbolizes exclusion: she is cast out even by those who are already marginalized par excellence: Mexican Indians. She exclaims, "How nice it would be to be able to live in peace with the townspeople, treating us like brothers and sisters and not like dangerous animals!" It is significant that she has been stigmatized by the sexual practices of her mother, a characteristic intrinsically associated with the female gender. The scriptwriter Mauricio Magdaleno protested because, he said, prostitution did not exist among the Indians.[34] But the film matters as a metaphor. María Candelaria is doubly marginalized: as an Indian but also as a woman and as a sexed being, which is made evident in the painting.

Fernández's indigenous women are continually sexually besieged by mestizo villains, but they avoid mixing with them. They act in a manner contrary to that of the director's own mother, who left her ethnic group in order to marry his mestizo father.[35] Indigenous women preserve culture and defend the land, but they also resignedly suffer an inexorable destiny. Their men can never defend them: the masculine role remains undermined.

María Candelaria is stoned to death by her own people. What indigenismo is invoked when racial purity is deposited in the naïve goodness of a woman and associated with atavism and submission? What indigenismo, when the rest of her group proudly displays its intransigence and barbarity? One herein observes a lapsus of El Indio: the indigenous is associated with a ferocious, indomitable nature that neither the sermons of the priest nor the proximity of the modern Mexico bordering Xochimilco can calm. The film distinguishes between "the indigenous," the collective represented by natural actors native to Xochimilco, and the natural aristocracy of his protagonist, "with the beauty of ancient princesses." In effect, Dolores del Rio does not look anything like the extras. The explicit discourse of the film insists on the Indians' goodness and authenticity, but the star is dressed by Armando Valdés Peza, one of the most famous haute couture fashion designers, following the norm already established in *La noche de los mayas* (Urueta, 1939), in which *huipiles*, or traditional dresses, were narrowed at the waist to flatter the actresses' figures.[36] Emilio Fernández recalls that he told the star she was representing a little Indian woman and not Cleopatra, but even so the glamour of the stars, the formalism of their style, and the idealization of the Indians goes against the kind of cinema that he wanted to make.[37] The old concept creeps onto the screen, contrasting the living Indian, devalued and sublimated by history, from the exalted ones "with the beauty of ancient princesses." María Candelaria is a turncoat from the past.

María Candelaria reveals the scarce resources with which Indians endure their lives. She is assisted only by her beauty, which wins her the painter's admiration, and her resignation, which seduces the priest. Lorenzo Rafael can count on the support of his community, but nothing more: his room to maneuver runs out in other spaces. Emilio García Riera has pointed out the force of criollo or mestizo characters who can put a name to the couple's disgrace and still help them, although once indigenous barbarity has been unleashed, they are impotent: the priest symbolizes the church; the doctor, science; the painter, art.[38] The relationship is always unequal: they address the Indians with the informal "you" and receive submission in return.

María Candelaria shows certain features of indigenous culture, such as the attachment to the land, that are biological in nature. When the young man considers emigrating, his fiancée dissuades him: "And our *chinampas*? And our flowers? We were both born here, and we have always lived here. This is our land: look how black and soft it is [she takes it in her hands]. How could you want us to leave? . . . They don't want us, but with outsiders it's even worse." The man looks at her, serious, and the scene unfolds in silence, with no background music: immobility is best, and the woman is its spokesperson. Moreover, the land has use value rather than exchange value, and the film never questions the property rights of the protagonist to her hut or the plot of land where she gathers flowers. When Don Damián wants to ruin her, he sends someone to kill her piglet, which symbolizes, more than anything else, an investment in her future and recognizes the importance assigned among the indigenous to animals.

At two points in the film, Náhuatl is spoken: first, when María Candelaria pursues Lupe, her rival in love, who by throwing a stone has broken her image of the Virgin of Guadalupe; she comes to blows with Lupe, throwing her into the water, and the woman threatens in her native language. Náhuatl is also spoken when Lorenzo Rafael leaves the market, irate, in order to avoid the painter who has noted his girlfriend's beauty. Both moments are not only action-packed but also angry. They are images contrary to María Candelaria's reaction when she talks back to the Virgin in a rage: "And you! Why won't you listen to me? You are too hard on us." The priest makes her repent her outburst and ask the image for forgiveness: docility speaks in Spanish.

One of the films derived from *María Candelaria* is *Maclovia*, which repeats many of its patterns: love between Maclovia (María Félix) and José María (Pedro Armendáriz), made difficult by society—as represented by the girl's father, Macario (Miguel Inclán), by harassment from the white man as a romantic rival, and by mestizos as authority figures, in this case the teacher and professional military officer who defend the Indians. In

Maclovia, an old mestizo soldier prevents the lynching and helps the couple escape, in a clear concession to Hollywood happy endings. However, indigenous isolation has in *Maclovia* the necessary setting of an island. The teacher tells the officer, "No native ever leaves the island. For them, it would be worse than death. Here they are born, here they live, here they die." Thus, the denouement of the couple fleeing augurs a new cycle of suffering for the protagonists, placing in doubt the ending's happiness.

Just as in *María Candelaria*, feminine beauty is an ambiguous value: it opens doors in life, but it also leads to problems. Thus, Maclovia chides God for not having made her more ugly. María Felix performs her beauty before humility: her figure is inappropriate, her gestures are not docile or tender, characteristics of Indian women according to Fernández. She cannot escape from the stereotype of the strong, tough woman who made her famous, and perhaps that is also why El Indio saves her from being stoned to death.

In *La perla*, Quino (Pedro Armendáriz) and Juana (María Elena Marqués) are a happily married couple, and she is the prototype of the docile wife. One scene defines her character neatly: she waits outside the cantina, curled up on the ground with her baby wrapped in a shawl, waiting for Quino to finish getting drunk so she can take him home. She watches him furtively in order to protect him.

Once the fisherman finds an enormous pearl in the sea and begins to envision a promising future, he starts laughing uncontrollably, with the arrogance and demeanor of someone who dares to challenge fate: he is filmed from underneath standing in the boat beside Juana. His laughter mixes with stentorian music while she cries: she fears that the balance of her life will be ruptured. Where he glimpses freedom and education for their son, progress and happiness, she suspects death and solitude. Ambition is alien to the indigenous man's desires, and Quino's breaks with the order of things. Although Juana never offers any arguments, her instinctive reaction turns out to be well founded: she is closer to nature, and the plot will go on to describe Quino's failure. Emilio Fernández does not allow his indigenous people either to assimilate to national culture or to find happiness in their own world, and his other films tell of the pain felt by those who set forth in search of other ways of life. In the final scene of *La perla*, the couple throw the great pearl back into the sea. With it go hope, education, well-being, and happiness.

The feminine essence and that of the indigenous is natural, not cultural or social. Nature is formless, ambiguous, chaotic, and should be molded in males by different means: tenderness, violence, authoritarian orders,

JULIA TUÑÓN

love, just to name a few. However, indigenous men are not successful in shaping the world: they lack resources and the words. In the beginning, nature was dominant, but culture prevailed and, with it came the destruction of the aboriginal world.

By Way of Conclusion

In Fernández's films can be discerned long standing elements that were constructed with the retrograde mentality of the times but expressed in the novel language of cinema for the benefit of mass audiences in the modern Mexico of the twentieth century.

On an explicit level, the indigenous characters of Emilio Fernández embody perfection: they are the most beautiful and purest racial group, the most delicate culture. However, through lapsus one observes that they are scenic beings, inscribed into nature, and that any change they attempt is impossible. They cannot modify the life that fortune has given them; they appear to resist progress, contradicting the purpose of a cinema that struggles against social injustice. Fernández constructs a stereotype that shows that the dignity, mystery, and stoicism of Indians cloak their inertia, submission, and ignorance. According to Ayala Blanco, "Fernández's indigenous may very well be docile lambs ripe for slaughter by Evil-worshipping whites."[39] In Fernández's films women are identified with Indians. All women are subjugated, thus indigenous women become a double metaphor for otherness and the quintessence of femininity.

But something disturbing remains: despite his failure, the Indian supports the nation, and he resists in the same way that the feminine, identified with nature, overwhelms and dominates. Through El Indio's cinema, the nation acquires a gendered character: essential Mexico is indigenous, ergo it is feminine and faces the tension implied by a modernity represented through criollos and mestizos—a struggle that expresses the one that exists between nature and culture. Although in all his films the Indians are defeated and the women vanquished, the feminine principle, the indigenous principle, dominates and conquers, albeit solely in order to preserve injustice and inertia.

Notes

1. Classic Mexican cinema, approximately dated from 1931 to 1952, tells stories for entertainment that follow the pattern of prologue, development, climax, and denouement. Such cinema was backed by a star system and classified by genre. The influence of Hollywood is clear.

2. For biographical background on Fernández, see Taibo 1986, Fernández 1986, and Tuñón 1988.

3. Tuñón 1992.

4. Ferro 1974, 246.

5. Tuñón 1988, 25.

6. Standouts include Gabriel Figueroa's cinematography, Mauricio Magdaleno's screenplays, Gloria Schoemann's edition, and actors like Pedro Armendáriz, Dolores del Rio, and María Félix.

7. Institutional cinema is understood as having its own means of representation and narration, with codes and conventions in both form and content that constitute a dominant filmic style that is understood and accepted by its audiences.

8. Tuñón 2002.

9. Tuñón 2000a; Tuñón 2000, 51.

10. Stavenhagen 1979, 11.

11. Ibid., 16.

12. Roger Bartra (1987) critizes the search for a supposedly eternal Mexican being.

13. Villoro 1987, 15.

14. Ibid., 102.

15. Ibid., 226.

16. Barre 1983, 18.

17. Ibid., 234.

18. Monsiváis 1977, 348.

19. Ayala Blanco 1968, 84.

20. Tuñón 1988, 84.

21. De los Reyes 1987, 190.

22. It is interesting to confront the concept of a profound Mexico with the imaginary Mexico defined by Bonfil Batalla 1990.

23. García Riera 1987, 53–54.

24. Tuñón 1998a.

25. By archetypes, I refer to longstanding mental patterns that refer one to the basic human drives. By stereotypes, I refer to the simplification of represented reality through either omission or deformation.

26. Ramírez 1983, 50.

27. Ibid., 50.

28. Ibid., 61.

29. Tuñón 2000, 51.

30. Ibid.

31. Hershfield 1999, 86.

32. "Noticiero Films Mundiales" 1943a, 16; "Noticiero Films Mundiales" 1943b, 16.

33. De la Colina 1985, 1.

34. Meyer 1976a, 30.

35. Fernández 1986, 36.

36. Meyer 1976b, 119.

37. Tuñón 1988, 48.

38. García Riera 1992, 68.

39. Ayala Blanco 1968, 196.

JULIA TUÑÓN

PART TWO

Reshaping the Domestic Sphere

"If Love Enslaves . . . Love Be Damned!"

Divorce and Revolutionary State Formation in Yucatán

STEPHANIE SMITH

On 16 May 1917, Yucatán's official newspaper, *La Voz de la Revolución*, published a letter written by Amelia Azarcoya Medina. Composed a week earlier and addressed to the state's revolutionary governor, General Salvador Alvarado (1915–18), the letter appealed for the governor's help regarding Amelia's divorce from her husband, the well-known and politically powerful notary Crescencio Jiménez Borreguí.

"I am a helpless woman who is longing to put an end to the sufferings to which my husband has subjected me," Amelia wrote, listing the many obstacles she had confronted in her struggle, which had lasted for over a year, to obtain a divorce from her abusive husband. According to her letter, she found it nearly impossible to retain a lawyer since her husband, a popular figure in regional politics and friend to a former governor, bribed and intimidated anyone who attempted to help her. When Amelia finally succeeded in taking her case before the state tribunals, the presiding judge displayed a marked indifference to her situation but treated her husband with the utmost respect. In fact, this same judge ordered the children to live with their father, ignoring the testimonies of Amelia and others who said that he had mistreated his children for years.

After the judge denied her request for a divorce, Amelia demanded "revolutionary justice" from local officials. But even after another six months of a new trial, she remained married, without her children, and without a cent, while her husband lived in their mutual home, maintaining his mistress and family and hosting parties. Describing herself as "one of the many victims who drags the weight of the heavy chain of slavery that until today the revolution has been impotent to break," Amelia insisted that the revolution correct past wrongs.

This letter was just the beginning of the story. For although Amelia was unable to obtain her divorce, the publication of her appeal so outraged her husband that he promptly took his wife back to court. Crescencio argued that his wife had sent the "scandalous" letter to General Alvarado with the sole purpose of damaging his honor and reputation. And now, in response to this public defamation of character, Crescencio demanded a divorce, which, of course, Amelia did not oppose. In the end, Amelia and Crescencio received their divorce, although in a surprising decision, the court found both spouses at fault and thus both lost custody of their children.[1]

Amelia and Crescencio's divorce case reveals much about the changing patterns of gender and the family, including the gendered meaning of divorce. With the liberalization of the divorce laws during the revolutionary era, divorce practices shifted from an overwhelmingly women-initiated process before the revolution to a mainly male-initiated process during the revolution and post-revolutionary consolidation.[2] Men like Crescencio, who generally avoided divorce before the revolution and instead preferred to simply walk away, began to seek divorce in growing numbers. In fact, husbands now sought to reclaim their honor by divorcing unruly wives who had fled the home or otherwise violated the sanctity of the marriage. For example, Crescencio agreed to a divorce only when the local newspaper printed Amelia's plea for help, exposing to the whole community her ardent desire to leave him. At that point Crescencio demanded an end to his marriage, thus ridding himself of an "unruly" wife who had publicly embarrassed him and regaining his honor in the process.

The meaning of divorce also changed for women. Although divorce was an option rarely used in the prerevolutionary years, it nonetheless offered women recourse to leave the most egregious marriages.[3] But after the national government legalized divorce in 1914, and although women still looked to divorce as an escape from abusive marriages, the number of Yucatecan women who sought divorces remained nearly constant.[4] Nonetheless, revolutionary officials presented legal divorce as a viable possibility for women, and thus it afforded women like Amelia an opportunity to influence public discourse about women's rights within the family. Amelia's fury at the corrupt judicial system and her letter to the local newspaper pressured the revolutionary government and Alvarado to fulfill the promise of allowing divorce for women needing relief. By demanding that revolutionary leaders carry out revolutionary ideals, women like Amelia participated in the everyday enactment of the revolution.[5]

In the end, Amelia's and Crescencio's divorce reveals both continuities and changes. For one, the legalization of divorce eliminated neither male sexual license nor female sexual subordination. Instead, divorce was but one more element in the movement toward the rationalization of family life, as the state assumed jurisdiction over functions previously reserved for the family. The privileging of men's social and sexual prerogatives during the revolution encouraged a growing number of men to ask judges to restore their masculine honor through divorce, while women received little help from the courts. Just as revolutionary rhetoric highlighted the idea of "proper" womanhood, revolutionary divorce cases demonstrate that most husbands believed that remaining married to a disobedient wife damaged their honor more than divorcing her.[6] In this manner divorce became a tool to restore masculine honor damaged by wives whose behavior did not fall within boundaries considered proper as defined by the patriarchal conventions of society.[7]

However, women managed to negotiate their place within revolutionary changes, writing letters to newspapers and public officials and learning to work within the revamped judicial system. When the courts failed to respond to their needs, as in most divorce cases, women practiced other means of negotiation. Mary Kay Vaughan argued that even while "the Mexican Revolution of 1910 was a quintessentially patriarchal event for rural women," women were nonetheless able to open "new spaces" for themselves.[8] Vaughan found that by the 1930s, however, government reformers envisioned a "modernization of patriarchy," subordinating the family to the "interests of national development" and rationalizing matters within the domestic sphere.[9] A study of revolutionary divorce cases reveals that the roots of the modernization of the family were, in fact, firmly entrenched within revolutionary reforms directed toward women.

"Modern" Divorce Laws, 1915–22

Before the Mexican Revolution, divorce entailed only legal separation, leaving couples without the ability to remarry.[10] Nonetheless, women and men did seek to dissolve their marriages through divorce. Between 1874 and 1915, women brought forward divorce cases more frequently than men, often speaking of divorce as an option that relieved them of their husband's verbal or physical abuse at home or that allowed them to leave a husband who had already abandoned the home.[11] Infidelity also precipitated divorce, leaving the wife with little other recourse.[12] A wandering husband could bring dire consequences for his abandoned spouse, as many times the wife told the presiding judge that her husband left her with no means to support herself or to feed their children.

Men rarely utilized the divorce laws, however, preferring to simply abandon the marital home. After all, a husband's honor remained unharmed if he walked away from the marriage. By contrast, appearing in divorce court could tarnish a man's honor as community members assumed that a husband would divorce only an unfaithful wife.[13] The court cases from this period reveal that men risked exposing their private lives by seeking divorce only in extreme cases and only when a high level of public humiliation already existed. For instance, Crescencio Cantillo declared that his spouse lived a "scandalous" life by being in a constant state of drunkenness; while drunk, his wife treated him poorly, calling him names in the street and throwing the dinner out onto the patio.[14]

The revolution, however, brought great changes for women in the area of divorce. In a 29 December 1914 decree Mexico's First Chief Venustiano Carranza declared divorce legal by defining marriage as a civil contract that partners could enter into or break by their own free will. Most important, divorce now left couples free to marry again.[15] On 9 April 1917, Carranza expanded his family legislation and issued the *Law on Family Relations*, which broadened the scope of the 1914 divorce law.[16] In Yucatán, Alvarado adopted Carranza's family and divorce laws in 1915 and, on 30 January 1918 he approved the new Civil Code of Yucatán, which contained provisions that allowed mutual consent divorces to be carried out at the couple's local civil-registry office.[17]

The revolutionary legalization of divorce responded to several issues. For one, revolutionary officials, who were engaged in a full-scale national attack on the Catholic Church, utilized divorce as a tool to chip away at the church's influence over social life in Mexico.[18] In Yucatán, the fight against religious ideology was particularly pronounced, as Alvarado closed churches, expelled priests from the state, and deployed divorce as a direct attack against Catholic concepts of morality, while promoting his secular version as an alternative.

Legalized divorce joined previous, nineteenth-century efforts to rationalize and modernize domestic matters. In formal law, civil-registry offices replaced the local church as the centralized location for conducting the business of family life, all entries on marriages, divorces, births, and deaths being carefully recorded in a standardized format.[19] This measure was intended in part to move statistical record keeping out of the hands of the church and place it under the state's regulatory control, making the movements of families more visible to policymakers.[20]

Despite the new divorce laws, however, initially it remained fairly uncommon for unhappy couples to file for divorce, especially outside the capital of Mérida and a few other urban centers.[21] Nonetheless, rich and poor, and Maya and non-Maya alike soon began to seek divorce.[22] Elite women often employed lawyers to represent them, helping to assure that their divorces would be favorably granted. In fact, the divorce cases of the wealthy could drag on for years through numerous appeals and the finagling of lawyers. However, those who lacked financial means could utilize public defenders to bring forward their cases as well.

When one examines who sought to end their marriages, however, one sees that a remarkable shift occurred in the number of women and men seeking divorce when compared to the prerevolutionary years. Now men took greater advantage of this option, while women largely continued as before.[23] To be sure, many factors discouraged women's use of divorce. For instance, politicians and judges often remained the same on the local level, making it unlikely that controversial reforms, like divorce, were translated into everyday life. Thus, corruption and personal factors could derail the most revolutionary ideals, as many judges refused to rule in favor of a woman attempting to divorce her husband. Furthermore, even while revolutionary officials like Alvarado expounded on the need to free women from unwanted marriages, they still argued that a woman's proper place was within the home as wife and mother.[24] As revolutionary ideology positioned women as married mothers, raising healthy families and taking proper care of their husbands, many judges attempted to rule out divorce as an option for women.

When women did bring forward divorce proceedings, they continued overwhelmingly to cite abuse as the primary reason. In these cases, the language deployed by the women reveals that while their marriages had been unbearable, they now believed that the revolutionary courts could provide an escape from their husbands. For instance, several women demanded divorces because they declared that their husbands and their families treated them as nothing more than mere "servants."[25] One woman said that after years of abuse, she was now "making use of the rights that the law resolves to me."[26] Another wrote that she had once believed that she would live happily by her husband's side for the rest of her life, although this illusion "passed like a gust of wind" soon after she married.[27]

Other wives refused to turn to the courts for help. However, those who bypassed the courts were not powerless before their husbands. Instead, it becomes clear in the women's testimonies in the cases of *men* asking for divorce that women also deployed alternative means of resistance within their unhappy marriages. For instance, Manuel Cauich brought his wife to court for divorce after she refused to have sexual relations with him and then abandoned their home.[28] In another case, María Porfiria Canche's husband brought her to court claiming that she constantly "disobeyed" him and that he had caught her in a "carnal act" with another man.[29]

In fact, many wives during this time preferred to flee their homes rather than go through the court system. In case after case of divorce brought forward by the husband, the wife's abandonment of the home remained the most often cited cause for the divorce. While the ability to leave the marriage offered the wife a viable alternative to divorce, the fact that some women abandoned abusive husbands rather than divorcing them reveals their lack of confidence in the judicial system.

Husbands occasionally stated in their court documents that they desired a divorce in order to marry another woman. In Mexico, as in other parts of the world, including the United States and France, ideas of romantic love became linked to modern notions of family.[30] In Yucatán, revolutionary officials began to promote the cultural modernization of Yucatecan families, promoting love-based marriage rather than contract-based unions. Mérida's revolutionary newspapers further printed articles and editorials promoting the concept of a marriage of love rather than obligation. In fact, these changing notions of marriage provided the foundation for Yucatán's new divorce laws of the early 1920s and would become even more important as the decade unfolded.

Carrillo Puerto and Divorce, 1922–24

Felipe Carrillo Puerto's socialist government took power on 1 February 1922. Like Alvarado, Carrillo Puerto advocated divorce to free women from the yoke of unwanted marriages and, as in many of his policies, pushed for even more radical changes. Certainly Carrillo Puerto drew on transnational intellectual currents, including the birth-control ideas of Margaret Sanger, socialist theories of revolutionary change, and the principles of the international movement for free love.[31] Following such trends, on 31 March 1923, Carrillo Puerto made divorce more accessible, describing marriage as "the voluntary union of a man and a woman, based on love, to form the home, dissolvable by means of divorce, which will be able to be asked for by both or only one of them."[32] In other words, either partner could seek divorce on the grounds of irreconcilable differences with or without the consent or knowledge of the other and with only one partner needing to appear at the civil-registry office.[33]

Love was now key to marriage, and divorce was to be a release from a loveless marriage. In theory, men and women could remain married until they no longer had feelings for each other, at which time they would easily end their marriage and part as friends. One article in the ruling party's magazine, *Tierra*, defended the government's position toward divorce. Appropriately titled "If Love Enslaves . . . Love be Damned!" it argued, "DIVORCE, and those other acts they need for the truthful triumph of free love, also has been unjustly condemned as dissolving factors of home life and of the sacred bonds of the family and society in general. There is nothing more erroneous, since divorce never will knock on the doors of the homes covered by the wings of happiness; therefore, there will never be able to be a law that breaks the bonds of the family nor of the wise societies."[34]

As in Alvarado's era and despite Carrillo Puerto's liberal ideas of law equating practice, the divorce law did not reflect women's everyday reality. In fact, as the 1920s progressed, men turned to divorce more than women did, and to an ever-increasing degree.[35] This ratio applied to both Maya and non-Maya couples, as Maya men appeared in court asking for divorce in even greater numbers as well. Although those growing numbers already included men with little financial recourse, Carrillo Puerto sought to ensure equal access to divorce and thus amended the tax code in June 1923 to allow a 75-percent discount for "poor" persons seeking divorce.[36]

That year brought great change to Yucatán as more and more unhappy spouses arrived from other countries to take advantage of the state's liberalized divorce law.[37] People now came from all over the world, including Britain, Canada, Italy, Germany, Russia, Hungary, Poland, Austria, and especially the United States. Carrillo Puerto actively sought out foreigners seeking divorce, molding the new divorce law to simplify the procedure for those arriving from outside Yucatán. From the beginning, the governor, arguing that he wished to make divorce easier for "philosophical" reasons, stated that it was immoral to make unhappy couples wait the required six months before they could divorce.[38] For those traveling from faraway places, the new law required only thirty days' residency in Yucatán before a divorce could be sought.[39]

The 1923 divorce law, including the requirements for divorce, was made available to foreigners. Yucatán's *Diario Oficial* published the law in English, and the Carrillo Puerto government distributed numerous copies to attorneys around the world—most extensively in the United States—to pass along to their clients.[40] Other individuals wrote directly to the governor to request the Yucatecan divorce laws in English, which they then received for the low price of 50 cents to cover the cost of the paper and postage.[41] Many people learned of Yucatán's liberal divorce laws through their lawyers or read of the law in New York papers.[42] Either way, the requests from men and women for information poured into Yucatecan state offices, via telegrams, handwritten letters, or on lawyers' official stationary. In return, brochures promised an easy divorce, a comfortable stay in a Mérida hotel, and a vacation among the antique Maya ruins as a bonus. Promotional information extolled the attractions of Mérida itself, with paved streets and a "constant state of cleanliness that is the wonder of foreigners." It further described the "natives" as "clean in their person and in their dress," as well as hospitable and friendly.[43]

Not surprisingly, the divorce law had its critics, both in Mexico and in the United States. The North American consul in Yucatán, O. Gaylord Marsh, condemned Yucatán's divorce law as an action of Mexican socialists, who served as puppets of the Russian Bolsheviks to undermine the morality of U.S. citizens. Marsh sent numerous memos to Washington about the "radical divorce laws," expressing concern that "matrimonially-bored" U.S. citizens would come to Mérida for a quick divorce without their spouse's knowledge. He wrote, "This is a treacherous and immoral piece of legislation, and it is a blow by an agency of Lenin at the very moral foundation of civilization." He railed against the divorce law's antireligious aspect, and contended that members of Yucatán's socialist government carried red cards that said, "Flee from the church . . . as from the plague."[44]

But the strongest opposition against divorce came from within Mérida. One article in the conservative local newspaper *Revista de Yucatán* described Yucatán as "the Mexican Reno."[45] Other newspapers fiercely opposed the concept of free love, which in theory allowed spouses to abandon each other at will. For instance, the antisocialist newspaper *La Lucha* carried a series of articles, all entitled "The Lies of Feminism." The author, Pilar de Fontanar, argued that the feminist propaganda of free love threatened Yucatecan homes, leading many a man to succumb to his animal instincts, to abandon his wife and children and run off with another woman. The author also warned that the new woman should herself be wary, since the man could leave her in turn.[46] Taken together the articles contended that the "lies of feminism" robbed the wife of her power, left her in disgrace, and created orphans of her children.[47]

The Aftermath of Change, 1925–30

Conservative opposition to Carrillo Puerto's reforms escalated, leading to the governor's assassination on 3 January 1924. At first, his death seemed to have little effect on the everyday practice of divorce.[48] But change was in the air. Although much of the animosity toward divorce focused on Carrillo Puerto himself, opposition to Yucatán's divorce law lasted well beyond his death, both in Yucatán and in the United States.

A question also remained about the legality of Yucatecan divorces in other Mexican states and in the United States. On 22 July 1925 the *New York Times* reported on the ruling of Connecticut judge Walter Pickett, who decreed that divorces obtained in Yucatán were invalid in the United States and argued that the divorces were "the output of a State into which many of the teachings of communism had crept and were without legal, international force."[49] This decision proved to be unfortunate for Milton Stone, who had already married his stenographer, Alice Larsen, after divorcing his first wife in Yucatán. Not only did Stone's first wife have him arrested on his return, Judge Pickett also sentenced the unhappy husband to sixty days in jail, although he later suspended the punishment in order to allow Stone to meet his financial needs.[50] Despite such problems, U.S. citizens continued to flock to Yucatán in the short term, indicating that such cases did little to dissuade others from seeking Yucatecan divorces.

By 1926, it was Yucatán's conservative elite who had proved to be effective in their continued opposition to Carrillo Puerto's concept of divorce. Indeed, changes as implemented by the Divorce Law of 1926, decreed on 17 April, reversed some of the most important elements of Carrillo Puerto's earlier divorce legislation. For instance, although divorce was still legal, spouses could no longer receive a divorce without the other partner's knowledge, "since this lack of knowledge imprints the standing law with an unquestionable hatefulness."[51] Furthermore, foreigners now had to reside six months in Yucatán, rather than thirty days, to receive their divorce.

Many Yucatecan husbands and wives tenaciously struggled to reverse earlier divorce decisions. They petitioned Yucatán's Superior Tribunals of Justice for help, and even the Supreme Court in Mexico City, which could overturn divorces granted by Yucatán's courts when it considered that a judgment violated an individual's constitutional rights.[52] In fact, in 1929 *La Lucha* printed an article warning Mérida society, and especially married women, not to find themselves victims of an "immoral" divorce law that the Supreme Court could rule as unconstitutional.[53] Nonetheless, Yucatán's governmental officials continued to protect the law's "revolutionary concepts" against continuing legal onslaughts, although after 1926 Carrillo Puerto's divorce law was left substantially weakened, and few couples continued to take advantage of their right to legal divorce.[54]

Conclusion

During the Mexican Revolution, "modern" concepts of marriage and divorce led to the liberalization of divorce laws. Revolutionary officials argued that divorce and family matters were matters to be administered by the state, rather than by the church. Nonetheless, while revolutionary ideals promoted a woman freed from the yoke of an unwanted marriage, modern concepts of proper womanhood constrained women to a narrowly defined, and certainly domestic, space within revolutionary society. Furthermore, as the 1920s unfolded, revolutionary officials promoted the notion of marriage based on love rather than a contract. The intertwining of discourse and everyday reality became a narrow tightrope on which women learned to balance themselves between these competing positions of the Mexican Revolution. The evolution of divorce from an overwhelmingly women-initiated process before the revolution to a mainly male-initiated process in the years that followed illustrated the contradictory construction of women's proper roles.

The revolutionary state was not a monolithic giant, however, as men and women with various social interests constantly challenged it and shaped it. In the end, even while revolutionary ideology defined the proper position of women as wife and mother, and even as some judges failed to carry out revolutionary changes, the revolution simultaneously produced opportunities that allowed some women to go the courts and to achieve changes that improved the conditions of their lives.

Notes

1. AGEY, FPJ, folio 002484, box 030–00 (1917). This chapter draws on several judicial groups found in the Archivo General del Estado de Yucatán (AGEY), as well as various municipal archives and the civil-registry office of Mérida. This work also benefits from the help of many people, including Jocelyn Olcott, Mary Kay Vaughan, and Gabriela Cano, due to their many smart suggestions through several versions. Barbara Weinstein, Temma Kaplan, Susan Gauss, and James Genova also read this piece more times than I can count, and I very much appreciate their support.

2. See Vaughan 1997; Cano 1998; Bliss 2001; and Deutsch 1991.

3. For studies on nineteenth-century Yucatán, including the roles of women, see Alejandra García Quintanilla (1982) and Piedad Peniche Rivero (1999).

4. Eileen Findlay (1999) includes a study of marriage and divorce in Puerto Rico.

5. Joseph and Nugent 1994a and 1994b.

6. On the issue of "modernizing" domesticity see also Schell and Blum in this volume.

STEPHANIE SMITH

7. See Caulfield 2000. Also see Beattie 2001.

8. Vaughan 1994, 106–7.

9. See Vaughan 2000. Also see Besse 1996.

10. Arrom 1994, 93. Also see Ramos Escandón 1987, 146–49.

11. For example, there were nineteen divorce cases in Fondo Poder Judicial (FPJ) for the years of 1872 through 1914. Of these cases, fourteen were brought by women, four by men, and one by both husband and wife. Silvia Arrom contends that divorce was "above all a female recourse" in the first half of the nineteenth century (1985, 206).

12. AGEY, FJ, Sección Civil, box 1, 1872, "Juicio de divorcio que sigue Doña Isabel Ceballos contra su esposo C. Eduardo Villamil, por sevicia."

13. da Silva 1989, 317–18.

14. AGEY, FPJ, folio 002623, box 027–00, 1914.

15. Rojina Villegas 1997, 376.

16. Carranza 1964. Also see Macías 1982, 76; Soto 1990.

17. *Diario Oficial,* Thursday, 27 May 1915. Also see *Ley sobre el divorcio* 1915. For the 1918 code see *Código Civil del Estado de Yucatán* 1918, 40.

18. On the Catholic Church see Kristina A. Boylan's essay in this collection.

19. *Legislación revoluciaria* 1918.

20. See, among others, James C. Scott 1998 on the rationalizing state.

21. For example, in 1916 there were 3,631 marriages in Yucatán, with 814 occurring in Mérida. Of the couples getting married, only six people had previously been divorced, four of whom lived in Mérida (*Boletín de Estadística: Organo de la Sección de Este Ramo del Gobierno Constitucionalist del Estado de Yucatán* 24, no. 5 [1917]). There were only 170 divorces in the city of Mérida for the years between 1918 and 1921 (ACREY, Libros 1, 2, 3, 4, 5 de Divorcio, 1918–1921).

22. Overall, in all types of court cases, including divorce, gendered conceptions of ethnicity were coded in other language. In this manner, women appearing before the courts for the most part did not specifically refer to themselves as Maya but rather expressed their needs in relationship to class, indicating that they were poor. Nonetheless, ethnicity continued to be a critical factor when women appeared before the courts, as revolutionary concepts of morality and honor were tied to ethnicity and class. Although women often may have presented themselves as "poor women," military commanders and local judges were nonetheless quite aware of whether the complainant was Maya or not. Indeed, ethnicity influenced the outcome of court cases, especially when deciding the amount of compensation awarded. While most courts considered marriage to be the sole path to restore a wealthy woman's honor, a poor or Maya woman's honor was instead replaced with monetary compensation. The amount owed to the woman also varied according to her social and cultural position. For examples see AGEY, FM, Valladolid, J, box 387, 48, 4 1 August 1915; AGEY, FM, Valladolid, J, box 387, 48, 3, 9 August 1915; and AGEY, FM, Valladolid, J, box 387, 48, 5, 26 August 1915. In these cases the revolutionary courts awarded young Maya orphaned girls monetary compensation rather than marriage after their bosses forced them into "illicit relations," which resulted in the women having children.

23. Out of seventy-five divorce cases filed in FPJ, only twenty-seven women asked for the divorce, while thirty-eight men came forward, and ten couples mutually sought divorce (AGEY, FPJ, 1915–1921).

24. Alvarado 1980, 107–20.

25. AGEY, FPJ, folio 002485, box 030–01, 1917. Also see AGEY, FPJ, folio 001168, box 028–00, 1915.

26. AGEY, FPJ, folio 000948, box 028–00, 1915.

27. AGEY, FPJ, folio 000791, box 031–02, 1918.

28. AGEY, FPJ, folio 001168, box 028–00, 1915.

29. AGEY, FPJ, folio 001168, box 028–00, 1915.

30. For a history of love in Europe, including changing notions of the importance of love in marriage, see Zeldin 1994, 83, 117. For a history of free love and sex radicals in the United States see also Passet 2003.

31. See Buck 2001.

32. *Ley de Divorcio* 1923, 9.

33. AGEY, FPE, Sección Gobernación, Series Leyes y Informes, box 785, 1924.

34. Trejo Camara 1923, 12.

35. For instance, there were twenty-four divorces in Fondo Poder Justicia for the years of 1922 through 1930. Of these, seventeen men asked for divorce, while only seven women implemented the divorce proceedings (AGEY, FPJ [1922–30]). Furthermore, in Mérida in 1924, there were 175 divorces registered for couples from Mexico, of which only thirteen women appeared; out of 128 foreigners, only sixteen women appeared (ACREY, Libros 8 and 9 de Divorcio, 1924).

36. The cost of divorce ranged from 60 pesos to 125 pesos, depending on whether a couple had an estate or whether they needed to appear before a judge (AGEY, FPE, Sección Gobernación, Serie Correspondencia, Leyes, box 780, 1923–24).

37. Although divorces did occur in some larger municipios such as Progreso, Ticul, Tekax, and, rarely, Valladolid, the capital of Mérida was, as before, overwhelmingly the site of more divorces than the smaller towns. For instance, from 11 May 1924 to 30 November 1924, there were 127 divorces in the capital, one divorce from a pueblo outside of Mérida, and only twenty-five divorces in the fifteen other departamentos and their surrounding towns (AGEY, FPE, Sección Justicia, Serie Registro Civil, box 794, 1924).

38. AGEY, FPE, Sección Gobernación, Series Liga de Resistencia Minutas, box 757 (1922).

39. AGEY, FPE, Sección Gobernación Series Leyes y Informes, box 785, 1924.

40. AGEY, FPE, Sección Gobernación, box 811, 1925.

41. AGEY, FPE, Sección Gobernación, box 811, 1925.

42. AGEY, FPE, Sección Gobernación, box 811, 1925.

43. AGEY, FPE, Sección Gobernación, Series Leyes y Informes, box 785, 1924.

44. USDOS, microfilm roll 148, 1910–29.

45. *La Revista de Yucatán*, 5 March 1923, 1.

46. "The Lies of Feminism," *La Lucha*, 28 July 1923.

47. "The Lies of Feminism," *La Lucha*, 14 July 1923.

48. In other words, during the year following Carrillo Puerto's death, the business of divorce continued as briskly as usual, with many couples still arriving in Mérida

to ask for divorce. For 1925, 307 couples appear in Mérida's books 10 and 11 for divorces. Of eighty-six divorces from Mexico, women appeared in only twenty. Of 174 foreign couples, only forty-four women appeared. Book 10 also includes four divorces decreed by judicial sentence, and both parties of one couple also appeared.

49. "Yucatán Divorces Held Invalid Here," *New York Times*, 22 July 1925, 21.

50. Ibid.

51. AGEY, FPE, Sección Gobernación, box 826, 1926.

52. On Supreme Court rulings on divorce see Varley 2000. For examples, see AGEY, FPJ, folio 007012, box 043–02 (1930).

53. "La Ley del Divorcio," *La Lucha*, 14 September 1929.

54. During 1926, 124 couples appeared for divorces in Mérida, with only eighteen women asking for divorce out of thirty-eight couples from Mexico, and fifteen women appearing out of fifty-nine foreign divorces. Toward the end of the year, however, sixteen of the divorces were by judicial sentence, and both of the partners appeared in eleven cases, reflecting the change in the divorce law during the year (ACREY, Libro 12 de Divorcio, 1926). Only forty-three divorces were reported in 1927, fifty-four in 1928, fifty-nine in 1929, and forty-eight in 1930 (ACREY, Libros 13, 14, 15, 16 de Divorcio, 1927, 1928, 1929, 1930).

111

Gender, Class, and Anxiety at the Gabriel Mistral Vocational School, Revolutionary Mexico City

PATIENCE A. SCHELL

In the summer of 1922 Chilean poet Gabriela Mistral arrived in Mexico to help secure the revolution. Feted throughout the capital, she gave lectures, attended banquets, and inaugurated educational facilities. In the talks she gave that summer Mistral emphasized a domestic, yet active role for women, and the newly opened federal vocational school bearing her name taught young women how to use their intelligence to better their homes. Yet the same newspapers that reported on Mistral's visit also reported—with shock—that feminist teachers at her namesake school promoted birth control in their classes. The ensuing scandal represented different points along a spectrum of gender models for women, revealing the multiple meanings of womanhood in revolutionary Mexico City. Vocational schools were a gendered space that incubated debates and prompted anxiety about women's place in the revolutionary period.

Women's Vocational Education in the Capital City

The capital's natural and human geography provide the backdrop for this discussion of women in education. In the revolutionary period, the population of Mexico City more than doubled, mostly due to migration, from

471,066 in 1910, to 615,327 in 1921, and rising to over a million in 1930.[1] The city was home to more women than men. For instance, in 1921 there were three times as many women as men in the age group twenty to twenty-four.[2] This city of women and migrants was also undergoing rapid spatial changes; population growth enlarged the physical space of the city, while infrastructure and transportation improvements such as tramlines knitted the urban environment together ever more tightly. The modern city also fostered a common culture of leisure and consumption available through popular spaces of sociability such as cinemas, dance halls, and cabarets that offered forums in which to contest and perform gender roles. The darkened auditorium of the cinema, for instance, offered the mixed-sex audiences possibilities not only for entertainment but also for sexual adventures.[3]

Yet it was not only in mixed-sex sites that gender roles started to bend and break: the virtually unisex spaces of women's vocational schools also opened opportunities to contest gender roles. Surviving photographs and lists of teachers show that only a few men—if any—were on staff. These men inhabited the schools' workshops, leaving the majority of the buildings to women: students, teachers, inspectors, and principals. The almost wholly unisex character of these schools did not safeguard traditional gender roles, which were challenged inside as well as outside the classroom. Debates on gender emerged in part because the revolution had undermined the hierarchies and social norms of the Porfiriato and had swept in new discourse, new behavior, new expectations, and new demands. Female and male workers organized and went on strike, Catholic women and men took to the streets, and young women adopted transnational fashions to become *chicas modernas* (modern girls). Through participation in such activities, women from diverse backgrounds unsettled conventional gender ideologies and participated in the project of state formation.

Vocational schools accidentally fostered debates about gender and women's public roles in society. Far from intending to subvert gender roles, the new revolutionary government intended adult education to meet demands for education, improve living standards, promote national economic development, and link citizens to the state through bonds of duty. In the first years of the Secretaría de Educación Pública (Ministry of Public Education, or SEP), vocational education received a high priority. The SEP operated seven vocational schools in 1922 in Mexico City, a number that rose to thirteen in 1926. Throughout these early years, more women than men attended SEP schools, and there were more schools for women. In 1926 these schools accommodated 13,050 women and 8,280 men students.[4] Ideological contradictions existed in the vocational system, however, as schools sought to train women for real life while using the model of the revolutionary family. In the 1917 Constitution, article 123 enshrined the "family wage" as the minimum wage. In the model revolutionary family, the woman—regardless of class—was a selfless, prudent, dedicated housewife and mother who did not have to engage in paid work because her sober, industrious husband supported her on this family wage.

Yet most women needed paid work to supplement their partners' wages or to support their families. Although SEP publications rarely trumpeted women's need for financial independence, policymakers accepted this exigency. The constitutional debates in 1917 acknowledged that working women had difficulty earning enough to support themselves and their children and that some became prostitutes out of economic necessity.[5] Women also turned to prostitution, according to legislators, because they lacked skills and employment opportunities. Moreover, elite and middle-class families depended on paid domestic labor for the orderly running of *their* homes. As cultured, formally trained mothers and homemakers, women might need to contribute to their household budgets but could only do so without threatening their femininity or challenging their subordinate employment status vis-à-vis men. As Susan K. Besse found in Brazil, "schools attempted to give girls a 'practical' education aimed at training them first and foremost for domestic and family life and second for earning a living (in an appropriate occupation) if and when it became necessary."[6] In Mexico, as Mary Kay Vaughan has argued, schools trained women for paid and unpaid domestic work, motherhood, crafts making in the home, and increasingly for clerical work in offices.[7] Individual skills courses included hat- and dressmaking, cooking, embroidery, drawing, and cleaning. The SEP curricula implicitly distinguished between skilled labor for women and men. Men performed skilled trades outside the home, in a workshop or factory setting, and earned a family wage. For women, a skilled trade meant an activity shoehorned between domestic chores to generate supplemental income.

While the focus on domesticity in vocational education indicates continuity with Porfirian education, the rationale behind these schools had changed. Domestic education now contributed to the process of "modernizing patriarchy," to fashion rational, orderly families raising the future workers who would strengthen Mexico and develop its economy.[8] Men had a financial responsibility to the domestic sphere, but no more: men's vocational schools offered no classes in paternity. The foundation of this family, then, was the modern, educated mother, who became a central

PATIENCE A. SCHELL

figure in government policy and public health rhetoric as early as the 1920s. As Ann Blum shows in her essay in this volume, it was through motherhood that women could participate in the revolutionary project.[9]

The state's attention to motherhood and the discursive importance of the mother, however, also turned maternity into a potent political weapon. In Chile, Argentina, and Uruguay, women used motherhood to gain a public voice, styling themselves as community caretakers. "Feminism" that promoted public service found support among women of diverse backgrounds, including groups opposed to the broader feminist goals.[10] In Mexico, too, feminists used maternity to justify a public role for women. In the textbook she wrote for her namesake school, Mistral emphasized that women's public service was based on mothering. In Mistral's vision all women mothered, even if they did not have their own children; thus, all women could justify participation in the social, medical, and welfare aspects of the revolutionary project.

Yet the revolutionary celebration of motherhood belied a strong mistrust of the flesh-and-blood women who raised Mexico's children. Poor and working women were historically objects of fear, scorn, lust, and government reform programs. For Porfirian elites, poor mothers seemed to willfully harm their children, allowing them to consume dangerous food, play in the streets, and sleep in rooms and beds crowded with other people. Although the revolutionary project inherited these prejudices, the explanatory rhetoric shifted to blame environmental conditions rather than the inherent degeneracy of the poor and working class, inducing social reformers and educators to work for the poor mother's redemption through formal education.[11] Through education and welfare programs the paternalist state adopted a maternal role, usurping the place of older female relatives to teach young women how to bring up their children, care for their husbands, and manage their homes.

Thus, SEP educational policy focused on motherhood and domesticity. In vocational schools women learned to prepare simple food, clean their homes, and care for children. Many vocational schools offered puericulture lessons to cultivate the scientific management of childhood and, drawing from the eugenics movement, emphasize care of infants and toddlers through understanding child development.[12] Several vocational schools operated contiguous "kindergartens," in which married women attending classes could leave their children, while señoritas could practice their training on live subjects, to the "infinite advantage" of their future children.[13] References to and promotion of puericulture, originating with French eugenicists, and the kindergarten movement, stemming from the educational philosophy of Friedrich Froebel and popular since the mid-nineteenth century, provide concrete examples of how deeply immersed Mexican educators were in transnational movements of public health and educational reform. Puericulture trained women to be active mothers, breastfeeding and playing with their children. The Mistral School did not offer separate puericulture classes, but incorporated maternal training into its overall program. A photo of the school's student body assembled on the patio depicted numerous young children, suggesting that the Mistral School also operated a contiguous kindergarten.[14]

Because women reproduced the depopulated nation, their physical well-being assumed vital importance, and each of the women's vocational schools emphasized an outdoor exercise program. All the vocational schools instructed girls and young women in sports considered appropriate for their "nature." Much like contemporary Brazil, Mexican educators considered physical education more important for women than for men because of women's reproductive role and designed sex-specific programs to reinforce gender ideologies. Fit, well-educated mothers also needed to learn how to keep house, or *trabajos manuales*, such as mending, ironing, and cleaning. Trabajos manuales also included learning a craft, so that women could make and sell products "to better . . . the home's material conditions."[15] Thus, the SEP promoted women's domestic piecework, professionalized home care, and taught scientific household management.

The reality of women's need for paid employment and the model of the revolutionary family translated into a confusing mix of ideologies at all levels of vocational education. Classes offered women income-producing skills while glorifying motherhood and taught women to care for their own children and homes while preparing working-class students to become domestic servants and middle-class students to hire them. Vocational schools promoted skills training as an independent, honorable means to earn a living working from home, yet these skills encouraged poorly remunerated domestic piecework. Women themselves tended to enroll for individual classes in order to learn a particular skill, instead of enrolling for a full-time degree.[16] Yet by enrolling for individual courses, students missed out on much of the ideological training. Other factors exacerbated these inconsistencies. The SEP inherited its curriculum from the Porfirian government and did not make reforming women's education a high priority, opting instead to layer new programs over old ones. Moreover, the programs offered at vocational schools reflected not the work of one individual but rather of SEP administrators, principals, teachers, and inspectors whose competing goals and priorities fostered further contradictions. Teachers, particularly, had autonomy inside their classrooms. Even though inspections theoretically occurred monthly, teachers were generally alone with their students and could teach as they saw fit. Additionally, courses responded in part to student demand for particularly useful skills; inspectors consistently noted that students enrolled in classes with practical applications. Yet the ideological inconsistencies present in vocational education also reflected the same normative gender ideologies that glorified motherhood, expected men to be the principal breadwinners, and ignored the fact that most mothers needed paid work.

These inconsistencies also reflected vocational schools' diverse student populations. For upwardly mobile urban families, the schools could polish their daughters' skills and decorum while training them in household management. For married women, individual courses taught particular skills and may have offered a welcome and legitimate reason to leave the domestic sphere. For women in financial need, skills training offered hopes for good employment. For rural migrant women, the schools may have acculturated them to urban life. For all students, vocational education offered a chance to socialize in a sanctioned female space. Thus, one vocational school could satisfy an array of educational and social needs for the surrounding community. Moreover, the core message of these schools communicated the importance of women and their work. Young women may have derived a new sense of self from vocational education, as they did in contemporary Italy.[17]

Clashing Gender Roles at the Mistral School

The Escuela Hogar Gabriela Mistral became a site of conflict precisely because it brought together women with different points of view about the purpose of women's education. The Mistral School, founded in 1922, initially operated in a rented building at 63 Sadi Carnot, just a few blocks north of the Alameda, serving students from the working- to middle-class neighborhoods of Guerrero, Santa María la Ribera, San Rafael, and Popotla, and the more upscale areas of Juárez and Roma. Demand for women's education was high here, and there was no comparable institution. From this central location, the school touted its goal of preparing women for the domestic sphere. The Mistral School took women's work seriously, cultivating intelligent, educated, involved mothers who did not depend on nannies and wet nurses, but personally oversaw their children's development and their homes' morality.[18] This new generation of highly educated homemakers would make a domestic revolution. When students sang the school's morning hymn, they intoned that their school was forming future wives. When students looked at the school's crest, they saw a woman nursing her baby with one arm and holding her toddler with the other.

Yet the SEP was inconsistent in the objectives it claimed for the school. An early report on vocational education claimed that the school would train teachers of domestic education, administrators of philanthropic institutions, and housewives, with additional specialized training for cooks, nannies, and washerwomen. The confused goals highlight the fact that even the SEP lacked a coherent plan for the school, while allowing the school to meet the needs of a diverse population. Moreover, occupations listed include those aimed principally at the middle class or aspiring professionals (teachers, administrators) and at the working class (cooks, nannies, washerwomen), offering separate tracks of education. Any focus on women's professional goals marks a clear break with Porfirian vocational education, while the training of women for domestic service suggests continuities in women's education and employment. Additionally, the new ideal of the active mother did not prevent the SEP from training women as nannies. It remains difficult to assess how seriously the SEP took women's professional training. No further evidence indicates that the Mistral School actually trained women to administer philanthropic institutions, and any unlucky enough to train as home-economics teachers found that there was no demand for their skills in primary or secondary schools.[19] The Mistral School did, however, train women for domestic service, the most significant source of women's employment in Mexico City.

The 1922 regulations described a school that would educate intelligent young women to run an orderly, rational home while giving them the means to support themselves and to better society through improving their own character.[20] Apparently written by the original teachers and headmistress, these regulations reflect, at least in part, the priorities of educated women living and working in Mexico City.[21] The regulations make frequent references to "morality," indicating that these professional women, already challenging gender roles through their work, may have felt under considerable pressure to demonstrate the compatibility of women's education and respectability. They also emphasized the importance of morality and good conduct in all levels of an institution that imparted professional training in domesticity. Teachers, who were to be aware of national and international developments in domestic science, also had to offer students an example of women who loved their work but maintained an independent and upstanding character. The authors of these regulations imagined the Mistral School as forming a community of women in which the teachers, students, and principal together bettered

Mexican society one orderly home at a time. The long periods of time each day that women spent away from family allowed for the creation of this sisterhood within the school, an alternative community based on relationships with peers.[22]

Within this sisterhood, however, divisions persisted perhaps of race and certainly of class. The school's records reveal an assumption that its students were not culturally indigenous. Indigenous people were objects for the students to study, different but deserving fair treatment. In her *Readings for Women*, Mistral describes the "Indian woman" whose clothing and manner situate her in a distant time and place. It is not known if indigenous women were actually students at the Mistral School, but sanctions against being dirty, late, and poorly dressed were likely understood racially and culturally. The focus on taste, decorum, and good manners possibly reflect another negative allusion to rural and indigenous people, encouraging acculturation to urban, middle-class behavior and consumption. By 1928, the Mistral School explicitly sought to attack prejudice. The school sought to "inculcate in the students' heart the good of all, making an abstract idea [out of] races, nationalities, and political parties."[23] The list itself suggests the continued polarization of Mexican society after the revolution.

The school, however, also sought to contain students' social aspirations. The 1928 revisions of the school's regulations enjoined teachers to help students select their trade to avoid "disillusionment" and failure. Teachers would dissuade students from focusing on professional careers, instead seeking satisfaction "in another class of work."[24] Teachers may well have harbored their own class and race assumptions, suggesting activities "suitable" for students' situations. A combination of pressure from teachers and students' own choices could have created de facto segregation, with working-class women enrolling in courses like cleaning while women with economic security attended courses on working with furs or embroidery.

Students, ranging in age from about fifteen to thirty, could be rowdy and undisciplined, perhaps partially explaining the focus on decorum in the school regulations. In 1926 the Gabriela Mistral students described themselves as the poorest among vocational-school students. A group photo of the whole school shows students diverse in age and economic background. Like their European and U.S. counterparts, these Mexican women took up the transnational rage for shorter skirts and hair. Photographs feature young, mestiza-looking women with bobbed hair and dressed in fashionably loose-fitting clothing, with skirts at mid-calf. The fashions that these women wore—styles revealing elbows and neckline—

Gender, Class, and Anxiety

challenged traditional feminine modesty. Such choices made a strong social statement and could have serious repercussions as Catholics campaigned against "immoral" dress and refused Communion to those clad "immodestly."[25]

The Question of the Sanger Pamphlet

In theory, families (often parents) of vocational school students could rest assured that education would enhance, not hinder, their daughters' moral development. The schools offered strict daytime supervision, and teachers received constant reminders of their responsibility for students' morals, both in and outside of class. Older girls and young women apparently attended school conditionally, based on the school's reputation and its teachers' high moral standards. Parents withdrew their daughters at any threat to decorum and innocence. This contingent attendance perhaps explains why school regulations frequently included a discussion of teachers' moral responsibility to their students. Yet educators and parents seeking to maintain young women's innocence battled the "immoral" spaces of the "marginal city." Behavior that the middle classes sought to contain in the domestic sphere, ranging from making dinner to making love, took place in public, not only in the poor and working-class neighborhoods but also in the city center.[26] The chances were high that these young women had seen more than decorum condoned. But what exactly did decorum mean? Traditional decorum meant not talking about sex, yet in the post-revolutionary period the Department of Public Health, partially responding to high rates of syphilis, sought to make sexual practice a public-health issue, through radio programs, pamphlet campaigns, presentations in cinemas, talks in public places, and posters in the street. The department also sought to remove the stigma associated with discussion of matters sexual, to make sexual knowledge another part of health awareness. The culture of ignorance was particularly damaging to young women who did not realize when their virginity was threatened and, according to social workers, became prostitutes as a result. It was not uncommon for young women to become pregnant without knowing how.[27] Converting sex from a taboo subject into part of a public-health campaign also brought it into the realm of public education.

Even though one department of the revolutionary state saw sexual matters as suitable for public discussion, the SEP swiftly intervened to censor "immorality" when the press picked up rumors that sex education was promoted in Mexico City's schools. The scandal that erupted exposed concerns about violating the trust of parents and of the nation. Parents expected high moral standards from education—discussion of sex was clearly not moral—and the nation as a whole needed women to reproduce. If women could choose not to be mothers, it threatened the very future of the nation. Giving women information about sex and fertility control undermined the cult of motherhood and women's most important role in society; moreover, the combination of population losses from the revolution and emigration to the United States meant that even feminists did not widely endorse birth control.[28] Thus, when a vocational teacher breached the dated moral standard, she risked not only her job but also—even worse—taking her students' innocence while violating the trust parents and the nation had placed in her. The birth-control scandal at the Mistral School exemplifies such a breach of trust.

To understand the tenor of the scandal, one must set the scene: summer 1922, Mexico City.[29] The newspapers closely covered the movements of the distinguished poet Gabriela Mistral, recently arrived from Chile at the invitation of Minister of Public Education José Vasconcelos to join in the revolutionary education effort. The scandal erupted shortly after Mistral's arrival, and newspapers carried articles both on Mistral's activities throughout the city, where she inaugurated libraries and gave lectures, and on the allegations that Margaret Sanger's birth-control pamphlets were being used in schools, particularly in Mistral's namesake school.[30] The original rumor held that the Sanger pamphlet had been distributed in primary schools, an exaggeration that surely offended the sensibilities of most Mexico City residents. Who would corrupt little girls? The fact that this rumor existed at all indicates some measure of public trepidation —fueled by purported SEP radicalism—about girls' education. In response to public pressure the SEP dispatched a male inspector to investigate. The teachers at the Mistral School all protested their innocence, while principals and students at other women's vocational schools unconditionally condemned Sanger's ideas. Several teachers at the Mistral School lost their jobs, ostensibly for economic reasons, but no doubt as a result of the negative publicity. Only after President Alvaro Obregón intervened were they rehired.

The SEP's investigation concentrated on Dolores Angela Castillo Lara, one of the teachers who was suspected, but never proven, to have used the Sanger pamphlet in her civics classes. According to the inspector's report, Castillo's classes scandalized some of her students, who reported this immorality to their parents and priests, who likely took the story to the press. Castillo remained outspoken in her beliefs about the role Mexican women should have in society. Even after the local papers accused her of immorality, the SEP inspector witnessed her teaching her students that

Gender, Class, and Anxiety

women should be publicly active, work for which their domestic role as wife and mother prepared them. Castillo went further by suggesting that women would be equal to men in the future. Castillo's students, however, did not all agree with their teacher, particularly with what she was alleged to have said when the inspector was not present. According to one student, Castillo told them that it was better to be "divorced three times than to put up with a husband's humiliation." The young woman in question took issue with Castillo's comments, saying that "self-denial and prudence were preferable to the scandal of divorce."[31] The fact that both women discussed heterosexual relations only in the context of marriage indicates that both framed their arguments within the strictures of middle-class mores. Poor and working-class Mexicans more often formed consensual unions, and no one alleged that Castillo went so far as to promote these unions or free love as an alternative to marriage.[32]

The controversy surrounding Castillo's civics class demonstrates the range of opinions regarding women's roles and experience in 1920s Mexico City. In the disagreement between Castillo and her student, Castillo promoted the view of the chica moderna, for whom marriage should be based on sexual attraction and companionship. Castillo's views on marriage and divorce coincided with those of politicians like Yucatán governor Felipe Carrillo Puerto and divorce-seeker Amelia Azarcoya Medina, for whom marriage should be a voluntary contract based on love.[33] Rather than accept a disagreeable marriage, a modern middle-class woman would seek divorce. Castillo's student promoted a traditional role of marriage in which the alliance served the extended family and individual happiness was subordinated to family honor. These opposing views pitted individual freedom and choice against responsibility to family and community. The conflict exposed a schism between traditional views, often anchored in Catholicism, and the emerging feminist discourse, as well as demonstrating the inconsistencies within a revolutionary ideology that could not always reconcile individual freedom with community good.[34]

While Castillo's feminism had no echoes in official SEP programs, other wings of the government had begun to rethink sexuality and family formation. Eugenics discourse was increasingly influential in government circles; as early as 1921, the topics at the First Congress of the Child, held in Mexico City, had brought eugenics discourse to the forefront of policymaking.[35] Eugenics promoted the idea that families should only have the number of children that they could support, which required some form of contraceptive practice. So any teacher discussing birth control could point to eugenics for justification. Moreover, since avoiding a "dishonorable" living was a principal goal of the SEP's education for women, and since

PATIENCE A. SCHELL

women became prostitutes partially through ignorance, the teachers could further justify sex education using the SEP's own rhetoric.

The tension between decorum and protecting young women appears in the collective defense that teachers at the Mistral School wrote to the SEP. They condemned the Sanger pamphlet and declared their goal of fostering their students' moral development while teaching them, "in a delicate, prudent, and discreet manner," everything women needed to know to be virtuous and to have a virtuous home. The teachers continued, expressing their frustration that the need for "discretion" and the abstract level of instruction actually kept students in ignorance. Due to their lack of knowledge, women made mistakes that left them with no other option but "vice," a term that could only mean prostitution. Thus, teachers agreed with social workers that ignorance led young women to prostitution and believed that they had a duty to answer students' questions honestly.[36]

If some teachers at the Mistral School in fact addressed sexual health and reproduction in their classes, it is possible that students' questions rather than teachers' initiatives raised these dangerous topics. Frustrated that decorum prevented them from defending their students against men's exploitation, the Mistral School teachers maintained that innocence did not equal sexual ignorance. Even if the teachers did not address reproduction, they promoted feminism, partially through linking the public and the private, using domesticity to justify a political role. Castillo, in her civics class, taught about female emancipation not only in the streets but also in the intimate spaces of a marriage. The scandal also showed how fine was the line in the public imagination between women demanding a larger public role based on their rights as mothers and wives and women shirking their reproductive roles as they demanded greater equality with men. New spaces for women, even if they were justified through domesticity, had the potential for subversion.

Conclusions

In Mexico the post-revolutionary period precipitated a crisis in and anxiety regarding gender roles, as revolutionary leaders sought to reconcile changes to women's lives that ruptured the strictures that had confided them in pre-revolutionary society. "Traditional" roles came under attack in a variety of ways. In the case of the Mistral School, such roles were "updated" to fit into the new discourses of scientific, rational modernity. Although vocational schools offered women a domestic education, they threatened established gender roles and acted as midwife to the independent chica moderna. Foreign and domestic influences converged to open new physical and metaphorical spaces for women, thus shifting expectations about their social roles. The revolution accelerated women's demands for educational and professional opportunities and raised expectations for greater rights, leading to the 1930s suffrage campaign. At the same time, images from outside Mexico offered models for how modern women might behave and look, cutting their hair, shortening their skirts, harboring career aspirations, and controlling the important decisions in their lives.

Revolutionary rhetoric and experiences gave women who demanded their own place in the nation a strong ideological justification, while traditional gender roles could bridge past and present. If vocational emphasis on the figure of the self-sacrificing mother had echoes in the past, that same figure could become the politically active mother, taking to the streets to defend her family and her community. SEP administrators valued women because of their domestic role, creating the Mexican nation in their kitchens and through their child rearing. Yet women's education, too, had the potential to subvert domestic ideals and to promote women's public activities. The mere existence of a school devoted entirely to women, staffed and run by women, proved not only the importance of women's work but also their capacity to achieve professional goals. Vocational schools offered Mexico City's women a space to make their own revolution.

Notes

1. Piccato 2001, 226 table 5.
2. Ibid., 22; Blum 1998a, 257.
3. Piccato 2001, 99–102. On cinemas in Mexico City see Bliss 2001 (88) and Rubenstein 1998 (312–23).
4. Schell 2003, 45.
5. Bliss 2001, 80.
6. Besse 1996, 119.
7. Vaughan 1977.
8. Vaughan 2000, 199.
9. See Blum in this volume. On motherhood and eugenics see Stern 1999 (369–97).
10. Lavrin 1995, 33–38. See Boylan 2000 and Schell 1999 (78–103) on Catholic women's activism.
11. Mistral 1967, xvii, 90–91. See Bliss 2001 (chap. 3), Piccato 2001 (chap. 3), and Buffington 2000 on views about the poor. The exaltation of motherhood combined with the degeneration of poor mothers has parallels in fascist Italy (De Grazia 1992, 60).

PATIENCE A. SCHELL

12. On eugenics in Latin America generally see Stepan 1991; on Mexico see Stern 1999.

13. AHSEP, Dirección de Enseñanza Técnica, Industria y Comercial 74/15, *Folleto de la Escuela Hogar "Sor Juana Inés de la Cruz,"* Publicaciones de la Secretaría de Educación Pública 7, no. 3 (1926): 23.

14. Secretaría de Educación Pública 1924, photograph "Gabriela Mistral Patio Central."

15. Besse 1996, 124–26; AHSEP, Departamento Escolar 44/59/3, Vasconcelos "Bases conforme a las cuales deberán organizar la educación pública federal," 12 February 1923.

16. Schell 2003, 145.

17. *Bulletin of the Pan American Union* 58 (June 1924): 582; De Grazia 1992, 146–47.

18. "La Escuela Hogar 'Gabriela Mistral'" 1922, 244 (article reprinted from *Excélsior,* 21 January 1922); Mistral 1967, 113; *Boletín de la Secretaría de Educación Pública,* nos. 3–4 (1923): 249. See Besse 1996 (104) for similar sentiments in Brazil.

19. AHSEP, Dirección de Enseñanza Técnica, Industria y Comercial 72/51/60, "Datos relativos a la organización de las escuelas de la DETIC," n.d. [1922]; *Boletín de la Secretaría de Educación Pública,* nos. 3–4 (1923): 236.

20. The following section is summarized from AHSEP, Dirección de Enseñanza Técnica, Industria y Comercial 72/4/1–24, "Instituting regulations Mistral School," 22 June 1922, Rosario Pacheco.

21. AHSEP, Dirección de Enseñanza Técnica, Industria y Comercial 72/51/56, "Nota relativa a la labor desarrollada por la Dirección de ETIC en los primeros meses del presente año," 17 June 1922.

22. Farnsworth-Alvear 2000, 116; Heather Fowler-Salamini's essay in this volume.

23. AHSEP, Dirección de Enseñanza Técnica, Industria y Comercial 74/18/2, "Finalidades de la Escuela," 21 November 1928, Elodia Chirón y Gómez. On racism in this period see Knight 1990 (71–113) and Mistral 1967 (61–62).

24. AHSEP, Dirección de Enseñanza Técnica, Industria y Comercial 74/18/2, "Finalidades de la Escuela," 21 November 1928, Elodia Chirón y Gómez, 2–3.

25. AHSEP, Dirección de Enseñanza Técnica, Industria y Comercial 68/21/3, Inspectora R. vda. de Macías to Director DETIC, 3 March 1923; Mistral 1967, xv; AGN, Obregón y Calles, 205-E-62, María González et al. to Obregón, 24 November 1926; AGN, Obregón y Calles, 205-E-62, secretary to González et al., 8 December 1926; photographs in Secretaría de Educación Pública 1924. See, for example, "Contra la moda y bailes modernos," *Excélsior,* 10 November 1922, 1.

26. Piccato 2001 (33) describes the social and spatial divisions in Mexico City as the "marginal city" and the "ideal city." See Bliss 2001 (87–92) for formal and informal sexual sites in post-revolutionary Mexico City.

27. Bliss 2001, 98–106.

28. Macías 1982, 98.

29. Schell 2003, 117–25; Schell 1998, 257–61.

30. Margaret Sanger (1879–1966), an early birth-control advocate from the United States, linked controlling fertility to women's emancipation (see Chesler 1992).

31. AHSEP, Dirección de Enseñanza Técnica, Industria y Comercial 68/11/3, Juan León to director DETIC, 22 August 1922.

32. See Piccato 2001 (113–16) on low marriage rates and consensual unions.

33. See Stephanie Smith's essay in this volume.

34. In her work on Brazil, Besse has found feminist writers attacking marriage and echoing Castillo's comment about preferring divorce to terrible husbands (1996, 40–48).

35. See Stern 1999.

36. These Mexico City teachers were not alone in finding that discretion often frustrated the need to protect young women. The ignorance of young Italian women, contemporaries of these Mexicans, made them, too, vulnerable to sexual exploitation. For a more detailed discussion of the defense see Schell 2003 (119); AHSEP, Dirección de Enseñanza Técnica, Industria y Comercial 72/7/17, letters in Mistral teachers without addressee, 10 August 1922. For similar convictions about young women's ignorance and sexual vulnerability among Italian reformers, see De Grazia 1992, 57.

〰
126

Breaking and Making Families

Adoption and Public Welfare, Mexico City, 1938–1942

ANN S. BLUM

Beginning in 1936, President Lázaro Cárdenas asserted that the federal government should strive to overcome the fundamental causes of social debility and to incorporate every Mexican into the production process. The state bore the obligation, based explicitly on revolutionary principles, to promote full integration through social-assistance programs. The newly established Ministry of Public Assistance absorbed existing child-welfare institutions and added to its fundamental obligations medical programs for mothers and children under the age of six to ensure the survival and future participation of those children in the national enterprise of production and consumption.[1] Within this context, formal adoption of children from public orphanages became more highly centralized and carefully scrutinized than it had been since the 1917 Law of Family Relations had reintroduced legal adoption.

Under Cárdenas's successor, Manuel Ávila Camacho, public-welfare policy promoted legal measures to solidify family bonds. In the administration's first two years, the ministry implemented 1,600 birth registrations, enacted 5,000 legitimations of children born outside of marriage, reviewed 1,000 applications to adopt state wards, and approved 155 of those cases.[2] In the context of consolidating revolutionary social-reform initiatives into a full welfare-state structure that linked assistance to production and consumption and defined legalizing family relations as aid, the adoption program raised key questions: what kinds of families did welfare officials seek to form to support national economic goals? What kinds of families did they endorse through legal instruments?[3]

The Revolutionary Family

Public welfare's adoption program highlighted women's roles in the national economic project and problematized the model of legal, state-sanctioned motherhood delineated in the review and approval of adoption petitions. Adoption records reveal contested constructions of motherhood deployed and acted on by welfare officials and social workers, would-be mothers, employers of domestic servants, and mothers seeking public assistance for themselves and their children. These cross-class interactions not only reflected the influence of nearly two decades of family-centered social reform focused on child health, child rearing, and domesticity, but also suggested that these programs had produced contradictory effects.

Starting in the early 1920s, federal reform initiatives generated a barrage of social programs implementing, as Mary Kay Vaughan has observed, a public appropriation of social reproduction. Public-health initiatives promoted hygienic sexual behavior and established pre- and postnatal clinics for mothers and infants. Health and welfare agencies deployed visiting nurses and social workers to instruct mothers in approved child-rearing and housekeeping techniques.[4] Recognized by the state primarily in their maternal roles, women needed children to participate in the national project. The adoption petitions not only testify to a strong link between maternity and emotional fulfillment for women from all walks of life but also suggest that many women claimed their adult status and gained access to participation in public arenas *as mothers*.

But negotiations over maternal qualifications—among state-employed social workers, adoption applicants, and mothers of children considered available for adoption—and the resolutions of many adoption cases suggest that evolving constructions of maternity not only rearticulated and perpetuated pre-revolutionary entitlements to family life structured around gendered notions of dependence but also reinforced a contradiction between motherhood and waged labor. Approval for adoption favored women who depended on a husband's income and who could afford to employ domestic servants. This pattern reflected a class-inflected understanding of motherhood that divorced the affective maternal role from domestic and waged labor and, in particular, devalued the motherhood of women who performed domestic service.[5] Legal adoption illuminated ways that separating affective motherhood from reproductive labor affirmed implicit

ANN S. BLUM

hierarchies ordering Mexico's "revolutionary family," the family model reflecting the structure and priorities of state consolidation and economic development.[6]

This model of motherhood was intimately linked to consolidating notions of protected childhood. During Mexico's mid-nineteenth-century liberal reforms, elimination of legal adoption from civil law favored informal adoption of minors for labor. By the late 1890s, Mexico City's federally administered orphanages oversaw a brisk traffic in informal adoptions, with some adoptions of young children occurring for the purpose of family formation, but the majority of older children being adopted for domestic service. The revolution accelerated the introduction of child-protection legislation incorporating broad international policy trends of the post–World War I era. Mexico's 1917 reintroduction of legal adoption as family formation dovetailed with a suite of initiatives promising significant social and cultural change in the meaning of childhood and the social value of children.[7] The 1931 Mexican federal labor code reinforced protective measures enshrined in the 1917 Constitution that limited child labor. Constitutionally mandated universal public primary education established that children belonged in school and that government-defined national curricula would shape modern citizens.[8] Reducing infant mortality and improving child health ranked among the revolutionary state's highest policy priorities. Urban mother-child clinics opened in working-class neighborhoods, and public schools taught health and hygiene to children and adults alike.[9] The juvenile court system, founded in 1926, focused on educating, readapting, and reintegrating young offenders into the social and productive mainstream, while child-welfare policy linked to national economic goals identified children and youth as vital national resources. Legal adoption served as one instrument among many for the state to restrict child labor, to define childhood as a protected life stage, and to mediate parent-child relationships and family formations, promoting affective nuclear families formed by contract.[10]

Forming Families by Contract

The 1917 Law of Family Relations, issued by decree by the Constitutionalist First Chief Venustiano Carranza, defined adoption as a contract available to married couples as well as to adult, unmarried men and women for forming a parent-child relationship.[11] A married woman could adopt independently of her husband with his consent. Catering to men who fathered children outside of marriage, the new law allowed a married man to adopt without his wife's consent, but if he did, he could not bring the adoptee to live in the conjugal home.[12] The law's preamble linked and affirmed affective and contractual family relations in stating that legal adoption "did no more than recognize the freedom of feelings and consecrate the freedom of contract."[13] Indeed, like civil marriage, adoption was dissoluble: except when the adoptee was a natural child of the adopting adult the law allowed for formal termination.[14] Although the law insisted that adoptive parents and children bore mutual responsibilities identical to those between parents and children by birth, provisions for termination perpetuated in law a widely held understanding of adoption as a temporary or limited relationship.

Ignoring colonial and pre-Reforma adoption statutes and declaring legal adoption new to Mexico, Constitutionalists asserted the modernity of families formed by adoption contract. But entrenched practices of informal adoption, like established attitudes toward divorce, proved resistant to legal innovation. At first not even Mexico City's public orphanages conformed to the law's stipulations: only presidential intervention in 1919 brought the orphanages into compliance.[15] Nevertheless, despite initial loose supervision, legal adoption in tandem with constitutional measures limiting child labor offered significant protections for state wards. By 1925 all recorded adoptions from the Mexico City foundling home were of infants and young children by couples and single women, emphasizing adoption as family formation.[16] This trend did not mean, however, that Mexicans ceased to view adoption, formal or informal, as a way to bring working minors into the household.[17]

The 1928 Civil Code, effective in 1932, fortified the connection between legal adoption and nuclear family norms in stating that only childless adults could adopt.[18] Married partners could no longer adopt independently of one another and had to consider the adoptee as their own child.[19] The legal age to adopt increased from twenty-one to thirty.[20] Critics, however, called for easing adoption procedures, lowering the age requirement, permitting people with children to adopt, and streamlining procedures for investigating applicants.[21]

Initially, Cardenista welfare officials provided flexibility by encouraging temporary placements. In the wake of the economic crisis of the early 1930s, the Cárdenas administration inherited severe overcrowding in the principal Mexico City orphanages and responded by initiating and publicizing a fostering program and paying foster families a stipend.[22] In 1938, however, a new policy promoted permanent adoptions. The new program, overseen by the Bureau of Social Therapy, a department within the Ministry of Public Assistance, centralized control and instituted rigorous background investigations of adoption applicants.[23]

ANN S. BLUM

Adoption and Domestic Service as Social Assistance

Before most adoption petitions passed to the bureau's lawyers, applicants submitted to the scrutiny of social workers' home visits and divulged their histories of infertility, ideas about family, and motives for adopting children. In turn, the social workers, who were from a variety of backgrounds but largely harbored middle-class values, became the gatekeepers of state-conferred maternity.[24]

Since the 1920s, proliferating public-health and welfare agencies had relied on in-house training to staff new positions for visiting nurses and welfare inspectors, work formerly undertaken by volunteer women's charitable groups. By the mid-1930s a social-work training program, based in the Secretariat of Public Education (SEP) and combining secondary education with courses in domestic skills, attracted young, primarily working-class students, while a short-lived program under the National Autonomous University's Faculty of Law offered a professional credential geared toward middle-class aspirants.[25] A June 1937 directive mandated that graduates of the SEP program fill all social-work positions in the Bureau of Social Therapy. Months later, however, when only eight out of forty staff members possessed the required credentials, a program administrator explained that unqualified employees had "entered anew by mere favoritism or by special appointment": even some supervisors lacked qualifications.[26] In 1942, welfare officials, still concerned by the lack of training, encouraged social workers already on the staff to enroll in or complete their studies at the university's School for Social Workers and sponsored internships and seminars for the students. While these measures soon produced "a notable improvement in the quality of work," their introduction in 1942 suggested that during much of this period, social workers did not adhere to a single official standard for evaluating adoption applicants.[27]

Indeed, social workers in the Bureau of Social Therapy brought potentially conflicting attitudes to their dealings with women seeking to adopt through public welfare and mothers seeking assistance. Social workers staffing community centers in working-class neighborhoods intervened in family crises. Emergency foster-care arrangements sometimes circumvented orphanage internment entirely, as community-based social workers distributed an aid applicant's children to private households until the precipitating crisis could be resolved. The social workers referred to such placements as "temporary adoptions," but some foster families became attached to the children and formalized the arrangements through permanent adoption. The same social workers ran an informal employment service, linking employers seeking domestic servants with women needing waged work.[28] Low wages and live-in requirements of domestic service may actually have impeded reunification of families separated by emergency measures. Legal adoption, moreover, rendered separation permanent, gave legal weight to the informal transfer of children across class lines, and reinforced differentials in class entitlements to family. With the policy emphasis on children as future citizens and producers and state endorsement of women's maternal identity, legal adoption also served to transfer valuable social capital to the emergent middle class.

Seeking Motherhood

Except in permitting single women to adopt, neither the 1917 family law nor the 1928 Civil Code fully recognized women's influence in changing Mexican adoption practice. By the late 1930s, in marked contrast to informal adoptions from public orphanages before 1917, married men initiated few petitions, single men even fewer, and officials screened such applications cautiously.[29] Adoption practices now centered on fulfilling women's understandings of family and maternity, but not necessarily within marriage. The desire for children among childless married and single women motivated the majority of the 160 adoption petitions analyzed herein, with wives initiating most of the 105 applications from couples, and single, divorced, or widowed women submitting 45 petitions. Some of the women applicants lived in comfort; others supported themselves with marginal commercial ventures, earning no more than a few pesos daily, but nevertheless acted on a strong sense of entitlement to motherhood and family life. Overall, these adoption petitions testify to the centrality of maternity for Mexican women's identity and fulfillment across the social spectrum.

In their letters of inquiry women wrote of their yearning for children. The home, clearly defined as the female sphere, was incomplete without children. One applicant, who had lost her own three babies in infancy, confessed to loneliness and unhappiness. Over the years, she had taken in little children, but their mothers or grandmothers would reclaim them, leaving her alone again. Another woman wrote, "As we are a married couple without children and find that something is missing in our home, permit me to beg you that you concede the great happiness [of granting our request]."[30] Most wife-initiated petitions from infertile or childless couples sought to adopt infants or toddlers, emphasizing a nurturing maternal role. Some petitioners also revealed the desire for the status that came from motherhood. An older married applicant who traveled to the capital from Zacatecas wanted to adopt orphan girls, two "little women," seven to fourteen years old. She saw adoption as a way to attain a reflected maternal identity: "When people see them all dressed up, it will seem like family."[31]

Single women applicants considered marriage irrelevant to their desire for maternal status and family life. One woman, a widow, applied to adopt on behalf of her daughter, who at twenty-two did not meet the age requirement. The mother told the disapproving social worker that her daughter had never been interested in marriage and planned never to marry.[32] Petitions also show that many single women had already brought children into their homes and sought only to formalize the arrangements. In 1939, a single woman applied to adopt a girl who had come to her four years earlier when the child's mother had died. The girl's father was in the army and could not care for her. To enroll the girl in school the woman needed to present the birth certificate, but it was in the father's name, and she "wanted it to look like the girl was her own daughter."[33] An unmarried normal-school teacher applied to adopt her brother's three orphaned, legitimate children. By 1939 the children had lived with her for four years and, as the social worker observed, viewed her as their mother.[34] Another woman petitioned to adopt her two-year-old niece; the girl's mother relinquished her parental rights, stating that she lacked the financial resources to support the child.[35] These last instances reveal persistence in the established role of unmarried women adopting to keep relatives within the family network.[36]

Like their married counterparts, single women who petitioned to adopt also sought emotional fulfillment. After four years in the capital, an employee in a dentist's office was lonely. An orphan herself, she applied to adopt a girl.[37] An office worker in the property registry who was the only unmarried sibling in her family applied to adopt a seven-year-old girl.[38] Such applications offer some insight into ideas about family among women in Mexico's emerging urban, salaried middle class: in addition to emotional fulfillment, these would-be adoptive mothers sought the social inclusion they believed maternity would confer. One unmarried insurance-company employee wrote in her petition to adopt a girl, "My object is to use the money that I spend in amusements on the girl, and in this way support my country and benefit an orphan who lacks everything."[39] By invoking patriotism, this applicant underscored the ways in which maternity represented public identity and offered access to participation in both social and political life.

New Norms, Old Family Forms

Women applicants generally wanted to adopt girls, pointing to a number of factors, including the divide between the social worlds of men and women. Girls were probably considered more docile than boys, but decades of informal adoption from public orphanages had also established a preference for girls and blurred the boundaries between adopting a family member and adopting a household worker. Indeed, the persistent pre-revolutionary ethos of protection and dependence that elided informal adoption with labor could trump formal adoption. One couple, denied adoption of an orphaned boy, learned that his fifteen-year-old sister had been released from the orphanage to work as a maid. The girl's employer had the surname Lorenzana, indicating that she or a parent had been abandoned to the Mexico City foundling home, where foundlings received the surname of the eighteenth-century clerical founder. The sister's employer, as the boy's godmother, sent him clothes, and his sister visited him weekly.[40] Although the sister, a minor, could assert no legal claim to her brother, the employer's involvement established a claim to the boy.

Protective legislation against child labor and the legal definition of adoption as family formation, however, mitigated exploitation in an increasing number of cases. The situation of a fourteen-year-old girl illustrated both expectations that adoptees perform domestic work and the state's role in enforcing legal protections. The girl had gone to live for a trial period with a brother and sister, proprietors of a fine yard-goods store. They explained that the girl behaved well, but that she was very serious and uncommunicative. She cried whenever letters arrived from her friends in the orphanage. The prospective adopters told the social worker that they bought the girl clothes and let her go to the movies with one of their nieces, but she remained discontent and finally faked illness in order to return to the orphanage. The caseworker found the girl taciturn, asserting only that she did not want to live with her prospective adopters because they made her do housework, which she considered a waste of time.[41]

To convince the girl to accept the arrangement, the social worker argued that formal adoption would oblige her adopters to treat and protect her as a daughter and to put her interests before those of other relatives. The girl responded that she preferred to live with a friend whose mother had offered her a place to stay. She wanted to continue learning dressmaking and believed that adoption would confine her to housework. The social worker insisted that in her friend's home the girl would have no security, that her friend's mother would favor her own daughter, and that in the end the girl would find herself without home or family. Still she refused to return. Nor was she forced to do so. The store proprietors requested permission to inquire whether other girls would accept their proposal.[42]

Officials wielded a new legal authority to deflect petitioners with blatantly exploitative agendas. An applicant from Michoacán complained of the difficulty of finding maids and sought to adopt a ten- or twelve-year-old-girl, "no matter how ugly," to care for an infant. The confiding reference to the maid's appearance may have been an allusion to the customary sexual exploitation of domestic servants by their male employers. The lawyer of the bureau refrained from direct criticism of the applicant's motives, but, citing the law, denied the petition on the grounds that adopters had to be childless.[43] In other instances, officials required assurances that the adopted child would receive a formal education. These measures reflected both legal intent and officials' optimism that adoption would confer middle-class status and opportunities rather than consign adoptees to domestic labor.

Thus, although the case files largely demonstrate that legal adoption reinforced the trend away from child labor, expectations established by the longstanding practice of informal adoption of girls for domestic service proved difficult to eradicate. In the instance of the girl who believed she was being adopted to work as a maid, the social worker ignored the evidence and argued that adoption promised the protection of family relations and home. Nevertheless, for the gatekeepers of formal adoption the relationship between motherhood and waged labor proved far more problematic.

Labor and State-Approved Motherhood

Adoption petitioners had to meet requirements beyond those stated in the Civil Code. Explicit criteria included good health, economic stability, and, for couples, proof of civil marriage. Applicants needed to present three letters testifying to their possession of the economic, social, and educational conditions that would improve the life and guarantee the future of the child.[44] These ostensibly concrete qualifications were open to interpretation, but even more so were qualitative criteria such as "correct behavior" or "honorable reputation." Furthermore, only after the social worker's interview with the applicant and favorable evaluation of the home environment could the case progress to the legal phase. Social workers' home-visit reports consistently reflect middle-class biases, especially regarding gender roles. In general, the review process screened applications from single women by class, preferring professionals, and screened couples for their conformity to a traditional gendered division of labor.

Evaluations of women applicants also turned on race. The social workers never remarked on male applicants' appearances but made scrupulous note of women's, especially skin color—the darker, the more likely that the social worker would find fault.[45] One social worker described a thirty-two-year-old applicant, originally from the state of Michoacán, as "dark, like a farm woman." Moreover, criticized the social worker, "She does not present the appearance of a well-dressed woman, despite the fact that she wears good things. . . . Her manner reveals scant culture."[46]

In the homes of single, working-class women prevalent attitudes toward women's waged labor predisposed social workers to perceive immorality or lack of approved domesticity. One such applicant, a widow, lived in a tenement and supported herself on the two pesos daily she made from her small shop. The social worker conceded, "This woman does not appear to be depraved," but disqualified the petition in part because the shop opened into the tenement, where she observed with distaste "an infinity of unkempt and half-dressed little ones." That the applicant had already raised one foster son, now twenty-two years old, whom all witnesses affirmed was a respectable person with a steady job in a stocking factory, failed to counterbalance the negative impression created by the señora's neighbors.[47] Nor could the applicant's self perception as a hard-working family provider counteract the social worker's preconceptions, which prevented her from observing differentiation among the tenement households.[48]

The approval process favored middle-class applicants, with taste in furniture and decor serving as a measure of class and culture. The home visit report condemned the application of a widow who earned her living making and selling sweets: "In addition to being of very poor quality, her furniture is ugly and uncared for."[49] By contrast, a caseworker exuded admiration for the tasteful acquisitions of a successful divorcée, a partner in a firm that made children's clothes. The petitioner herself had been adopted informally at the age of three when her mother left her with the family that raised her. Married for thirteen years, during which time she had not worked, she divorced her husband in 1935 for living with and fathering children by another woman. In 1938, having reached the required age, she petitioned to adopt an eight-year-old girl whom she had fostered for a year. At the time of this girl's formal adoption, the woman was furnishing a newly purchased house, complete with garage and patio, in a fashionable neighborhood. Two years later, she applied to adopt

ANN S. BLUM

again. The first girl, the social worker observed, loved the applicant as if she were her true mother, had finished primary school, was studying dressmaking, and expressed enthusiasm about the prospect of a companion.[50] Although the applicant's divorce and career might seem to contradict approved models of dependent domesticity, her luxurious home and staff of servants instead represented the pinnacle of tasteful consumption and class-based concepts of modern maternity that distinguished affective mothering from domestic labor.

For couples lacking such means, social workers tended to recommend approval of petitions when the wife devoted herself to housework and maintained acceptable standards of domesticity. Evaluations largely reflected the criteria emphasized in child-rearing and domestic-hygiene brochures distributed by other public agencies; the majority of the advice literature presumed a middle-class home and a housewife without external distractions.[51] But rather than cite specific lapses of prescribed hygiene, such as inadequate ventilation or plumbing, social workers couched both positive and negative perceptions in qualitative terms that reflected the female applicant's moral character. For example, after the visit to the home of a former hairdresser married to the proprietor of a clothing stall in La Lagunilla market, the social worker noted approvingly, "Within their means they live with sufficient comfort. . . . She does not have to work to help her husband." She described their small apartment, "furnished very modestly, but reflecting the activity of the señora as a good housewife. . . . They seem to be very good people."[52] Another couple from Amecameca, state of Mexico, presented a marriage license describing them as "mixed race." The wife could not sign her name. The social worker described the applicants as members of the "peasant class, but," she continued, "one sees that they are very decent people in their manners and dress, they show a neatness and cleanliness in their clothes and persons."[53]

For married working-class applicants, the wife's paid work presented the steepest obstacle to adoption approval. For example, both members of one working-class couple had completed primary school and finished their commercial course. He worked as a driver, and she had a sewing business specializing in children's clothes. Although this couple employed a maid, the wife's work probably prejudiced the social worker against their case. The infant girl they selected was denied them because "she had been requested by other people who were in a better economic position and had more time to attend to her."[54] The señora's persistence, however, later prevailed, and the couple adopted a baby girl.[55] Immediate approval rewarded another couple living on less than four pesos a day, probably because the wife did not leave home to work and because the child they selected had not been "requested by people in a better economic condition." The social worker considered their apartment "a real home."[56]

When social workers chose to construe class as an obstacle, however, the wife's need to do her own housework justified denying the petition. Another applicant and her husband had both completed primary school. He made about 4 pesos daily working in a dairy store. One of the less-judgmental social workers gave their home environment a negative evaluation: "It cannot be beneficial for the minor, since the petitioner has to dedicate herself exclusively to housework for not having the money to pay a maid, and, although she appears to be an affable and kind person, she lacks a favorable education."[57] Their first petition was denied. When they applied again, the wife had a sewing job outside the home and brought in an extra 30 pesos a month. Unfortunately, the most fastidious social worker performed the second home visit. Of their apartment house she wrote in obvious disgust, "So many people live here that one hears a loud murmur as in the markets." There were "many dirty children playing in the patio and in the corridors, offering a very disagreeable appearance." She told the couple that they would have to move to adopt, but her report recommended denying their application because of their income.[58] Married or single, women who worked for wages and who could not afford a maid became suspect in their capacity to care for a child.

Mothers and Maids

Even as the state centralized the regulation of formal adoption, informal networks continued to transfer children across class lines. Because formal, legal adoption was still a novelty, many adopters pursued both informal and formal means, especially when seeking infants. Although petitioners preferred infants and toddlers, often only older children were available through public welfare.[59] One couple seeking an infant withdrew their application after waiting over a year, and other files of couples requesting babies record no outcome, suggesting that they either let the matter drop or pursued other means.[60] Couples who obtained infants through informal networks not only avoided the intensive scrutiny of the review process but also enjoyed the tacit approval of the social-work staff. A college-educated couple sought to legalize the status of an infant girl whom they had acquired by informal means, in the meantime passing the baby off as their own. One of the people writing a testimonial for them noted that the señor "is enchanted since becoming a father, he is mad for the little daughter born a few months ago." The social worker noted coyly in her report that she had refrained from comment.[61] She also refrained from investigating the child's history.

The intersection of official and unofficial means reveals the networks circulating children across class lines, often through the employment of maids. A couple from Guerrero, for example, applied to adopt a six- or seven-year-old boy to be the companion of another boy they had raised, born in their house to a Guatemalan maid and "given" to the wife.[62] Officially, adoption required the consent of a surviving parent or relative.[63] But in relations between employers and domestic servants, the unequal positions of class and power put into question the nature of consent.

The case of Señora Flores Vda. de Trujillo, a recently widowed mother of six, illustrated the pressures to relinquish to their employers that domestics could experience, as well as the conflicts of interest produced by using domestic service as emergency aid. When Flores arrived in Mexico City from rural Michoacán, she was about to give birth to her seventh child. The Red Cross put her up in a hotel for the birth, but subsequently she lived in a construction site with her newborn and three-year-old daughter. When she approached the public-welfare system for aid, she had not eaten since the day before and could not nurse the infant. A social worker took Flores, with her two youngest, to work as a servant in a private home in a fashionable neighborhood.[64]

A few weeks later Flores returned to the Ministry of Public Assistance and reported that she had quit her job and was now living with a friend, and that on leaving her position, she had given her baby to her employer's daughter. The social worker chastised Flores for giving her daughter away, although she affirmed that the mother had the right to do so.[65] Then, together, they proceeded to the employer's home to verify the story. The employer reported that Flores was not accustomed to serving and that she showed indifference to and refused to nurse her baby. In addition, the employer had offered to send Flores out of the city to stay with relatives, to pay for the journey, and to put all her older children in Catholic school. The social worker recorded that the family had fed the three-year-old at their own table, bathed her, and given her clothes and medical attention. Concerning the infant, the employer claimed that Flores had signed a paper consenting to the informal adoption, although out of Flores's hearing the social worker confided that the paper had no legal value. A visit by the social worker to the luxuriously furnished home of the employer's married daughter found the baby asleep in her cradle and the daughter distraught that the baby might be taken from her. The social worker reassured her that she would do everything to facilitate the adoption process, in the interest of securing the future of "our special concern, the baby."[66]

A number of factors combined to shift the social worker's focus from aiding Flores to facilitating her baby's adoption. Flores's rejection not only of domestic service as a solution to her needs but also of her employer's offer to educate her older children suggested that further efforts to improve her situation would prove fruitless. Meanwhile, she had found a place to live. Most important, voluntary relinquishment of her baby indicated a lack of maternal sentiment, while the prospective adoptive mother not only enjoyed a secure economic position but also demonstrated her emotional attachment to the baby. Yet from Flores's perspective, the employer's lavish attentions to her three-year-old and offers to educate her older children may have appeared as pressure to separate her from her children and to relinquish her infant. This case and its outcome illuminate vividly public welfare's conflicting roles in the postrevolutionary politics of class and maternity and call into question which mothers were actually the beneficiaries of adoption in the context of public assistance.

In another instance dating from 1942, during the Ávila Camacho administration, the social worker evinced sympathy for a mother's duress and appreciated the strength of her maternal feelings, but offered no material assistance to the family. Poverty and depression made this mother contemplate giving up her seventh child, whose birth she awaited. The family, also migrants from Michoacán, lived in a tenement for the indigent. The husband was rheumatic and unemployed. The couple learned about the welfare system's adoption program through an employee at the public cafeteria where their children ate breakfast. When the social worker visited the expectant mother in the hospital, she found her suffering physically and depressed over her dilemma. She had not discussed adoption with her husband; she stated that they understood their responsibility as parents. "She had the idea she was going to die," recorded the social worker. Still, the woman withheld her consent to adoption. Impressed by her tenacious maternal sentiment, the caseworker nevertheless made no recommendation for aid to support the mother's wish to keep her child, in effect encouraging relinquishment.[67]

From September 1941 through August 1942, public-welfare officials processed 1,000 adoption applications from married couples and approved 155. The significant acceleration of the adoption program initiated in 1938 must be seen in the context of the policy shift that took place under the Ávila Camacho administration and emphasized legalizing and normalizing families and promoting children's placement in stable home and family environments for optimal development. To meet these goals, public welfare expanded the number of group homes and revived programs facilitating temporary placements. Yet policy statements also explicitly asserted that "the indigence of the mother must not be reason to separate her completely from her children" and recommended grants or pensions to stabilize households in need.[68] These measures reflected international policy trends moving away from the institutional internment of children and toward home-based assistance.

In this context the social worker should have immediately provided assistance to support this couple's ability to maintain their family intact and provide for the awaited baby. Her failure to do so testified not only to the critical ways in which state agents mediated public policies but also to the persistence of biases favoring the acquisition of children by families of means in the modernizing domestic economies of postrevolutionary Mexico.

Conclusion

By the late 1930s, proliferating community-based welfare programs and centralized oversight of legal adoption created multiple intersections where the paths of mothers and would-be mothers crossed, where female social workers assessed their worthiness for motherhood, and where officials used legal instruments and public policy to arbitrate the movement of children out of their families of origin and into approved households.

Children's circulation in this complex social economy followed class-based differentials in the value of women's reproductive labor. The ideal adoptive mother could afford to delegate domestic work to a maid and devote herself to the child. Working-class women who held to traditional divisions of labor that kept them in the home and dependent on a husband's support also received approval for legal adoption. The very kinds of paid work that permitted women to keep their children with them during the day, whether a shop opening into the tenement courtyard or a sewing machine in the living space, disqualified them for state-conferred motherhood. Women who worked as domestics, perceived as doubly dependent —on state assistance and on their employers—remained vulnerable to temporary or permanent separation from their children.

The social workers' judgments appeared to contradict policy in other branches of the federal government. Reclaiming maternity from conservative Catholics in the wake of the Cristero crisis, federal agencies during the Cárdenas administration articulated and promoted a secular version of motherhood linked to national development through ceremonies such as the Department of Labor's 1936 Homage to the Proletarian Mother and Mothers' Day ceremonies coordinated by the SEP. Under President Avila Camacho, public Mothers' Day rituals on a mass scale distributed labor-saving appliances, including pawned sewing machines, to working-class mothers. Moreover, under both administrations, the proliferation and expansion of neighborhood-based programs such as day-care centers and factory crèches, mothers' clubs, and public cafeterias provided important resources supporting single, working mothers in their efforts to sustain family coherence.[69]

Yet, the adoption cases spanning both administrations revealed enduring contradictions at the intersections of motherhood, nation, reproductive labor, and waged work. Whether policy priorities linked assistance to production or emphasized family legalization, two primary considerations qualified a woman for state-conferred motherhood: either she devoted herself to housework and did not work for wages; or she enjoyed the services of a maid, separating the status of affective motherhood from the more burdensome aspects of reproductive labor. The virtues of motherhood remained an entitlement based on dependence on a male breadwinner or access to the reproductive labor of women in a lower social and weaker economic position.

Notes

1. Secretaría de la Asistencia Pública 1940, 16–19.
2. Secretaría de la Asistencia Pública 1942, 255, table 9. The 1,000 applications and 155 adoptions were not archived with the adoption petitions analyzed for this paper.
3. See also Nelson 1990.
4. Vaughan 2000; Bliss 1999; Blum 2003; Stern 1999.
5. Blum 2004.
6. See García and de Oliveira 1994, 26; Ginsburg and Rapp 1991.
7. Jara Miranda 1968, 26–35; Gordon 1999, 119–20; Weiner 1991; Zelizer 1994.
8. Vaughan 1982.
9. Schell 2004.
10. For comparison with Argentina see Guy 2000.
11. *Ley de relaciones familiares* 1917; Blum 1998a.
12. *Ley de relaciones familiares* 1917, cap. 8, art. 220–36, pp. 67–71; ibid., cap. 8, art. 221, pp. 67–68; ibid., cap. 8, art. 222, p. 68.
13. Ibid., p. 6–7; ibid., cap. 2, art. 13, p. 24.
14. Ibid., cap. 8, art. 233–34, p. 70; ibid., cap. 8, art. 235, p. 70.
15. AHSSA, Beneficencia Pública, Establecimientos Asistenciales, Casa de Niños Expósitos, file 15, folder 4, "Acuerdo para que las adopciones de niños se reglamenten en la Ley de Relaciones Familiares," August 1919.

ANN S. BLUM

16. AHSSA, Casa de Niños Expósitos , register 58, 1924–25.

17. Secretaría de Gobernación, Beneficencia Pública del Distrito Federal, *Reglamento para el Hospicio de Niños* (1924), art. 46, p. 16. See also the records of the Mexico City juvenile court, founded in 1926, at the Archivo General de la Nación (AGN), Consejo Tutelar para Menores Infractores.

18. Código Civil (10 de octubre de 1932), cap. 5, art. 390 and 404, in Instituto Interamericano del Niño 1961, v.3, 3:30–32.

19. Ibid., cap. 5, art. 391, in Instituto Interamericano del Niño 1961, 3:31.

20. Ibid., cap. 5, art. 390, in Instituto Interamericano del Niño 1961, 3:30.

21. Padilla 1937.

22. Gutiérrez del Olmo 1993.

23. This analysis is based on 160 adoption petitions between 1938 and 1942 (AHSSA, Beneficencia Pública, Asistencia (As), Asilados y Alumnos (AA), files 32–34, folders 1–3).

24. See Gordon 1988, 12–20.

25. Valero Chávez 1994, 50–58; Sanders 2003, chap. 4. See also Millan 1939, 162–66.

143

26. AHSSA, Beneficencia Pública, Dirección, Oficialía Mayor, box 7, folder 11, 7 October 1937.

27. Secretaría de la Asistencia Pública 1942, 271.

28. AHSSA, Beneficencia Pública, Dirección, Oficialía Mayor, box 7, folder 11.

29. Blum 1998a, chap. 6 and 9.

30. AHSSA, Beneficencia Pública, As, AA, file 32, folder 1, 1940; AHSSA, BP, As, AA, file 32, folder 3, 1942. See also AHSSA, Beneficencia Pública, As, AA, file 34, folder 8, 1939.

31. AHSSA, Beneficencia Pública, As, AA, file 32, folder 1, 1940.

32. AHSSA, Beneficencia Pública, As, AA, file 34, folder 7, 1938.

33. AHSSA, Beneficencia Pública, As, AA, file 32, folder 3, 1939.

34. AHSSA, Beneficencia Pública, As, AA, file 34, folder 6, 1939.

35. AHSSA, Beneficencia Pública, As, AA, file 34, folder 15, 1940.

36. Twinam 1999; Larissa A. Lomnitz and Pérez-Lizaur 1987.

37. AHSSA, Beneficencia Pública, As, AA, file 32, folder 1, 1939.

38. AHSSA, Beneficencia Pública, As, AA, file 32, folder 1, 1941.

39. AHSSA, Beneficencia Pública, As, AA, file 32, folder 1, 1942.

40. AHSSA, Beneficencia Pública, As, AA, file 32, folder 1, 1941.

41. AHSSA, Beneficencia Pública, As, AA, file 32, folder 1, 1941.

42. AHSSA, Beneficencia Pública, As, AA, file 32, folder 1 1941.

43. AHSSA, Beneficencia Pública, As, AA, file 32, folder 2, 1942.

44. AHSSA, Beneficencia Pública, As, AA, file 32, folder 3, Roberto García Formentí to Jefe del Departamento de Terapía Social, March 1940.

45. AHSSA, Beneficencia Pública, As, AA, file 32, folder 1, 1939; AHSSA, Beneficencia Pública, As, AA, file 32, folder 3, 1939.

46. AHSSA, Beneficencia Pública, As, AA, file 32, folder 3, 1941.

47. AHSSA, Beneficencia Pública, As, AA, file 32, folder 1, 1939. For comparison with fostering in Brazil see Cardoso 1984.

48. Larissa A. Lomnitz and Pérez-Lizaur 1984.

49. AHSSA, Beneficencia Pública, As, AA, file 32, folder 3, 1941.

50. AHSSA, Beneficencia Pública, As, AA, file 33, folder 11, 1938–1943.

51. See Ochoa 1921; AHSSA, Salubridad Pública, Higienie Infantil, box 10, folder 14, Cartas [números 1–12], Servicio de Higiene Infantil Post-Natal, Departamento de Salubridad, D.F., 1934. See also Vaughan 2000.

52. AHSSA, Beneficencia Pública, As, AA, file 32, folder 1, 1941–1942.

53. AHSSA, Beneficencia Pública, As, AA, file 33, folder 3, 1938.

54. AHSSA, Beneficencia Pública, As, AA, file 34, folder 1, 1939.

55. AHSSA, Beneficencia Pública, As, AA, file 34, folder 1, 1939.

56. AHSSA, Beneficencia Pública, As, AA, file 34, folder 14, 1940. See also AHSSA, BP, As, AA, file 34, folder 9, 1940.

57. AHSSA, Beneficencia Pública, As, AA, file 32, folder 3, 1941–1942.

58. AHSSA, Beneficencia Pública, As, AA, file 32, folder 3, 1941–1942.

59. AHSSA, Beneficencia Pública, As, AA, file 32, folder 1, 1941.

60. AHSSA, Beneficencia Pública, As, AA, file 32, folder 1, 1941–1942.

61. AHSSA, Beneficencia Pública, As, AA, file 34, folder 17, 1939.

62. AHSSA, Beneficencia Pública, As, AA, file 33, folder 2, 1939.

63. Código Civil (10 de octubre de 1932), libro 1, tít. 9, De la tutela, cap. 5, art. 492, in Instituto Interamericano del Niño 1961, v. 3, 41.

64. AHSSA, Beneficencia Pública, As, AA, file 32, folder 3, 1940. The woman's name has been changed.

65. AHSSA, Beneficencia Pública, As, AA, file 32, folder 3, 1940.

66. AHSSA, Beneficencia Pública, As, AA, file 32, folder 3, 1940.

67. AHSSA, Beneficencia Pública, As, AA, file 32, folder 3, 1942.

68. Secretaría de Asistencia Pública, *Informe de labores, 1941–1942*, 254–55, 285.

69. Secretaría de la Asistencia Pública 1940, 51; "Nueva Forma el 10 de Mayo," *El Nacional*, 9 May 1938, p. 8. See also Buck 2002.

PART THREE

The Gendered Realm of Labor Organizing

The Struggle between the "Metate" and the "Molinos de Nixtamal" in Guadalajara, 1920–1940

MARÍA TERESA FERNÁNDEZ-ACEVES

During the 1920s and 1930s, Guadalajaran society experienced a unique cross-fertilization between secular feminists and working-class women in the convergence of four processes: the building of the new revolutionary state, church-state conflict, rapid economic modernization in the tortilla industry and related change in labor-force participation, and the rise of a modern trade-union movement. These processes opened the way for women to mobilize and politicize and led to a more active role for women than either the church or the revolutionary state had desired.[1] The story of women's organizing in the tortilla industry, in particular, challenges myths of women's passivity and demonstrates both the extent and the limits of working women's mobilization in this period of Mexican history.[2] Gender and class differences became culturally significant and politicized within a revolutionary context in which male-dominated institutions and social movements—the Catholic Church, the postrevolutionary state, and trade unions—struggled for hegemony.

Rise of Radical Regional State Politics

Guadalajara was Mexico's second largest city. Like the cities in Puebla and Veracruz, it had textile and light consumer-goods industries serving a primarily regional market.[3] Unlike Puebla and Veracruz, the state of Jalisco and its capital city of Guadalajara produced no strong autochthonous revolutionary movement. Although a radicalizing, anticlerical liberal tradition from the nineteenth century existed among some sectors of the working, artisan, and middle classes, it was eclipsed in the early years of the revolution by the rise of a multiclass Catholic social and political movement that promoted the principles of Pope Leo XIII's Rerum Novarum of 1891. This movement grew when in 1914 General Manuel Diéguez brought the Constitutionalist revolution to Jalisco in the form of harsh anticlerical measures.

From Diéguez's arrival through the 1920s, radical and anticlerical governors—Manuel M. Diéguez (1914–19), Basilio Badillo (1921–22), José Guadalupe Zuno Hernández (1923–26), and Margarito Ramírez (1927–29)—introduced important labor, agrarian, and educational reforms to build a mass base that would offset Catholic power.[4] They favored improved working conditions for urban and rural male and female workers and encouraged them to organize and strike. They relied on a liberal, secular labor movement of workers, artisans, and teachers that had radicalized through exposure to anarchosyndicalist and communist ideas during the revolution.

The Catholic and secular labor movements and women's mobilizations fed off one another and negotiated with the state in a dialogical fashion rather than being directed by the government or church. In fact, popular forces were more radical than the revolutionary state or the church hierarchy.[5] In the 1920s, the contest between Catholic and secular organizations intensified as both fought to control public space, gain recognition, and obtain civil, social, and political rights. Under Governors Zuno and Ramírez, secular labor, agrarian, and women's organizations gained political recognition and increased their numbers, while the urban Catholic movement suffered from effects of state repression and the Cristero Rebellion (1926–29), the Catholics' war against the government that ravaged western Mexico.

MARÍA TERESA FERNÁNDEZ-ACEVES

The Radical, Secular Women's Movement and
Labor Politics in the 1920s

As opportunities opened to subaltern groups to organize and influence the postrevolutionary state, radical women formed female or mixed-sex unions—textile workers, teachers, and food-processing workers—and joined Zuno's Confederación de Agrupaciones Obreras Libertarias de Jalisco.[6] Female and male workers demanded the implementation of their constitutional labor rights, but they encountered resistance from foremen who ridiculed the Constitution of 1917. Working women became advocates of Zuno's labor initiatives: his Board of Conciliation and Arbitration in the new Labor Department, his labor laws of 1923 and 1924, and his creation of a new Colonia Obrera where workers could live.[7] In large part, Zuno encouraged women's organizing to offset the formidable presence of women in the Catholic movement. Like Veracruz's populist governor Adalberto Tejeda, Zuno implemented paternalist policies to create loyal male and female supporters.[8]

In the 1920s secular women organized twenty-six different organizations.[9] The most influential was the Círculo Feminista del Oriente (CFO), in part because their members joined state labor, health, and educational bureaucracies. Established in 1927, the CFO emerged from anticlerical schoolteachers' and radical women workers' participation in secular worker and women's organizations from the 1910s. Some CFO founders of middle-class backgrounds radicalized when they campaigned with the teacher-led Centro Radical Feminino (CRF), the city's first feminist organization, against Catholic labor organizations in the textile factories. Others attended the CRF's anticlerical iconoclast school at the Casa del Obrero Mundial. Women teachers and manual workers began to radicalize their anticlericalism through exposure to anarchosyndicalist and communist ideas. They promoted the image of a "New Woman" in the public sphere: radical, anticlerical, and political.

In the mid-1920s radical female textile workers, although expelled or fired by owners who favored Catholic organizations, continued working politically with schoolteachers, organizing other male and female workers, and pressing for workers' rights at the Labor Department. Still, after almost a decade of political participation and struggle, working conditions for women had not changed significantly. The replacement of women workers in modernizing industrial sectors continued. Communist-oriented male unionists showed little interest in female workers, and the Catholic movement preferred to ensconce them at home. The situation began to change in the second half of the 1920s, when ousted women textile workers and feminist teachers witnessed the beginning of the displacement of women tortilla workers. Taking advantage of the government's and Catholics' preoccupation with the Cristero War, they began to organize a more radical women's movement through the formation of the CFO.[10]

Taking a leadership role was María A. Díaz, a textile worker with a combative class perspective nurtured by her experience during the transition from mutualism to anarchosyndicalist-inspired unionism and her fight against Catholic textile unions. Díaz advocated for a single compulsory union, dues payments, and obligatory worker attendance at union meetings to strengthen solidarity and to fight against "traitors to the working class." Her participation in the textile workers' movement and clashes among competing labor organizations taught her the crucial role of discipline, loyalty, and militancy in creating a strong union. Her code of honor was informed by the violence she experienced when she was almost killed by a priest and foreman of a textile factory.[11]

Along with María Díaz, Guadalupe Martínez became a CFO leader. Martínez came from a family that embraced nineteenth-century liberal, anticlerical traditions. Her mother was a textile worker and a relative of Díaz, and her father, an electrical worker, had been a founding member of the anarchist-leaning Casa del Obrero Mundial in Guadalajara in 1915. As a militant public-school teacher, Martínez embraced the revolutionary discourse of social justice for the working class.[12]

The CFO pledged to fight for the moral and material improvement of women workers. Like the Catholic movement and more moderate state-associated women's organizations, it campaigned for a moralization of society but one that championed a non-Catholic morality. In contrast to state-allied women reformers, it did not promote domesticity at the expense of women's right to work outside the home. The CFO's notion of female morality rested on rights to jobs, decent wages, and education as well as civil and political equality. They modeled a New Woman, a politically informed, revolutionary citizen, antithetical to the stereotype of the submissive, religiously obsessed Catholic female prevalent in the rhetoric of male revolutionaries.

The CFO helped unionize women seamstresses, domestic servants, shoemakers, and tortilla, oil-cooking, and cracker workers. Its members took note of one of the most significant technological revolutions in twentieth-century Mexico—the introduction of the corn mill—and proceeded to organize women tortilla workers to defend their rights. The CFO's success in this sector was greater than among textile workers because those unions did not compete with the Catholic and Confederación Regional Obrera

Mexicana organizations and because Governors Zuno and Ramírez lent significant support to regional and local labor organizations. Because the tortilla industry remained scattered in work sites dispersed throughout the city, it could not be closely supervised by a small, united group of owners and the church. Moreover, the armed rural resistance of the Cristero Rebellion had diverted the attention of Catholics from the city.

The Corn Mills

In Mexico women have made tortillas since pre-Hispanic times.[13] For centuries, women made tortillas at home in a long production process that took at least six hours. The production process began to change in the late nineteenth century and early twentieth with the introduction of mechanized corn mills (*molinos de nixtamal*). The mill effected a technological revolution within and outside the domestic realm. The new tortilla industry created three distinct workplaces outside the home: corn mills, dough shops, and tortilla factories.

Initially, there were two types of mills: the industrial corn mill, which used steam or electricity to grind large quantities of *nixtamal* (soaked and softened maize kernels), and the *maquilero* corn mill, which helped individual families to grind nixtamal. By 1929, there were five types of corn mills distinguished by the amount of nixtamal ground.[14] The industrial corn mills created five occupations: *nixtamaleros/as* (male or female workers who soaked and softened the maize kernels), *cebadores/as* (male or female workers who cut lime for the nixtamal, supervised the corn mills, and fed ingredients to the machine), *boleras* (female dough-ball rollers), *recaudadoras* (female dough-sellers), and *conductores de masa* (men who carried large quantities of dough from corn mills to dough shops). By 1930, women and men in the mills fought for the skilled and better-paid positions of cebadores and nixtamaleros. The other positions were not disputed between male and female workers.

The second workplace was the dough shop. After the mid-1920s, some corn mills had dough shops, while others remained separate from the mills. Generally, only women worked in these shops, as *expendedoras de masa* (female dough-sellers). The third workplace was the *tortillería* (a tortilla workshop or factory) where women made tortillas manually. Each tortilla maker ground approximately 20 to 30 kilograms of dough a day on the *metate* (grinding stone), making 300 to 450 tortillas.[15] By the late 1920s and early 1930s, there were different types of tortillerías, some linked to large or small corn mills and others including family-owned workshops that did not hire unionized workers.[16] The dough shops and tortillerías

The Metate *and the* Molinos de Nixtamal

paid workers piece-rate for the amount of dough sold or the number of tortillas made.

From 1900 through the 1920s, the tortilla industry grew rapidly in response to the demand of expanding social groups, particularly the middle classes with little time to devote to tortilla making and little money to hire servants to make them.[17] Workplaces were all over the city. Most employed few workers. Generally, the mills and tortillerías were in the old barrios of Guadalajara, where there were better services, dense populations, and dynamic economic and social interaction. Most were in middle- and working-class districts with big markets and churches. The tortilla-worker unions were primarily located in the middle-class Hidalgo neighborhood and near downtown. Ease of contact among people appears to have facilitated politics and social mobilization.

The number of male and female workers changed as the industry grew: the greater the mechanization at the mills, the greater their masculinization; the lesser the need of new technology at dough shops and tortillerías, the greater their feminization. In 1920, women dominated the tortilla industry, constituting 65 percent of workers, and they increased their share to 87 percent by 1930, concentrating in dough shops (97 percent female workers) and in tortillerías (99 percent).[18] Within the corn mills, however, by 1930 the workforce included 150 women (51 percent) and 145 men (49 percent). As men increasingly occupied the positions of nixtamalero and cebador, female labor-force participation in the mills declined. By 1940, women represented only 30 percent of the workers as mills increased their size and skilled positions to process larger quantities of nixtamal. Women protested the masculinization of skilled jobs, deploying traditional gendered divisions by insisting that all tortilla work belonged to women.

Working Conditions in Corn Mills

Until 1927, the tortilla industry remained unregulated. Owners abused workers, and the government did not control the prices of products and services.[19] Work in the mills began between 3:30 and 4 A.M., as nixtamaleros/as had to have the dough prepared by six in the morning. They stayed at work until 5 or 6 P.M. Because wages depended on the amount of dough prepared and sold, longer working days brought more money.[20] Male and female workers complained of owners' breaking verbal agreements, arbitrary firings, deplorable hygienic conditions, and low wages that were often not even paid in full.

After protesting to the Labor Department and Boards of Conciliation and Arbitration about their denial of constitutional rights, tortilla workers' began to unionize into mixed- and single-sex unions. The first union, linked to the Mexico City–dominated Confederación Regional Obrera Mexicana, was a mix-sex, ineffectual organization. In 1926 the Zunista Confederación de Agrupaciones Obreras Libertarias de Jalisco promoted the formation of three unions: the Unión de Trabajadoras en Molinos de Nixtamal (a female union of nixtamaleras), the Unión de Trabajadores en Molinos de Nixtamal (a mixed-sex union), and the Unión Social de Expendedoras de Masa (a female union for dough shops).[21]

In 1927 the Unión de Trabajadores en Molinos de Nixtamal promoted the implementation of an internal regulation of working hours, work tasks, compulsory holidays, and the obligations of owners and workers.[22] In 1928 another union, the Unión de Trabajadores y Trabajadoras en Molinos para Nixtamal, obtained the first collective contract establishing minimum wages, a seven-hour workday, a four-hour workday on Sunday, a fifteen-minute break, and double pay for overtime. Moreover, the male and female corn-mill workers and female sellers of dough agreed that those workers who were not members of unions could not maintain their positions.[23] However, in 1928, twenty-eight labor inspections in different mills showed that none had followed those regulations.[24] With demand dwindling as the Depression hit and people returning to the countryside with the conclusion of the Cristero Rebellion, small-mill owners contended that they could not pay the high salaries demanded by the unions and asked permission from the Labor Department to reduce the number of workers or close their mills.

After several years of appealing to the Jalisco Department of Labor and noting the increasing conservatism of its policies, organized male and female workers on 19 May 1930 complained to the federal Ministry of Industry that mill owners had violated the first collective contract of 1928.[25] They argued that owners had reduced their salaries with state government approval and that the mills had not maintained the required distance from one another, negatively affecting competition and driving wages down. Resisting the conservative turn of state labor leaders, the tortilla workers persuaded the federal Ministry of Labor to demand a plan for amelioration from the state Board of Conciliation.

On 21 May 1930, the Jalisco Board of Conciliation and Arbitration admitted extreme exploitation in the industry and identified multiple reasons for it. The return migration from city to countryside following the end of the Cristero War reduced demand and forced some mills to close. Disputes among Confederación Obrera de Jalisco (COJ) leaders impeded close supervision over mandated hiring of unionized workers. Mill owners

The Metate *and the* Molinos de Nixtamal

had taken advantage of these divisions to hire non-union workers and to evade the contract. Further, attempts to unify the tortilla workers had caused divisions among workers and unions. These divisions in turn prompted the formation of new unions recognized by neither the owners nor the old unions and thus outside the collective contract.[26] Absent from the report were the conflicts between men and women over jobs and between masculine and feminine notions of work.

The Rise of the Male-Dominated Trade-Union Movement, the CFO, and Tortilla Workers

As in Puebla, the 1930s gave rise to a process of conservative governance. Jaliscan politicians allied with Plutarco Elías Calles—Mexican president (1924–1928) and jefe máximo (1928–1934)—destroyed the regional independence created by Zuno and came to control state politics by the early 1930s. The weakening of the Catholic social movement, the Cristero Rebellion, and the church-state accords of 1929 all facilitated the ensuing domestication of the labor movement. The ruinous impact of the Depression on Jalisco's mining, textiles, and railroad industries—all centers of labor radicalism—exacerbated this development.[27] Governor Sebastián Allende (1932–1935) promoted worker domestication through his ambitious public-works program of street, road, and highway construction. Many male workers became clients of the government and government-affiliated unions. Female and male service workers also swelled the ranks of state-allied organized labor.

The critical intermediaries were the new leaders of the COJ—Carlos Sánchez Lara, Alfonso González, and Heliodoro Hernández—who between 1929 and 1932 transformed the COJ from an autonomous, combatant, and communist organization into a moderate ally of Allende and Calles.[28] In the midst of the Great Depression, COJ leaders sought to avoid boycotts, strikes, shutdowns, lockouts, and sabotages.

Ironically, militant women in the tortilla industry and the CFO worked well with the COJ and, in particular, with Hernández, who controlled bus and taxi drivers' unions and sought to expand his power by allying with different kinds of workers. By exchanging favors and loyalties and promoting discipline, Hernández expanded his base in order to gain control of the labor movement. He influenced the Board of Conciliation and Arbitration, ran for the state congress, and extended his power into the economic arena by creating a company of union buses that provided jobs for his loyal followers. Hernández worked strategically with women to expand his base and found in the CFO a potential ally. For their part, CFO

MARÍA TERESA FERNÁNDEZ-ACEVES

women believed they could work with the new COJ leadership because they shared a core notion of women's role as non-Catholic revolutionaries. They thought such an alliance would increase their power in pushing for women's agenda.

The life histories of Catarino Isaac, a male leader of nixtamaleros, and Anita Hernández Lucas, a female leader of *torteadoras* (women who made tortillas by hand), illustrate the relationships between Hernández and male workers and his interactions with women workers and the CFO. Hernández introduced Catarino Isaac's family to the corn mills and the labor movement after the death of Isaac's father, a sweeper in a public market.[29] Because Isaac's family was in great economic need, Hernández secured them jobs in Guadalajara's biggest corn mill. There, Isaac's mother and sisters worked as boleras and expendedoras, while he worked as a *repartidor* (dough deliverer) and *cargador* (dough carrier) from the age of eight. Later on, Catarino Isaac became a nixtamalero, joined the union, was elected to the union's executive committee, and married the daughter of the leader of the Sindicato de Trabajadores en Molinos para Nixtamal y Similares. By strengthening his kinship ties, Isaac learned the skills necessary to succeed in the labor movement: negotiation, personal loyalty, and discipline. After his father-in-law's death, Isaac succeeded him as union secretary-general. Equally important was Isaac's relationship with Hernández, who treated him as a son and guided his union career. As a loyal disciple, Isaac ensured his actions dovetailed with Hernández's policy of safeguarding skilled positions for men. After a long debate among male and female workers, unions, and owners, Isaac became the powerful leader of the tortilla industry and implemented a gender policy that confirmed the separation of male and female unions, reserved skilled jobs for men, and relegated women to unskilled positions. According to Isaac, all the unions would fight together for their labor rights. To compensate his loyal followers, Isaac also applied Hernández's economic policy within the tortilla industry, offering small loans to buy mills.

Isaac's gender policy reflected his role inside his own family. After the deaths of his father and father-in-law, he became the male breadwinner and head of the household. His mother and sister continued working at the mills but in positions perceived as feminine. They could be members of the CFO and militant women workers only with Isaac's permission.

Like Isaac, Anita Hernández Lucas lost her father during the revolution. Her mother obtained a pension from General Álvaro Obregón and moved the family to Guadalajara where she found work as a torteadora and occasional candy vendor. All of Hernández Lucas's siblings died from illness or accidents, underscoring the problem of inadequate child care for

The Metate *and the* Molinos de Nixtamal

workingwomen. Only Anita and her mother survived. They worked at the different corn mills—most often from 3:30 a.m. until 6 p.m. Her mother took her to union meetings, where they met the textile leader María A. Díaz, the schoolteacher Guadalupe Martínez, and the union boss Heliodoro Hernández. They also attended CFO meetings, where they met other women leaders, among them, Jovita Robles of nixtamaleras and Refugio Santa María of dough-shop workers.

The CFO trained tortillería leaders and, indirectly, their rank and file on the principle that women workers should have the same rights and benefits as their male counterparts, including equal pay for equal work, acceptance in all jobs, and more female labor and health inspectors. The CFO helped to organize women in small shops and mills cross the city and to convince them that political struggle and unionization were dignifying processes.

In 1936, when Anita Hernández Lucas's mother was elected secretary-general of the Sindicato Elaboradoras de Tortillas, she rejected the position and asked the union leadership to give it to her daughter. Members of the union agreed and made Anita leader of the torteadoras. As a leader, she worked tirelessly to improve working conditions. Guadalupe Martínez taught her to read and write, as she did with other female tortilla workers. Through this intersectoral, interclass, and intergenerational experience, torteadoras like Anita Hernández Lucas learned the basic skills they needed to defend their labor rights.

In his interactions with María A. Díaz, Guadalupe Martínez, Anita Hernández Lucas, and other workers, Heliodoro Hernández stressed the values of honesty, education, respect, and discipline.[30] He warned them not to become agitators but encouraged them to assume their worker identity with pride and vigor. While he helped them to abandon their submissive attitude toward owners and foremen, he also taught them that the union's honor-and-justice committee would expel anyone suspected of disloyalty or a lack of solidarity.

Political Revolution at the Corn Mills

By 1930, as the tortilla workers fought for their labor rights, two groups within the COJ fought to control and unify them. One faction was led by the labor leader and federal deputy Nicolás Rangel Guerrero who relied on the male nixtamalero Timoteo Robledo (leader of the Unión de Trabajadores y Trabajadoras en Molinos de Nixtamal) and the female dough worker Isaura Camacho (leader of the Unión Social de Expendedoras de Masa), and included their respective rank-and-file constituencies. The other group followed labor leader Hernández, whose supporters included

Catarino Isaac (of the recently created Sindicato de Trabajadores de Molinos de Nixtamal de Guadalajara), Jovita Robles (leader of the Unión de Trabajadoras en Molinos de Nixtamal), and their memberships. Each group included different unions that fought to control jobs. Timoteo Robledo's group protested vigorously when Hernández became labor representative of some tortilla workers at the Board of Conciliation and Arbitration. Robledo argued that that role was only for the representatives of industry-specific unions, not for outside labor leaders.[31] Although Robledo complained several times, Hernández continued to represent and organize the group led by Isaac and Robles.[32]

While both groups sought unification, they refused to resolve their differences because their leaders fought to control the COJ. Recognizing the negative impact of this dispute, a group of women workers in February 1930 created a single-sex union, the Unión de Trabajadoras en Molinos de Nixtamal, and launched a fierce protest against their male co-workers at the Board of Conciliation and Arbitration.[33] In this crucial act, the nixtamaleras showed their ability to counteract perceptions of women as weak and unskilled workers. In their response to male discrimination and to hostile or patronizing attitudes, their self-perceptions diverged markedly from the positions articulated by male unions that minimized women's work and sought to displace it.

On 18 February 1930, the new union's leader, Jovita Robles, with backing from the CFO, complained to the Board of Conciliation and Arbitration of the "dirty" work performed by several unspecified organizations that aimed to destroy the unions by asking owners to give cebadora and bolera positions only to men. She denounced this action as criminal and unfair because even if women had not been the first to organize in the industry, they were certainly veterans. She told of male co-workers attacking them and threatening to take their jobs, or receiving money from owners to bypass the collective agreement in order to fill positions with men only. She denounced those co-workers who attempted to "destroy workers' organizations" as betrayers of the revolution and the working class. Further, the women she represented refused to pay union dues as long as male leaders failed to fight for women's issues and continued to spend such hard-earned contributions drinking in cantinas. The women had decided to form their own union to decide on their needs as women and let the men resolve their own issues.

Although the formation of an all-female union turned out to be part of Heliodoro Díaz's plans to eliminate his enemies, Jovita Robles's apparently heartfelt rhetoric illuminated the intersection of gender and class in a period of rapid economic change and intense political struggle. She

The Metate *and the* Molinos de Nixtamal

asserted that the corn mills belonged to women, not men. Like the female coffee sorters of Veracruz, she denied that women lacked skills for mill work.[34] She linked traditional cultural notions of gendered work with a bid for modern equality. Although she recognized the existence of a new gendered division of labor within corn mills that required both men and women, she wanted the same rights for men and women in the same positions.[35] Robles's claim exposed the embittered power relations between male and female mill workers, with men manifesting their hostility in physical violence, political corruption, and the use of denigrating, misogynist language.

Although women of the Unión de Trabajadoras en Molinos de Nixtamal sought to preserve female jobs in the industry, conflicts between male leaders prevented their success. In 1931, the differences between the two political factions intensified as each group asked owners to employ only their members. Owners took advantage of the dispute to hire nonunionized workers.[36] Without the approval of Timoteo Robledo's groups, Heliodoro Hernández signed a collective agreement with mill owners that replaced the first collective contract of 1928.[37] Hernández and "his" tortilla workers denounced Robledo's workers as traitors dividing the working class and tried to get their official, legal representation denied.[38] More internal division and violence ensued. On 30 December 1931, María Martha Guillén, a dough-shop worker, was killed when mill workers tried to force an owner to hire unionized workers. Some owners used the chaos and tragedy to threaten workers and to refuse to sign another contract or recognize labor rights.[39] The situation became so dire that President Pascual Ortiz Rubio intervened in early 1932 and ordered the signing of a collective agreement to implement the workers' rights granted by the Federal Labor Law of 1931.[40] This became the third industry-wide agreement ratifying the 1928 contract.

Again, owners disregarded it and fired workers.[41] By the end of 1933, mill labor leaders remained divided. In the tortilla industry one group continued to be led by Robledo, while the other was represented by Isaac and supported by Heliodoro Hernández.[42] Women workers were also divided in their support for these groups.[43] In 1934, because they had been forced to leave their mill jobs, Timoteo Robledo's and Isaura Camacho's group sued the governor, the municipal president, the president of the Board of Conciliation and Arbitration, the general inspector of police, and the head of the Security Commission. They lost their case. According to their rivals—Heliodoro Hernández and Catarino Isaac, who were clearly favored by Jalisco state and municipal institutions—they were expelled from their unions, and as nonunionized workers, they had neither rights nor jobs.[44] To add to the melee, internal divisions wracked and split the women's union. When its reunification favored Jovita Robles, she expelled members of the rival group for divisiveness and disloyalty.[45] Thus, women did not form a solid sisterhood, nor did revolutionary male workers have a monopoly over the discourse of class and revolutionary betrayal and disloyalty that masked factional disputes.

By 1934, the leaders of nixtamaleros—Isaac and Robles—and tortilla unions associated with Hernández had won a significant battle: they had converted their third collective contract of 1932 into law. In 1935 the tortilla-industry unions and supporters of Hernández sought to obtain fixed salaries for all workers and demanded a new labor contract through a general strike.[46] On 9 September 1935, corn-mill owners and the unions signed the fourth collective contract, which established a fixed wage of 1.50 pesos daily in the mills and dough shops, a regulated workday, annual vacations with salaries, double pay for overtime, paid holidays, and Sunday rest.[47] Nonetheless, the torteadoras were still paid by the piece.

Despite the agreement, owners did not pay what they had promised.[48] In late 1935, workers struck to demand the fulfillment of the contract.[49] Whereas the expendedoras sought to have their right to a fixed wage honored, the torteadoras asked that their workday comply with the Federal Labor Law of 1931 and that they get 3 cents for each kilogram of dough produced.[50] In 1936, nixtamaleras and expendedoras struck again to demand the implementation of their legal contract.

As a result of the consolidation of the CFO and Heliodoro Díaz's faction, "enemy" female unionists and nonunionized women workers lost their jobs while the working conditions of female "loyalists" gradually improved. In 1941, a report from the Investigative Office of the Labor Conditions of Women and Minors pointed out that cebadoras, boleras, expendedoras, and *molineras* (women corngrinders) had a minimum wage, paid compulsory Sunday rest, maternity leave, and eight-hour workdays. By contrast, the torteadoras did not have a minimum wage. They worked by the piece and had long workdays and no maternity leave.[51] Their conditions were very similar to the *boneteras* (knitwear workers) in Puebla. By the late 1940s, all unionized women tortilla workers won demands to receive wages for holidays, annual vacations, and maternity leave. They even exacted a monthly contribution from owners for their basketball team.

The women who kept their jobs actively participated in the labor parades and those that commemorated the revolution on 20 November. In these parades they accompanied women of the CFO and other women's unions. Through their participation in the parades, women of the tortilla

159

industry enhanced their familiarity with the language of the Mexican Revolution, which they had acquired through their work struggles. At the same time, they linked their efforts to those of the international working class, inscribed in the memory of the Haymarket martyrs of Chicago. In short, they forged identities as women of the revolution and of the international working class.

By 1940, men had taken over the skilled jobs and a hierarchical, gendered division of labor functioned to keep women in unskilled, lower-paid positions. Women accepted the male-dominated COJ that reaffirmed a gender ideology that separated masculine, skilled from female, unskilled jobs. After the COJ became the Federación de Trabajadores de Jalisco and affiliated with the all-powerful, national Confederación de Trabajadores de Mexico, Hernández and Isaac unified the tortilla unions into one federation and divided it into female and male sections. They retained the female leaders, who maintained their loyal militancy in their union organizations, the CFO, and the official party until their deaths some forty years later. They had consolidated and subordinated themselves as a political family within a male-dominated, boss-rule unionism.

Notes

1. For similar developments elsewhere in Latin America see Weinstein 1997, Farnsworth-Alvear 2000, Hutchison 2001.
2. Fernández-Aceves and Orejel Salas 1987; Keremetsis 1983; Keremetsis 1984a; Lailson 1987.
3. See Gauss and Fowler-Salamini in this volume; Ramos Escandón 1987; Ramos Escandón 1990; Ramos Escandón 1998; Ramos Escandón 2003; Gutiérrez Álvarez 2003.
4. Aldana Rendón 1988; Tamayo 1988a, 97, 134, 171, 191, 245–50; Tamayo 1988b, 34–37, 38, 43; Moreno Ochoa 1959, 126, 141–44.
5. See essays in Joseph and Nugent 1994b; Fernández-Aceves 2000, 310–22.
6. AHJ, Ramo de Trabajo, T-9–926, exp. no. 2132. Tamayo 1988b, 34–37.
7. Tamayo 1988a, 248–50.
8. See Fowler-Salamini in this volume.
9. Fernández-Aceves 2000, 123, 361; Fernández-Aceves and Orejel Salas 1987; Lailson 1987, 59–82.
10. AHJ, Ramo de Trabajo, T-7–927, exp. no. 2470.
11. Fernández-Aceves 2000, 194–98.
12. Ibid., 200.
13. Bauer 1990, 1–17; Pilcher 1998, 11, 100–106.
14. AHJ, Ramo de Trabajo, T-2–929, T-142, exp. no. 3667.
15. In contrast with this handwork, in 1907 a man proposed to sell a tortilla machine that could make 300 tortillas in one hour (see AHJ, Ramo de Beneficencia, 1907).

MARÍA TERESA FERNÁNDEZ-ACEVES

16. AHJ, Ramo de Trabajo, T-7–934.

17. Vaughan 1997, 5, 43. Pilcher 1998, 100–101.

18. Fernández-Aceves 2003.

19. AHJ, Ramo de Trabajo, T-9–925, exp. no. 1700.

20. Keremetsis 1984a, 57.

21. AHJ, Ramo de Trabajo, T-1–926.

22. AHJ, Ramo de Trabajo, T-2–927.

23. AHJ, Ramo de Trabajo, T-2–931/4943.

24. AHJ, Ramo de Trabajo, T-2–927, caja T-15 bis "D," exp. no. 7310.

25. AHJ, Ramo de Trabajo, T-2–930, caja T-163, exp. no. 4286.

26. AHJ, Ramo de Trabajo, T-2–929, caja T-138, exp. no. 3526.

27. Romero 1988, III, 115.

28. Tamayo 1985, 149–50.

29. Agapito Isaac, interview by author, Guadalajara, Jalisco, 15 March 2002; Anita Hernández Lucas, interview by author, tape recording, Guadalajara, Jalisco, 17 August 1996 and 8 August 1998.

30. Anita Hernández Lucas, interview by author, tape recording, Guadalajara, Jalisco, 8 August 1998.

31. AHJ, Ramo de Trabajo, T-1–930, caja T-153, exp. no. 3905.

32. AHJ, Ramo de Trabajo, T-9–930, caja T-155, exp. no. 3950. AHJ, Ramo de Trabajo, T-9–930, caja T-153, exp. no. 3904.

33. AHJ, Ramo de Trabajo, T-1–930, exp. no. 3898.

34. AHJ, Ramo de Trabajo, T-1–930, exp. no. 3898. See Fowler-Salamini in this volume.

35. Joan Scott 1996; Fernández-Aceves 1996, 226–29.

36. AHJ, Ramo de Trabajo, T-7–931, caja T-37 bis "A," exp. no. 8400.

37. AHJ, Ramo de Trabajo, T-1930/3905.

38. AHJ, Ramo de Trabajo, T-7–931, caja T-195, exp. no. 5086.

39. AHJ, Ramo de Trabajo, T-7–932, caja T-216, exp. nos. 5407, 5408.

40. AHJ, Ramo de Trabajo, T-4–932.

41. AHJ, Ramo de Trabajo, T-2–933; AHJ, Ramo de Trabajo, T-2–933, caja T-19, exp. nos. 7503, 7504, 7508; AHJ, Ramo de Trabajo, T-7–933, exp. nos. 5612, 7696, 5590, 5830, 5843, 5593, 5590, 5844.

42. AHJ, Ramo de Trabajo, T-9–933, caja T-236, exp. no. 5806; AHJ, Ramo de Trabajo, T-2–933, caja T-237, exp. no. 5840.

43. AHJ, Ramo de Trabajo, T-9–934, caja T-42, exp. no. 8809.

44. AHJ, Ramo de Trabajo, T-2–934, caja T-240, exp. no. 5928.

45. AHJ, Ramo de Trabajo, T-2–933, T-9–934, T-3–934.

46. AHJ, Ramo de Trabajo, T-3–935, caja T-260, exp. no. 6562.

47. AHJ, Ramo de Trabajo, T-2–935, T-2–934, caja T-243, exp. no. 6003.

48. AHJ, Ramo de Trabajo, T-3–935; AHJ, Ramo de Trabajo, T-8–935, caja T-260, exp. no. 6568

49. AHJ, Ramo de Trabajo, T-3–935, caja T-260, exp. no. 6571.

50. AHJ, Ramo de Trabajo, T-3–935.

51. Fernández-Aceves and Orejel Salas 1987, 188.

Gender, Work, Trade Unionism, and Working-Class Women's Culture in Post-Revolutionary Veracruz

HEATHER FOWLER-SALAMINI

The gendered process of working-class formation was evident among the workingwomen (*la mujer obrera*) who labored in heterosexual spaces in the Veracruz coffee-export industry between 1920 and 1945. Their oral history helps reconfigure conceptions of the workingwomen in terms of how they perceived themselves as mothers, workers, trade unionists, and community. Recent studies on Mexican women textile, clothing, and tobacco workers have emphasized the agency of women workers.[1] Here, a grassroots perspective reveals the advantages as well as disadvantages that gender-segregated enclaves created for workingwomen. The Veracruz coffee sorters constructed their own unique community to legitimate themselves as workingwomen and to juxtapose it with working men's culture. Work experiences, union activities, and social activities in public spaces contributed to the formation of a set of values, understandings, and practices that questioned bourgeois provincial norms of patriarchy and working-class women. Workingwomen also challenged gender ideology and conceptions of working-class women's honor held by male workers.

These workingwomen existed within the socioeconomic and political context of a paternalistic workplace culture and an emerging Mexican post-revolutionary state, which was seeking in the 1920s and 1930s to exert its control over regional, reformist movements intent on expanding workers' rights.[2] Moreover, bitter conflicts emerged between rival male-dominated social movements vying with each other to mobilize and control peasants, workers and tenants, and women.[3] During this period, gender became one of many issues that labor leaders manipulated to consolidate their power bases. When regional, state, and national actors sought to take control of the coffee-sorter unions, women were forced to contest their right to work in public spaces. In fighting for gender-neutral demands they appropriated behaviors and language most commonly associated with male trade unionists rather than with housewives.

The state of Veracruz produced almost half the nation's 48 million tons of coffee and had the largest coffee-export industry in the mid-1930s.[4] Coffee production and processing was concentrated around five central highland provincial towns, located less than a hundred miles west of the port of Veracruz: Coatepec, Córdoba, Huatusco, Jalapa, and Orizaba.

Engendering the Post-Revolutionary Mexican Coffee-Export Industry

Susie Porter cogently argues that modernization and industrialization negatively affected women's employment in Mexico City's traditional textile, clothing, and tobacco industries during this period, while women found alternative work in other female-dominated and mixed-sex occupations, in particular the consumer industries.[5] This may explain why so many women entered the coffee mills in the first half of the twentieth century in the states of Veracruz, Chiapas, and Oaxaca. The Mexican export-coffee industry emerged in the 1890s in response to an enormous increase in demand for coffee in the United States and Europe and to the skyrocketing price of the commodity on the international market. Consumer demand for a high-quality coffee bean pushed Mexican and foreign exporters to invest in machinery to clean the beans more thoroughly and efficiently during the Porfiriato. However, the collapse of world prices during the 1927–28 season led to retrenchment and consolidation in the industry. Exporters were reluctant to replace machinery or fully mechanize their mills, as they had already done in Brazil and Colombia, most probably because they only controlled 2 percent of the U.S. market in the late 1930s. So they continued to employ thousands of female workers to sort and classify the coffee beans manually, the most labor-intensive stage of coffee preparation.[6]

Coffee mills (*beneficios* or *factorías*) were not really processing plants, for their primary purpose was simply to prepare coffee for the world market. This involved removal of the outside layers of the coffee cherry, followed by polishing, cleaning, and classifying its two beans. The new urban mills simply mechanized the cleaning and shelling processes, which had been accomplished manually in the countryside since the end of the nineteenth century. These work processes were largely defined by two interlocking gendered social patterns of Mexican society: patriarchy and the gendered division of labor in agricultural production. Men used their greater physical strength to remove the outer layers of the coffee cherry in wooden mortars. When entrepreneurs built "wet" mills (*beneficios húmedos*) and "dry" mills (*beneficios secos*) to prepare export grade coffee, they hired men as skilled laborers to operate the machinery that washed, depulped, dried, hulled, and polished the beans. On the other hand, sorting and classifying grades of coffee had always been considered "women's work," an extension of rural domestic work.[7] As mill owners brought inside the final cleaning and sorting stages, they hired women and children to perform the manual, unskilled labor. Smaller mills employed twenty to fifty sorters, while larger mills in Córdoba, Coatepec, and Orizaba utilized 100 to 500 women during the height of the harvesting season.

Work in the dry mills was organized around gender-segregated tasks and spaces. The machinery that first removed the two, thin inner layers of the coffee bean, then polished and classified the coffee beans occupied space on the ground floor, where male machine operators and stokers labored. Male loaders carried the green coffee upstairs to the large sorter workshop (*salón* or *sala*) lined with windows or out back to a smaller workshop (*taller*) attached to the end of the building. In these all-female workshops, women manually removed the remaining impurities as well as the discolored and disfigured beans.[8] This monotonous task required a high level of finger dexterity, good concentration, and considerable patience. The average worker could clean 110 to 160 kilos (10 to 12 *arrobas*) a day. At the piecework wage in the early 1930s, a permanent worker could earn approximately 1.50 to 1.80 pesos per day for four to six months a year.

Mexican industrial censuses did not include seasonal workers, so no accurate figures exist on the number of women and men employed in the Veracruz coffee-export industry. One can only estimate based on the union membership lists for the five towns in the central coffee belt. In 1936, 2,942 unionized sorters worked in twenty-two coffee mills in the five principal coffee towns—a figure roughly equivalent to the number of female workers employed in the state's textile and garment industries. Moreover, for every unionized sorter there were probably two to three nonunionized sorters laboring on small- and medium-sized farms. The gender ratio of the workforce was very uneven in the dry mills: for every five female workers there was roughly one male worker.[9]

Paternalism and Gender Relations on the Shop Floor

Paternalism on the shop floor dated back to the nineteenth century, when factory owners tried to re-create the patron-client relations of the hacienda and cottage industry within the factory. Owners continued these authority patterns on the shop floor to maintain discipline and to keep the workers and their families content up through the revolution.[10] Post-revolutionary owner-labor relations in family-owned Monterrey, Atlixco, and Tlaxcala factories were strikingly similar. Factory owners established personal bonds of obligation in order to create paternalistic systems of control. Owners and administrators consistently imposed paternalistic societal values on workers in the workshop to keep them compliant and discourage unionization, despite worker resistance.[11] Paternalism was further reinforced by the revolutionary state and the national labor confederations to encourage submissive behavior among women workers in the 1930s.[12]

Paternalist labor relations continued to predominate in the Veracruz coffee mills throughout the 1920s, 1930s and 1940s. Yet, worker-management relations in the semi-mechanized agro-industry were less rigid than in the more mechanized industries. Much as with domestic labor, rhythm of work in the sorter workshops was driven by the manual worker's motivation rather than by the machines. Yet, mill work brought provincial women into new heterosexual work spaces hitherto off limits to them. Former coffee sorters in their interviews constantly emphasized the fluidity in their relations with male authority figures in order to legitimize their identity as workingwomen. In so doing, they sought to reconfigure their representation of themselves as women, wives, and workers.

In her study of Colombian textile workers Ann Farnsworth-Alvear argued, "Doing factory work meant being in close proximity to persons outside one's family circle for most of the day, and more than the 'vertical' relationship to a mill-owner or administrator, it was this 'horizontal' relationship to large numbers of other women and men that made a mill job different."[13] This work experience was also true for coffee sorters. They recalled their work experiences in terms of the opening up of horizontal relationships with the fellow workers, male and female, who were nonfamily members.

The sorters considered the mill owners their principal patrons or benefactors. The permanent workers almost always represented the relations between mill owners and themselves as harmonious and not antagonistic. The owners had always treated them with "respect." Respect, associated with their ability to be hard workers but also with their honor as women, was one of the dominant themes in the sorters' narratives. The women accepted the paternalistic environment as part of the gendered reality, for the workers felt that the owners looked after them. "There were no clashes," a number of Córdoba workers recalled. Don Ricardo Regules "knew how to treat the sorters," and "he talked with them," giving the impression that they were treated fairly. The workers usually associated the Regules family with good wages: "The Reguleses were good to us. Humberto, Ricardo, and their father paid us well." Others made a distinction between Don Ricardo and his two sons: "The sons did not behave well. When they inspected the coffee they always found some bad coffee beans." Ricardo Sr. and Ezequiel González "were noble and good bosses." The workers had less kind words for Tirso Sainz Pardo and his nephew Julián, who were described as "demanding" and at times "hard-hearted."[14] In Coatepec, Adelina Texon and Alicia Limón echoed these same sentiments, reiterating that the owners treated them with "respect."[15] The mill managers were characterized along the spectrum from good to demanding, but in general they were not described in negative terms.

The sorters' representation of the mill owners was influenced to some degree by a collective memory of the not-so-distant past, when the mill owners, managers, and workers shared a similar socioeconomic status. Many mill owners had arrived in Veracruz as part of a wave of Spanish, Anglo-Saxon, German, Italian, and Arab immigrants beginning in the 1880s. These immigrants had begun to become part of coffee elite or nouveau riche only in the late 1920s. Former Córdoba sorters and residents could still recall when these men had been humble immigrants, not much different in status from themselves. Their grandmothers and mothers related how these Spanish immigrants had arrived penniless and almost illiterate from northern Spain between 1900 and 1920 to begin a new life.[16] Stories still circulate about the affairs some of them had had with sorters, market vendors, and rural women. Those who had married sorters had done so before they had became wealthy.[17] Thus, in their collective memory the sorters could equate these Spaniards' past economic and social status with their own. Brígida Siriaco recalled conversing on the shop floor with Ricardo Regules Sr., using the familiar form of speech.[18] Such recollections, however, did not affect the basic economic, social, and ethnic disparity between the workers and their bosses, and the workers always recognized their dependence on the owner's goodwill for their economic livelihood.

Discipline in the sorting workshop was under the control of the most highly skilled female workers rather than a male supervisor. Chosen for her sorting ability and knowledge of coffee, the receiver or supervisor (*encargada*) was responsible for quality control on the shop floor. In the 1920s, when paternalism remained strong in the beneficios, the mill owners appointed a trustworthy employee (*empleada de confianza*) to this post, a practice that continued unchanged in the small workshops throughout the 1930s. Since the encargada worked under an individual contract, the manager could fire her at will if he was not satisfied with her performance. After the passage of the Federal Labor Code of 1931, the larger Córdoba and Coatepec sorter unions won collective contracts, which included the right to elect their own receivers.[19]

The paternalistic authority formerly exercised by the Córdoba and Coatepec mill owners began to erode once the receivers and union's work committees assumed immediate responsibility for maintaining discipline on the shop floor. The receivers had to enforce the work rules by discouraging the sorters from engaging in small talk, so the sorters could better concentrate on their work. The sorters remember distinctly how union leaders also required them to remain quiet and to refrain from talking loudly or singing when they worked. If a sorter began to flirt with an administrator or a mill owner, the receivers and/or union leaders reprimanded her for inappropriate behavior. However, the sorters did not use unkind words to refer to their beloved union leaders who enforced discipline.[20]

The sorter workshops, where hundreds of women sat side by side performing monotonous work for hours, were quite conducive to the transgression of paternalist authority. For example, Inés Reyes Ochoa, who liked to sing and act in her spare time, was notorious for her singing. The stern Spanish mill owner, Tirso Sainz Pardo, was so irritated by her behavior that he sent her across the street to another mill, where the receiver was stricter. However, Inés continued to sing without being disciplined further.[21] As she was a respected union leader who served frequently on the union's executive committee in the 1930s, management could ill afford to fire her. In short, coffee sorters seized everyday opportunities to resist the discipline of the workplace and to assert their individuality.

The sorters' characterized their relationships with the mill's male workers as professional but cordial. Management always saw male workers as a distraction for female workers and a disruption to the work routine within the workplace. It continually discouraged them from entering into each other's space, striking up conversations, or flirting.[22] Nevertheless, they shared the same socioeconomic origins and were often family members, so sorters were bound to strike up conversations, enter into affairs, or even marry their male fellow workers. Since they emptied their baskets of cleaned coffee down the chutes to the stirrers (*graneleros*) below, the sorters were more likely to develop relationships with these unskilled workers than with machine operators.[23]

Bitter antagonism arose between the women's and men's leadership in the mid-1930s, when the men's unions left the Regional Confederation of Mexican Workers (Confederación Regional Obrera Mexicana, or CROM) and joined the Mexican Workers Confederation (Confederación de Trabajadores de México, or CTM). The strong-willed Córdoba female leaders forbade rank-and-file members from talking with the men at work, because they were afraid that they might defect to the CTM.[24] That the leaders feared this kind of mixed-gender interaction suggests that sorters were actually engaging in new forms of heterosexual social behavior. Opportunities to socially interact with nonfamily members of both genders on the workshop floor modified the sorters' perceptions of themselves not only as women but also as workers.

State Politics, Trade Union Rivalries, and the Appropriation of Masculine Behavior

Veracruz's two most avid proponents of social reform in the 1920s, Governors Adalberto Tejeda Olivares (1920–24, 1928–32) and Heriberto Jara Corona (1924–27) supported trade-union organization and peasant mobilization to confront the still-dominant conservative landowning and commercial elites. Both governors tried to minimize labor violence to maintain a favorable relationship with the center while at the same time encouraging popular mobilization. Tejeda publicly cultivated a hands-off position towards Luis Morones and his powerful patronage machine, the CROM, while Jara was much more confrontational, which led President Plutarco Elías Calles to remove him from office. Both politicians initiated far-reaching legislation to improve worker wages, benefits, and access to housing. In the face of violent strikes, interunion conflicts, and urban unrest, they personally intervened to mediate conflicts peacefully or, in the event of urban violence, ordered troops into the cities to restore peace.[25] Neither of them seemed particularly concerned with the plight of the woman worker per se, although they both supported equal rights for women. However, they did create political and social conditions favorable to workingwomen's mobilization.

Veracruz coffee-export workers were unable to organize on their own during the post-revolutionary period primarily due to mill-owner resistance, so they called on outside male labor, peasant, and political organizers to assist them in their efforts. Women workers usually organized long before male workers in large part because they represented a significantly larger percentage of the mill workers. The CROM, Communist Party, Peasant League, and local tenant unions played key roles in mobilizing coffee sorters in Jalapa, Córdoba, and Coatepec during the 1920s and in Orizaba and Huatusco in the early 1930s. However, rival male-dominated labor confederations and peasant organizations collaborating with state and local politicians competed with each other to dominate and manipulate these women's unions so as to incorporate them into their respective power bases. Although their demands to freely elect their union leadership and retain their jobs were gender-neutral, workingwomen, spurred on by their male labor advisors, began to exhibit militant, unruly, violent behavior patterns commonly displayed by union men. As Deborah Levenson-Estrada has argued for Guatemala, women had entered into public spaces "dominated by men who . . . conceptualized trade unionism and qualities such as militancy and solidarity as masculine."[26] Thus, women's working-class activism tended to mirror men's working-class activism during periods of intense labor mobilization. Women workers felt obliged to appropriate masculinized behavior to legitimize their gender-neutral demands in ways that they would not have considered socially acceptable in their domestic lives.

In 1932, Governor Tejeda's key sociopolitical organization, the Veracruz Peasant League of Agrarian Communities and Peasant Unions (Liga de Comunidades Agrarias y Sindicatos Campesinos), accelerated its efforts to wrest control of Córdoba's rural and urban unions away from the CROM. With the CROM facing internal divisions due to the political marginalization of Luis Morones, the league seized the opportunity to make inroads where Tejedistas controlled the municipal governments. As the largest union and possibly the easiest to manipulate, the women's sorters union was chosen as a target. The CROM-controlled bakers' union and the local tenant union had originally organized ninety female workers into a city-wide union with the motto "For the Rights of Women" in 1925.[27] For seven years the CROM, from its stronghold in Orizaba just twenty miles away, had exercised its influence over the Córdoba Coffee Sorter Union (Sindicato de Obreras Escogedoras de Café de la Ciudad de Córdoba, or SOECCC). During the course of the intraunion conflict, leaders as well as rank-and-file members appropriated behaviors that closely resembled male practices associated with trade unionism. Members of two rival unions took to the streets, closed down the coffee mills, engaged in fist fighting and rock throwing, attacked law-enforcement officers, occupied the CROM's regional headquarters, and harassed Cromista municipal authorities.

The discontent among the rank and file in the SOECCC first erupted due to local economic conditions and internal union politics; many sorters had been laid off due to the Depression, and they were disenchanted with the lack of turnover in the all-female leadership. The common trade-union practice of *continuismo* had set in. Certain union leaders had held positions on the executive committee almost continuously since the SOECCC's founding in 1925. Dissidents sought the support of the newly elected Tejedista mayor and Jalapa-based Peasant League, which were more than willing to offer their support. After a majority of the SOECCC's 1,200 members dutifully "reelected" Luz Vera secretary-general in January, 406 dissident sorters voted to suspend Luz Vera and other leaders on account of their poor level of performance and the union's bad financial and social situations. The dissidents also agreed to sever all ties with the CROM, claiming they were trying to win back their "autonomy." They contended that the CROM had collaborated too closely with the Mexican state and announced they would follow a more "revolutionary" orientation as a proletarian organization.[28] The language of the dissidents revealed the same sense of betrayal that María Teresa Fernández-Aceves found among female trade unionists reacting to corrupt and irresponsible leadership in Guadalajara.[29] By breaking with the officially recognized SOECCC union, the dissidents immediately lost their jobs, for the union's 1931 collective contract had guaranteed its right to a closed shop.[30]

Thrown out of work, groups of Tejedista-affiliated dissidents stationed themselves on 1 February at the entrances to the coffee mills to prevent Cromistas from entering the workshops, thus paralyzing the coffee-export industry. For days the barricade continued, while the two groups of women screamed back and forth at each other in the streets. The State Conciliation and Arbitration Board (Junta Central de Conciliación y Arbitraje, or JCCA) finally issued a resolution to end the dispute by supporting the officially registered CROM-controlled union. However, the board's decision was not considered judicially binding, so the dissidents refused to abandon their positions in the mill entrances.[31] When the federal labor inspector proposed that the two groups meet amicably in joint assembly, the conflict escalated further. The two groups confronted each other on the street, throwing punches and hurling stones that they had torn up from the streets. After a fifteen-minute melee, the municipal police, followed by federal troops, intervened to break up the conflict. Twenty women were arrested, and three were badly injured. The dissidents refused to give up their struggle. In the following days they proceeded to attack and injure Luz Vera and to occupy in collaboration with Tejedista municipal authorities the recently opened regional CROM federation headquarters, hoping to seize the documentation necessary to win the JCCA's official recognition.[32] With the conflict within the SOECCC no closer to settlement, Governor Tejeda personally intervened, calling for the reintegration of the two groups so that the dissident minority could regain their jobs.[33] This solution only papered over the underlying rivalry between Governor Tejeda and Eucario León, the former Santa Rosa textile worker and secretary-general of the CROM, for control over Veracruz's largest women's union. The outside intervention by male regional leaders was clearly reflected in the split within the union's leadership.

By December 1932, Governor Tejeda had completed his second term in office, and his peasant organization and armed state militia was about to be challenged by the center. To block his political aspirations to run for the presidency in 1934, Jefe Máximo Calles instructed President Abelardo Rodríguez to disarm Tejeda's state militias and create a rival peasant league. Meanwhile, the dissidents, finding themselves outnumbered and outmaneuvered, made one last attempt to regain their jobs. They organized a separate union, the Majority Group of Coffee and Tobacco Sorters of the City and Region of Córdoba (Grupo Mayoritario de Escogedoras de Café y Tabaco de la Ciudad y Región de Córdoba) and adopted the anarchist-inspired, gendered motto "For the Emancipation of Organized Women."[34] However, the group's position became increasingly desperate, for its members had been out of work for more than eleven months; it therefore reapplied for official recognition of its union, which the JCCA did grant, most probably because Tejedistas still controlled its leadership. Within days, Luz Vera sent an irate letter to President Rodríguez protesting the JCCA's decision and forcing the state board to reverse itself.[35] Unhappy with this outcome, the dissidents vented their frustration by taking to the streets of Córdoba once again, throwing the Cromista president of the Municipal Board of Conciliation into the fountain in the central plaza. On 2 February, with the support of the Tejedista-affiliated Ursulo Galván Center and of municipal council members, the dissidents stationed themselves for a second year at the doors of the five largest coffee mills to prevent workers from entering the premises.[36] To avoid further violent confrontations, the mill owners decided to lock all the workers out, appeal for police protection, and terminate their contract with the SOECCC.[37]

The women's control of the mills' entrances continued for seven days from 2 February through 8 February, during which time several bloody clashes broke out between women of the two rival unions. Meanwhile, loyal male and female Cromistas from around the state flooded into Córdoba to menace and insult the Tejedistas. The newly elected Cromista leader of the SOEEC wrote threatening letters to the JCCA: "We are ready to take control of the mills by force in order to take justice into our own hands." When the municipal police tried to break up coffee sorters' protests, they yelled insults at them and tried to disarm them. As tempers flared, the municipal police shot a worker, and the workers retaliated by wounding a policeman. Order was not restored until 7 February, when the state's secretary of government, who had arrived in Córdoba to personally resolve the conflict, instructed the federal army to intervene to disarm the police loyal to the Tejedista mayor and restore order around mills. Twenty women were arrested, and others were sent to the hospital.[38] The next morning the federal forces set out to dislodge the Tejedistas from the mills, but the dissidents abandoned their posts peacefully. Immediately the Cromistas reentered the mills, and the mills began functioning again. To resolve the employment problem of the 700 Tejedista sorters, Governor Gonzalo Vázquez Vela arranged for the U.S. firm Hard and Rand, which had probably been employing nonunion labor, to hire the workers.[39]

The military resolution of the Córdoba sorters' intraunion conflict represented one of many defeats suffered by Tejeda in early 1933 as his power base was dismantled by the center. It also was a major setback for the SOECCC, which continued, like many men's unions in the Orizaba-Córdoba region, to be under Eucario León's domination and revealed an inability of the rank and file to replace its entrenched and coopted leadership.[40] However, it does illustrate how in order to protect their right to work workingwomen resorted to disruptive, aggressive, and at times violent behavior, attacks on unpopular leaders, and foul language, all reminiscent of male trade-unionist behavior.

Building an Alternative Working-Class Women's Culture

Through their working experiences and new horizontal relationships established with nonfamily members in the mills, the street, and union halls, coffee sorters began in the 1930s to build an alternative working-class women's culture, which was different from working-class men's public culture. Their social activities outside the home challenged provincial norms of trade unionism, patriarchy, and their own reputation as "street women." There was a basic contradiction between gender and class for workingwomen, unlike for working men. Men could really conflate "class" and "male" for themselves. However, the tension between the ideal of representing unions, militancy, and class as male and the reality that unionism, militancy, and class were both male and female could not be eradicated.[41] Susie Porter argues that Mexico City's lower-class women constructed notions of respectability and honor, which intertwined gender and class in ways different from bourgeois norms and those of lower-class men. Workingwomen were represented within two paradigms: one of industrial paternalism and the other of middle-class norms of femininity. Both shared the idea of female vulnerability. These paradigms separated honor as a private virtue for women from honor as a public virtue based on family reputation, protection, and economic status. Women workers on the other hand fought to win "respect" as disciplined, hardworking workers in order to retain their wage earning capacity.[42] In detailing their life histories, former Veracruz coffee sorters similarly strove to represent themselves as a community of hardworking workingwomen intent on supporting their families within the bourgeois norms of respectability and honor. They also sought respect as good providers, faithful mothers, maintainers of the household, and morally upright wives.

In these five provincial towns of central Veracruz, which ranged in population from 6,000 to 45,000 inhabitants in 1930, women had been raised to work primarily within the household. Their income-producing activities contributed to the family economy, but they were not paid for their labor. Family members strictly monitored women's movements outside the home. Provincial women seldom ventured out alone, except to buy food or to run errands. To do so threatened their reputation as "honorable" women and their desire for "respect" as loyal daughters, wives, and mothers. Male family members discouraged and even punished their wives and daughters for leaving the house unaccompanied or for talking to people on the streets.[43]

Respect and happiness were two dominant themes that ran through most workingwomen's life histories, whether they were meatpackers in Argentina, textile workers in Mexico City or the Bajío, or coffee sorters in Veracruz. They took considerable pride in their accomplishments as workers and their ability to support their families, a pride they expressed in terms of their own genuine satisfaction and the respect they received for their roles as economic providers for the family.[44]

Veracruz sorters likewise expressed great satisfaction in their work ethic and their ability to provide for large extended families. One sorter, Cecilia, felt "proud to be able to earn enough to buy food each day" to support her ten children after her husband left her.[45] Estela Velázquez, a happily married, retired sorter with nine children, articulated the same sentiments: "It gives me pride even today . . . because . . . I raised my children honorably . . . with much pride because the work allowed me to gain experience, and more education; just think, work never honors a person; it is the person who honors the work."[46]

Although former sorters portrayed their work outside the home as an economic necessity, they seemed to recognize the inherent contradictions between the reality of their private lives and the ideal of good housewife they wanted to represent in the public sphere. As a consequence, they constructed an identity that encompassed both roles, as housewives and as workers, to downplay this tension. In so doing they created a collective gender identity, which glossed over the seeming contradictions between the two identities. Enriqueta Salazar Báez legitimized women's work by comparing it to a good husband: "The best husband is work."[47] On the other hand, sorters wanted to be remembered as superwomen, women who could bring home the paycheck and also be responsible housewives and mothers. To rationalize the two roles they frequently referred to each other as *madronas*, women of strong character who, like workingmen, did not want to be crossed.[48]

On the shop floor, they developed new and strong friendships with their co-workers as they chatted over the click-click of the foot-pedal machines. The gender-segregated workshop provided them with a more open space to develop their own public culture. Unlike textile workers and tortilla workers, they did not have to be constantly attentive to the rhythm of their machine, to the danger of getting their clothing or limbs caught in the machinery, or to continual confrontations with male workers.[49] They sang in unison, shared notes on family heartaches, marriages, and children, and developed a special camaraderie based on their common personal experiences. Cecilia Sheridan's excellent ethnographic study of Coatepec sorters emphasizes this same social intercourse. "The women sorters succeeded in creating their own space: 'their workshop,' one could call it. As they sat next to each other with their attention fixed on the conveyor belt carrying the coffee, there were no communication barriers."[50] That they referred to each other as *compañera* suggested that they shared a common identity. As they labored side by side in their monotonous work, they swapped stories about their personal lives, tragedies, illnesses, abortions, births, husbands, and so forth. "Almost the majority of them passed the time talking. . . . But the hands were working. . . . You are talking to your compañera who was on one side of you, or the other side of you, and here comes the belt. . . . Many times we talked about our domestic problems . . . pregnancies, boyfriends, husbands, about everything we talked, and one or the other of them would make comments."[51]

These newfound friendships led them to spend leisure time together in public places.[52] As Kathy Peiss has so cogently argued, wage-earning women "experienced the rhythms of time and labor more similar to men's than married women's, and shop-floor cultures reinforced the notion that leisure was a distinct realm of activity to which workingwomen could demand access."[53] They walked to work and home together, went to the movies, and attended union meetings and dances together. When they married, they became each other's godmothers (*comadres*) and shared babysitting chores.[54] This community of women interacted with each other both on and off the shop floor, which represented a significant change from the ideal vertical male-female gender dynamics found in most working-class households.

Although they had little time to socialize outside of their workplace because of myriad domestic chores, their common work experiences were reinforced when they met at their weekly union meetings, dances, Labor Day marches, and pilgrimages to the Virgin of Guadalupe. They distinctly remember leaving their husbands or companions at home, and walking in groups, sometimes holding hands, to the union hall for these organized activities, sometimes returning alone home late at night.[55] In these public places they continued their conversations about home, work, and boyfriends, their complaints against the mill owners, and the local gossip of the neighborhood. This newfound sociability led to the use of language about private life in public spaces. Even mill administrators recalled the ways in which sorters developed their own street banter, streetwise behavior, greater independence from their family responsibilities, and a greater sense of their self-worth.[56] In other words, they were subverting the conception of a working-class culture as exclusively male, organized around cantinas and sports, by constructing an alternative female one.

To the upper and middle class (*la gente decente*) living in these towns, workingwomen represented a direct threat to the maintenance of their patriarchal value system and their morality. One of the legacies of the nineteenth century was the middle-class view that women did not belong in the workplace. "The factory represented a potentially threatening space within which employers, overseers, and workers might violate norms of femininity."[57] Women's penetration of public spaces frequented by men, whether it was in the coffee mill, the market, the union hall, the dance hall, or the cantinas, represented a stigma to the reputation of an honorable family woman. As soon as a Mexican woman abandoned her children to enter the factory or work on the streets, she was identified as a loose woman.[58] When hundreds of women entered the mills each day to work alongside male workers, the townspeople felt even more threatened by changing gender roles. Moreover, the fact that some sorters frequented bars and worked as prostitutes to make ends meet reinforced this image. The Friday- and Saturday-night union dances, where women went unaccompanied by men, led to even more raised eyebrows.

When the Coatepec sorters went on strike for higher wages and the right to organize in the late 1920s, mill owners and townspeople employed this middle-class gender ideology to question the workers' morality as honorable women.[59] In so doing they sought to cast aspersions on the credibility of the women's economic demands. Townspeople yelled at them in the streets, calling them "prostitutes" and "dark gals" (*chivas prietas*). The sexual and racial meanings of these terms cast a shadow over the workingwomen. Moreover, with the CROM-affiliated unions vigorously supporting the state's anticlerical campaign, devout Catholics even used the term "dark gals" to insinuate that the sorters were religiously disoriented women. The priests went so far as to threaten to excommunicate any woman who joined the union.[60]

To the well-off townspeople the sorters were social deviants or sexually promiscuous women who had strayed far from proper womanly behavior. For this reason, they were frequently referred to as "street women." Priests and mill owners, the two most powerful authority figures in these towns, continually admonished them to behave properly. The sorter María del Carmen recalled bitterly how an Orizaba priest chastised a group of sorters before their 12 December pilgrimage to the statue of the Virgin of Guadalupe: "Even the priest told us: don't go and cave in to the reputation that you have. Behave yourselves! We were doing nothing wrong because many of the women had brought their children, their grandfathers, their grandmothers along. We were nothing more than that for the townspeople. We were all bad, and I was only a young girl. . . . I did not even know what movies were. We grew up in a world of hypocrisy, and this is the way I was judged."[61] The sorters categorically rejected these stereotypical representations in their narratives, repeating, time and time again, the same phrase: "We were not street women." Many temporary workers defended themselves against these charges by arguing that they did not even earn enough money to afford the food and drinks sold at the dances.[62]

176

Conclusions

At first in the 1920s, the post-revolutionary milieu provided spaces for labor activism and state patronage, which benefited workingwomen. But by the end of the decade, a three-way struggle developed, involving the consolidating central state, regional actors, and women's unions. These same political processes played out in the Guadalajara tortilla industry and the Puebla textile and garment industries, and in most cases workingwomen were the losers. In Veracruz, this struggle reached its culmination in 1932 and 1933, when the federal government took steps to disarm and politically marginalize the progressive Tejedista movement. During this process, the rivalry between the CROM and the Tejedista Peasant League played out within the Córdoba coffee-sorters' union, with unfortunate consequences for union autonomy. In seeking to defend their gender-neutral demands, rival groups of sorters appropriated masculine behaviors in order to protect their constitutionally guaranteed worker rights.

177

Despite these political reversals, former sorters in their narratives sought to represent themselves as a community of heroic and honorable workingwomen who had entered the labor force out of economic necessity to support their families. In new heterosexual public spaces they developed nonfamily social relationships with other sorters, their male co-workers, and their bosses. Their union-related social activities influenced them to represent themselves not as isolated individuals but as a community of women who shared similar concepts of women's work and workingwomen. Respect was anchored in their ability to be simultaneously a good wife and mother and a sustainer of the family, not a street woman. In this way they developed an alternative working-class women's culture.

Notes

I would like to thank Teresa Fernández-Aceves, Susan Gauss, Leticia Gamboa Ojeda, Thomas Klubock, Jocelyn Olcott, and Mary Kay Vaughan for their very helpful comments on an earlier version of this chapter. Whatever errors remain my responsibility. The research for this chapter was partially funded by a Fulbright-García Robles Lecturer/Scholarship in 1998–1999 and a Bradley University Research Award. All translations from Spanish are by the author.
1. Ramos Escandón 1998, 71–92; Lear 2001; Porter 2003, 73–118; Fowler-Salamini 2002, 34–63.
2. Meyer 1977; Benjamin and Wasserman 1990.
3. Fowler-Salamini 2002; Wood 2000; Novell 1996, 55–75.
4. Rodríguez-Centeno 1993: 96.
5. Porter 2003, 3–49.

6. Brazilian conveyor belts are pictured in *Tea and Coffee Trade Journal* 74 ([March 1938]: 11). For Colombian mechanization see Bergquist 1986, 351–52.

7. Sartorius 1961 [1858], 175.

8. Secretaría de la Economía Nacional 1933, 45–46, 61–66.

9. For more extensive discussion of the coffee-mill working conditions see Fowler-Salamini 2003 (102–12). Dirección General de Estadísticas 1934, 233 table 20.

10. Lear 2001, 348.

11. Snodgrass 1998, 115–36; Crider 1996, 26n14; Leñero Franco 1984, 46–52.

12. Vaughan 2000, 194–214; Olcott 2003, 45–62.

13. Farnsworth-Alvear 2000, 116.

14. The author conducted interviews with open-ended questions between 1999 and 2003 with former sorters and their children. They had worked in the mills in the 1930s and early 1940s in Córdoba, Orizaba, and Coatepec. The interviews with Estela Velázquez Ramírez of 13 May 1999, Brígida Siriaco García of 6 June 2000 and 3 July 2001, Lino Alejandro Gómez Reyes of 13 May 1999, and María del Carmen Ríos Zavala of 9 May 1999 were tape-recorded. They were transcribed by Gerardo Cirruelo Torres, Universidad Autónoma de Veracruz. All translations were done by the author. As the remainder of the interviews were not tape-recorded because of the age of the interviewee or the nature of the venue, the researcher had to rely on her field notes.

15. Adelina Texon, interview by author, Coatepec, Veracruz, 9 July 2001; Alicia Limón, interview by author, Coatepec, Veracruz, 10 July 2001.

16. Tirso Sainz Pardo, who had arrived in the 1910s to work for his older brother as a lowly muleteer, would become the major partner of the largest coffee-export business by the 1930s in Córdoba. When Ricardo Regules Baranda arrived, he worked in a grocery of another Spanish immigrant for a number of years before he accumulated enough capital to open his the coffee-trading business.

17. Alejandro Lino Gómez Reyes, interview by author, Córdoba, Veracruz, 19 July 1999; Rosa González (pseud.), interview by author, Córdoba, Veracruz, 12 March 1999.

18. Siriaco García, interview by author, Córdoba, Veracruz, 3 July 2001.

19. AGEV/JCCA, collective contract between José Vallejo and Sindicato de Trabajadores en General de la Industria del Café en el Estado de Veracruz, sec. no. 21, 1939; AGEV/JCCA, Fondo Sindicatos, no. 524, exps. 14 (Huatusco) and 136 (Jalapa), individual contract between Juana García and Mario Fernández, 29 November 1939; Brígida Siriaco García, interview by author, Córdoba, Veracruz, 3 July 2001; López Osorio, interview by author, Córdoba, Veracruz, 18 February 1999; Antonio Díaz Sanabria (mill administrator), interview by author, Coatepec, Veracruz, 4 July 2002.

20. Siriaco García, interview by author, Córdoba, Veracruz, 6 June 2000 and 3 July 2001. In Colombia, the young teenage sorters were at the mercy of male foremen who monitored their output (see Bergquist 1986, 352).

21. Gómez Reyes, interview by author, Córdoba, Veracruz, 13 May 1999; Siriaco García, interview by author, Córdoba, Veracruz, 6 June 2000.

22. Siriaco García, interview by author, Córdoba, Veracruz, 6 June 2000.

23. Díaz Sanauria, interview by author, Coatepec, Veracruz, 10 July 2001.

HEATHER FOWLER-SALAMINI

24. Siriaco García, interview by author, Córdoba, Veracruz, 6 June 2000.

25. Falcón and García Morales 1986, 135–37, 234, 239–40; Domínguez Pérez 1986, 37–56, 97–131.

26. Levenson-Estrada 1997, 208; see also Tinsman 2002, 271–72. Susan Gauss argues in this volume that working-class masculinity revolves around pro-family and pro-union behavior patterns where militancy, violence, solidarity, loyalty, and responsibility as the primary breadwinner are primordial.

27. AGEV/JCCA, Sindicatos, 1932, exp. 18, Sindicato de Escogedoras, Founding Act of Sindicato de Escogedoras de Córdoba, 6 February 1925; AGEV/JCCA, Sindicatos, 1932, exp. 5, folio 6; AGN, Departamento de Trabajo, Conflictos, Córdoba, no. 329, 1925; Sheridan Prieto 1983, 29–30.

28. AGEV/JCCA, Sindicatos, 1932, exp. 18, Córdoba, Act, 24 January 1932.

29. See Fernández-Aceves's essay in this volume.

30. The Federal Labor Code of 1931 made exclusion clauses legal but not obligatory. However, they were a standard feature of collective contracts negotiated by CROM affiliates after the mid-1920s. Middlebrook 1995, 96–97.

31. *El Dictamen*, 7 February 1932, pp. 2, 4; AMC, no. 411, exp. Sindicato y Uniones, Tejeda to Valverde, 4 February 1932 (tel); AGEV/JCCA, Sindicatos, 1933, exp. s.n, Labor Dept memorandum to Provisional Governor Francisco Salcedo Casas, 6 February 1933.

32. "En Córdoba las escogedoras de café libraron ruda pelea," *El Dictamen*, 14 February 1932, p. 13; AMC, exp. 1, Sindicatos y Uniones, no. 411, Undersecretary of Government to Municipal President (16 February 1932).

33. *El Dictamen*, 24 February 1932, pp. 17, 19; AGEV/JCCA, Sindicatos, 1933, exp. s.n, Labor Dept, Memorandum to Provisional Governor Salcedo Casas, 6 February 1933.

34. AGEV/JCCA, Sindicatos, 1933, exp. s.n, Majority Group of Coffee and Tobacco Sorters of the City and Region of Córdoba to JCCA, 28 Deceember 1932.

35. AGEV/JCCA, Sindicatos, 1933, exp. s.n, Carmen Hernández to Provisional Governor Salcedo, 26 December 1932; AGN, Acervos Presidentes, Abelardo L. Rodríguez, 561.8/13, Luz Vera (Secretary General of Sindicato) to Abelardo L. Rodríguez (28 December 1932) and Provisional Governor to Abelardo Rodríguez, 6 Feb 1933.

36. AGEV/JCCA, Sindicatos, 1933, exp. s.n., Carmen Hernández, letter to the editor, *El Globo* (Veracruz), 26 January 1933; AGEV/JCCA, Sindicatos, 1933, exp. 66, Eduardo Valverde and Odilon Zorrilla to President of the JCCA, 3 February 1933 (tels); *El Dictamen*, 3 February 1933.

37. AGEV/JCCA, Sindicatos, 1933, exp. 66, Cámara Nacional de Comercio de Córdoba to JCCA, 3 February 1933 (tel).

38. AGEV/JCCA, Sindicatos, 1933, exp. s.n., Report of Santiago Mota Barrientos to Provisional Governor, 8 February 1933; AGEV/JCCA, Sindicatos, 1933, exp. 66, Ramona Martínez to Enrique César Jr. (president of JCCA), 4 February 1933 (tel); AGEV/JCCA, Sindicatos, 1933, exp. 66, Isauro González to JCCA, 4 February 1933 (tel).

39. AGEV/JCCA, Sindicatos, 1933, exp. s.n., Report of Santiago Mota Barrientos to Provisional Governor, 8 February 1933; AGEV/JCCA, Sindicatos, 1933, exp. 66, Gonzalo Vázquez Vela to JCCA, "Acuerdo," 6 March 1933; AGN, Acervos Presidentes, Abelardo L. Rodríguez, 561.8/13, Provisional Governor, Francisco Salcedo Casas to Abelardo Rodríguez, 8 February 1933.

40. Aurora Gómez-Galvarriato Freer contends that the decline of the CROM nationally did not lead to a weakening of its Orizaba organization; in fact, as secretary-general Eucario León strengthened its role in the confederation (1999, 320).

41. Levenson-Estrada 1997, 224.

42. Porter 2003, xv, 119–21, 132.

43. Sheridan Prieto 1983, 22–23, 42; Wilson 1990, chap. 2; Leñero Franco 1984, 50.

44. James 2000, 162; Radkau 1984, 96; Wilson 1990, 176–77.

45. Cecilia Hernández de Huerta, interview by author, Córdoba, Veracruz, 20 July 1999; María del Carmen Ríos Zevala, Orizaba, Veracruz, 9 May 1999.

46. Estela Velázquez Ramírez, interview by author, Córdoba, Veracruz, 13 May 1999.

47. Enriqueta Salazar Báez, interview by author, Coatepec, Veracruz, 12 June 2002.

48. Ibid. Velázquez Ramírez, interview by author, Córdoba, Veracruz, 13 May 1999.

49. Correspondence with Leticia Gamboa Ojeda, 13 June 2002, in author's possession. Leñero Franco found no sense of community among Tlaxcalan female textile workers in the 1980s, for they suffered cultural discrimination on the shop floor because of the gender hierarchies and paternalism; this kept workingwomen isolated, without friendships outside the factory, and in continual competition with other women over who was a better mother or could more easily capture a man (1984, 46–52).

50. Sheridan Prieto 1983, 42–43.

51. Siriaco García, interview by author, Córdoba, Veracruz, 3 July 2001.

52. Verena Radkau uncovered a similar type of social experience among women textile workers (1984, 96); Porter 2003, 16.

53. Peiss 1986, 6.

54. Velázquez Ramírez, interview by author, Córdoba, Veracruz, 13 May 1999; Báez Salazar, interview by author, Coatepec, Veracruz, 12 June 2002; and Ríos Zavala, interview by author, Orizaba, Veracruz, 9 May 1999.

55. Ibid.; Siriaco García, interview by author, Córdoba, Veracruz, 7 June 2000; Limón, interview by author, Coatepec, Veracruz, 10 July 2001.

56. Ibid; Velázquez Ramírez, interview by author, Córdoba, Veracruz, 23 March 1999; Díaz Sanabría, interview by author, Coatepec, Veracruz, 10 July 2001 and 4 July 2002.

57. Porter 2003, 132.

58. To this day, upright Veracruzanos place the coffee sorter in the same category as the prostitute. They still represent undesirable, marginal women on the fringes of provincial urban society.

59. Porter 2003, 64–65, 114–15, 175.

60. Sheridan Prieto 1983, 30; Texon and Díaz Sarauría, interview by author, Coatepec, Veracruz, 9 July 2001; Ríos Zavala, interview by author, Orizaba, Veracruz, 9 May 1999.

61. Ríos Zevala, interview by author, 9 May 1999.

62. Jesús Baltazar, interview by author, Córdoba, Veracruz, 13 May 1999; Ríos Zavala, interview by author, Orizaba, Veracruz, 9 May 1999.

HEATHER FOWLER-SALAMINI

Working-Class Masculinity and the Rationalized Sex

Gender and Industrial Modernization in the

Textile Industry in Postrevolutionary Puebla

SUSAN M. GAUSS

During the labor conflicts of the 1920s and 1930s, male-dominated textile unions in Puebla enforced gendered ideals of workforce rationalization that emphasized working-class masculinity as a means to build solidarity and loyalty among male laborers.[1] To bolster masculinist forms of union militancy, they promoted concepts of working-class femininity identified with home-based domesticity.[2] These gendered prescriptions had their origins in pre-revolutionary transitions in the Pueblan textile industry and accompanying shifts in the sexual division of labor. Yet, amid struggles involving unions, regional leaders, and the state over local and regional authority in the 1920s and 1930s, unions redefined these ideals to feed revolutionary workforce militancy.[3] By the 1940s, however, conservative shifts in ruling-party consolidation encouraged unions to shed this militancy in favor of promoting their male workers as responsible working-class citizens. The unions, in turn, advanced scientific definitions of healthy, modern, working-class motherhood as the foundation for social peace and nationalist economic growth. In this way, the gendered process of working-class formation emerged at the heart of post-revolutionary state-building and industrial modernization.[4]

The emphasis that unions placed on reproductive politics was backed by the post-revolutionary promulgation of protective legislation for women workers. While legislation mobilized unions in defense of working women's rights, it also promoted domestic ideals that justified women's continued segregation in low-paid, unskilled labor. This not only met the demands of masculinist union politics but also reflected ideas about industrial and domestic rationalization emanating from the United States.[5]

The textile industry in Puebla provides fertile ground for examining the complexity of post-revolutionary gender and labor politics. In the early 1900s women were almost totally absent from most sectors of the Pueblan textile industry; by the 1940s, they still comprised less than 5 percent of the legal textile labor force there.[6] Yet, from the inception of the textile industry in the nineteenth century until at least the 1950s, women dominated *bonetería* production, or the manufacture of knitwear, especially socks and stockings.[7] Unions and owners even promoted women's employment in bonetería, considering it an extension of women's domestic duties and natural affinities for conditions and tasks in this particular industry. The 1917 Constitution and the 1931 Labor Code entitled bonetería workers to move into political-legal spaces previously closed to women. Though they claimed the special protections provided for women workers, they also demanded rights traditionally perceived to be the preserve of male laborers, including the right to a family wage.[8]

While unions ensured the continued segregation of women into low-skilled jobs, women's dominance of bonetería and mobilization for workers' rights revealed the fragility of the male breadwinner/female homemaker duality underpinning union authority and industrial modernization. In Puebla, textile unions contended that women workers remained a threat to the male workforce, despite women's virtual invisibility in the industry. Even the Confederación Regional Obrera Mexicana (CROM), which had been among the most successful in excluding women from its ranks, vigorously promoted domesticity to underscore the alleged challenge that women workers presented to male jobs and union authority. In some ways, women's labor was a threat to the CROM. As state patronage offered women access to new forms of public participation, domesticity preserved local spheres of male authority. Moreover, women working in bonetería were an important base of support for the anti-CROM Federación Regional de Obreros y Campesinos del Estado de Puebla (FROC) during the union struggles of the 1940s. In the end unions gained from these seeming threats because they encouraged solidarity, loyalty, and militancy within a male workforce often at odds with a corrupt and politicized union leadership.

Joan Scott maintains that gender is "a primary way of signifying relationships of power" that "are not always literally about gender itself."[9] In Puebla, high rates of workforce segregation in conjunction with widespread union conflict encouraged labor leaders to adopt gendered prescriptions as a potent means to essentialize differences between male workers in order to build factional solidarity and union authority. Yet it was within the factories and unions themselves, as contested social and cultural spaces, where communal ideas about masculine honor and female domesticity were defined and deployed to meet the demands of violent union struggles.[10]

By the 1940s, conflicts among unions, regional leaders, and the state over local and regional authority intersected with threats to job security posed by machinery modernization, President Miguel Alemán's ambivalent commitment to Puebla's textile industry, and U.S. efforts to manipulate Mexican production to complement its own industrial goals. By promoting home-based maternalism, labor leaders hoped to assure their survival by conforming to the project for industrial modernization and social peace underpinning the increasingly conservative rule of the Partido Revolucionario Institucional (PRI). In doing so, Puebla's textile labor force became identified with the ideal of a politically active, unionized, male, working-class citizen who eschewed the violence of previous generations. Consequently, though state consolidation and industrial modernization offered women new rights that challenged historic understandings of working-class femininity, they also justified women's continued exclusion from the modern textile labor force.

The Reconstruction of Regional Authority and the Modern, Male Textile Worker

The growing influence of unions in the post-revolutionary period enabled them to play a significant role in the unfolding struggle between the central government and regional political leaders. As Heather Fowler-Salamini and María Teresa Fernández-Aceves suggest, unions artfully negotiated these struggles in their fight to claim the rights recently granted to their workers.[11] In the process, unions sought to consolidate their own regional political authority, as well as their role in the masculinization of Mexican industrial development.

During the 1920s, Puebla's textile industry suffered waves of strike activity, often in relation to union factionalism stemming from the CROM's corrupt domination of its labor force. Until 1928, Puebla lacked a political leader capable of uniting, and restraining, these diverse social movements. The weakening of the CROM after it lost favor with national leaders in 1928 and the rise of the populist Governor Leonides Andreu Almazán (1929–1933) suggested an end to the contentious 1920s. Governor Almazán forged an alliance with the anti-CROM predecessor of the FROC, harnessing its militancy to his budding populist political machine. However, textile-owner resistance to this progressive alliance and ongoing union factionalism continued to spark labor conflicts.

The military and political rise of the conservative governor Maximino Ávila Camacho (1937–41) promised to provide a resolution to the region's unrest. With military force, the backing of President Lázaro Cárdenas and the CROM, and a detente with textile owners, Governor Ávila Camacho attempted to reconcile political rifts and persistent labor conflicts, if only to consolidate his own regional authority.[12] Yet, Ávila Camacho's success at incorporating unions into his conservative project and ending labor unrest was incomplete. His alliance with the CROM, as well as his repression of the regionally dominant FROC, reignited conflicts between the longtime rivals. Though the FROC's political influence waned, it continued to dominate key labor sectors and to use targeted strikes to challenge *avilacamachismo*. This further weakened the FROC, however, since both President Cárdenas and the ruling-party-allied Confederación de Trabajadores de México (CTM), with which the FROC was affiliated, declined to sanction its militancy against Governor Ávila Camacho. The FROC's exile from mainstream politics, as well as from the CTM, was sealed when it refused to back ruling-party candidate and Governor Ávila Camacho's brother, Manuel Ávila Camacho, in the 1940 presidential elections. Soon thereafter, the FROC broke from the CTM. Struggling for political survival in the face of both regional and national abandonment, the FROC continued to use strikes to contest the authority of avilacamachismo into the early 1940s. Therefore, despite some success in coopting FROC leaders, rank-and-file intransigence constrained conservative efforts to extend state control over labor.[13]

The interference of municipal authorities in labor politics further complicated the resolution of union conflicts. While unions regularly forged alliances with municipal leaders, they also condemned local authorities for politicizing labor affairs for their own ends. For example, the FROC accused the CROM of enjoying protections due to its alliance with municipal authorities in Atlixco, including those provided by a judge whose brother was a local CROM leader and self-professed enemy of the FROC. The CROM countered that municipal authorities were arming local opponents of avilacamachismo so they could assassinate pro-*avilacamachista* workers.[14] In another conflict, the CTM accused a local police commander, who was also a FROC member, of killing one of its workers because of the worker's ardent loyalty to his union. The FROC in response charged local CTM leaders with manipulating the murder to propel themselves into lucrative public positions.[15]

The ability of municipal authorities to exploit labor conflicts was circumscribed by collective contracts, the 1931 Federal Labor Law, and tripartite commissions comprising union, owner, and government representatives. Jointly, they granted unions important powers over hiring and firing, work rules, and labor relations.[16] In return for these benefits, the ruling party sought labor's complicity both in elections and in its project for industrial development. By the 1940s, the historic dependence of textile workers on owners had been supplanted by a state-labor alliance that protected and empowered unions while buttressing the authority of the PRI.

These powers enabled unions to compel worker loyalty during labor conflicts. This was especially critical in light of worker hostility to union leaders, who they often alleged were enemies of the working class because of their arbitrary use of power.[17] Already by the late 1920s, workers protested that while they had recently been able to "break the chains of capitalist slavery" through revolutionary struggle, they were now suffering under a "new oppression" created by union leaders trying to enslave workers for their own political purposes.[18] Worker solidarity and militancy built on bonds of masculinity therefore became critical in union efforts to maintain workforce discipline and union legitimacy.[19] Union leaders manipulated masculine norms and patronal relationships with workers to gain rank-and-file allegiance on the shop floor, within unions, and in the larger community.[20] As a result, workers' identities and union loyalties reflected to masculine codes of honor.

These masculine codes were vital in channeling the community violence that continued to permeate union culture through the 1930s and 1940s. Though not ubiquitous, violence exaggerated codes of honor by reinscribing them with a militancy in service to unions. While attacks often occurred between workers from unions competing for control of a factory, they also frequently reflected the settling of community or personal disputes. In this context, low-level daily violence, punctuated by extreme examples, such as the murder of five workers in 1947 and 1948 during conflicts between the CROM and the CTM, became a measure of union strength and loyalty.

While militant union rhetoric remained a staple of local labor conflicts in the 1940s, union leaders revealed that they understood the growing limits of this rhetoric at the national level. For example, union newspapers portrayed a 1944–1945 conflict over control of the Fábrica San Juan Amandi as a tale of betrayal, relying on masculine ideals to punish union disloyalty. CROM leaders cast doubt on the loyalty of first-shift workers, labeling them Judas Iscariots for joining another faction of the CROM, led by Eucario León. The federation compared them to the second-shift workers, who were commendable for their " 'unbreakable loyalty'" as demonstrated in their ability to distinguish León's split as an act of betrayal. The CROM went on to characterize the first-shift workers as immoral, disruptive, and cowardly assassins whose leaders' personal goals overshadowed their loyalty to union honor.[21] According to the CROM, the first-shift workers were undermining the dignity of Mexican syndicalism, as well as public law and order, with their lack of respect for legal union authority.

These turncoats were also accused of betraying their class, gender, and nation. The CROM claimed that the first-shift workers had made a deal with the factory's owners that prevented second-shift laborers from entering the workplace, an act that betrayed the 1942 Labor Unity Pact, wherein unions had pledged their commitment to aid in meeting national production goals during the war.[22] Most important, by forcing 120 families into the streets, they betrayed the code of masculine honor that respected men's efforts to care for their families.

Though news reports represented the struggle as a conflict over labor, communal, and family values, unions understood the limits of their militancy at the national level. The conflict originally centered on efforts by the first-shift union to gain control of the second shift, whose minority union enjoyed legal protection. Soon, it escalated into firings and violence. In the ensuing struggle second-shift labor leaders Hermelindo Soriano and Agapito Hernández were murdered. Despite the violence and militancy by workers of both unions, each appealed to their legally protected rights within the factory to petition the government to intervene on their behalf. To bolster their position, they emphasized the immorality of the opposing leaders, who they argued were fostering factionalism and engaging in backroom manipulations that undermined social peace.[23]

In post-revolutionary Puebla, gender-segregated textile factories were masculine spaces wherein laborers drew on revolutionary legacies of violence and honor to attempt to establish their place as legitimate workers and secure union authority. Despite the growing limits of militant rhetoric at the national level, by impugning the masculinity of traitors and encouraging solidarity and militancy among its members, unions tied class action to the social construction of the violent, male, unionized textile worker. Through their state-granted powers, unions became arbiters of factory and community life and enforced gendered assumptions about working-class identities.

Union Discrimination and Bonetería Workers

Powers over hiring and firing became the most important tools with which textile unions executed their ideals about the sexual division of labor. In Puebla, these powers allowed unions to hire exclusively men at most of the large cotton-textile factories. Women's exclusion from much of the industry, however, reinforced the historic concentration of women in bonetería. Women made up over 80 percent of the workforce in bonetería between 1935 and 1950.[24] Common assumptions about women's suitability for this type of production justified their segregation. As one Mexico City owner summed up with regard to perceptions about women working in bonetería, "Even though women have a more delicate condition and get sick more often than men, the management prefers them because they apply themselves to their work and create fewer problems for the company."[25] The industry's small factories, lower wages, and older machinery also help explain women's segregation in bonetería.

In the late 1930s, most women in the industry worked with individual contracts that exposed them to high levels of owner abuse. Prominent industrialist Jesús Rivero Quijano characterized the industry as populated by women exploited "in unhygienic conditions, with neither limits on their daily shifts nor a just salary scale."[26] Unions welcomed the opportunity that women's exploitation in the industry offered them to contest owner authority within factories.[27] For example, CTM leader Blas Chumacero denounced the factory owner Francisco Álvarez for forcing his predominantly female laborers to work excessive shifts without overtime pay, for maintaining rudimentary and unhygienic conditions, and for denying women their legally guaranteed maternity care. The immediate catalyst for Chumacero's intervention was Álvarez's alleged assault on three women, whom he slapped across the face and locked in a closet. Chumacero noted that Álvarez's behavior was particularly cowardly since it targeted women. He justified his special defense of the women by noting that for many years Álvarez had denied women workers their legal rights. He found this especially objectionable, since the "feminine sex . . . due to its moral and material daintiness should be the object of consideration."[28] Amid post-revolutionary labor conflicts, unions sought to protect women as a pretext to curb owner prerogatives in factories.

"Fraternidad Feminina": Women Workers in the Fight for the Nation

In 1942, approximately one-third of all bonetería workers were affiliated with the FROC. By 1952, the FROC controlled roughly three-quarters of bonetería workers, much of the expansion comprising factories previously affiliated with the CROM and the CTM.[29] Unlike in the Veracruz coffee industry and the Guadalajara tortilla industry, as described by Fowler-Salamini and Fernández-Aceves, there was little apparent competition among union federations to organize women working in bonetería, possibly because of the smaller relative size of the factories.[30] Yet, due to its own political marginalization by the late 1930s, the FROC may have treated women workers more seriously than other labor federations.[31]

Mobilizations in bonetería therefore contributed to the FROC's continuing survival and militancy in Puebla. For example, bonetería workers from Puebla were critical in forcing through a collective contract in the late 1930s, despite significant opposition from other regions. They pressured for its passage by emphasizing that workers in the industry were the worst paid. After its passage, they criticized the government's delay in making it obligatory.[32] The 1940 collective contract promised to relieve some of the industry's more extreme abuses through establishing work norms and protections. Many factories in Puebla signed the contract, including El Musel, La Palma, La Cibeles, El Aguila, La Especial, and El Cometa, all of which were dominated by women. Yet, though unions representing the required two-thirds of workers signed the contract, making it binding throughout the industry, many factories did not sign.[33] Women working in the industry therefore struggled to compel the enforcement of minimum wage, social security, and health and safety standards.

Undaunted, bonetería workers challenged owners' efforts to break the contract. For instance, in 1942 a bevy of women union leaders from bonetería factories in Puebla joined to denounce owners for upsetting production and for promoting union factionalism. They urged President Ávila Camacho to force owners to honor their contractual obligations while emphasizing that workers' contributions to national welfare should not be attained through salary reductions that impeded their ability to maintain a home.[34]

Furthermore, the prevalence of foreign ownership in the industry placed these women on the front lines of Mexico's revolutionary struggle to achieve independent, industrial modernization. In contrast to Monterrey, where, Michael Snodgrass maintains, the predominance of domestic capital and paternalistic practices potentially muted worker militancy, bonetería production was controlled largely by foreign owners and managers.[35] In 1935, 62 percent of the industry's managers in Puebla were foreign born.[36] With the rising censure of foreign entrepreneurs in the 1930s, nationalist resentments infused workers' efforts to challenge management. For example, in 1941, the CTM complained that women working in bonetería were victims of Jewish and Arab piracy that forced them to work inhuman shifts of twelve to fourteen hours with low salaries.[37] And Blas Chumacero stepped in to defend women workers who had been assaulted by the Spanish owner of a bonetería factory by demanding that the owner be expelled from Mexico.[38]

By appealing to post-revolutionary legislation supporting collective contracts, women working in bonetería challenged owner and union paternalism that confined them to lower-paying jobs. They promoted their equality as working-class citizens and their right to earn a family wage at a time when women's rights were still tentative.[39] In fueling nationalist antagonisms toward dependence on foreign investment, women workers successfully gained rights in the industry by portraying foreign owners and managers both as men reprehensible for their affronts to female workers and as parasites preying on Mexico's wealth.

The Rational Sex: Industrial Crisis, Labor Politics, and the Modern Mother

During the 1940s, labor unions transformed their message of militancy into a politics of national unity that mirrored conservative shifts in post-revolutionary state building and industrial modernization. Conflicts still frequently erupted into violence at the local level, and militancy reigned in local rhetoric. Yet, the changing national climate induced unions affiliated with the CTM and CROM to promote responsible working-class citizenship among its male workers, while reinforcing home-based maternalism. By trumpeting their defense of middle-class family models as the foundation for industrial modernization and social stability, they hoped to secure their regional and national survival. The FROC, for its part, echoed this conciliatory shift at the national level, even as it continued to mobilize bonetería workers and shun the rhetoric of domesticity.

Declining real wages and scarcities during World War II deepened tensions in Puebla's textile labor force. Postwar inflation caused by deteriorating trade conditions and the 1948 peso devaluation further compounded anxieties.[40] Despite census statistics that indicated only a mild drop-off in jobs, factory stoppages and disputes over machinery modernization contributed to public perceptions that the size of the textile labor force was shrinking.[41] The uneven commitment of the Alemán admin-istration to Puebla's ailing textile industry intensified these perceptions.

Further jeopardizing the industry and its workforce were conflicts be-tween labor and owners over machinery modernization.[42] Mechanization had already occurred in much of Puebla's textile industry by the early 1900s.[43] In the 1940s, however, textile industrialists pressured the govern-ment for the right to import more modern machinery because it would force the renegotiation of the collective contracts that were sheltering workers. Owners hoped machinery modernization would enable them to displace thousands of workers, create a more dependent and pliable work-force, and restructure labor-owner relations to upset the state-labor al-liance that protected union privilege in the factories.[44] Labor organiza-tions uniformly contradicted owners' proposals. Unions feared that a decrease in the size of the workforce and the deskilling of previously skilled jobs that would accompany machinery modernization would un-dermine their authority. As the battle with owners heated up during the mid-1940s, unions consistently opposed the renegotiation of collective contracts, since their abrogation was the only means to make machinery modernization economically and politically feasible.[45]

Threatened by postwar decline, machinery modernization, and a na-tional project for industrial modernization that imperiled Puebla's textile industry, unions affiliated with the CTM and CROM struggled to maintain their local authority by building solidarity and loyalty among their male workers. To do so, they emphasized the threat that workingwomen posed to the jobs of male laborers, despite women's virtual absence from the industry. For example, unions applied the specter of betrayal to women by manipulating beliefs about women's divided allegiance to workplace and home. They argued that women were suspect as union loyalists and threatened the gender norms and job differentiation that underpinned union power. Just as they had highlighted exaggerated forms of mas-culinity and urged men to be loyal, strong, and violent, they exhorted women to be self-abnegating in service to the nation.[46]

Unions deployed common conceptions about the essential, divergent interests of working-class men and women in order to build unity among their largely male workforces. They defined the interests of women work-ers as stemming from their responsibilities as wives and mothers. They stressed the benefits and duties inherent in modern motherhood, em-phasizing its ties to female domesticity and its foundations in morality, health, and hygiene.[47] Unions even portrayed women workers as neglect-ful of their families and children. One 1950 news article, for example, describes a woman worker sadly trudging to work, tears streaming down her cheeks as she watched other mothers playing in the parks with their children: she missed her children and lamented not being at home to raise them. Women workers, the article concluded, were selfish in choosing to leave their kids in the care of others, or even worse, the care of the street.[48] The same divided loyalty between factory and home that prevented workingwomen from being viewed as loyal union members also precluded them from being viewed as proper mothers.

While uncertainty aggravated conflict in Puebla in the 1940s, unions found that the ruling party's wartime promotion of class conciliation and national unity meant that their political survival increasingly depended on good relations with national leaders. President Alemán secured this shift with expanded antistrike legislation and cold war politics that justified his repression of leftist labor leaders in the CTM during the *charrazo* beginning in 1948, which destroyed the left's position within the labor movement by restructuring the radical railway, oil, and mining unions.[49] Many labor federations confronted this transition by portraying the militancy of their counterparts as disrespectful to both the state and revolutionary ideals. They, in turn, used labor mobilizations as an oppositional narrative against which they posited their own worth as respectable citizens.

In Puebla the FROC's militancy, along with its enduring resistance to collaboration with avilacamachismo, had made its unions the target of repression in the early 1940s. Under the weight of these attacks, the FROC was politically weakened. Even after it established a pact of collaboration with the CROM in 1940, the sheer dominance of avilacamachismo left it struggling for political relevance. By the mid-1940s, the FROC recognized the political boundaries of its militancy, choosing conservative collaboration in an attempt to survive. It pursued a more conciliatory line with the ruling party by affiliating with the Confederación Proletaria Nacional (CPN) beginning in 1942 and attempted to improve its relationship with avilacamachismo after 1945. Moreover, it increasingly shunned the use of work actions for political gain. Despite this shift, the FROC continued to stand apart from the CTM and the CROM in important ways. Evidence suggests that unlike CTM- and CROM-affiliated unions, the FROC eschewed the rhetoric of female domesticity, instead focusing on organizing the female-dominated bonetería industry and backing later-1940s strikes for better wages and working conditions in the industry. Nevertheless, coupled with the predominance of the CROM and CTM in the Puebla textile industry, growing collaboration at the national level meant that the impact of FROC efforts to promote female unionization was muted.

By portraying its members as responsible working-class citizens, the CROM confirmed that it understood that laws and social peace, rather than militancy, were now the paths to labor privilege and authority. For example, when appealing for state assistance in a 1948 labor dispute, the CROM opened by outlining a range of positive acts it had performed in Puebla, including the construction of schools, hospitals, and public-recreation facilities and the formation of transportation and food cooperatives.[50] During a 1946 conflict, the CROM accused the CTM of provoking labor agitation that threatened to reignite the labor factionalism in Atlixco that had marked that region's descent into conflict and violence after 1933.[51] In doing so, the CROM sought to demonstrate its own political maturity and honorable character.

With unions now bridled by both union leaders and the state, ideals of domesticity remained prominent in union discourse. Indeed, home-based maternalism affirmed unions' commitment to the family as the foundation of economic growth and social stability. Unions even attempted to educate women about modern forms of Mexican motherhood. They relied on the discourse of science and *mestizaje* that was being used to support a growing body of post-revolutionary paternalistic attitudes and social policies. For example, women workers were pressed by labor federations to uphold the purity of the Mexican race by not marrying foreigners. Though reflecting concerns about the "spiritual unity" of the nation, these entreaties also revealed labor's continued resentment against foreign owners amid the economic fallout after World War II and U.S efforts to shape Mexico's postwar production to feed its own industrial aims.[52]

By the 1940s, transnational pressures confirmed forms of masculinity that transferred the threat of economic decline onto women's bodies. Unions constructed an ideal of the modern mother who was to be the progenitor of both a pure Mexican race and a truly national Mexican industry. She would be responsible for raising honorable, healthy, hardworking children, who would embody the birth of a moral and productive industrial nation. In this way, the emergent emphasis on industrial growth through the rational exploitation of Mexico's primary resources was projected onto women's bodies, as women literally became the producers of modern mestizaje. The rhetoric rendered invisible women workers who in increasing numbers labored unprotected in often abysmal conditions and almost always low-paid positions.

Conclusion

The persistence of politicized strike activity in Puebla into the early 1940s demonstrates the importance of the post-Cárdenas era in resolving long-standing labor militancy. Even in states such as Puebla, where the avilaca-machista political machine secured regional conservative rule in alliance with the ruling party by the mid-1930s, not until the global economic and ideological shifts of the 1940s created the conditions for conservative ruling-party consolidation did the unions shed their militancy. Throughout these decades, gendered beliefs traversed the fictive boundaries between household, community, and factory amid union struggles to establish authority. Though the rhetoric of domesticity had long provided the justification for gender segregation in the textile industry, its form shifted in the 1940s, as union leaders promoted the sexual division of labor as an extension of resource rationalization. In Puebla, this was refracted through the political and productive demands placed on male laborers and the reproductive norms imposed on women. The masculinization of union and workplace identities belied, however, the efforts of women workers to gain rights as working-class citizens and to engage in the post-revolutionary battle in defense of national industry. Nonetheless, this post-revolutionary Mexican woman was to be a modern producer while submitting to patriarchal privilege in the household, workplace, and union.[53]

In the end, the dilemma that workingwomen presented to unions had less to do with their presence in the labor force than with the affront that the image of the woman worker posed to the ideals of masculinity that underpinned union power emerging at the core of post-revolutionary PRI authority. This was exacerbated by challenges to the workforce presented by transnational pressures that encouraged the underdevelopment of major areas of the world, including Mexico, and plans for industrial modernization that threatened textile production. In this climate, unions manipulated gendered beliefs about working-class identities in order to define and defend the workforce on which their local, regional, and national power rested. In the end, efforts by union leaders to affirm union power fostered exaggerated forms of masculinity and an ideal of working-class femininity defined by modern, home-based domesticity and the rationalization of women's reproductive capacities.

Notes

I would like to thank Mary Kay Vaughan, Jocelyn Olcott, Temma Kaplan, Tom Klubock, Greg Crider, Stephanie Smith, Teresa Fernández-Aceves, and Heather Fowler-Salamini for their insightful comments on this essay.

1. Greg Crider's argument that labor leaders fostered rivalries to discourage workers from uniting in opposition to them sheds light on the multiple and often contradictory ways in which unions managed workers (1996, 112–13).

2. For more on the rise of ideologies of female domesticity see Vaughan 2000 and Arrom 1985. On masculinization in Latin American industry and the domestication of women workers see Weinstein 1997.

3. William Sewell argues that workers reinscribed dominant cultural norms with revolutionary meaning after the French Revolution (1980).

4. Two excellent studies on gender, class, and state formation in Chile are Rosemblatt 2000 and Klubock 1998.

5. Vaughan 2000, 195–99.

6. AGN, Fondo Secretaría de Trabajo y Previsión Social, Actas de Visita, Dirección General de Previsión Social (DGPS), Secretaría de Trabajo y Previsión Social (STPS), 1941–52. See also Secretaría de Economía Nacional 1936; Keremitsis 1984b, 492–98.

7. Susie Porter notes that women were concentrated in bonetería production in Mexico City at the industry's outset in the late nineteenth century (2003, xiii). I include bonetería under textiles because it is categorized in industrial censuses as part of the textile industry.

8. Porter 2003, 50–51, 74, 174, chap. 7.

9. Joan Scott 1988, 42, 45.

10. For a discussion of space as a site of contestation over power in the postrevolutionary period see Vaughan 1999 (275–82).

11. See their essays in this volume.

12. Márquez Carrillo 1983; Pansters 1990; Valencia Castrejón 1996.

13. Malpica Uribe 1984; Talavera Aldana 1976, 227–99; Estrada Urroz 1997; Ventura Rodríguez 1984.

14. AGN, Fondo Lázaro Cárdenas, 442.1/32, telegrams from the FROC, Atlixco, to President Lázaro Cárdenas, 22 June and 25 June 25 1935; AGN, Fondo Dirección General de Gobierno, 2.331.8(18)17520, c. 35-A, exp. 85, letter from Federación Local de Sindicatos Obreros y Campesinos "Domingo Arena" de la Región de Tehuacan, FROC, 24 April 1936; and AGN, Fondo Dirección General de Gobierno, 2.331.8(18)17520, c. 35-A, exp. 85, telegram from the CROM, Atlixco, to the Secretaría de Gobernación, 30 April 1936. For a history of textile workers in Atlixco see Gamboa Ojeda 2001.

15. AGN, Fondo Manuel Ávila Camacho, 432/553, correspondence about the conflict at the Fábrica San Juan Xaltepec, Tehuacan, Puebla, 11 January–15 May 1944.

16. Bortz 1995, 3–69; Zapata 1976; Franco 1991; Crespo Oviedo 1988.

17. AGN, Fondo Dirección General de Gobierno, 2/331.9(18)/18, c. 64-A, exp. 116, letter from Sindicato de Trabajadores de la Industria Textil y Similares de la República Mexicana, to President Alemán, 25 April 1948.

SUSAN M. GAUSS

18. AGN, Fondo Departamento de Trabajo, c. 1460, exp. 4–10, letters from various unions and peasant leagues to President Plutarco Elías Calles and other government agencies, 5 September–24 September 1928.

19. Deborah Levenson-Estrada argues that militancy, solidarity, and trade unionism became heavily masculinist in Guatemala in the 1970s and 1980s (1997, 208).

20. Crider 1996, 6, 112–13.

21. "El Caso de la Fábrica 'San Juan Amandi,'" *Germinal*, 6 May 1944, 1, 4.

22. "'San Juan Amandi,' Segundo Turno, ha estado usando de enorme paciencia," *Germinal*, 13 May 1944, 1, 4; "Surge Nueva Fricción en la Fábrica de 'San Juan Amandi,'" *Germinal*, 6 January 1945, 1, 6; "Reina el caos en 'San Juan Amandi,'" *Germinal*, 3 February 1945, 1.

23. AGN, Fondo Manuel Ávila Camacho, 432/423, correspondence dealing with conflict at San Juan Amandi.

24. AGN, Fondo Secretaría de Trabajo y Previsión Social, Actas de Visita, Dirección General de Previsión Social, Secretaría de Trabajo y Previsión Social, 1941–52; Secretaría de Economía Nacional 1937.

25. AGN, Fondo Gonzalo Robles, c. 75, exp. 5, visit by the Banco de México to "La Perfeccionada, S.A.," 23 October 1945.

26. Rivero Quijano [1930s], 6–7.

27. AGN, Fondo Lázaro Cárdenas, 521.6/5, document from Blas Chumacero, Secretario FROC, Puebla, to President Cárdenas, 6 November 1934.

28. AGN, Fondo Manuel Ávila Camacho, 432/423, letter from Blas Chumacero, CTM, to President Manuel Ávila Camacho, 22 March 1944; AGN, Fondo Manuel Ávila Camacho, 432/423, letter from Gustavo Díaz Ordaz to Secretario Particular de la Presidencia de la República, 23 March 1944.

29. Actas de Visita from thirty-three bonetería factories demonstrate that the percentage of workers organized independently or remaining nonunionized was between 16 and 20 percent during the 1940s and early 1950s (AGN, Fondo Secretaría de Trabajo y Previsión Social, Actas de Visita, Dirección General de Previsión Social, Secretaría de Trabajo y Previsión Social, 1941–52).

30. See their essays in this volume.

31. The FROC could have organized female-dominated factories because it concentrated in representing smaller factories; during the 1940s, it controlled few factories as large as two hundred workers (AGN, Fondo Secretaría de Trabajo y Previsión Social, Actas de Visita, Dirección General de Previsión Social, Secretaría de Trabajo y Previsión Social, 1941–52). I thank Jocelyn Olcott and Greg Crider for pointing out the potential links between the FROC's incorporation of women and the organization's struggle for survival.

32. Census statistics confirm that bonetería workers earned considerably less than their counterparts in cotton-textile production. However, inconsistencies in data collection hinder exact comparisons. Secretaría de Economía Nacional 1936; Secretaría de Economía Nacional 1937; AGN, Fondo Lázaro Cárdenas, 521.6/5, telegrams from numerous factories in Puebla, September–November 1940; and AGN, Fondo Manuel Ávila Camacho, 444.2/305, Comisión de Estudios, Presidencia de la República, Memorandum Acerca de la Queja que Presentan los Industriales Boneteros de Jalisco, Contra el Contrato Obligatorio de la Industria, 8 August 1941.

33. Secretaría de Trabajo y Previsión Social 1941, 279.

34. AGN, Fondo Manuel Ávila Camacho, 444.2/305, telegrams from Ana Sosa, Josefina González, and others to President Ávila Camacho, 29 January 1942.

35. Snodgrass 1998, 115–16.

36. Secretaría de Economía Nacional 1937.

37. "Boneteros Rebeldes a un Contrato Ley," *Acción*, 26 July 1941.

38. AGN, Fondo Manuel Ávila Camacho, 432/423, letter from Blas Chumacero, CTM, to President Ávila Camacho, 22 March 1944.

39. For more on post-revolutionary debates about women's rights to a family wage see Olcott 2003, 47–48.

40. Estrada Urroz 1980, 356–57.

41. Cited in Estrada Urroz 1997, 24–25.

42. Letter from the Comisión Mixta Especial de Modernización de la Industria Textil del Algodón y sus Mixturas to the Secretaría de Trabajo y Previsión Social, 15 August 1947, Instituto Mora, D.F.

43. Ramos Escandón 1988, 84.

44. Daniel James considers a similar effort by Argentine factory owners to transform the "balance of forces" in factories (1981, 375–402).

45. "Sobrevendrá un desastre en la industria textil," *Novedades*, 29 November 1943; "Temen que desplace la Nueva Maquinaria a Numerosos Obreros," *El Nacional*, 13 December 1944; AGN, Fondo Manuel Ávila Camacho, 523/116, correspondence from Fidel Velázquez and Blas Chumacero to President Ávila Camacho, 30 November 1944; AGN, Fondo Gonzalo Robles, c. 75, exp. 4, interview with Jesús Rivero Quijano by Banco de México, 5 March 1942.

46. For an example of the CROM's use of this imagery see "Mujer," *Germinal*, 20 October 1945; "Hombre, Bendito Seas!" *Germinal*, 20 October 1945; "Dos Mujeres," *Germinal*, 23 February 1946; and "Para las Madres de Verdad," *Germinal*, 22 May 1943.

47. "Higiene de la Madre que Amamanta," *Germinal*, 10 August 1946.

48. "Sección de la Mujer," *Reivindicación*, 5 August 1950.

49. Middlebrook 1995, 110–55; Carr 1992, 142–86.

50. AGN, Fondo Manuel Ávila Camacho, 432/328, letter from CROM, Puebla, to Adolfo Ruiz Cortines, Secretario de Gobernación, 14 July 1948.

51. AGN, Fondo Manuel Ávila Camacho, 432/423, letter from Federación Sindicalista de Obreros y Campesinos, Cámara del Trabajo del Distrito de Atlixco, CROM, to President Ávila Camacho, 22 February 1946.

52. "Sección de la Mujer," *Reivindicación*, 4 February 1950.

53. Olcott 2003, 49.

PART FOUR

Women and Revolutionary Politics

Gendering the Faith and Altering the Nation

Mexican Catholic Women's Activism, 1917–1940

KRISTINA A. BOYLAN

Muy lento voy a cantar,	*Slowly I shall sing*
la canción del agrarista	*The song of the agrarian*
Los que con tantos sudores	*Those who by the sweat of their brow.*
Señores capitalistas	*Capitalist sirs*
(coro) Ay ay ay	*(Chorus) Ay ay ay*
Lucharon por nuestro anhelo	*They struggled for our desires*
Murieron muchos hermanos	*Many brothers died*
Que Dios los tenga en el cielo	*May God keep them in heaven*

This version of "The Agrarian's Song," sung by 73-year-old María Guadalupe Díaz in 1997, seems oxymoronic: had anyone wished for God to keep the agrarians in heaven?[1] Telescoping memories of events or influences in an oral interview is not uncommon, and, after sixty some years, understandable. However, rather than interpreting her version of this song as the product of a muddled memory or retrospective rationalization, one can instead discern something about the real experiences of the religious conflict in Mexico, as revealed from "this very reorganisation of the memory," which can be "a precious indication of how a people's consciousness is constructed."[2] In Tizapán el Alto, Jalisco, in the late

1920s and 1930s, Catholic activist women ran a school with a doctrinally sound curriculum as per the church leaders' requests, but they charged tuition beyond the means of most villagers. Not only was Díaz's family unable to afford the Catholic-school fees, but her father was an *ejidatario*, served in municipal government, and supported the new, socialist public school by sending his children. But he and his wife, Elpidia Solís de Díaz, also sent their children to catechism classes that the activists coordinated in the absence of the parish priest. Díaz did not consider herself less Catholic for having attended the socialist school or for remembering it fondly. Tizapán had only a primary school, and Díaz attended for only three years—not enough time, she joked, for her to convert to atheistic socialism.[3] Díaz's experience shows the impact of Catholic women's activism in twentieth-century Mexico. While Díaz was not kept out of the revolutionary regime's public-school system, as hard-line ecclesiastical leaders and Catholic activists would have wished, she was nevertheless exposed to and appreciated a cultural and social worldview alternative to that of the state. Thanks to the actions of the local churchwomen, Tizapán, a site of radical campesino organizing, also remained a place where Catholicism could be expressed and practiced.

According to Manuel Castells's simple formulation, "space is the expression of society," and in revolutionary Mexico a fierce contest was fought over geography in its traditional sense: the "historically rooted spatial organization of our common experience."[4] The revolutionary government and independent, radical activists sought to purge Mexico of the Roman Catholic Church's remaining social influence, completing the campaign against its economic, political, and social presence that had begun during the reform era of the previous century. Controlling public discourse was a requisite part of this project; so in its attempt to create a new society, the revolutionary government tried to exclude the Catholic Church from public venues outside of church buildings (and sometimes from those buildings as well), from schools, and from political, civic, and labor organizing. In reaction to the regime's idea of altering their society to erase its religious content, the Mexican population had a variety of responses, ranging from cooperation, to foot-dragging, to outright resistance and rebellion.

Women played a large role in these contests and could be found acting all along this spectrum, selecting and incorporating different ideas regarding religion and public participation into their own project of creating society, whether they called it revolutionary or not. Numerous women who identified as Catholic participated in overt and tacit forms of protest against the anticlerical laws. Over the years, a significant number distin-

KRISTINA A. BOYLAN

guished themselves with a heightened level of mobilization. Despite being rhetorically assigned to the home and largely lacking access to formal channels of political power, higher education, or leadership within the religious institution that was core to their identity, these women participated in the social debates of their day with notable effect. Catholic women activists used their gatherings, activities, and influence on their leaders and community members to circumvent formal prohibitions on religious content. While not able to formally alter the laws and policies crafted toward the end of the armed revolution, Catholic women activists enjoyed considerable success—from reopening churches and schools to infusing Mothers' Day celebrations with religious content—in challenging the revolutionary regime's attempts to impose its discipline on public spaces and discourse and in substantially reshaping the "pedestrian rhetoric" of their communities and country.[5] During the Catholic women's mobilizations from the 1910s through the 1930s, rural women and children like Elpidia Solís de Díaz and her daughter María Guadalupe were often the objects of secular and religious social reform but also had their own, objective power to judge whether to keep or remove religious practice from their lives and to accept or reject political and social change.

Historians acknowledge that Catholics resisted the revolutionary regime's attempts to diminish church influence in Mexican society and that women spearheaded "everyday peaceful resistance," which undermined the state's anticlerical social policies at least as much as men's violent attacks or officials' indifferent enforcement.[6] But not much has been said about *how* these women mounted such a challenge, nor about *why* they did. To these ends, one must consider the spaces, physical and conceptual, that both ecclesiastical leaders and their critics assigned to Catholic women, and those that they came to occupy in post-revolutionary Mexico.[7]

Catholic Rhetorical Roots

The Pauline biblical letters were often used by critics of religious affiliation to demonstrate how Christianity conceptualized women as inherently subordinate to men. Indeed, Catholic leaders often repeated the analogy that husband was to wife as Christ was to the church to indicate proper channels of respect and obedience.[8] Another popular adage stated, "A woman outside her home is like a sacred vessel outside the temple that is in danger of being profaned."[9] Early-twentieth-century Catholic rhetoric portrayed women as weak and easily corrupted but also as potentially seductive and corrupting. For both reasons, the church argued that maintaining purity, doctrinal adherence, submission to authority, and passivity were women's best guards against worldly contamination and contaminating others.

However, masculine authority came with a proviso. Christianity had freed both men and women from the bonds of "pagan" society; thus, it was no more acceptable to "enslave" or exploit women for enjoyment or profit than it was to subjugate the church. The Vatican globally and squarely condemned feminist and radical proposals to emancipate women through the secularization and state regulation (or deregulation) of marriage, divorce and family law, free love, birth control, salaried work, and workplace organization. Pontiffs from Leo XIII (1878–1903) onward decried such secular practices, claiming that they eroded women's dignity, which Christians should preserve as essential to moral society. Secular emancipation did not grant women rights but replaced them with "abandonment of the home where [woman] reigned as queen, and her subjection to the same strain and working hours" as men.[10] In the late nineteenth century and early twentieth, increasing numbers of women sought wages or education, often of necessity, but Catholic leaders insisted that women's ultimate focus remain the household and family.[11]

Despite women's purported weakness, the church also saw them as potential agents for strengthening its position and its standards of morality. In 1908 Pope Pius X (1903–14) instructed women to be "sweet, silent and stay at home," but the next year he exhorted women to undertake, like the recently beatified Joan of Arc, "duties outside the family circle that involve others."[12] Proponents of Catholic social action resolved this contradiction by casting women's activism as an unfortunate necessity, but one that fit in with the duty of wives and mothers to protect their loved ones. By extension, this duty could include educating children, other family members (even husbands), and peers, and supporting social and even political movements that safeguarded church institutions and teachings.[13] Furthermore, this extra-domestic duty was increasingly seen to include participation in the Catholic Action organizations that were formed to harness lay people's enthusiasm and ability to act in civil society in Europe and Latin America in the early twentieth century. Ordained and lay authors described the composition of this "apostolate in society," which had strictly delineated gender roles and demarcations of public and private life, but never excluded women.[14]

Catholic women activists utilized this logic to justify their church participation, their defense of religion, and their rejection of secular, reformist social programs. In Mexico, Refugio Goribar de Cortina, three-time president of the Mexican Catholic Women's Union (Unión Femenina

Católica Mexicana, or UFCM), used the same biblical citation to upbraid Mexican men for falling short of their obligations to guide their families (and by extension, the country) in the Catholic faith. Women, in turn, were exhorted to use their influence on men in order to restore a Christian direction to Mexican society. Women had proven their moral superiority and capacity to instruct and lead in the past, Goribar de Cortina asserted, and needed to do so again.[15]

Mexican Catholic Women's Organizing through the Armed Revolution

Barbara Ann Miller describes Guadalajaran Cristero leader Anacleto González Flores as unusually "aware of the great dormant resource of Mexico, its women."[16] The characterization of Catholic women activists as "dormant" up to the 1920s bespeaks the effect of "separate spheres" ideologies, for Mexican women had participated in Catholic mutual-aid societies, trade unions, and pious associations since the early nineteenth century. After the reform wars, Catholic women's associations became more visible and began to play a greater role in preserving a space for Catholic practice amid social and economic changes in the early twentieth century.[17]

In 1911 the Mexican Jesuit Alfredo Méndez Medina, later the first director of the Mexican Social Secretariat (Secretariado Social Mexicano, or SSM—the umbrella organization for Catholic social action groups, founded in 1920), suggested creating a Mexican Catholic women's association. While he agreed that women should remain at home and that Catholic labor activists should campaign for men's "family wages," he admired the European Catholic women's associations that he had seen while traveling. From the start, his vision for a laywomen's activist organization subverted any narrow, domestic restriction on women or suggestion to eradicate women's waged labor and public participation. Méndez Medina's plan assigned women to very public venues: founding and running educational and recreational centers, libraries, catechism programs, women's trade unions, employment agencies, and consumer leagues, as well as aiding Catholic men's organizations.[18]

In response to industrialization, Catholics already had begun organizing women's labor associations, which together had about 10,000 members by the beginning of the twentieth century and served as more than "token responses to the new social concerns being expressed in Rome."[19] Rather, they allowed the Mexican episcopate to build on, modify, and direct lay people's existing work. Probably for this reason, Archbishop of

Mexico José Mora y del Río approved Méndez Medina's idea and appointed another Jesuit, Carlos M. de Heredia, to found a national Catholic women's organization. Building on an existing Mexico City women's group that he advised, Heredia formally established the Association of Catholic Ladies (Asociación de las Damas Católicas, ADC) in 1912 to offer aid to the poor and education against "ignorance." One of the ADC's first projects was to provide material aid and moral support for the newly founded Catholic association for young men, the Mexican Association of Catholic Youth (Asociación Católica de la Juventud Mexicana, or ACJM). The ADC also established and maintained schools and organized visits to hospitals and prisons, providing them with morally sound reading materials. In Mexico City, the ADC held weekly meetings to discuss social and cultural concerns and began publishing a periodical, *Mexican Catholic Woman* (*La Mujer Católica Mexicana*). The group founded chapters in dioceses from Chiapas to Saltillo and gradually adopted the name Union of Mexican Catholic Ladies (Unión de Damas Católicas Mexicanas, or UDCM).

In 1913, following Méndez Medina's vision, the UDCM expanded its support for Mexican workers, collecting supplies and funds to open night schools and workers' halls. The UDCM received requests for financial support from several independent workers' newspapers and dedicated funds to religious congregations' free schools for children. The UDCM also covered expenses and supplied religious images for the SSM's Center for Catholic Students. Soon afterward, the violence that followed Victoriano Huerta's coup induced some UDCM members to flee Mexico and curtailed the activities of those who remained. Declining donations and increased demand for food drives, soup kitchens, and medical supplies strained the UDCM's finances. Some regional chapters disappeared entirely, and the UDCM stopped printing *Mexican Catholic Woman*. Others, like the Guadalajara UDCM, led by Catalina Palomar de Verea, continued their projects despite their archbishop's exile and led protests when local revolutionaries attempted to implement anticlerical legislation.[20]

Numerous priests were harassed or exiled during the armed conflict, and many continued to be afterward. The church invited women to perform more community work, and increasing numbers accepted the opportunity. Catholic women's organizing enjoyed a revival as the revolution's military conflict waned. In 1920 the UDCM began publishing a new monthly periodical, *Catholic Lady* (*La Dama Católica*), prepared to convene women from across Mexico for its first national assembly, and cultivated contacts with the Geneva-based International League of Catholic Women.[21] During the early 1920s, the UDCM concentrated on evangelization, charitable works, and morality campaigns targeting the growing print, film, and music industries, dances, and women's fashions. Members encouraged lapsed Catholics to attend Mass, partake in the sacraments, and worship in their homes, which included reciting the rosary, practicing private devotions, maintaining altars, and arranging "enthronements," consecrations of households to specific iconic images.[22] They devoted particular attention to "legitimizing" common-law and civil unions into Catholic marriages—a significant choice of words, since the Mexican government had not considered religious marriages legally binding since the liberal reforms of the 1850s.[23]

In 1919 the UDCM's ecclesiastical advisors encouraged Catholic women to take advantage of the gaps in the financially challenged Mexican government's provision of public education by founding more free Catholic schools. Catholic women continued to provide support for orphanages, hospitals, and campaigns against prostitution and the spread of venereal disease. As requested by the SSM, the UDCM lent financial and spiritual support to existing women workers' societies and sponsored conferences to organize Catholic women's unions in cities from Monterrey to San Miguel de Allende. These included trade unions for seamstresses, telephone and tobacco workers, and a Catholic teachers' syndicate, all of which later joined the National Confederation of Catholic Labor (Confederación Nacional Católica de Trabajo, or CNCT). Both the UDCM and working-class Catholic women's organizations participated in campaigns for the "moralization" of Mexican workers. According to Randall Hanson, some contemporary observers weighed Catholic women's groups against those of the other two Catholic action groups of the 1920s—the all-male Knights of Columbus and the ACJM—and deemed the women's to be more vigorous.[24]

Catholic Women in Action during and after the Cristero Rebellion

The UDCM formally obeyed Pius XI's (1922–39) mandate against violence and partially disassociated itself from the National League for Defense of Religious Freedom (Liga Nacional Defensora de la Libertad Religiosa, or LNDLR) when that coalition of Catholic organizations endorsed armed rebellion against the post-revolutionary government. However, the UDCM continued active protests and boycotts of industries dominated by government unions, and never entirely broke with the LNDLR. Some local chapters of the UDCM continued to coordinate efforts with the belligerent organization, and as late as May 1928 the UDCM central committee signed a LNDLR memorial to the pope objecting to a negotiated peace with the government.[25]

Other Catholic women's organizations were transformed by their challenge to Calles's policies of extreme limitation of religious practice and autonomy. In 1927, led by their president, María Gollaz, and their lay advisor, Luis Flores González, members of Guadalajara's Union of Women Office Workers (Unión de Empleadas Católicas, or UEC) and of other Catholic, working-class women's unions formed the Women's Brigades of Saint Joan of Arc (Brigadas Femeninas de Santa Juana de Arco, or BF).[26] Almost all of the BF's 25,000 members worked outside their homes, although some had lost their jobs when they refused to join state-sponsored or radical unions; others were CNCT members. Middle-class members were largely office workers and public schoolteachers who had lost or left their jobs due to the secularization of education. Women in rural areas joined as well, many of whom had been directly involved with the church through the UDCM, sodalities like the Daughters of Mary, catechism, adult education, or other programs. Predominantly young and single, BF members often came from the UDCM's counterpart for young women, the Association of Young Women Catholics (Juventud Católica Femenina Mexicana, or JCFM), although others were married homemakers. Many emerged from the first "revolutionary generation," which came of age amid challenges to the weight of tradition and propriety on Mexican society (and on women) and during the heyday of Catholic social-action campaigns.[27]

Organized into cells and headed by women in military-like ranks, the BF smuggled arms and ammunition to the Cristeros, raised money, and provided food, medical supplies and nursing, information, and other support, including some participation in active combat. Claiming that the Cristeros lacked papal authorization, the Mexican episcopate refused to appoint chaplains for the Cristeros or their auxiliaries. Instead, the BF relied on lay leaders and independently acting clergy for advice. Members took an oath not to reveal the organization's existence or details of their work—even when lives were threatened—to anyone besides BF supervisors. However, the BF never advocated disobeying spiritual leaders or family members, and superiors required members to keep detailed records of their work. Very few members were apprehended during the year and a half of their greatest activity, although they feared arrest, torture, and rape at the hands of government soldiers.[28]

As one of the few who were apprehended, María Gollaz decided she could no longer work in Guadalajara without jeopardizing her colleagues, so she left for Mexico City, where she approached the LNDLR and proposed that they cooperate.[29] On 22 June 1928, she and Mexico City LNDLR leader Miguel Palomar y Vizcarra agreed to incorporate the BF into the LNDLR, with the BF recognizing the LNDLR as its sole superior organization but preserving its own autonomous structure, leadership, and capacity to recruit and initiate work throughout Mexico. Palomar y Vizcarra initially welcomed the BF's collaboration but soon opposed its independence. Within several months, he complained to Archbishop of Guadalajara Francisco Orozco y Jiménez that the BF, still based principally in that archdiocese, contributed to the region's separatism from the LNDLR's unified resistance. However, Orozco y Jiménez, who had long been appreciative of Catholic women's organizations, did little to reprimand the BF. Meanwhile, the BF disregarded LNDLR pressure to replace their founding leaders with more compliant ones.

The Cristero field leader General Enrique Gorostieta cited the LNDLR's harassment of the BF as evidence of its inability to direct a rural guerrilla war from Mexico City. Luis Beltrán y Mendoza, the LNDLR representative in Guadalajara, countered that it was unnatural and dangerous to have women subject to military orders, discipline, and pressure; this, he claimed, would cause the women to become impervious to the guidance of the clergy. Surely, he argued, their organization would degenerate into favoritism and infighting, though he offered no evidence of this. The LNDLR also founded its own women's group, the Guadalupan Legion (Legión Guadalupana), which apparently did not gain support from many women or men involved with the Cristero cause. Palomar y Vizcarra finally resorted to church structure, sending his appeal for the BF's dissolution to the Mexican episcopate and, higher, to the Vatican. Oddly, in his petitions, Palomar y Vizcarra maintained that the BF's secrecy was wrong because the women hid their actions not only from their husbands, but also from their country. Despite its repeated exhortations to Catholic resistance, the Holy See reiterated its condemnation of secret societies and ordered an investigation. The Mexican episcopate's theological commission determined that the BF's secrecy violated church teachings; it also declared that, given women's inherent inability to work together well, the BF and any group that lacked guidance from male ecclesiastics and lay supervisors would be doomed to failure. Although neither Beltrán y Mendoza nor Palomar y Vizcarra offered much evidence to support such claims, both the Vatican and the Mexican episcopate ordered Orozco y Jiménez to declare the BF illicit, which he did on 7 December 1928, threatening members with excommunication if they continued their work.[30] Meanwhile, the LNDLR's inferior knowledge of local terrain and power structures became obvious. Without the BF, ammunition supplies to the Cristeros declined, and their military campaign deteriorated drastically up to the June 1929 peace accords. The LNDLR never considered restoring the BF's former autonomy, even as the armed movement degenerated.

James Scott points out that the people who take teachings most seriously sometimes become the most dangerous to the regimes that train them. The mobilized women of the BF had taken the admonition to defend their faith to an extreme. In doing so, they violated Catholic norms for women's behavior and Mexican law, precipitating condemnation from their own church as well as from the government. The overwhelming objection on the part of these male leaders to women's autonomous contributions showed that their fear of women's actions that could threaten the patriarchal organization of church and home overrode demonstrations of women's cooperation and effectiveness. Archbishop of Mexico Pascual Díaz Barreto instructed SSM director Miguel Dario Miranda to collect and destroy the BF archives, although it remains unclear whether he intended to eliminate the organization's influence or to protect the persons involved from further persecution.[31]

In his dissolution order, Orozco y Jiménez told BF members that they could work with local Catholic projects if they changed their organization's name and leaders and accepted ecclesiastical supervision. The BF reemerged, in altered form but with the same name, and in Mexico City rather than in Guadalajara. In July 1929, Apostolic Delegate and Archbishop of Morelia Leopoldo Ruíz y Flores delivered the Vatican's approval of a new, domesticated BF. In August, Díaz Barreto communicated the new stipulations to Gollaz and other BF members, appealing to them to support the church's new, unifying lay organization, the Mexican Catholic Action (Acción Católica Mexicana, or ACM), with "unconditional obedience." Gollaz agreed, needing funds to support the organization's abandoned members. On 13 September 1929, two women in Mexico City, María and Berenise Ortíz, replied to the archbishop on "Brigadas Femeninas de Santa Juana de Arco: Consejo General [General Council]" stationery, offering their "submission."[32]

Over the next several years, the Mexico City–based BF appealed to former members to rejoin the church's campaigns. In the first edition of BF's new periodical, *El Informador de las Brigadas Femeninas de Santa Juana de Arco* (*Informer of the BF of Saint Joan of Arc*), editor Berenise Ortíz thanked Archbishop Díaz Barreto for his "truly paternal goodness in placing our organization under the immediate command of the [SSM]."[33] (Díaz Barreto also appointed its ecclesiastical advisors.) Despite the women's obsequious tone, they apparently had not given up on the organization's interpretation of its role. The BF committed itself to teaching catechism in working-class, urban neighborhoods and in isolated rural areas, and to providing technical training for financially challenged women like its own members—an effort that preceded the UFCM's efforts by several years and other Catholic programs by decades.[34] Yet, the *Informador* publicly reprimanded those women who continued to engage in "activities . . . condemned by our superiors."[35] The BF's campaigns to support charities, seminaries, schools, and libraries closely paralleled those of other approved women's organizations. The post-Cristiada BF remained small and poorly publicized, with membership in the hundreds. It was subsumed into the UFCM in 1935, though it continued to hold its own biennial meetings until at least 1940.[36]

Not many ex-*brigadistas* saw the resuscitated BF as worth joining, and many shifted from religious activism to private or professional life. Some joined religious orders, and others worked as lay teachers in the private Catholic schools founded clandestinely in the 1930s and more openly from the 1940s onward. Other teachers opted for public schools, believing that the state offered a better way to support themselves and to educate more children.[37] Gollaz later told her son that while some ex-brigadistas joined the new ACM, "many got married afterward" and stayed at home; she herself married Flores González, her fellow UEC organizer, in 1930. Flores González continued to organize for Catholic causes, which Gollaz supported, but chronic depression kept her housebound. She refused to record her past, seeing the exercise as pointless after the destruction of the BF's records. Gollaz only obliquely acknowledged her role in the BF—she named one of her daughters Celia, her own nom de guerre.[38]

Women in Catholic Action

Even though the church reacted fiercely against militarized women activists and sought to control them as part of its appeal to reclaim public space, it still identified women as a vital part of the new ACM. SSM organizers, including JCFM president Sofía del Valle, traveled throughout Mexico to help found diocesan committees, which, paralleling church structures, oversaw parish groups. The UFCM central committee, based in Mexico City, and ecclesiastical leaders communicated with these diocesan organizations through the UFCM monthly newsletter, *Acción Femenina* (*Feminine Action*), and through correspondence and visits, strategies that diocesan committees reproduced on a regional level. The UFCM encouraged all members to attend its biennial general assemblies, and in alternate years the dioceses and parishes held assemblies, where members reported on their work, held seminars, and planned for the next two years.

The ACM statutes mandated that every UFCM group have an ecclesiastical assistant, but women comprised the organization's leadership and during the 1930s often worked in the absence of the clergy.[39]

The membership of the UFCM grew steadily. In 1932, the UFCM counted 13,465 active, dues-paying members. By 1936, 67,775 were registered, and in 1940 the UFCM had 149,514 members.[40] The UFCM sponsored the JCFM, many of whose activists cited positively that it provided opportunities to leave home and take part in projects of which their families approved; many of them also continued to participate in the UFCM even as they grew older or got married. JCFM membership also increased rapidly, from 8,601 in its first year, to 31,107 in 1934, to 102,491 in 1942.[41] By comparison, the Sole Front for Women's Rights (Frente Único Pro Derechos de la Mujer), a coalition of state-affiliated and radical feminist organizers, optimistically estimated its membership at 50,000 at the height of its mobilization for women's suffrage and social reform.[42]

The degree to which anticlerical laws would be enforced was unclear immediately following the peace accords, and Catholics hoped for more aperture. Catholic women activists began planning to support clergy, women religious (women who have taken religious vows), and Catholic institutions, as church leaders gauged the reactions of federal, state, and local officials and radical activists. To focus efforts, the UFCM strategically divided into "sections" reminiscent of the UDCM: religious instruction, support for priests and seminaries, mothers, and enthronements, with additional, optional sections including Catholic schools, charitable works, and one devoted to encouraging women to develop personal piety.[43]

Catholic leaders knew that early contact with children was crucial to instilling religious practices, and women's assumption of this duty, once assigned to priests or seminarians, helped continue a process that anticlerical legislation was meant to interrupt. Some exiled priests were able to return to their parishes in the early 1930s, but others were delayed or restricted in their movement. Church leaders identified the actual and potential mothers and wives in the UFCM and JCFM as ideal catechism and schoolteachers, for which they were encouraged to continue their own education. Women catechists worked with children in parishes in cities and towns, and some organized courses in rural areas.[44]

The UFCM also focused on maintaining public morality. UFCM members criticized immodest fashions, music, dances, and entertainment in articles in *Acción Femenina* and *Juventud* (*Youth*, the JCFM's periodical). In Chihuahua, some activists even monitored the entrances to churches to prevent women they deemed "immodestly" dressed from entering. The UFCM also collaborated with the Mexican League of Decency, founded

KRISTINA A. BOYLAN

during the 1930s to monitor movies and other media, by publishing their recommendations in ACM magazines and distributing their flyers at Masses and meetings.[45]

Following earlier models, and paralleling the increased efforts of the state, the UFCM reopened and inaugurated adult-education programs, night schools, day-care centers, hygiene and health services, workers' associations (including muted forms of the CNCT), and social organizations. The UFCM ran clothing and food drives for those who had endured natural disasters and for the urban and rural poor, including indigenous communities. While the UFCM advocated charity rather than structural change, it nevertheless attenuated indigence and crises.[46]

While in some dioceses the UFCM remained a small, elite organization, in others (notably Mexico and the central-western dioceses) it took in a broader membership, including white-collar employees and, in some cases, rural and working-class women. Some UFCM members thus became more conscious of workingwomen's needs and advocated practical plans for addressing them. Belatedly adopting revolutionary language, the UFCM announced at the 1938 General Assembly that it would group its efforts among peasants, blue-collar workers, white-collar workers, and professionals into one section: working classes. The UFCM recognized that many women—including some in their ranks—needed and wanted to work and dispensed with the mandate barring women's salaried employment.[47]

Catholics protested the government's 1933 sexual-education-curriculum proposal and the amendment of constitutional Article 3, which made public education "socialist" rather than "secular" in all schools and prohibited confessional education in advanced as well as primary schools. The UFCM participated in petitions, school boycotts, and rallies coordinated by the National Parents' Union (Unión Nacional de Padres de Familia).[48] The Mexican episcopate decreed that Catholic parents were to withdraw children from socialist schools and asked the UFCM to offer alternatives.[49] However, Article 3 mandated the incorporation of all private schools with more than nine students into the Ministry of Public Education, and they were required to follow its guidelines and pass government inspections. UFCM activists then organized small home schools, but, their size notwithstanding, the fact that they followed Catholic curricula violated laws proscribing religious activity outside of churches, and in some regions local officials sought out the schools and penalized their teachers, students, and supporters. Nevertheless, the UFCM ran approximately 2,500 schools by 1936. While they could not have taken in more than a small percentage of Mexico's school-age children (a lack of written records makes quantification difficult), their symbolic value proved important for Catholics

Gendering the Faith

and irritating to the state.[50] JCFM members taught in and supported the home schools, and their organization sustained its own Advanced Institute for Feminine Culture in Mexico City until 1954.[51]

Part of the rationale for the 1934 closure of remaining Catholic schools was that their teachers were not state-educated or licensed. Some women religious who had run schools since the late nineteenth century hired licensed, lay teachers to comply with this regulation, but this proved expensive. (Nuns, in contrast, worked for their keep.) By 1935, the government enforced prohibitions on religious communities, the schools run by women religious were closed, and the UFCM's work to support convents and their institutions became illegal. For several years, the UFCM procured housing and supplies for women religious. Some sent their children to nuns' classes in private homes, but enrollment fell because of the risks involved. Many women religious lost their main source of income and had to rely on charity or low-paying piecework to survive.[52] Conditions for women religious did not improve until the end of the 1930s, when diminished enforcement of anticlerical laws allowed them to resume more public work.

During the early 1930s, the UFCM central committee ordered members to collect funds to support both legally and clandestinely working priests. Restrictions on religiously oriented higher education made it nearly impossible to train seminarians within Mexico, and fears of the disappearance of Mexican priests ran strong.[53] In 1937, the Vatican granted the Mexican episcopate an alternative, the Montezuma Seminary in Arizona, for which the UFCM raised funds and collected supplies. However, in the early 1940s Montezuma Seminary students constituted nowhere near the majority of Mexican seminarians, which indicated the persistence of underground seminaries in Mexico that the UFCM also supported.[54] These institutions replenished the supply of Mexican-born priests, who would be constitutionally eligible to minister pending the relaxation of church-state tensions and of federal and state restrictions.

At first, the UFCM responded cautiously to the constitutional restrictions on public religious activity and displays. As the UDCM had done, the UFCM visited homes and encouraged devotions like enthronements in order to aid absent or overextended parish priests and to extend Catholic practices beyond churches.[55] The UFCM also continued the UDCM's practice of promoting Catholic marriage among those in consensual unions and civil marriages, especially in light of the 1927 Civil Code, in some cases offering to pay the fees for church ceremonies to "legalize" these marriages.[56]

Civic events like the state-sponsored Mothers' Day offered Catholics

KRISTINA A. BOYLAN

opportunities to fuse civic and religious cultural practices. Bishops advocated holding Masses for the day, Catholic protesters petitioned the government to allow public celebrations honoring the "mothers of the nation's future," and the UFCM campaigned to make Mothers' Day a Catholic holiday in practice, if not in name. The UFCM president Refugio Goribar de Cortina dispensed with private-sphere rhetoric when she dedicated UFCM energies to this effort, according it almost as much importance as their campaign to encourage Mexican Catholics to comply with their annual Easter obligations, which were central to Catholic practice.[57]

Catholic women also participated in protests to publicly practice their faith that involved civil disobedience. Guadalajara Catholics were arrested for leaving churches with visible crosses on their foreheads on Ash Wednesday in 1932 and 1933. In 1937, women led thousands of Veracruz Catholics to occupy churches after government agents killed an adolescent girl when dispersing a clandestine Mass in Orizaba with gunfire. The protest forced Governor Miguel Alemán to open churches and allow more priests to officiate.[58] Elsewhere, as tensions diminished and local officials wearied of enforcing anticlerical laws, Catholics again enacted public religious displays with little or no response. By 1940, the UFCM could cite a pilgrimage and outdoor Mass honoring Our Lady of Ocotlán (Jalisco) as one of many pious actions reclaiming public space nationwide.[59]

Other 1930s Challenges

The 1929 peace accords left many Catholic rebels discontented; renewed state animosity in the early 1930s compounded their sense of victimization. Along with outbursts generated by land, educational, and anticlerical reforms, a more cohesive Second Cristero Rebellion (Segunda Cristiada) emerged by the early 1930s. Several thousand continued to fight, supported by the remainder of the LNDLR, its Guadalupan Legion, and families, communities, and some clergy. However, they lacked widespread support among Catholics, as many feared government retribution and heeded the bishops' prohibition of armed movements. Some attacks on schoolteachers and other state representatives were religiously motivated, and many were brutal, but not all rural violence was attributable to armed Catholics' seditious organizing, as some union leaders, schoolteachers, and military and other state personnel averred. Nevertheless, the labels "Cristero" and "fanatic Catholics" were employed widely and effectively to justify military campaigns, *ejido* grants, support for socialist education, and other state-building projects.[60]

The National Sinarquista Union (Unión Nacional Sinarquista, or

UNS), an offshoot of the Segunda Cristiada mobilizations, was founded in 1937. The sinarquistas rejected the pragmatic approach of the bishops and the ACM, rallying instead around their purist conception of loyalty to God, country, and family (in that order), which facilitated accusations of fascist sympathies. The UNS was strongest in the central-western region, but gained notoriety for supporting Salvador Abascal's movement to re-open churches in Tabasco in 1938. Sinarquismo appealed to those less concerned with defending the institutional church than with regional and personal autonomy, expressions sometimes couched in terms of xeno-phobia, anti-Semitism, and machismo.[61] Catholic women mobilizing as women seem not to have played much of a part in secular, fascist move-ments, as some male Catholic university students did for Luis Rodríguez's Gold Shirts or the Catholics who supported General Saturnino Cedillo's uprising in 1938.[62]

Female sinarquistas's roles were described in gendered rhetoric similar to that employed by the ACM. Aside from exhortations to place country before family, the sinarquista woman's rules of conduct closely resembled those of the UFCM member. They, too, were to uphold high standards of purity, obedience, devotion, and modesty while mobilizing in the streets, schools, and other public venues. Also, they were to maintain virtue among their families and impel their male relatives to direct action for God and country. Women were crucial to the formation and growth of the UNS, and they later organized formally, founding the Woman's Section (Sección Femenina, or SFUNS) in 1945. The SFUNS established community chapters, schools and literacy programs for children, and, in 1948, a wom-an's adult-education center in Mexico City that offered academic, re-ligious, and practical courses.[63]

There are no estimates available of the number of female sinarquistas during the 1930s or 1940s. Even though women vigorously promoted sinarquismo, male UNS leaders disapproved of their assertiveness and ac-tively worked to stifle women's activity outside of home and church. Ac-cording to Laura Pérez Rosales, a high proportion of sinarquista women remained unmarried by choice; even as they extolled women's abnegation and selfless devotion, they valued the more independent existence they could lead as activists. Although women sinarquistas differed in their evaluations of church leadership and Mexican politics, their beliefs regard-ing religion, morality, and education were similar to those of their UFCM counterparts. And, although they diverged in the order of priorities — God, family, and then country—UFCM members shared with women sinarquistas the desire to use their organization to defend Catholicism while circumventing certain restrictions on women's behavior and activity.

KRISTINA A. BOYLAN

Catholic women activists also refrained from commenting on women's suffrage, which was again debated publicly in Mexico toward the end of the 1930s. Some government officials gave as their rationale for denying women the vote the fear of a Catholic backlash; one was said to comment, "If they achieve their objective ... we'll soon have a bishop for president."[64] The ruling party proclaimed a gradualist approach, maintaining that women should not exercise suffrage until they had been "duly prepared by their social and educative effort."[65] Ironically, church leaders echoed these sentiments. Despite decades of women's mobilizations on the church's behalf, ecclesiastical authors cast women's voting, should it come to pass, as an "unfortunate necessity," and Catholic clergy expressed doubts that the majority of Mexican women were educated sufficiently for the responsibility.[66] This, along with the Mexican episcopate's caution regarding pointed commentary on politics during the late 1930s, may be why the UFCM remained silent on the issue. However, many individual members supported conservative opposition parties like the National Action Party (Partido de Acción Nacional), founded in 1939, and the Revolutionary Party of National Unification, which supported opposition candidate Juan Andreu Almazán in 1940. Even without the vote, many Catholic women activists lent these political parties logistical and financial support.[67]

Conclusion: Women's Spaces in Postrevolutionary Mexico

Idealizations of women's purity, piety, and domestic loyalty have provided strong rhetorical force for those who equate the home with women's behavior and activity.[68] The home has been, in Doreen Massey's words, "coded female." Whether women are truly, completely restricted to their homes or not, the mother of the household often functions as its "stable symbolic center," beloved when she is there, provoking panic or anger when she is not. The mandates for social organization of industrializing, capitalist economies, which contradictorily demand women's participation in a larger labor force and their generally unpaid reproductive labor in the home, at best coexist uneasily with patriarchal social models that rest on women's "anchoring" the home for breadwinning yet transient males. Thus, the social changes that remove women from the home, however profitable, generally disrupt, disturb, and provoke protest.[69]

Mexican women had moved and worked both inside and outside the home for centuries before foreign investment and domestic political and economic changes presented increased opportunities for women's waged labor. While the ideal for the home to be a haven populated by women was articulated by revolutionary as well as Catholic leaders in pre- and post-revolutionary Mexico, its popularity does not amount to a conflation of women and the home.[70] Rather, persistent, vociferous protests against women circulating outside the home imply that women were not limited to such a "sphere."

Lived experiences in revolutionary Mexico complicate the simplistic portrayal of the home as a wholly private space versus the public spaces of the street, the workplace, and government, not to mention that of women's occupying the home solely or primarily. Households were, by and large, not sealed enclaves in post-revolutionary Mexico; rather, they were ideological battlegrounds, leaving no home front for women or men to observe without participating. Government education and hygiene programs sought to reform Mexican homes; Catholic catechism programs and encouragement of household devotions and symbolic dedications challenged the state's efforts. Neither left the home undisturbed as a "private" space under the sole jurisdiction of its inhabitants.

When comparing the Catholic mobilizations of the 1930s with the beginnings of the SSM's liberation theory focus in the 1940s, scholar Carlos Fazio concludes that women-dominated Catholic movements of the 1930s in essence created a "good girls' house" (*casa de niñas bien*), a focus on personal piety and domesticity that needed to be replaced by community mobilization as soon as anticlericalism abated.[71] But the actions of these niñas bien had strong implications outside the casa as well as inside it for decades. Religious practice began at and permeated the home, but was ultimately intended to be a public endeavor, with participants engaging in actions visible to their churches and communities. Enthronements publicized personal piety and the dedication of household space to Catholicism, but also demonstrated a demand for religious practice and clergy ministering outside of church buildings. Catholic organization meetings, catechism classes, and home schools transformed private homes into public spaces. Catholic doctrine may have placed women in the home, but living—let alone defending—it required public action.

Lay volunteers and activists can link a distant religious hierarchy to ordinary people.[72] In general, Catholic activists, the majority of them women, strengthened the church in Mexico when its social standing had deteriorated due to leaders' intransigence. The ACM's stated purpose was not to change laws or government, but to help the hierarchy reach the broader population. Even the dissenting women who participated in the Segunda Cristiada or the UNS carried the Catholic message to rural areas. And these activists rallied their countrymen to demand both the right to practice their religion and greater latitude for their church as a whole.

KRISTINA A. BOYLAN

Mexico exemplifies a society in which the "midwives" of later, progressive religious movements were women activists who put Catholic social teachings into effect earlier in the century, sometimes reshaping or even making Catholic policy in the process.[73] Women's activism helped build the Catholic social-action movement from the Porfiriato through the 1920s. In the 1930s, after the government explicitly banned confessional labor organizations, the UFCM was one of the first Catholic groups to redesign and sustain its campaigns for workers. In the mid-1940s, as the SSM again developed more militant programs for workers and peasants, they found early and constant support in women activists like Emma Galán, JCFM president during the late 1930s. The UFCM, the JCFM, and other women's groups continued to affiliate with the SSM and participated in its studies of the Second Vatican Council reforms. Leonor Aida Concha, who worked on indigenous-rights issues in the 1970s and presently directs the Catholic feminist organization Women for Dialogue, was recruited by the JCFM in the early 1940s and traces her inspiration to combine religion and social work to the organization.[74]

The church's survival strategy in post-revolutionary Mexico prioritized clarification and regulation of distinct roles for clergy, women and men religious, and laity. Church leaders identified laywomen as the sustainers of religious and moral practices within the home, and this was their central contribution to the ACM's "secular help for the hierarchy."[75] Church leaders in Mexico emphasized the regulation of Catholic practices among women, seeking to avoid aberrations like the BF and the UNS. Toward the end of the 1930s, the Mexican church hierarchy again emphasized the UFCM's and JFCM's moral content over their community roles, highlighting the complementary role that Catholic women's groups should play to those of men. Overall, Mexican church leaders remained ambivalent about women's public activities. Bishops and clergy recognized the desperate need for Catholic women's activity at a time when the clergy's capacity to act was limited and laymen's support was low, and some applauded women's accomplishments. But others insisted on limited roles for women in the church and in society. Church leaders asked Catholic women to work actively for the church yet remain obedient and unchallenging in their participation—not unlike some radical and state leaders studied elsewhere in this volume.

In great part, the UFCM and JCFM answered this expectation and did not overtly challenge Catholic paradigms for women. Many loyally supported the church hierarchy after the 1929 peace accords and were rarely linked to violent protests or support for the UNS and other dissidents. Their work helped to offset Mexican women's defection to anticlerical government

Gendering the Faith

programs or radical groups. Church leaders' one constant complaint regarding the ACM was that women outnumbered men and were more active, which problematized their portrayal as ancillaries or auxiliaries. Through the ACM's peak in the 1950s, women's membership eclipsed that of men's and formed its "most forceful nuclei."[76]

Nevertheless, the boundaries of Catholic women's social and civic engagement had expanded during the post-revolutionary period, both according to the needs of the times and according to women's inclinations. The public-private divide offered by the Mexican church in the early twentieth century and reinscribed following violent conflicts and social upheaval domesticated neither Catholic religious practice as a whole nor women's participation in it. It was not meant to do the former completely; even negotiation-oriented church leaders like Pascual Díaz Barreto demanded that lay Catholics stand up, albeit cautiously, against government policies that affronted the church. Paralleling some secular women's movements, these calls to action mobilized a significant number of lay Catholic women to engage in activities that overstepped the boundaries of both the domestic realm and the law. In their continued testing of the limits of the revolutionary regime's laws, these women provided much of the force of the "everyday" but essential resistance that wore down the will of many Mexican radicals and officials to press the anticlerical program.[77]

Although it remains difficult to quantify the impact of the UFCM on post-revolutionary Mexican political or legal affairs, they clearly formed an organized, energetic, and critical part of opposition campaigns against socialist education, the one area in which Catholic resistance won a clear victory. Other policies and practices that the church opposed—including land reform, agrarian mobilization, and government control over church properties and the presence of its clergy—remained in effect throughout the period and beyond, though they were gradually eased. Catholic schools cautiously opened, clergy and women and men religious slowly emerged into public life, and Catholics engaged in more public religious practices, processes visible in the long term but difficult to attribute exclusively to individual efforts.

Catholic women's activism consisted of more than a mechanical response of a small elite to the mandates of its canonical leadership. Though couched in conservative rhetoric, it provided women with opportunities to change conditions, not only in homes and churches but also in schools, workplaces, and streets. Many realized that there would be no return to the pre-revolutionary social order that some of their leaders desired, but saw room for adaptation in post-revolutionary Mexico. Catholic women activists' actions pushed the boundaries of public discourse and of women's—even Catholic women's—spaces. They helped join the religious and social traditions of Mexico's past to its post-revolutionary present and set Mexican society on a course different from those imagined by both revolutionary and church leaders.

Notes

1. María Guadalupe Díaz and Elpidia Solís de Díaz, tape-recorded and transcribed interview by author, Tizapán el Alto, Jalisco, 14 March 1997. All interviews herein cited were tape-recorded and transcribed. For the entirely secular version of the song, see Lerner 1979, 106.

2. Thompson 1988, 137–38.

3. María Guadalupe Díaz and Elpidia Solís de Díaz, interview by author, Tizapán el Alto, Jalisco, 14 March 1997; for agrarian organizing in Jalisco see Craig 1983.

4. Castells 1999b, 378, 411.

5. The phrase is Michel de Certeau's, quoted in David Harvey 1993, 214.

6. Fowler-Salamini and Vaughan 1994, xxii; Knight 1996, 317.

7. Throughout I use James C. Scott's explorations of forms of resistance available to subordinates (1990); Doreen Massey's articulations of gendered spaces assigned to women (1994); Christine E. Gudorf's analysis of women's participation in religious movements and "repatriarchalization" (1983); and David Harvey's understandings of how different forms of spatialization can inhibit or facilitate processes of social change (1993, 206).

8. Eph. 5:23–24. For criticism, culled from multiple sources, see Castells 1999a (23).

9. Quoted by María Refugio H. de Puga (CIDOC, microfiche no. 2354, "La socia de la UFCM en el hogar y en las costumbres sociales," *Segunda Asamblea Diocesana*, León, Guanajuato, 14–16 October 1935, 6). Mary Vincent finds the same quote, from Msgr. Luigi Civardi's *Manual of Catholic Action*, used by right-wing Spanish women in the 1930s (1990, 112).

10. Werth, Mihanovich, and Mihanovich 1955, 41–43.

11. Miller 1981, 322.

12. De Grazia 1992, 11, 22. De Grazia examines Catholic Action as one of the roots of women's fascist organizing in 1920s and 1930s Italy.

13. Vincent 1990, 114–19.

14. These terms were used repeatedly by church leaders. See Civardi 1935 for citations spanning forty years.

15. AHUFCM, I Asamblea General (1932), Goribar de Cortina, "Restauración Cristiana de la Familia," 1–10; AHUFCM, II Asamblea General (1934), "Informe," 1–2; AHUFCM, III Asamblea General (1936), "Informe," 3, 11; AHUFCM, IV Asamblea General (1938), "Informe," 1–2.

16. Miller 1984, 304.

17. Arrom 1985, 34; Adame Goddard 1981, 20–27; Ceballos Ramírez 1991.

18. Ceballos Ramírez 1991, 123; Hanson 1994, 175–78; Miller 1984, 304; Vaca García 1998, 196.

19. For this judgment see Gotschall 1970, 153; for Catholic women's labor organizations see Fernández-Aceves in this volume.

20. "La UDCM en el 20 Aniversario de su Fundación" 1933, 3–4; "Orígenes de las Damas Católicas" 1937, 7, 16–17; Hanson 1994, 180–86; Hanson 1997, 3–11; for Guadalajara see Dávila Garibi 1920.

21. AHUFCM, Sección de Correspondencia, Serie Liga Internacional Católica Femenina, caja 13.

22. Enthronements were popularized by the Jesuits in the nineteenth century (McSweeney 1980, 49–50).

23. Schell 1999. For alternatives to marriage imagined by revolutionary Mexicans see Smith in this volume.

24. Bliss 1997; Hanson 1997, 14–15; Hanson 1994, 407; Miller 1984, 304–5; O'Dogherty Madrazo 1991; Schell 1999.

25. Hanson 1997, 17–22.

26. Meyer 1973–1974, 2:146–47, 2:289–91, 3:124; Tuck 1982, 23–25, 37–38, 101–3; Vaca García 1998, 242.

27. Meyer 1973–1974, 1:60–62, 3:120–22; Miller 1981, 60–61; O'Dogherty Madrazo 1991, 153–54; Vaca García 1998, 197–98, 214, 238, 242.

28. Jesús Flores Gollaz [Flores's and Gollaz's son], interview by author, Guadalajara, Jalisco, 28 April 1997; Miller 1981, 29, 68–69. Interestingly, there are similarities between the structure of the BF and subsequent organizations like the UFCM and that of the women's organizations of the Mexican Communist Party (see Olcott in this volume).

29. Jesús Flores Gollaz, interview by author, Guadalajara, Jalisco, 28 April 1997. Vaca García 1998, 258–59.

30. Meyer 1973–1974, 3:122–23; Miller 1981, 70–74, 86, 92–95; Tuck 1982, 103; Vaca García 1998, 245–54. The Guadalupan Legion later mobilized women to support the Segunda Cristiada, the Second Cristero Rebellion of the 1930s (Miller 1981, 117).

31. James C. Scott 1990, 104, 107; Jesús Flores Gollaz, interview by author, Guadalajara, Jalisco, 28 April 1997; Tuck 1982, 103.

32. AHAM, Fondo Pascual Díaz Barreto, gabinete 197, folleto 69, "Brigadas Femeninas"; Miller 1981, 115.

33. "Agradecimiento," 1930.

34. AHAM-PDB, Fondo Pascual Díaz Barreto, gabinete 197, folleto 69, "Brigadas Femeninas," G. Aguilar to P. Díaz Barreto, 28 June 1929; G. Aguilar to the Secretaria Episcopal, 8 October 1929.

35. "Importantísimo," 1931; for additional reprimands, see "La Acción Católica y la Acción Política," 1931.

36. For UFCM statistics see below; AHAM, caja Acción Católica, folleto 74–71, L. G. Oñate and M. Buelna to L. M. Martínez, 12 September 1939.

37. Miller 1981, 99–100; Vaca García 1998, 275–77.

38. Jesús Flores Gollaz, interview by author, Guadalajara, Jalisco, 28 April 1997.

39. For a critical perspective on this independence see Tromp 1937. Also see Proyecto de Historia Oral, Instituto Nacional de Antropología e Historia–Instituto de Investigaciones Históricas y Instituto de Investigaciones Dr. Jose Maria Luis

Mora, PHO/4/11, Alicia Olivera de Bonfil, interview by Sofía Del Valle, Mexico City, 3 November 1972 and 14 February 1973; Méndez 1980.

40. AHUFCM, II Asamblea General (1934), "Informe," 3; AHUFCM, II Asamblea General (1934), "Reglamento de Centros en el extranjero"; AHUFCM, III Asamblea General (1936), "Informe," 12; AHUFCM, IV Asamblea General (1938), "Informe," 1; AHUFCM, V Asamblea General [1940], CIDOC, microfiche no. 2347, 23.

41. AHUFCM, I Asamblea General (1932), María Luisa Hernández, "La instrucción como fundamento de las socias de la UFCM"; AHUFCM, III Asamblea General (1936), "Informe," 10; AHUFCM, IV Asamblea General (1938), "Informe," 7. Also "M." 1937; María del Rosario Ortíz de Salazar, interview by author, Guadalajara, Jalisco, 7 May 1997.

42. Cano 1991a, 284; Macías 1982, 142; E. Tuñón Pablos 1992, 111. However, Jocelyn H. Olcott (2000 and this volume) and Stephanie Mitchell (2002) stress that the FUPDM does not account for all progressive secular women's organizing, especially in rural areas.

43. AHUFCM, III Asamblea General (1936), "Informe del Comité Central"; for more detail see Boylan 2000.

44. Arnold 1973, 50, 60–64; Boylan 2000, chap. 4; Contreras 1940.

45. USDOS, 812.404/1912; AHUFCM, III Asamblea General (1936), "Informe," 10; AHUFCM, IV Asamblea General (1938), "Informe," 7; María del Rosario Ortíz de Salazar, interview by author, Guadalajara, Jalisco, 7 May 1997.

46. "Circular No. 8" 1937; AHUFCM, III Asamblea General (1936), "Informe," 7, 9–10; AHUFCM, IV Asamblea General (1938), "Informe," 10–11. For state efforts see Lerner 1979.

47. AHUFCM, II Asamblea General (1934), "Informe," 8; AHUFCM, III Asamblea General (1936), "Informe," 9.

48. Torres Septien 1992; "Conclusiones aprobadas" 1935; Lerner 1979, 10, 41, 44–45, 70, 82.

49. AHUFCM, II Asamblea General (1934), "Informe"; Episcopado Mexicano 1935.

50. Lerner 1979, 39; SSM, Carpeta *Episcopado–Informes, 1924–1931*, Miguel Dario Miranda, "Seis Años de Actividades del Secretariado Social Mexicano, 1925–1931"; AHUFCM, III Asamblea General (1936), "Informe." For school attendance figures see *Sexto Censo General de la Nación* 1940, 4. Also see *New York Times*, 25 November 1934, sec. 1, p. 18; USMIL, Military Attaché, Mexico, report no. 5677, 30 October 1934.

51. Miller 1981, 135–38; Proyecto de Historia Oral, Instituto Nacional de Antropología e Historia–Instituto de Investigaciones Históricas y Instituto de Investigaciones Dr. Jose Maria Luis Mora, PHO/4/11, Alicia Olivera de Bonfil, interview by Sofía Del Valle, Mexico City, 3 November 1972 and 14 February 1973.

52. Consuelo Ardila, RSJC, interview by author, Guadalajara, Jalisco, 16 November 1996; María del Rosario Alejandre Gil, interview by author, Guadalajara, Jalisco, 13 May 1997; Parsons 1936, 73–75, 120–22; SSM, Carpeta *Episcopado–Informes, 1924–1931*, J. Aviña L., "Datos sobre la actual persecución religiosa . . . ," 27 March 1935; SSM, Carpeta *Episcopado–Informes, 1924–1931*, J. Aviña L., "Informe rendido . . . acerca de las actividades docentes de algunas Casas Religiosas," 2 May 1935.

53. *Mexicano* 1968, 24–26 art. 3, 331–33 art. 130.

54. Galindo Mendoza 1945, 22; Parsons 1936, 254–57; Vera 1998, 22–27; Salvador Sandoval Godoy, interview by author, Guadalajara, Jalisco, 14 June 1997.

55. *Mexicano* 1968, 89 art. 24; on enthronements as symbolic opposition against state and radical agents in the 1930s see Becker 1995, chap. 4.

56. AHUFCM, I Asamblea General (1932), R. Goribar de Cortina, "Restauración Cristiana de la Familia"; AHUFCM, I Asamblea General (1932), Hernández, "La Instrucción como fundamento." See also Smith in this volume.

57. Tuñón 1999, 100; F. Orozco y Jiménez, 1930.

58. USMIL, Military Attaché, report no. 3686, 18 December 1931; USMIL, Military Attaché, report no. 3697, 29 December 1931; USDOS, 812.404/1074 (1931); USDOS, 812.404/1945–1950; *New York Times*, February and March 1937.

59 "La UFCM en Ocotlán" 1940.

60. Miller 1981, 117; Meyer 1973–1974, 1:329–83.

61. Aguilar V. and Zermeño P. 1992, 17–30; Meyer 1979.

62. Knight 1991, 293–95; Prewett 1941, 155.

63. Pérez Rosales 1992.

64. As cited by Morton 1962, 13.

65. Robles de Mendoza 1931, 84; Macías 1982, 142. For more detail on Mexican women's suffrage campaigns see Olcott in this volume.

66. Paredes 1937.

67. María del Carmen Solano Vega, interview by author, Guadalajara, Jalisco, 27 May and 13 June 1997; Macías 1982, 144; Sherman 1997, 119, 126.

68. Barbara Welter identified this mentality of double standards for women as it developed in the nineteenth-century United States (1966).

69. Massey (1994), 179–80.

70. See the essays in this volume, especially those by Blum, Schell, and Smith.

71. Fazio 1997, 9.

72. Gudorf 1983, 233.

73. Carole Ann Drogus makes this case for Brazilian women activists of the 1930s, whose actions created an environment in which the teachings of liberation theology could be developed and spread in later years (1997, 12, 15, 27–28).

74. Dussel 1981; Galán G. 1947; Fazio 1997; Velázquez H. 1978, 17–22; Escontrilla Valdez 2000, 56–58; Leonor Aida Concha, interview by author, Mexico City, 12 November 1996.

75. Gudorf 1983, 235; "Ayuda laica a la jerarquía" 1937.

76. Pérez Rosales 1992, 172, 179–80; Barranco V. 1996, 64–65.

77. This follows James C. Scott's formula of effective hidden resistance, with one key difference: these women helped *resacralize* rather than *desacralize* public space (1990, 193–97). It may be that criticisms of institutional authority and fundamentalism have dominated theoreticians' understanding of religion (see also Castells 1999a, 12–27), given these two authors' indications that such actions are negative. More work is needed to explore cross-culturally the varieties of religious experience and the positive attributes of people mobilizing to practice as they please.

KRISTINA A. BOYLAN

The Center Cannot Hold

Women on Mexico's Popular Front

JOCELYN OLCOTT

I n May 1937 Anne Kelton Wiley, a member of the U.S. National Woman's Party and an activist in the Equal Rights Amendment movement,
traveled through central Mexico with the well-heeled suffragist Margarita
Robles de Mendoza as her guide. Her tour culminated in Mexico City,
where, in a speech to a small audience of twenty-five members of the Sole
Front for Women's Rights (FUPDM), she held up the "drama and frightful
effort" of the U.S. suffrage movement as an example for its Mexican
counterpart.[1] María del Refugio "Cuca" García, a longtime communist
militant and the FUPDM's secretary-general, responded with a mix of gratitude for Wiley's solidarity and of resentment at her implication that
Mexican women had not yet demonstrated the courage of their convictions, and she pointed out that although the U.S. suffragists offered
inspiration, the FUPDM struggled in the context of a "semi-colonial country." Women "helped make the revolution," García explained to the foreign visitor. "The gunpowder from the battlefields passed through our
hair many times without making us turn back, but the government of our
country, when the revolution was ended and they had taken advantage
of our services, sent us home, saying that the place of a woman is in
her home."[2]

García's thinly veiled antipathy emerged from her own encounter with
Mexican electoral politics. With the organizational and financial support

of the Mexican Communist Party (PCM), García and another FUPDM member, Soledad Orozco Ávila, had campaigned for and reportedly won nominations as National Revolutionary Party (PNR) congressional candidates, but the PNR refused to seat them, citing ongoing disputes about women's citizenship status. García's bitterness belied the language of unity that characterized most FUPDM interventions. "I was nominated for the Federal Congress by 10,000 votes, but was not allowed to take my seat," she explained. "I wish to make this promise as a fighter for my rights. I do not care for the decisions of the National Revolutionary Party. The National Revolutionary Party does not represent the will of the people. I will go back to my District for the June elections because the people will back me. This shows that the people are with the women and, helped by them, we will open the doors of Congress to all the country's women."[3]

García's strident insistence reflected the accumulated challenges to gendered practices and ideologies since the revolution. Men and women in both reality and representation inhabited a range of gendered identities during the 1920s and 1930s. Cultural renderings, often self-consciously didactic and polemical, offered novel images of womanhood in which women transgressed the ascribed femininity of self-sacrificing motherhood and traditional piety, but remained women. They carried guns, read books, worked shoulder-to-shoulder with their *compañeros*, and unswervingly supported the newly progressive post-revolutionary government. Although notable largely for contrasting with dominant depictions of *rebozo*-draped, subjugated, and pious women, new archetypes of femininity—the workingwoman, the self-possessed *indígena*, the modern girl, and the suffragist—joined those of the camp follower and the abnegated mother.

These representations emerged not from the imaginations of artists and writers but from the heterogeneous array of women's organizations that proliferated in the wake of the revolution. Against a backdrop of mass mobilization and elastic femininity, women's political organizing entered what some scholars have dubbed the golden age of women's activism. Offering a tentatively affirmative answer to the question of whether the Mexican Revolution galvanized the nation's women *as women*, feminist scholars have often pointed to the 1935 formation of the FUPDM.[4] Culminating two decades of feminist militancy—from the 1916 feminist congresses to the National Congresses of Women Workers and Peasants of the early 1930s—this federation bridged the ideological and partisan divides of the 1920s and early 1930s, and endeavored to fashion a national women's movement.

The emphasis on the FUPDM, however, has left students of Mexican women's activism with a central conundrum: why, at a moment of unprecedented strength and consolidation, did women fail to secure their principal objective of suffrage rights? The coincidence of FUPDM-fostered unity and the exasperating deferral of suffrage may not be as paradoxical as it seems. What at the time appeared to be the crowning victory for the Mexican women's movement in fact marked the beginning of its decline. The FUPDM's consolidation and political incorporation defanged and straitjacketed what had been a multivocal and often radical women's movement. Within the FUPDM, women activists attenuated their critiques of government policies as they struggled to establish their credentials as "good citizens" and loyal supporters of the new regime.

Given these constraints, the front failed to secure even suffrage, the goal that most unified the organization's leadership. For suffrage, with its foundations in liberalism, links to a masculinized conception of citizenship, and implicit validation of existing political practices, remained among the least disruptive of the women's demands. Most women called for greater recognition of and relief from their arduous reproductive labors of bearing and raising children, nursing and feeding family members, and maintaining households and communities. Many sought gender equity in labor and land reforms, including wage parity and collective plots for organized women. A few even advocated for a wholesale revision in the gender ideologies that undergirded Mexican society, questioning the sexual, social, and political practices that reinforced Mexican patriarchy. Women activists debated demands such as mothers' wages and a quota system granting equal government representation, making voting rights seem a relatively modest request. With its 1938 incorporation into the ruling party, however, the FUPDM not only closed down the dissent and debate that had sparked many activists' commitment and dynamism during the 1920s and early 1930s but also rendered the organization strategically incapacitated when post-revolutionary leaders failed to honor their promises.

The answer to the conundrum presented earlier rests largely on the reconfiguration of citizenship during the late 1930s.[5] Between the armed struggle and the late 1930s, the marker of civic engagement had shifted from the ability to mobilize constituencies to the ability to demonstrate loyalty to the post-revolutionary regime. Women failed to secure suffrage because the FUPDM—by 1937 the focal point of suffragist activism—had relinquished the leverage of a dissenting organization and because, particularly after the ruling party's restructuring along corporatist lines, individual voting rights seemed irrelevant to women's most pressing concerns.

The Center Cannot Hold

Cardenismo, the Popular Front, and the Political Culture of Organizing

Three factors contributed to activists' decision to form the FUPDM: support for women's organizing within the government of Lázaro Cárdenas (1934–40), the Mexican Communist Party's 1935 commitment to form the Popular Front, and activists' own frustration with the division and discord that characterized early 1930s efforts to fashion a national women's movement. These three elements provide crucial context for understanding the organization's eventual inefficacy and the conditions under which women activists fostered and strove to maintain unity.

Alarmed by the vitality of Catholic women's organizing, the ruling PNR sponsored a series of national congresses during the early 1930s to encourage secular women's organizing. The congresses, however, became battlegrounds for combat between PNR women (*penerristas*) and those of the semi-clandestine PCM. The former feared that women's needs would always receive short shrift within larger, male-dominated organizations, while the latter argued that all-women's organizations would divide revolutionary movements and ultimately remain marginalized and powerless. At the 1931 congress, penerrista organizer María Ríos Cárdenas (no relation to the president) advocated a unified feminist organization, arguing, "Syndicalism, having conquered many benefits for workers, does not resolve women's problems. We need purely feminine organizations that are made by and for us."[6] Communists, challenging the existence of a "feminine class," saw only those allied with the exploited and those allied with the exploiters.[7] Each side repeatedly accused the other of betraying Mexican women to serve the interests of their respective parties.

Second, a political culture of organizing emerged in Mexico during the 1930s. Beginning with the PNR's 1929 founding and accelerating during the Cárdenas presidency, the post-revolutionary government encouraged popular organizing to shore up its legitimacy. Organizing, in this sense, connoted both enabling and disciplining political activism. The Cárdenas government constructed an institutional infrastructure that simultaneously created openings for traditionally disenfranchised groups and closely circumscribed their activities.[8] Cárdenas advanced women's activism, vocally supporting women's social, economic, and political rights during his campaign and throughout his presidency. Most importantly for FUPDM organizers, the Cardenistas fashioned a corporatist state, wherein official institutions would represent "interest groups" of labor, peasants, the military, and the "popular sector." As a result, groups scurried to establish their credentials as "organized" entities that would enjoy recognition as legitimate representatives, necessarily flattening identities to reflect the official mapping of social groups. The PNR's 1938 reorganization into the Party of the Mexican Revolution (PRM) marked the political culmination of this transition to corporatism.

For its part, the Communist Party hailed the PRM as the institutionalization of the Popular Front. The PCM's dramatic volte-face with its 1935 adoption of the Popular Front strategy provides the third important contextual element for understanding the FUPDM's creation and eventual dissolution.[9] By then, the mounting threat of fascism and other counterrevolutionary and antirevolutionary movements both in Mexico and abroad fostered the sense that the proliferation and fragmentation of left-leaning organizations had become dangerously counterproductive. Analogous to the relationship between the Mexican Labor Confederation (CTM) and the labor movement, the FUPDM, created just one month after the Comintern congress proclaimed the Popular Front campaign, brought together a broad swath of women from the ruling party, the PCM, and other center-left organizations. Intensifying its "boring from within" strategy, the PCM trained organizers to enlist women into the PNR and promote welfare-state programs, such as school breakfasts, universal child care, and postnatal health services, pushing the ruling party toward the PCM's political priorities.[10] The Popular Front strategy inspired optimism in the PCM, which envisioned a coalition government like Leon Blum's in France.[11]

Within four years, communist women activists had redefined their relationship to the governing regime, from lambasting the ruling party to promoting its hegemonic control. The progressive leanings of the Cardenistas, the cooperative spirit of the PCM's Popular Front campaign, and the promise of making significant gains in women's rights and opportunities induced leading women activists to put aside their differences. The FUPDM leadership, however, found itself caught between two masters —the expectation of mobilization and the imperative to demonstrate allegiance. The PCM, which had once mandated that the women within its ranks reject all ruling-party overtures, now insisted that they embrace the post-revolutionary regime. In adopting this strategy, communist women activists found themselves on a path of less resistance, but no less under the thumb of male officials and partisan politics.

Structures and Strategies

The FUPDM adopted the PCM's organizational structures and the PNR's emphasis on building a cross-class, women-only membership to pursue a two-pronged strategy of fighting for both immediate gains, such as motorized corn mills and land reform, and the long-term political aims of securing suffrage and combating fascism.[12] The leadership remained dominated by communist militants, with Cuca García, long the instigator of anti-PNR attacks, at the helm. This combination of communist organizational discipline and the ruling party's big-tent politics united a broad array of women's groups under the FUPDM's umbrella.

Building a united front required more than simply rewriting organizing priorities. Women like Cuca García and Ana María Hernández, who had spent the first half of the decade exchanging barbs, found themselves making common cause as members of the front's original executive committee. Even the FUPDM's cultural aspect marked a significant departure for communists. While PCM meetings often included folk songs, revolutionary ballads, and the "International," violin and vocal compositions of contemporary European composers punctuated the FUPDM's inaugural plenary.

The organization's main objectives—women's suffrage and opposition to fascism—occupied the common ground between these two parties that had so often opposed one another. These twin goals reflected not only the Comintern's 1935 resolutions but also mirrored Cárdenas's commitment to women's political rights and growing concerns about fascism, which intensified with the 1935 conflicts with the Gold Shirts and the 1937 founding of the fascist National Sinarquista Union.[13] By making women's suffrage and antifascism their top aims, FUPDM leaders participated in linking fears about women's political rights to the rise of fascism, but inverted the argument to contend that only through state incorporation could women fend off fascism.[14] They argued that women were, in fact, indispensable to challenging the fascist threat.

In keeping with penerrista preference, the FUPDM was run by and for women. Its range of associations allowed it to count on broad support in its struggle for public resources. When, for example, Cuca García demanded public funding for the FUPDM-organized May First Maternity Clinic in Mexico City, she secured endorsements ranging from the communist-dominated railroad workers' union to the elite, feminist Union of American Women. The confederation bolstered its legitimacy by promoting the temperance and public-health campaigns that enjoyed widespread support and coincided with women's traditional duties.

The FUPDM adopted three organizing strategies to integrate its immediate and long-term objectives. First, it self-consciously developed organizing structures, establishing committees, cultivating leadership and solidarity ties, and formulating agendas for mobilization. Second, the front maintained a sensitivity to local contexts and needs, allowing local leaders to serve as intermediaries between rank-and-file membership and national entities. As the organization's magazine explained, "In every place where a group of the FUPDM is installed, we must struggle for the local demands of particular interest to women . . . always linking these demands with those contained in the general program."[15] The headquarters remained in Mexico City, but the national office dispatched organizers throughout the country. Finally, the FUPDM maintained transnational connections, cultivating alliances abroad among other communist and Popular Front organizations, feminist groups such as the U.S. National Woman's Party, and multilateral organizations such as the League of Nations and the Pan-American Union.

The Local and the Global

The organization claimed a membership of 35,000 in 1936 and 50,000 by 1939.[16] These figures doubtless exaggerated the front's size, but, much like the ruling party's membership accounting, they represented an expansive understanding of the confederation's membership as including the members of all affiliated organizations. These membership claims—even ignoring the question of their credibility—masked wide variations in the meanings of front membership in different parts of the republic. Some chapters maintained closer ties to the PCM, and others to the ruling party. Local economies and political climates defined the possibilities available to front activists. Cities, ports, agricultural collectives, and rural villages all had different objectives for establishing FUPDM chapters.

The front's complexion as a national confederation reflected local politics and cultures as much as the agenda of the FUPDM headquarters in Mexico City. Local chapters often made potentially more disruptive demands than women's suffrage, provoking substantial and occasionally violent resistance when they sought control over tools of production, access to cultivable land, and limitations on patriarchal privileges. The FUPDM chapter in Tenabo, Campeche—a southeastern state dominated by a rural, ethnically Maya population—reported that local authorities had imprisoned and "savagely stripped and beaten" one FUPDM officer.[17]

In the port city of Salina Cruz, Oaxaca, meanwhile, the FUPDM worked closely with CTM dock workers' and petroleum workers' unions, which supported FUPDM protests against rampant inflation and its efforts to secure better working-class housing.[18] However, the sixty FUPDM members who demanded employment in the traditionally male space of the docks met with CTM resistance. "There are jobs in the loading-dock offices," they wrote to President Cárdenas, "that women could fill with greater efficiency, such as the positions of wholesaler, time keeper, and squad leader." They argued that they should not be denied these jobs "for the sole fact of not being recognized as a union."[19] Subsequently, the organization's officers insisted "that the unions, employers, and workers in general understand that women have the right to work" and "that women workers not be the object of harassment and evasions."[20]

Similar experiences played out in many contexts, despite PCM and government support for wage-earning women. FUPDM activists generally garnered more support from male allies when they remained within the realm of domestic concerns such as food prices and housing standards. When they transgressed these boundaries, they often encountered "harassment and evasions." The Salina Cruz organizers also highlighted the importance of official recognition. Although FUPDM members viewed themselves as an organized group meriting the attendant benefits, CTM members clearly saw them as encroaching on their territory and undermining union control.

The creation of the FUPDM's Acapulco chapter similarly demonstrated the importance not only of official recognition but also of unity and internationalism. Acapulco, Mexico's largest Pacific-coast port, had incubated radical politics since before the revolution.[21] In 1934, only days after delivering campaign speeches that endorsed the arming of Guerrero's agrarian radicals and lambasted "voracious capitalism," Cárdenas founded a chapter of the National Feminine League.[22] The following year, under the leadership of the tireless activist María de la O, the ninety-six founding members of the Union of Revolutionary Women of Acapulco allied with that port's male-dominated stevedores and day-laborers union as well as other women's labor unions such as the Syndicate of Red Women.[23] By March 1936, however, divisions within the National Feminine League precipitated an organizational split, creating the rival First Red National Feminine League of Acapulco (hereafter, the Red League), which identified itself as a "leftist" women's organization.[24]

A month after the Red League's creation, FUPDM activists arrived from Mexico City to bring peace among Acapulco's estranged women's organizations. Ofelia Domínguez Navarro, a communist and Cuban national representing the FUPDM's Mexico City offices, relied on local teachers and organizers to call on "women without distinctions of political or religious creeds, [to] unify on the basis of this solidarity pact, through which they will be able to struggle for their demands."[25] To promote unity, the governing body included delegates from each member organization, which pledged to organize FUPDM locals throughout the state. The organizers laid out a wide-ranging program that included issues as varied as opposing inflation and discounted women's wages; agitating for maternity clinics and labor laws compatible with childbearing; and taking stances against "humiliating treaties," the payment of the national debt, and "imperialist war." Using an arsenal of press campaigns, demonstrations, and "any act that [would] procure the mobilization of the greatest number of women," the chapter echoed the PCM priorities of combating fascism and "capitalist imperialism." To cement the peace, the new confederation organized a "solidarity meal" the following Sunday.

The strategy of integrating campaigns for local, tangible gains with international objectives such as fighting imperialism defined the FUPDM and the Popular Front. For Domínguez, one newspaper explained, "as for any good socialist, borders and nationalities do not exist."[26] Not only did expatriate activists like Domínguez organize in Mexico, but FUPDM leaders also attended international women's congresses and maintained international networks of contacts with like-minded women's organizations that supported its efforts. This web of connections, from neighborhood meetings to ruling-party conferences to transcontinental congresses, reinforced the organizers' roles as intermediaries among these different levels, giving them legitimacy as negotiators of women's rights.

FUPDM activists often became political brokers between communities and the government. Setting up production cooperatives, improving labor conditions, and procuring motorized corn mills and potable water garnered allegiance among rank-and-file members. In turn, the organizers' ability to mobilize large numbers of women behind government-sponsored programs promoting school attendance, family nutrition, and community-sanitation campaigns endowed the FUPDM leadership with the political capital to lobby the administration on issues of particular importance to its membership. Consistent mobilization and personal connections enabled the organization to gain endorsements from political leaders at the highest levels.

Many FUPDM leaders had already held positions as intermediaries between policymakers and grassroots women's organizations. Having worked as public schoolteachers, they drew on the John Dewey–inspired "action pedagogy" training received in normal school and used their positions as teachers and organizers to promote the FUPDM. Not surprisingly, FUPDM petitions nearly always included requests to fund school improvements, objectives that probably more closely reflected the organizers' priorities than the members'. Furthermore, the front maintained close ties to the PCM-influenced teachers' unions and the Ministry of Public Education (SEP). By 1937, the job description for the secretary of women's affairs of the Yucatán teachers' union included the directive "To struggle for the ideological preparation of women within the [union]. To advocate for equal constitutional rights for men and women. To struggle so that the female membership of the [union] supports the FUPDM, each [female teacher] being an organizer for the same among the laboring and peasant classes."[27] Many FUPDM endeavors such as congresses and cooperatives utilized the SEP's bureaucratic structures, and the SEP acknowledged that its only real success in organizing women and youth had been in "collaboration with already established organisms" such as the Socialist Youth and the FUPDM.[28]

While each FUPDM local took on regional characteristics, the central demands of healthcare, temperance regulations, labor-saving devices, support for cooperatives, and school improvements remained nearly uniform throughout the country. These issues held a central place in FUPDM organizing programs not only because most women genuinely favored them but also because they enjoyed explicit government endorsement. The organizations' programs thus developed through a process of negotiation that accommodated both members' cooperation and state support. FUPDM activists, many of them communists and fellow travelers, carefully navigated the terrain between rank-and-file members and the policy objectives of the PCM and the ruling party.

Much like the PCM during these years, the FUPDM leadership struggled with its ambivalent relationship to the post-revolutionary regime, trying to maintain autonomy while enjoying the legitimacy that accompanied cooperation and a more mainstream presence in the political culture. To be sure, cracks occasionally appeared in the façade of unity, as when Cuca García critiqued the PNR. This tension between ambivalence and unity became more pronounced as the FUPDM increasingly centered its efforts on the struggle for women's suffrage and endeavored to navigate the murky terrain of revolutionary citizenship. In the post-revolutionary decades, policymakers and public intellectuals linked three masculinized experiences with citizenship: military service, wage labor, and political activism. During the second half of the 1930s, secular women activists endeavored to define women's compulsory service, unpaid labor, and political activism as equivalent markers of citizenship.[29]

Suffrage on the Popular Front

In an August 1937 speech in the port of Veracruz, Cárdenas declared his support for women's full citizenship rights, including the rights to vote. and be elected to public office. The FUPDM, seeing an imminent strategic victory and following the Popular Front's embrace of electoral politics, threw itself wholeheartedly behind its suffrage campaign. Given the organization's strength and size and the president's open support, success seemed near at hand. Telegrams poured into both the presidential residence at Los Pinos and the FUPDM offices, offering premature congratulations on having won the suffrage battle. This victory, however, proved illusory; women would not vote in a federal election until 1958.

The FUPDM's stance reflected the communists' "Unity at Any Cost" campaign, and the perceived opportunity for meaningful and legitimated political participation created a strong incentive to achieve consensus within the FUPDM to gain a place at the corporatist bargaining table alongside the CTM and the Mexican Peasant Confederation. Following a February 1938 women's congress, the FUPDM joined several other prominent women's organizations in stating, "Unification is of the highest importance. . . . [It] is the solution to our needs."[30] With each step that the suffrage bill took toward passage and each overture that the Cárdenas administration made to give organized women a voice in decision making, FUPDM leaders increasingly shifted their strategy from militant demonstrations and hunger strikes to establishing themselves as responsible, reasonable political actors working within the official channels established by the post-revolutionary regime. They seemed certain that gaining their long-sought-after political rights required only that they prove their fidelity.

Meanwhile, in an effort to demonstrate its discipline, the FUPDM leadership marginalized dissenting voices. Leading activists such as Juana Belén Gutiérrez de Mendoza and Concha Michel, who called for increased mobilization rather than an emphasis on political rights, found themselves pushed to the confederation's periphery.[31] To Gutiérrez de Mendoza and Michel, emphasis on suffrage rights simply imitated fruitless, masculine approaches to political and social change. Many other activists did not openly dissent from the FUPDM's suffrage agenda, but neither did they engage it. Particularly in rural areas, the ballot box remained a less-important instrument of change than more informal political tools such as patronage networks and public demonstrations.

While the elusive objective of women's suffrage guided the FUPDM's leadership in Mexico City, many regional chapters continued to focus on more immediate goals, such as establishing production cooperatives and obtaining basic medical care. Even as the leaders in Mexico City demonstrated in front of Los Pinos, FUPDM organizations from the Yucatán peninsula wrote to Cárdenas during his regional tour, issuing petitions that overwhelmingly ignored the suffrage issue. The predominantly indigenous women of the FUPDM in Chichimilá, Yucatán, solicited a first-aid kit, electrical service, a corn mill, and three sewing machines, but did

The Center Cannot Hold

not mention suffrage among their demands.[32] Similarly, the indigenous FUPDM members in Hampolol, Campeche, pointed to the social and economic rights that the Cardenista revolutionary ideology ascribed to their class rather than demanding formal political rights. Describing the FUPDM of that community as "totally unified in struggling for the social and economic improvement of our husbands and children and likewise in supporting your government," they requested support for a women's hat-making cooperative, "since women are an indispensable factor in the class struggle and in the vanguard of the Revolution."[33] Apparently, when the FUPDM chapters in the Yucatán had the president's ear during his regional tour, they emphasized not the suffrage battle that captured headlines in Mexico City, but rather their own local concerns and contributions to constructing a "revolutionary" society. Invoking the prevailing political rhetoric, they made claims as workers—and thus as revolutionary citizens —supporting the regime's cooperative-building agenda.

Although suffrage demands did not remain absent from FUPDM concerns outside Mexico City, a corollary existed between urbanization and emphasis on suffrage. FUPDM locals in port cities and state capitals often included the right to vote among their priorities, with the women of Tepic, Nayarit, referring in 1939 to suffrage as "one of the things we need most."[34] While FUPDM chapters in municipal seats, smaller towns, and *ejidos* occasionally included suffrage among their demands, more immediate issues such as health care and land tenure generally received the most weight and attention to detail, with petitions for suffrage often tacked on at the end of a letter, in a pro forma fashion. Thus, while the FUPDM claimed tens of thousands of women as members, they hardly held uniform priorities.

What Price Unity? The Cost of Co-optation

The FUPDM's and PCM's commitment to "unity at any cost" had its price, however. Much like the embarrassing reversal that had subordinated the PCM to the CTM leadership in June 1937, the FUPDM's decision to claim political space within the PRM tied its hands, preventing it from posing the credible challenge to the regime that remained necessary to force the suffrage amendment's passage.[35] As the front gained bureaucratic influence, it sacrificed its capacity for dissent. Further limiting the FUPDM's leverage was the fact one year after its founding, the ruling party launched its own efforts to organize women. The ruling party's Agrarian Department set up Women's Leagues for Social Struggle under the control of the local governments.[36] Thus, even before the ruling party's 1938 reorganization, it began eroding the FUPDM's primacy as the "Sole Front," with significant consequences for the organization.

Esthela Jiménez Esponda, a communist activist and the FUPDM's education secretary, wrote to Cárdenas that the front had "succeeded in controlling the majority of peasant women [in the western state of Nayarit], counting no fewer than 70 to 75 Women's Leagues in the state," including one in the village of Heriberto Casas.[37] That league had gone through all the appropriate channels to acquire a corn mill. However, Susana Larios, the Agrarian Department representative charged with organizing Nayarit women, had informed the league that neither the National Ejidal Credit Bank nor the Agrarian Department could help unless it changed affiliations from the FUPDM to the Agrarian Department. Accordingly, the FUPDM chapter set about establishing a new organization affiliated with the Agrarian Department. Outraged that a branch of the state-party would undermine the FUPDM's efforts by dividing and misleading the peasantry of Heriberto Casas, Jiménez Esponda reminded Cárdenas that the PRM's guiding tenets specifically forbade the establishment of competing party-affiliated organizations. Indicating that the FUPDM had "always openly supported your frank and progressive policies and have endeavored to avoid any conflicts with the dependencies of your government," she candidly informed Cárdenas that allowing such behavior would "remain a damaging precedent by the department, which is on a higher level than us, as an official dependency counting on greater economic resources, while our organization counts only on the reduced dues of the unionists and the efforts and sacrifices of the same." She recounted Cárdenas' promise to the Yucatecan FUPDM delegation that "the Agrarian Department only had instructions to organize women with the aim of obtaining a corn mill, but it did not have cause to control the organizations, which remained absolutely at liberty to affiliate with whomever they wanted." She reiterated their agreement that "in order to avoid conflict with the Agrarian Department, the Front should not organize where [the Agrarian Department] organized, understanding that the Agrarian Department remained subject to the same conditions. That is to say, not to organize where we were already organized. But this case demonstrates the reverse."[38]

It remains unclear from the documentation how this issue was resolved. The National Ejidal Credit Bank in Mexico City maintained that it had never interfered with the Women's Leagues "except in special cases" and had no knowledge of the Heriberto Casas case.[39] No new league registration exists for Heriberto Casas for the remainder of the Cárdenas presidency, implying that the FUPDM retained control. Indeed, the FUPDM remained relatively strong in Nayarit, and the state's women continued to form affiliates even after the FUPDM had disintegrated, indicating that the front's hegemonic control over the region had a lasting influence.[40]

However, this exchange illuminates more than a territorial conflict between the two primary institutions organizing women during the Cárdenas period. First, it underscores the fact that pragmatic gains such as corn mills induced women to change allegiances. These improvements most likely meant more than the revolutionary regime's endless, unfulfilled promises. For many women, relief from the arduous *metate* (grinding stone) held more immediate value than even education and medical services, which often remained halfhearted, ramshackle efforts.[41] After all, women labored for hours every day over the metate; labor-saving devices such as corn mills and sewing machines promised liberation from chronic exhaustion and the possibility of leisure time.

Second, Jiménez Esponda's response to the Agrarian Department's machinations allows informed speculations about the FUPDM's expectations of PRM incorporation. To be sure, the divvying up of organizing tasks and the pledge of noninterference indicates early suspicion on the FUPDM's part. Indeed, Jiménez Esponda candidly pointed out the inequality of resources at the disposal of the FUPDM vis-à-vis the Agrarian Department and called on Cárdenas and his new party to intervene on behalf of the underdog, as he had always pledged to do. The government's promise to even out conflicts between unequal parties—workers and employers, peasants and landowners, women and men—supposedly justified the creation of an all-encompassing corporatist state. This episode, however, raised the troubling question of how the state would act when it was one of the unequal parties. Jiménez Esponda invoked the ruling party's own moral economy, calling on Cárdenas to protect the FUPDM's right to organize and to mobilize women, as well as the right of women themselves to affiliate with whichever organization they preferred without jeopardizing state support.

Finally, Jiménez Esponda's appeal demonstrates an enduring clientelism that characterized popular organizing during this period. She emphasized that the FUPDM had always supported Cárdenas's regime and had taken pains to avoid conflict with the ruling party. In exchange, she expected the paternalist shelter of the state—ironically in this case from one of its own branches. As in all patron-client relationships, the association between the front and the Cárdenas regime remained one of uneven reciprocity. However, having committed itself to the ruling party via the PCM's "Unity at Any Cost" campaign, the FUPDM retained very little leverage. An attack on the ruling party would undermine the very project in which the front had so recently invested itself. Indeed, the waning animosity between the ruling party and the PCM, culminating in the reorganization of the former, eliminated the rivalry that had fueled the debate over women's political rights.

Conclusions

The FUPDM leadership's decision to incorporate into the restructured ruling party can only be understood within this matrix of factors of corporatist consolidation (and its implications for the meaning of citizenship), rising concerns about fascism, and the PCM's fast-evaporating support for an oppositional women's movement. After the ruling party's March 1938 reorganization, the PCM retreated from the project of recruiting women, particularly as its internal crises and divisions shifted the leadership's focus from the extroversion of the early Popular Front years to the introversion of self-criticism and purges. The communist newspaper, *El Machete*, stepped up its coverage of women's issues throughout the early 1930s, with Consuelo Uranga as one of its editors. In 1937, in the heat of the women's suffrage campaign and growing radicalism on the part of the FUPDM, the newspaper had doubled in size, increased its coverage of women's issues within larger stories of labor struggles and land conflicts, and added a "Women's Activities" page. By May 1938, however, the paper had reverted to a smaller format and included only passing mention of women's organizing activities for the remainder of the Cárdenas presidency.

The PCM, the most vocal and consistent proponent of women's suffrage, had moved from opposition to détente to complicity in its relationship with the ruling party, and its most active members, including those in the FUPDM leadership, generally coordinated their efforts with the PCM's agenda. Further, as the FUPDM leader Esthela Jiménez Esponda pointed out, her organization could not possibly compete with the state resources. Unable to beat the PRM in the race to organize women, the FUPDM decided to join it. The common cause of fighting fascism replaced the PCM–ruling party animosity that had characterized the early 1930s, inducing the ruling party to put its resources into attracting women from its right rather than from its left.

From the perspective of midlevel organizers and rank-and-file members, these lines among parties and institutions were not so clearly drawn. Once the PCM adopted its Popular Front tactic, relationships among different organizations became quite fluid as party memberships overlapped with those of unions or agrarian communities and of women's organizations. Different groups' objectives did not always coincide neatly, particularly as their relationships constantly shifted. Tying one's beliefs to the ruling party or the PCM would have been like trying to hit a moving target. Further complicating matters, local incarnations of national parties and organizations often had a flavor of their own, reflecting the lines of ideological, class, and cultural difference that characterized that locality. Nonetheless, as a radical opposition movement, the PCM and its women militants had enjoyed power far beyond their numbers. As a part of an impotent and ultimately mythical Popular Front, the communist militants confined themselves within a ruling party that defeated the leading item on their agenda. While the FUPDM left an enduring legacy of organizational infrastructure, its principal objective of national women's suffrage would elude women activists for two decades.

Notes

1. AGN, Ramos Presidentes (RP), Lázaro Cárdenas del Río (LCR), exp. 544/1, Anne Kelton Wiley to Lázaro Cárdenas, 30 September 1937; *Equal Rights*, 15 July 1937, 102–4.
2. *Equal Rights*, 15 July 1957, 102–4.
3. Ibid.
4. Cano 1991a; Cano 1993; Macías 1982; Rascón 1979; Soto 1990. The most complete work to date on the FUPDM is Tuñón Pablos 1992. For a review of this historiography see Cano 2000.
5. For a more extensive discussion of Mexican women's revolutionary citizenship see Olcott 2005.
6. *El Universal*, 4 October 1931, 9.
7. *El Universal*, 3 October 1931, 9.
8. Olcott 2005.
9. Carr 1992; Carr 1994.
10. CEMOS, doc. 000128, PCM circular from Consuelo Uranga and Elodia F. Cruz, 12 January 1938.
11. For sanguine predictions about the Mexican Popular Front see the PCM newspaper *El Machete* and the CTM newsletter *Mexican Labor News*.
12. On practical and strategic gender interests see Molyneux 1985.
13. Jean Meyer reports that women never formed less than a quarter of the sinarquista militants (2003, 68).
14. See, for example, AGN, RP, LCR, exp. 433/121, Cuca García's statements at the congress of the Frente Popular Anti-imperialista, 27–28 February 1936.
15. *Mujer Nueva*, no. 1 (November 1936): 2, cited in Tuñón Pablos 1992, 70–71.
16. The 35,000 figure is cited in AGN, RP, LCR, exp. 544/1, letter from the FUPDM, Tampico, Tamaulipas, 6 September 1936. The 50,000 estimate appears in Millan 1939, 165.

17. AGN, RP, LCR, exp. 542.1/2012, FUPDM, Tenabo, Campeche, to Cárdenas, 8 April 1937. Although surnames in the documents often appear indigenous, they reveal little about the meaning of ethnic identity for the women involved. The Tenabo women, for example, couched their appeals as "peasant women who know the bitterness of their class" rather than as indigenous women (see AGN, RP, LCR, exp. 151.3/1365, FUPDM, Tenabo, Campeche, to Cárdenas, 29 July 1937).

18. AGN, RP, LCR, exp. 521.8/24, Liga Acción Femenina, FUPDM, to Cárdenas, 8 January 1936; AGN, RP, LCR, exp. 151.3/879, Liga de Acción Femenina Pro-Derechos de la Mujer, CTM and FUPDM to Cárdenas, 15 March 1940; AGN, RP, LCR, exp. 151.3/879, CTM to Cárdenas, 10 May 1940.

19. AGN, RP, LCR, exp. 151.3/879, FUPDM, Salina Cruz, Oaxaca, to Cárdenas, 29 December 1937.

20. AGN, RP, LCR, exp. 151.3/879, Liga de Acción Femenina Pro-Derechos de la Mujer, CTM and FUPDM, Salina Cruz, Oaxaca, to Cárdenas, 15 March 1940.

21. Gill 1956; Vizcaíno and Taibo 1983.

22. On the Liga Nacional Femenina see AGN, RP, LCR, exps. 437/112 and 136.3/20. For Cárdenas's Guerrero campaign speeches see Cárdenas 1978, 127–29.

23. AGN, RP, LCR, exps. 437.1/147, 534.3/45, and 433/481, Unión de Mujeres Revolucionarias de Acapulco, 16 February 1935. On María de la O, see Flores Arellano and Román 1992.

24. AGN, RP, LCR, exp. 437/112, Primera Liga Nacional Femenina Roja to Cárdenas, 7 May 1936.

25. AGN, DGG, 2.312 (9) 21, caja 6, exp. 37, FUPDM, Acapulco, Guerrero, 27 June 1936.

26. *Redención* (Villahermosa, Tabasco), 7 March 1936, p. 1.

27. Sindicato Único de Trabajadores 1937, 23–24.

28. Secretaría de Educación Pública 1938, 488.

29. Olcott 2005.

30. *El Machete*, 19 February 1938.

31. AGN, RP, LCR, exp. 544.6/24, Instituto Revolucionario Femenino, 28 September 1938; Gutiérrez de Mendoza 1936; Michel 1938.

32. AGN, RP, LCR, exp. 609/152, FUPDM, Chichimilá, Yucatán, to Cárdenas, 15 August 1937.

33. AGN, RP, LCR, exp. 136.3/2590, FUPDM, Hampolol, Campeche, to Cárdenas, 20 August 1937.

34. AGN, RP, LCR, exp. 151.3/1300, FUPDM, Tepic, Nayarit, to Cárdenas, 20 July 1939.

35. The post-revolutionary regime consistently sought to co-opt dissident organizations, but the importance of both organized dissent and armed resistance in compelling policymakers to grant suffrage rights was expressed explicitly during the 1917 Constitutional Convention (see *Diario de los debates del Congreso constituyente de 1916–1917* 1922, 601–3).

36. Olcott 2005.

37. AGN, RP, LCR, exp. 437.1/726, Jiménez Esponda to Cárdenas, 12 August 1938. After Cuca García left the party in 1940, Jiménez Esponda succeeded her as the head of the PCM women's department.

38. AGN, RP, LCR, exp. 437.1/726, Jiménez Esponda to Cárdenas, 12 August 1938.

39. AGN, RP, LCR, exp. 437.1/726, Secretary of Organization, Banco Nacional de Crédito Ejidal, to Cárdenas, 6 September 1938.

40. See AGN, RP, Manuel Ávila Camacho (MAC), exps. 151.3/230, 556.63/143, 546.2/70, and 136.3/1057, correspondence from Ligas Femeniles Pro-Derechos de la Mujer.

41. Bauer 1990; Keremetsis 1983.

JOCELYN OLCOTT

Epilogue

Rural Women's Grassroots Activism, 1980–2000:

Reframing the Nation from Below

LYNN STEPHEN

From 1980 to 2000 Mexico underwent the consolidation of a neoliberal economic policy, and its state-sponsored ideology shifted from a nationalism based on revolutionary symbols and ideas to a neoliberal globalism that posited Mexico as a strong player in the global economy and downplayed the country's uniqueness. Neoliberal policy paradigms specifically targeted women and families while decreasing state support for services and goods that women often depended on and were responsible for procuring, such as medical services and basic foods. During this same period, Mexico witnessed the proliferation of nongovernmental organizations (NGOS) attempting to provide some of the services and economic supports that the government had abandoned. In addition, a wide range of Mexican social movements either emerged or consolidated in the 1980s, notably feminist movements, urban movements, human-rights movements, and indigenous and peasant organizations. In the 1990s, the most influential social movement that had repercussions throughout Mexican society was the Zapatista movement, represented by not only the Zapatista Army of National Liberation (EZLN) and its base communities in Chiapas but also the other movements that emerged during the political opening the EZLN created, most notably that for indigenous rights.

The combination of neoliberal economic policy, a change in state-sponsored discourse from revolutionary nationalism to global capitalism, second-wave feminism, the rise of several social movements (feminism, Zapatismo, indigenous rights), and the presence of NGOs geared toward women refashioned women's organizing in rural Mexico. At first being a response to state policy initiatives aimed at increasing women's economic and political participation at the local level, women's organizing came to involve participation in significant national movements, then the creation of spaces of critical dialogue within these movements through challenges to gendered assumptions about women's roles. Involved in this process were a wide range of organizations and movements and their various relationships to changing economic policy and discourses of nationalism and globalization. Common to each, though, was a "strategic essentialism" in the struggle for recognition and a new gendered political space, which homogenized the participants within a particular movement, glossing over the contradictions and conflicts inherent in social-movement formation.[1]

The Legacy of Rural Women's Organizing: From the Mexican Revolution to the 1960s

Rural women's fame as participants in armed struggle dates to before the Mexican Revolution, when they achieved mythic status as *soldaderas* working behind the lines as cooks, doctors, nurses, entertainers, spies, and arms smugglers, or on the front lines commanding troops. María Quinteras de Meras fought in ten battles with the army of Francisco Villa while Angela "Angel" Jiménez fought for the Constitutionalist faction, insisted on being called by the masculine version of her name, and threatened to shoot anyone who tried to seduce her.[2] And, as documented by Gabriela Cano, Carmen Amelia Robles Ávila, known as Amelio Robles, cut a figure of stunning virility as an original Zapatista guerilla.[3] Kristina A. Boylan demonstrates that women also took up strategic positions through the counter-revolutionary Catholic struggle against official anticlerical campaigns.[4] In short, rural women have long engaged in armed struggle when necessary and used their organizational and tactical skills to support armed action and social movements.

Women in the Mexican countryside participated in agricultural production, wage labor, and property ownership—including land, with its related rural-income producing activities—before and after the Mexican Revolution, giving them a significant stake in the revolution's outcome and rendering them the targets of post-revolutionary policy development and political organizing.[5] As Jocelyn Olcott shows, rural women's organizing, particularly in the 1930s, responded broadly to the national government's and official party's concerns with counteracting Catholic mobilizations among women and with promoting developmentalist policies and political incorporation.[6] Policymakers encouraged the semiautonomous organizing of the Sole Front for Women's Rights (FUPDM) and at the same time marginalized it through government programs and official organizations. Women teachers often operated simultaneously in the FUPDM and government bureaucracies and organizations. The deliberate incorporation of girls and women into rural schools as students and teachers in the 1920s and 1930s increased rural women's literacy, involved them in union organizing, and provided them with limited rural leadership roles.[7] In addition, efforts to promote socialist education in the 1930s under the presidency of Lázaro Cárdenas involved rural women in local- and state-level committees such as the Committee against Vice, the Committee for Peasant and Worker Homes, the Committee for the Proletarian Child, and the League of Mothers of Families.[8] In Oaxaca during Cárdenas' tenure, educational activities increased, as did teacher militancy. Rural and urban women participated in these efforts. Teachers, including women, organized in local agrarian communities. In 1938, for example, during the First Regional Peasant Convention celebrated in the Vanguard School of San Antonio de la Cal near Oaxaca city, women were among the seventy-two delegates from a variety of communities who discussed agrarian reform, irrigation, the collectivization of work, and the role of women.[9] Women's participation in a wide range of local committees during the 1920s and 1930s was an important part of nation-building, later reflected, in the 1970s and 1980s, in the creation of Agro-Industrial Units for Women (UAIMs), which were used by the government to directly link women to state institutions and organizations such as the National Peasants' Confederation.[10]

During the 1930s, the Cárdenas government dispatched many people to the countryside to organize *ejidos* (agrarian collectives). In many cases, groups of men petitioned for land, but often women's auxiliary groups or local mothers' groups formed as well. Many ejidos included a few women, often widows, as founding members. Article 97 of the Ley de Dotaciones y Restituciones de Tierras (Law for the Endowment and Restitution of Land), written in 1927 to interpret the implementation of Article 27, defined eligible *ejidatarios* as "Mexican, males over eighteen years of age or single women or widows who are supporting a family," thus reinforcing Porfirian land-distribution policies.[11] Rural Oaxacan cultural norms established widowhood as a woman's primary route to land ownership well before the Mexican Revolution.[12] Single mothers may also have been transformed into widows on paper to ease municipal authorities' burden of caring for them. Thus, agrarian politics and organizations included women both before and after the Mexican Revolution. While women were not formally named as ejido authorities after the revolution, some participated in the discussions, debates, and often contentious battles involved in occupying ejido lands granted by presidential decree.

Rural women were indoctrinated in the rationalization of the domestic sphere as policymakers and others urged them to register births and learn about new scientific ideas about nutrition, hygiene, and disease, and about how to structure their houses for health and comfort.[13] Neverthe-less, new technologies such as the *molino de nixtamal* (corn mill) and the programs promoted by teachers, FUPDM organizers, policymakers, nurses, and others not only reinforced patriarchy but also fostered ideas about women's rights and possibilities in the larger world. Such contact and the experiences of women who became politicized and learned leader-ship skills through the realms of education, ejido formation, and agrarian development projects from the 1930s through the 1960s undergirded the rural women's organizing that came of age beginning in the 1970s. While independent peasant organizations and other social movements were im-portant in this process, so were contact with state agencies, the formation of new kinds of organizations that became known as NGOs, and the influence of second-wave feminism. And women's roles in the Mexican Revolution provided the Mexican government with a strategic hook to draw women into the legacy of revolutionary nationalism.

Rural Women and the Revolutionary Legacy, 1970–1991: The extension of Ejidatario Rights to All Women and the Creation of UAIMs

The appropriation of the goals and symbols of the Mexican Revolution has anchored the Mexican state's twentieth-century construction of na-tionalism. Chief among these symbols is the figure of Emiliano Zapata and, through him, the right to land.[14] Through the establishment of 28,000 ejidos and agrarian communities between 1915 and 1992, built rhetorically on the legacy of Zapata, rural communities who received land established direct ties to the ruling party (the Partido Revolucionario Institucional until 2000) and its governments. As many historians have suggested, some ejidos remained closely bound to the state while others existed in regional political constellations far removed from the circuits of centralized state power.[15] For example, while the central region of

Nayarit has been more closely linked to agrarian policies and politics stemming from the center, areas such as the Lacandón jungle of Chiapas clearly remained outside the central state's sphere of influence until quite recently.

During the process of land distribution (most accelerated in the 1930s, but ongoing until 1992), few women received access to land. However, earlier agrarian codes such as that of 1934 did not prevent women from holding elected posts in ejidos if they were ejidatarias with full rights, observed good conduct, and resided in the community for at least six months prior to the election. Helga Baitenmann suggests that in practice, many women ejidatarias voted in assembly meetings.[16] The significance of this of course depends on how many women ejidatarias there actually were in any given community and whether or not they could consistently exercise their voting rights.

Until the federal Agrarian Reform Law of 1971, the only women eligible for ejidal rights were single or widowed female heads of households. Despite women's contributions to household income and subsistence, laws did not include married women as heads of household when there was a male present.[17] Only under Article 200 of the Agrarian Reform Law of 1971 did men and women become equal with regard to their ability to qualify for ejidal rights. The law stated that ejidatarios must be "Mexican by birth, male or female, older than sixteen or of any age if they are supporting a family."[18] With the passage of that law, women were no longer required to be mothers or widows maintaining a family to qualify for land rights. The 1971 law preserved the notion that ejidos were inalienable and that use rights could only pass to a family member, making it likely that women would be named as successors. The law also allowed women to hold any position of authority (*cargo*) within ejidos.

Most important, the 1971 law called for the creation of UAIMs, which provided for special agricultural and small industrial projects for the majority of women who did not have access to ejido land as ejidatarias. The language of the law indicated that "the organization of women would be stimulated because they would be incorporated into the 'productive process.' In some cases, government rhetoric went on to suggest that this would eventually lead to reducing gender inequalities."[19] The creation of UAIMs in the 1970s resembled the 1930s creation of the Ligas Femeniles de Lucha Social, (referred to in Olcott's essay as Women's Leagues for Social Struggle) both having the goal of making women "productive," although in the 1930s such organizations were directed less toward agricultural production than toward "complementary" activities such as sewing and milling cooperatives. The number of UAIMs that were established in Mexico is difficult to ascertain. One study found that 8,000 UAIMs had been legalized, but only 1,224 were officially registered and only 1,112 had received credit.[20] In 1993 only 15 percent of Mexico's ejidos had registered UAIMs, and an even smaller number of UAIMs actually functioned.[21]

UAIMs allowed women to receive communal land from agrarian communities and plots from ejidos. The amount of land they received as a group, however, equaled the amount given to one ejidatario. Whether a UAIM had four members or forty, it still received the allocation of one ejidatario. The existence of a UAIM also allowed its membership to have one collective vote in the ejido organization—again, equivalent to one ejidatario. The 1971 law granted UAIM members access to receive credit and government resources for small development projects, but these funds were usually funneled through the ejidos, often resulting in problems for women who lacked direct access to the funds and depended on male leadership.

Ignoring the fact that most rural women were already deeply involved in agricultural and other forms of rural production, the logic behind UAIMs reflected the assumption in 1970s international-development programs that pushing women into agricultural production would reduce inequality between men and women by translating women's economic participation into greater authority. However, little was done beyond changing the law to make UAIMs a reality. No efforts were made to organize women, defend their rights within ejidos, or provide them with credit, technical training, or access to markets for their products. In addition, the law did nothing to address continued inequities in local political cultures where community assemblies and decision making often remained the province of men.

There were some efforts to form UAIMs in the 1970s, during a period of economic expansion fueled primarily by the state-owned oil sector, which offered collateral for spending programs funded by international lending agencies. Rural women depended on subsidized basic food items, internal price supports paid to rural corn and other producers for their products, as well as access to healthcare through rural health clinics. While Mexico's 1970s social-welfare programs were modest, they were widely available, rather than reduced and targeted at the poorest, as they later were. Although rural women benefited from some of these programs, they had been less carefully cultivated as a political constituency than rural men since the 1940s.

The Mexican government promoted UAIMs in the 1970s, 1980s, and 1990s in large part to gain better political access to rural women—a project it had ignored for several decades. UAIMs were created on state terms and used state support. The creation of UAIMs, as well as of other government programs that involved women through their role in the family, created a new constituency that could not only receive resources but also be cultivated to support the PRI politically. This goal became even more important in the late 1980s and the 1990s as social-welfare programs shrank, rural producers were hard-hit by lower prices and eventually by competition from North American grains, and the PRI had to work harder to hang onto its rural supporters. While the UAIMs languished in the mid- to late 1980s, by the 1990s they were reclaimed by the National Peasants' Confederation and in some states by the Women in Solidarity Program, a welfare program targeting women. In some contexts this drive to reclaim the UAIMs may have also been fueled by a strategy to co-opt potentially subversive organizing campaigns. In this sense, the revival of the UAIMs suggested parallels with Olcott's analysis of the Agrarian Department's attempts to sideline the FUPDM in the 1930s by creating its own women's organizations.

In 1991, UAIMs gained independent judicial and financial status, allowing them to receive funds directly from the government and international-development agencies. While this independent financial status decreased their dependence on local authorities, it also fostered increased reliance on bureaucrats from agencies such as the Ministry of Agriculture or the Ministry of Agrarian Reform. Rather than increase their autonomy, the change often strengthened their clientelist relations with the federal government and made them more directly accessible to be mobilized for political purposes.

This effort occurred in tandem with independent peasant and producer organizations' efforts in the late 1980s and early 1990s to cultivate women's participation as well. In Chiapas by 1991, women participated in the EZLN's armed struggle and formed a central part of its strategy for organizing in base communities. Catholic and Protestant churches in Chiapas also organized women. Christian-based community organizing clearly represented something very different from the counter-revolutionary organizing in the 1920s and 1930s, as examined by Kristina A. Boylan.[22] While that organizing focused on defense of the faith from government attack, Christian-based community organizing, inspired by Vatican II and liberation theology, deployed faith to pursue goals of social justice and equality.

During the 1990s under the Salinas government, many UAIMs depended on the Solidarity Program of social welfare for their funding. Women's participation in both the national Women in Solidarity Program and community solidarity committees often had mixed results, increasing their reliance on state governors and their supporters but giving them

Epilogue

skills that they could transfer to their own projects. Their political perspectives and skills differed, however, from those of rural women who came of age in independent organizations and opposition movements.

Mexico's Urban and Rural Social Movements in the 1980s and 1990s: Experimenting with Women's Organizing

In the 1980s and 1990s, the revolutionary nationalist legacy waned as globalization came to define Mexican economic policy and national identity, at least as projected from the center. While Mexico's government loosened its social-welfare obligations and oriented its policies toward global market integration and free trade, other currents bubbled in Mexican society, including the revitalization of grassroots social movements in a variety of sectors. Many of these movements emerged from strands of the Mexican left linked to the student movement of the 1960s. Student organizers, working from a Maoist philosophy that emphasized building a mass movement from the bottom up, succeeded in both the countryside and the urban periphery. While many of these movements included both men and women, women organized discrete entities within some of them or formed their own organizations.

In urban areas these movements began in the early 1970s in the northern states of Chihuahua, Nuevo León, and Durango, and in the southern state of Oaxaca, creating new channels to express the needs of the urban poor. In some cases, the organizations delivered services that the state did not; in other instances, they pressured the state to deliver what it was supposed to. In 1980, approximately twenty-one organizations and seven hundred delegates attended the first national congress of urban popular movements in Monterrey. At a second congress held a year later, the National Council of the Urban Popular Movement (CONAMUP) was created to focus on improving urban living conditions and democratizing Mexican society. Two years later, the CONAMUP formed the Women's Regional Council to address demands particular to women, who remained marginalized within the organization, and to promote local women's councils. The Women's Regional Council combined issues of urban survival with programs to combat domestic violence and rape and to improve women's health and nutrition. They also focused on providing women with leadership skills for political organizing.[23]

In the countryside, ejido unions gave way to regional peasant organizations that focused not only on the struggle for land but also on production requirements such as credit, farming inputs, transportation, and marketing outlets. Chiapas was a good example of this process. Encouraged by the 1971 Federal Agrarian Reform law, which allowed ejidos to unite into larger productive units known as unions of ejidos, catechists, activists, and representatives from many indigenous communities convened in the 1974 Indigenous Congress in San Cristóbal de las Casas, Chiapas, to formulate solutions to the many complaints about lack of control over the productive and marketing process in the highlands and the colonized areas of the Lacandón jungle. In 1976, three regional ejido unions brought together two or more communities. These included Ejido Union, United in Our Strength (Quiptic Ta Lecubtecel) in Ocosingo; Ejido Union, Land and Liberty (Tierra y Libertad) in Las Margaritas; and Ejido Union, Peasant Struggle (Lucha Campesina) in Las Margaritas.[24]

Two sets of Maoist-oriented organizers participated in these efforts. The first, members of the Union of the People, included advisers to the Catholic Church who helped to prepare the Indigenous Congress. Later, a second group of organizers, who belonged to People's Politics, sought to apply the Maoist "mass line" to organizing nonviolently for socialism. Neither group sought to directly organize women in relation to distinct demands, but many women joined in their activities and could often be seen in marches and other public political activities. In 1979 People's Politics joined with other nonviolent groups and became known as Proletarian Line, a statewide organization that in some places had a stronger presence than did the Mexican government.[25]

Born out of the three regional ejido unions formed after the Indigenous Congress, the Union of Unions and Solidarity Peasant Organizations of Chiapas came out of a struggle to help people to market their coffee and other goods. It focused primarily on peasant appropriation of the production process and formed "the first and largest independent campesino organization in Chiapas, representing 12,000 mainly indigenous families from 170 communities in 11 municipalities."[26]

Many other sources of independent peasant organizing besides the Union of Unions emerged in Chiapas in the 1970s and 1980s.[27] Many of these organizations brought a language and symbolic system that reclaimed Emiliano Zapata and the struggle for land. The National Coordinadora, Plan de Ayala (CNPA), which takes its name from Zapata's 1911 plan to redistribute land, was founded in 1979 with ten regional peasant organizations.[28] In the 1980s, CNPA's principle demands included "the legal recognition of longstanding indigenous land rights; the distribution of land exceeding the legal limits for private property; community control over and defense of natural resources; agricultural production, marketing, and consumption subsidies; rural unionization; and the preservation of popular culture."[29]

Epilogue

Participants in CNPA included indigenous peoples with communal land or no land, smallholder peasants, peasants who were soliciting land, and some groups of small producers and agrarian wage workers. CNPA was also one of the larger independent peasant organizations where women attempted, albeit unsuccessfully, to establish a permanent presence.

During the 1980s, as in many "mixed organizations" connected to the urban left, the CNPA began to debate whether to organize an autonomous women's branch. The first such effort came in 1981, but the national organization decided that an autonomous women's presence would invite internal division. A second attempt, during a 1984 CNPA congress, created a women's commission charged with organizing a national meeting of peasant women to be held in 1986. The CNPA mobilized women around issues related to health, education, job creation, social services, and the cost of basic goods. The official report from the 1984 CNPA meeting underscored the commission's considerable dissatisfaction about women's role in the organization. Reflecting the early 1980s influence of urban grassroots feminist movements, the report noted that women had little role in official negotiations with the state, received little political training, and had not participated in choosing authorities or reached positions of authority themselves within the CNPA. The commission enumerated particular problems related to women and asked for financial support, child care, and other resources that would allow them to participate more fully in the CNPA. The official report also encouraged the inclusion of women's specific demands among those the organization adopted, requested that women receive ejidal plots regardless of their marital status, and urged that the CNPA include at least one woman in its directorate.[30] Some of these demands reappeared in the 1994 Zapatista "Revolutionary Law of Women," presented at a Chiapas women's convention held in 1994, and in the critiques rural, indigenous women made in the 1990s debate on the meaning of indigenous autonomy.

By the mid-1980s in rural Chiapas, a wide range of grassroots movements existed that allowed some organizers to cross over to the armed organization of the EZLN. Some of these organizations had debated the utility of autonomous women's organizing and had women within them who raised gender-specific concerns and challenged male-dominant leadership. Although organizations such as the Union of Unions did not have such open debate, the increasing presence of women's movements and specifically grassroots feminist organizations and NGOs in Mexico during the 1980s eventually had an impact on rural women's organizing, particularly in Chiapas.

Second-Wave Grassroots Feminism and Women's NGOs: Bringing a Gendered Analysis to Social Movements

Analysts of the development of Mexican feminisms have characterized the movements as limited in their impact and defined by factionalism and the inability to form sustained, broad-based coalitions until the 1980s.[31] Second-wave feminism of the 1970s drew on consciousness-raising groups of primarily middle-class women who also began to make cross-class connections in 1975, following the United Nations World Conference for International Women's Year. They focused on issues such as the legalization of abortion, stricter penalties for violence against women, support for rape victims, and connecting the personal and the political.[32] The mid-1970s saw the first feminist publication, the creation of a center for rape victims, and a large number of public demonstrations and assemblies. In 1979 the National Front for Women's Rights and Liberation (FNALIDM) formed, uniting feminist groups with labor unions, gay organizations, and leftist political parties. Co-optation by political parties and strong differences in perspectives began to arise, resulting in the demise of the FNALIDM in the early 1980s.

In the 1970s, women also participated in a range of other social movements, including leftist political groups, labor unions, liberation-theology-inspired Christian-based communities, relatives of the disappeared, and groups such as the CONAMUP. These nonfeminist spaces for political activism did not bring women into contact with self-defined feminist organizers in a sustained way until the mid-1980s. Mexico City's devastating 1985 earthquake stands as a watershed for Mexican social movements. The enormous responses and the strong presence of women within them initiated a new era of broader-based feminist organizing as well as the emergence of NGOs specifically focused on women.

After the 1985 earthquake, several new loosely allied networks—that included the Network Against Violence toward Women, the Feminist Peasant Network, and the Network of Popular Educators—developed a discourse characterized as *feminismo popular*, or grassroots feminism, an important strain of second-wave Mexican feminism that had lasting influence on rural women's organizing.[33] Grassroots feminism "integrates a commitment to basic survival for women and their children with a challenge to the subordination of women to men" and "challenges the assumption that issues of sexual assault, violence against women, and reproductive control are divorced from women's concerns about housing, food, land, and healthcare."[34] In many ways, the grassroots feminism of the 1980s and early 1990s focused on linking class and gender issues. Not until the mid-1990s, when indigenous women from Chiapas began to participate, did Mexico's women's movements include ethnicity as an additional basis for women's inequality.

After the Mexico City earthquake, poor women emerged as key leaders in neighborhood associations, such as the Coordinating Committee of Earthquake Victims, and also in the September 19th Garment Workers Union, an association of unemployed garment workers whose factories had been destroyed in the earthquake.[35] In 1987 women began to mobilize and participate in a widespread public debate about the importance and meaning of democracy in Mexico. Within organized women's sectors, "democracy at home" as well as "democracy in the government" were topics of heated discussion. The economic crisis of the 1980s with its devastating effects on women and their families, mobilized many to participate in the 1988 elections. Many united behind the opposition candidacy of Cuauhtémoc Cárdenas, believing that change might be possible. Two other women's organizations formed at that time as well, signaling the continued possibility for coalitions. The Benita Galeana Coordinating Committee—named after a prominent communist activist at the precise moment that the Mexican Communist Party dissolved itself to create the Party of the Democratic Revolution—brought together women from thirty-three urban groups, unions, NGOs, and political parties, and mobilized them around issues of low-income women. It focused on building democratic processes at home, at work, and in the political system, working against all forms of violence and generating conditions (economic and otherwise) that support life beyond survival.[36] The other organization, Women Fighting for Democracy, pulled women together from outside of political parties to work for political change.[37] While much of the successful coalition-building work between women's organizations centered in urban areas, the emergence of women's NGOs also began to affect the discourses and strategies promoted by some rural organizations.

Mexico's economic crises of the 1980s and a shift to neoliberal economic policy fostered growth in both social movements and NGOs developing in spaces parallel to those inside the Mexican political system and welfare structure. As stated by María Luisa Tarrés in an insightful analysis of the rise of women's NGOs in Mexico, "Women's NGOs are thus created in a changing and political context that defied the popular perception of the state as the depository of social welfare, populism as a form of political relationship, and Marxism as the political alternative of the popular sectors. This changing context in turn leads to a different set of demands, which instead of falling within the general category of 'social justice' are presented as a set of citizens' rights that in order to become effective presupposed the existence of a democratic government."[38] In this discussion of "democracy," NGOs and movements adopted and elaborated feminist discourse to suit their own purposes, bringing self-defined feminists into direct contact with women across a wide range of social movements, including organized rural and indigenous women.

NGOs in Mexico generally work in tandem with particular social movements. Those in NGOs usually have much more education, professional training, and higher incomes than the populations they serve. In NGOs, students, professionals, and activists offer their technical, organizational, and ideological support to popular sectors, a tradition Tarrés traces to "the support groups (comunidades de base) of the Catholic Church as well as to the vanguard of the left."[39] Thus NGOs' support not only for women's movements but also for women in movements where men and women militated together brought them into sustained contact with self-defined feminists, including many feminist activists from the 1970s and 1980s. In her study of Mexican NGOs that work with women Tarrés documented ninety-seven NGOs in Mexico by the end of the 1990s, with significant growth beginning in 1984. Ten NGOs dedicated to gender issues formed in 1984, 1987, and 1990.[40] Tarrés names San Cristóbal de las Casas, Chiapas, along with Mexico City and Tijuana, Baja California, as important cities for NGO development.

The case of San Cristóbal was unusual, as most women's NGOs formed in more urbanized areas. The presence of organizers from semiclandestine leftist groups in the 1970s and 1980s as well as the fact that the ex-bishop Samuel Ruiz in Chiapas followed the tenets and strategies of liberation theology were also significant. In her investigation of women in the gender-focused NGOs Tarrés analyzes four specific sectors that served as activist training grounds: ecclesiastic-based communities linked with the Catholic Church's liberation theology, semiclandestine leftist groups such as Línea de Masas (Mass Line), leftist Mexican political parties such as the Mexican Worker's Party and the Unified Socialist Party of Mexico, and feminist discussion groups.[41] Three out of these four sectors were well represented in Chiapas social-movement organizing in the 1980s.

The Gendered Politics of Zapatismo: The Motor for Rural Indigenous Women's Organizing of the 1990s

In late 1991, the Mexican Congress ratified a change to Article 27 of the Mexican Constitution, ending the government's obligation to provide land to landless petitioners and permitting, but not requiring, the privatization of communally held land such as ejidos and agrarian communities. To facilitate the proposed changes, the agrarian attorney general's office set up a massive outreach and education campaign and created a special land-measuring and -titling program to facilitate and even encourage the privatization of previously inalienable, communally held ejido land.[42] Potentially privatizing almost half of the Mexican territory went along with opening up Mexico for further foreign investment and privatizing the economy as much as possible—two key neoliberal aims. This political move discouraged Mexico's rural population from making land claims. In Chiapas's Lacandón jungle, where each new generation since the 1970s faced a land shortage, this unwelcome news pushed some activists, including women, in regional peasant and producer organizations that had tried to operate within the Mexican political system to the side of armed struggle. In eastern Chiapas, they joined the EZLN, most rapidly from 1992 to 1994.

In Chiapas, contact among grassroots feminists in NGOs, members of regional peasant organizations, and clandestine EZLN organizers who recruited and cultivated women in their underground organizing produced a context receptive to women's perspectives. The emergence in the 1990s of a nationally projected political discourse linking inequalities rooted in gender, class, and ethnicity stemmed in part from the 1994 Zapatista uprising and subsequent consolidation of a national indigenous-rights movement. The women's organizing that emerged within Zapatismo and among indigenous women in Chiapas and elsewhere in Mexico built on previous grassroots movements (gendered and otherwise), but because it emerged at a moment when the Mexican government faced a legitimacy crisis and challenges from strong opposition movements, it moved onto the national stage in ways that similar, earlier messages (such as those of the women in CNPA) could not. The Zapatista rebellion opened up a forum for a national debate on the rights of Mexico's indigenous peoples. Indigenous women and their allies moved into that forum, engaged in a gendered analysis and critical dialogue with government officials and indigenous leaders, and demanded a reexamination of what it meant to be a gendered indigenous citizen of Mexico. They also demanded the consideration of indigenous peoples' basic rights within gendered contexts. Thus, the most politically, economically, and culturally marginalized women rewrote their national epitaph as victim to establish a strong political voice. Women's roles within the EZLN formed an important part of this process.

With regard to women's participation, the EZLN is perhaps best known for two things: first, roughly 30 percent of its militants, including some of the top posts in its military command structure, are women; second, it produced the "Revolutionary Law of Women" which appeared simultaneously with the "First Declaration from the Lacandón Jungle" on 1 January 1994.[43] The "Revolutionary Law of Women" states,

> First, women have the right to participate in the revolutionary struggle in the place and at the level that their capacity and will dictates without any discrimination based on race, creed, color, or political affiliation.
>
> Second, women have the right to work and to receive a just salary.
>
> Third, women have the right to decide on the number of children they have and take care of.
>
> Fourth, women have the right to participate in community affairs and hold leadership positions if they are freely and democratically elected.
>
> Fifth, women have the right to primary care in terms of their health and nutrition.
>
> Sixth, women have the right to education.
>
> Seventh, women have the right to choose who they are with and should not be obligated to marry by force.
>
> Eighth, no woman should be beaten or physically mistreated by either family members or strangers. Rape and attempted rape should be severely punished.
>
> Ninth, women can hold leadership positions in the organization and hold military rank in the revolutionary armed forces.
>
> Tenth, women have all the rights and obligations set out by the revolutionary laws and regulations.[44]

Many viewed such demands as "feminist" in tone since they accorded with some of the 1970s Mexican feminist demands. The history and meaning of these demands, however, differed significantly from those of middle-class, Mexico City feminists. In addition, the law reflects some of the issues raised by the Women's Commission of the CNPA in the mid-1980s, including the rights to education, training, and healthcare, to hold leadership positions in the movement, and to a just salary.

While it is tempting to read the "Revolutionary Law of Women" as the EZLN posing a serious challenge to women's subordination, the situation is much more complex. The EZLN operates on many levels, in many different contexts, and the participation and possibilities for women within these spaces vary significantly. Full-time insurgents live in separate camps with very specific rules for how men and women should interact. There, men and women expect equal treatment, and women may command male subordinates. Insurgents receive literacy training, sexual education, and a range of other information and experience that socializes them in a

way very different from their home communities. While significant ex-
perimentation in gender roles may take place among the men and women
who live completely separated from their communities and train as full-
time armed insurgents in special camps, in Zapatista-based communities
women often continue to struggle for recognition and participation in
decision making. The high levels of militarization and paramilitarization
that characterized the Mexican government's counterinsurgency strategy
cut off changes in the structure of community politics and organization
that began to develop in 1994–1995.

Women have assumed an in-your-face role in the low-intensity conflict, physically confronting soldiers and police and attempting to force
them to leave the communities they have invaded. They have also assumed a public political role in relaying stories to reporters, videogra-
phers, anthropologists, and other outsiders about how they repelled the
army from their community—or tried to. And the ongoing presence of
hundreds of young men from the Mexican army living in encampments
within indigenous communities has encouraged prostitution and increased the sale and use of alcohol and drugs. All of these changes have
generated discussion and action that did not previously exist in some
communities.

Thus both Zapatismo and the conditions of the low-intensity war have
produced new openings for questioning gender roles at the local level, but
have also generated conditions that shape the ways in which such changes
are explored. The result is contradictory. Women have become Zapatista
comandantes, but at the local level women who are mothers of young
children may be unable to either leave their home or community to attend
political meetings and discussions. While community assembly protocol
allows women and even children to speak, other conditions for encouraging women to do so may not exist.

Since the mid-1990s, Zapatista communities have pressed hard for
legislation of the 1996 San Andrés Accords on Indigenous Rights and
Culture signed by the EZLN and the Mexican government. The accords lay
the groundwork for significant changes in the areas of indigenous rights,
political participation, and cultural autonomy. Most important, they recognize the existence of political subjects called *pueblos indios* (indigenous
peoples/towns/communities) and give conceptual validation to the terms
"self-determination" and "autonomy" by using them in a signed agreement. The accords emphasize that the government takes responsibility
not only for reinforcing indigenous peoples' political participation and
representation but also for guaranteeing the validity of internal forms of
indigenous government. The accords further note that the government

promises to create national legislation guaranteeing indigenous communities the right to associate freely with municipalities that are primarily indigenous in population, to form associations between communities, and to coordinate their actions as indigenous peoples. The Mexican government did not legislate these accords, but instead implemented in 2001 a greatly watered-down version that ignored many of the core ideas of the original accords. Nevertheless, Zapatista communities proceeded to implement the spirit of the accords, with women playing a key role in the process.

Ethnographic analyses of indigenous communities in Chiapas and elsewhere that have attempted to implement the spirit and content of the San Andrés Accords and to validate local judicial customary practices and laws emphasize an ongoing challenge between defending "collective rights without silencing other subordinated voices, both individual and collective."[45] In her analysis of gender and ethnicity in a Zapatista community that has struggled to live out the San Andrés Accords, Shannon Speed suggests that focusing analytical efforts on establishing whether or not "individual or collective rights should have primacy is unproductive and obfuscating."[46] Instead, she argues, women's rights are constructed at the intersection of collective and individual rights, and insisting on a conceptual dichotomy between the two will deny the lived experience of indigenous women in Chiapas. Speed's analysis reflects the words of EZLN Comandante Esther's 2001 statement to the Mexican Congress.

> Primarily it is we women who are triply exploited. First, for being indigenous women. And, because we are indigenous, we don't know how to speak Spanish and we are disrespected. Second, because we are women who don't speak Spanish they say that we are fools, that we don't know how to think. We don't have the same opportunities as men. Third, for being poor women. We are all poor because we don't have adequate nutrition, decent housing, education, or healthcare. Many of our children die in our arms of curable diseases. Because of this triple exploitation it is necessary that all indigenous women raise our voices, unite our hands so that we are taken into consideration and our rights are guaranteed. I am making a call to all of you that we fight without stopping until we have achieved dignity as women and as indigenous peoples.[47]

Esther and other Zapatista women have modeled an understanding of indigenous women's rights that suggests that ethnic and gender rights can potentially unite collective and individual rights and can function together in an expanded sense of citizenship. In August 2003, Zapatista women were a strong presence when the EZLN inaugurated the creation of five *caracoles* (literally "shells," but implying points of communication that are the seats for five Juntas de Buen Gobierno, or Good Governance Councils). Currently, thirty Zapatista Autonomous Municipalities in Rebellion feed into the five juntas. The juntas are subject to all revolutionary Zapatista laws, including the "Revolutionary Law of Women," but the local cultural forms of governance through which these laws are interpreted can vary. Thus, the gendered implications of what the Good Governance Councils mean on the ground can vary from place to place, but within this variation, Zapatista women have stood firm in their insistence that ethnic rights and gender rights can go together.[48]

Conclusions: Identity Politics in Women's Organizing

Understanding the evolution of grassroots organizing among rural women in late-twentieth-century Mexico requires consideration of a multitude of factors. Rural Mexican women's movements emerge in particular places, at particular historical moments, and in relation to other social movements. From 1980 to 2000 in Mexico, several significant changes occurred that significantly affected the form, strategies, goals, and identities of rural women's movements. These included a change from government-sponsored nationalist ideology centered on the claims of the Mexican Revolution to neoliberal globalism promoting Mexico as a player in global economy; the influence of grassroots second-wave feminism in a wide range of social movements and NGOs; and an increase in the number and consolidation of social movements and NGOs that attempted to organize and militate for many sectors of the Mexican population, which established a strong current of opposition to the government and attempted to hold the government accountable according to the law and the services it claimed to provide.

In this historical and political context, rural women's movements can be understood to have shifted from a more passive position, responding to government initiatives that integrated women into the rural economy and cultivated their political loyalties, to a more active position, openly questioning the inequalities women suffered in relation to their ethnic and class positions as well as positively proposing the rights rural, indigenous women should enjoy within national law, their home communities, and the organizations that represent them. Proposals for rural women's rights in the late 1990s incorporated the issues of reproductive sexuality, violence against women, land and labor rights, political participation, and leadership in local and national contexts.

By the beginning of the twenty-first century, rural and indigenous Mexican women captured new political space and audiences that permitted them to truly sit at the table of national decision making. For the first time in history, an indigenous woman held a cabinet-level position in the government, one aimed specifically at addressing the issues of Mexico's indigenous citizens. It remains to be seen, however, whether the overtures of President Vicente Fox to indigenous peoples, including women, from 2000 to 2006, will lead to real power-sharing or whether his economic agenda will simply continue the ongoing economic and political marginalization of Mexico's rural and indigenous inhabitants. If the opening continues, rural and indigenous women will no doubt continue to operate in it. If the opening closes, rural and indigenous women at least have some experience, tools, and models for continuing their struggles.

Notes

1. On "strategic essentialism" see Spivak 1989, Spivak 1990, Spivak 1993. Many anthropologists and indigenous intellectuals have written about the competing tendencies of anthropologists to deconstruct essentialist notions of "Indians" and ethnicity, while those working within indigenous movements strategically deploy essentialism in order to be considered legitimate as well as to create a unifying discourse for specific political efforts (see Montejo 2002; Warren 1998; Field 1999; Jackson 1999).

259

2. Cano 1997, 1359.
3. See Cano's essay in this volume.
4. See Boylan's essay in this volume.
5. See the excellent case studies in Fowler-Salamini and Vaughan 1994.
6. See Olcott's essay in this volume.
7. Vaughan 1994.
8. Stephen 2002, 52–53.
9. Martínez Vásquez 1994, 135
10. See Olcott in this volume.
11. Botey Estapé 1991.
12. Chassen-López 1994, 27–50.
13. Vaughan 2000, 202.
14. Stephen 2002.
15. Rubin 1997; Ana María Alonso 1995.
16. Baitenmann 2000, 25.
17. Baitenmann 1997; Fowler-Salamini and Vaughan 1994; Stephen 1991.
18. Botey Estapé 1991.
19. Villarreal 1994, 6.
20. Arizpe and Aranda 1986; Villarreal 1994, 6–7.
21. Robles, Aranda, and Botey 1993, 32.
22. See Boylan's essay in this volume.
23. See Stephen 1997, 11, 148; Mogrovejo Aquise 1990.
24. Neil Harvey 1994, 29; Neil Harvey 1998, 79–83.
25. Neil Harvey 1998, 79–82.

26. Neil Harvey 1994, 30.

27. Neil Harvey 1994; Neil Harvey 1998.

28. Another important regional peasant organization that developed in the 1970s and had an increasing presence in the 1980s in Chiapas was the Independent Central of Agricultural Workers and Peasants (CIOAC), which initially organized Tzeltal and Tzotzil agricultural workers into unions on coffee and cattle ranches in the municipalities of Simojovel, Juitiupan, El Bosque, Pueblo Nuevo, and Solistahuacan in Chiapas. The CIOAC also became a strong presence in the Tojolabal *cañada* and was based in Comitán (see Mattiace 1998). Like the Emiliano Zapata Peasant Organization (OCEZ) and the CNPA, while the name of the organization did not signal ethnically based demands, CIOAC documents reflect an awareness of indigenous identity and politics through the acknowledgment of indigenous claims to lands historically denied and defense of indigenous forms of government, religion, and language and of the need to struggle against efforts to assimilate indigenous peoples.

29. Paré 1990, 85.

30. Documentos del Movimiento Campesino 1984, 123–26.

31. Lamas 1998, 106; Tarrés 1998, 133.

32. Lamas, Martínez, Tarrés, and Tuñón 1995, 324–35.

33. Ibid., 336.

34. Stephen 1997, 2.

35. Lamas, Martínez, Tarrés and Tuñón 1995, 337; Carrillo 1990; Stephen 1989.

36. Maier 1994, 41–45; Stephen 1989.

37. Lamas, Martínez, Tarrés and Tuñón 1995, 340.

38. Tarrés 1998, 132–33.

39. Ibid., 133.

40. Ibid., 134–45.

41. Ibid., 143.

42. Cornelius and Myhre 1998, 1.

43. Ejército Zapatista de Liberación Nacional, "First Declaration of the Lacandón Jungle," 1994, http://www.ezln.org/documentos/1994/199312xx.en.htm.

44. "La ley revolucionaria de las mujeres" 1994, 8. My translation.

45. Sierra 2002, 13.

46. Speed 2006.

47. Original at http://www.ezln.org. My translation.

48. Hernández Castillo, Speed, and Stephen 2006.

Final Reflections

Gender, Chaos, and Authority in Revolutionary Times

TEMMA KAPLAN

The Mexican Revolution, like the Russian and Chinese revolutions that followed, transformed social and political relations over the bodies of women. With great determination, revolutionaries attacked the dictators, czars, emperors, and generals who controlled the old governments, not always realizing that, following the overthrow of old regimes, some people would fight to free themselves from all social constraints, including those of gender. Revolutions undermine prevailing systems of authority and inadvertently weaken the patriarchal systems through which most governments rule. Revolutions initially reduce the authority of men over women, elites over the subaltern, and dominant ethnicities over those they exclude from power. But liberating people from repression under the old regimes also presents challenges to the new revolutionary governments. In the process of reestablishing some form of social order, post-revolutionary governments frequently invent new constraints, trying to stave off the sense of chaos that almost invariably follows the destruction of the old regime of authority.

The essays in this volume tell the story of how women of all races and classes negotiated within various systems of authority to achieve particular political and social goals. Mexicans occupying different places in the social structure and promoting different plans attempted to shape society in their own image and according to their own desires, opening up new spaces and introducing new visions. Elsewhere, men and women fought for analagous goals, for although every revolution is to some degree unique, social conflicts often follow similar patterns.

Like Russian and Chinese revolutionaries, Mexican authorities periodically attempted to end social strife by reordering gender arrangements or by introducing new forms of patriarchy. Over the decades following the initial revolutions, Mexican, Russian, and Chinese revolutionary governments, including women officials, periodically attempted to speak for groups of women who had not participated in the revolutionary changes. Eager to overcome old systems of social relations, these governments sometimes targeted women as those whose conditions of life needed reform. Taking women as symbols of what had been wrong with former regimes, the new governments tried to alter the conditions of women's lives, sometimes pitting them against the older women and men in their ethnic or national group.

Some governments actually attempted to help women change their own lives. Revolutionary authorities in China, for example, sent cadres into the countryside to hear about the bitterness in women's lives. In Soviet central Asia in the 1920s, Russians decided that in landlocked Muslim countries such as Uzbekistan, which lacked male factory- and dockworkers, women constituted what they called a "surrogate proletariat."[1] Of course, there is a great difference between those instances in which groups of women presented their own views and those in which women became symbolic of other social issues, but widespread consciousness that gender differences constitute a challenge to those undertaking social change has emerged in a variety of settings.

Historically, new leaders rush to establish their authority and quickly cut off debate about competing goals and practices. Revolutionary governments privilege certain systems of affiliation over others. Although they sometimes evoke fraternity, as in the French Revolution, or the notion of sibling bonds, as in the nineteenth-century Taiping Rebellion in China, most governments re-impose centralized political authority and patriarchal systems of rule.

Patriarchy serves as a model for all hierarchical systems. In most patriarchies, authority and autonomy are linked to masculinity, which can be synonymous with real and symbolic fatherhood, with virility, and with strength. Patriarchal governments justify themselves on the basis of protecting the weak and dependent, including those marked as feminine, who occupy a subordinate place in the social hierarchy. But maternal power rests on women's support for the existing social system and acceptance of its rules about the proper place of women and mothers. Mothers and other women outside the control of men, such as most of those who appear in this volume, disrupted patriarchal systems and, in risking the stability of their homes, schools, and workplaces, confronted not only the government but also the men of their classes and ethnic groups.

Authority repeatedly came into question during the Mexican Revolution and the socially contentious periods that followed. Conceived in war like all the other great twentieth-century revolutions, the long Mexican Revolution brought into focus many fundamental issues concerning relationships among authority, gender, and revolution. Sometimes activists envisioned new social arrangements completely different from the ones that preceded them. The process engendered sporadic periods of revolutionary effervescence, which sometimes exploded old hierarchies of gender, race, and class. People seeking social change sometimes overcame their fear of social disorder and allowed men and women to stretch their notions of permissible forms of masculinity and femininity. Those categories, fixed as they seemed at any historical moment, frequently became objects of contention when questions of power and authority emerged.

Chaos and Order

Mary Douglas confronted questions about social disorder in her classic anthropological study, *Purity and Danger*. According to Douglas, authorities regulate social order, imposing taboos and marking some activities as unclean and dangerous. She defined dirt as "matter out of place," arguing that social order, not hygiene, dictates observation of certain dietary and sexual taboos. Innovation can even become synonymous with rebellion, especially with regard to challenging gender roles. Hoping to ward off the danger of disorder, most societies establish rules and punish those who transgress them.[2]

Interpolating from Douglas, it is possible to argue that those in power impose taboos to buttress their authority, which partially rests on observing established gender relations. Although the content of gender varies enormously, masculine and feminine behavior appears "natural." Violating that behavior threatens chaos, and those in authority police the boundaries of gender in order to maintain social order. Because acceptance of gender norms marks social order in most countries, even deviations as seemingly trivial as haircuts and unique forms of dress elicit the wrath of those seeking social stability. From a mixture of fear and anger, those who equate survival with maintaining their authority repress those who violate established codes. Conflict in trade unions, refusal to follow established marriage or family patterns, and even unusual behavior in public places can, by disrupting conventional practices, threaten such people, whose moral panic sometimes takes the form of authoritarian behavior. According to Douglas, the blurring of boundaries, especially about sexuality and food, frequently appears as a political or social threat. Political defeat, rejection, or repression of one's class, race, or ethnic group leads to a sense of pollution that can only be overcome by reestablishing one's masculinity, often viewed in sexual, class, and racial terms. Although seemingly far removed from affairs of state, Douglas's insights have a great deal to say about the ways in which revolutionaries try to shape everyday life in order to re-impose their authority and reestablish social order.

During and after revolutions, those in power have commonly introduced new patriarchal systems to regain control over society. Whether the new order is based on fraternal bonds or the rule of fathers and potential fathers, the system usually entails an idealization of masculinity. Paradoxically, so long as masculinity remains unchallenged, men and women may enjoy a wide range of behavior, as Gabriela Cano demonstrated in her study of the transgendered Amelio Robles, who spent his life as a soldier and a cowboy. Stories of women passing as men appear in many cultures and historical periods, particularly when the women act as soldiers.[3] Maxine Hong Kingston described how women warriors brought social justice to repressed communities, and Estelle Friedman has written about heroic Civil War soldiers, whose sexual identities were revealed when they were wounded in battle.[4] During wartime, the disruptions of everyday life lead ordinary people to distinguish between soldiers who help them and those who attack them. The soldiers depend on one another for survival, and the esprit that unites the group requires emphasizing similarities, which has led military forces to segregate themselves by race and sex. But when race and sex are hidden, solidarity establishes a sense of social stability. In the circles in which he traveled, Amelio Robles masqueraded as a he-man and enhanced the masculinity of those around him.

For men trying to assert a revolutionary sense of authority, homosexuality could threaten social order. According to Cano, although Amelio Robles comfortably lived his life as a man, Manuel Palafox, a homosexual, was disparaged since he supposedly rejected masculinity. Openly gay, he was thought to be politically seditious and a threat to social stability. And Bayard Rustin, longtime civil-rights activist and advisor to the Reverend Martin Luther King Jr., like so many gay political activists remained closeted rather than have the movement he helped launch suffer ignominious attacks, linking his sexuality with disorder.[5] If certain forms of masculinity were associated with patriotism, any rejection of one entailed a rejection of the other. By this standard, heterosexual coupling became patriotic, but homosexuality, especially if linked to effeminacy, undermined authority.

Working-class women could even challenge social stability through their dress and demeanor. Christine Stansell wrote about the threat presented by the early-nineteenth-century New York working-class women known as the Bowery Girls. They appeared too young, affluent, and carefree to be considered acceptable as honest workingwomen.[6] Their ribbons and free movements around town outside the control of men presented further threats to patriarchal social order. The possibility of women singing on the job presented a similar challenge, which was one of the reasons why unions prohibited it, according to Heather Fowler-Salamini.

With the sense of stability even more tenuous after the Mexican Revolution, men of every generation often acted as if social stability depended on not only controlling women but also having women openly show deference to male authorities. Women who kept their feminine identities but entered male space as students in vocational or professional schools or as workers in agriculture or industry faced the greatest repression. The loose clothing and bobbed hair women students wore in the Gabriela Mistral vocational school that Patience A. Schell described and the vocational and professional students whom Anne Rubenstein discussed faced the kind of violent hazing that Amelio Robles eluded. Robles might cross from one gender to another, but he did not challenge masculinity. The *pelonas*, or bobbed-haired women, did, however, and, in the summer of 1924, male students attacked them in front of a vocational night school and outside the Medical School in Mexico City, humiliating them by shaving their heads. While violence against women occurs in many different contexts, the humiliation of the pelonas requires further explanation. Following World War I, when inflation, along with the loss of markets, swept Mexico, the increased independence of women of all classes challenged masculinity and, through it, the authority of the Mexican revolutionary order. Thus, as one eyewitness in Rubenstein's account noted, short hair may have caused a "moral panic" among the boys. Mary Douglas might point to the threat presented by "matter out of place."

Women who seemed to undermine authority faced violent retribution. Even before Mexican flappers, New Women, turned their attention to transforming gender norms in the 1920s, Chinese communist women cut their hair. Like the socialist schoolteachers in Mexico who went into rural areas to raise the level of literacy and introduce isolated peasants to the possibilities revolutionary society might offer, Chinese women activists ventured into the countryside. Mexican women schoolteachers sometimes suffered rape and murder. Likewise, Chinese women who wanted to educate peasants faced isolation and danger for living outside the control of men. The Chinese women who were part of the May Fourth nationalist movement of 1911 demanded full rights for women as citizens. To advertise their own freedom from Chinese feudalism, many leftist women exchanged their long, single, black braid for bobbed hair. Young women moved through the cities and the countryside, working with the poor and persuading—sometimes even forcing—women who wanted social change to cut their hair. Altering one's body image by cutting hair or taking up new dress styles indicated other ruptures with the past, a fact adversaries clearly noticed. When Chiang Kai-shek and the Kuomintang Party attempted to destroy communist forces between 1925 and 1927, the nationalist army targeted short-haired women for rape and murder, killing Mao Tse-tung's first wife along with thousands of communist women teachers.[7]

The violence men direct toward women who violated hair and dress codes had less to do with the women themselves than with the fact that they were outside the control of men and showed it. Masculine competition for authority in China and in Mexico frequently took place over the bodies of women, which calibrated the degree of male power. When women challenged that power in word, deed, or dress, authority came into question. Women who deviated from so-called traditional behavior —and many who continued to dress as they had before the revolutions— become symbolic of alterations in the body politic that put social order in danger.

The Russian revolutionaries thought that headscarves and veils indicated backwardness and associated revolutionary progress with winning women away from such forms of customary dress. In order to educate the peasants, the revolutionaries embarked on a massive, but short-lived literacy campaign, directed toward women as well as men.[8] The Russian peasant woman, symbolized by the stooped-over grandmother, or babushka, wearing her headscarf, was to be transformed into the modern woman worker in the field, dressed in her coveralls, her bobbed hair blowing freely in the wind. But massive shortages and famine in the late twenties detracted attention from educating rural women in Russia.

Russian revolutionaries had an even more daunting task of establishing social order as they attempted to transform Soviet territories in Uzbekistan, Turkestan, and Kazakhstan.[9] With little or no support for the revolution from the male population, revolutionary authorities devoted their attention to their version of "liberating" Muslim women in Uzbekistan.

TEMMA KAPLAN

The women wore veils called *paranji*, which resembled burqas, and the Russians viewed them as impediments to women's entry into modern society. Russian revolutionary women activists worked with Muslim women, teaching them to read and training them in technical skills. Often against the authority of their families, some of the girls embraced their new opportunities. But the policy of encouraging—maybe even forcing—the young women to unveil themselves without ensuring their protection resulted in huge massacres of women thought to have dishonored their fathers, brothers, and husbands. There is no more striking example of the way social engineering to replace the patriarchal authority of one group by the authority of another has resulted in greater harm to the women whose bodies were fought over.

Colonial officials elsewhere also attempted to reorganize gender relations to establish their own authority and reduce the patriarchal rule of those they conquered. Government attempts to feminize and naturalize whole groups of people helped authorities gain and maintain control over them. Historians and literary critics focusing on the process of colonization have argued that imperialist governments mute gender differences among the colonized and treat both men and women of the colonized group as feminine in order to enhance authorities' sense of their own masculinity. Men of that subordinate group increasingly take refuge in domestic life.[10] Implicitly, the idealized indigenous people whom Julia Tuñón discusses in her essay on the films of Emilio Fernández were feminized by being associated with nature. Anthropologist Sherry B. Ortner's now classic article asks if women are to nature as men are to culture, pointing out that the association of the natural world with femininity robs women of agency and presumes that they are not rational beings who act in the world.[11] For Mary Douglas, the division many cultures make between the natural and the rational world contributes to the illusion of control while discriminating against those who are naturalized. Being cast as having natures that prevailed over reason hurt both men and women. Nature can be benign or vicious, but nature threatens when it is out of control. Associating women in general and men of certain races or ethnicities with nature removes them from the rational world. If they have fixed human natures, they cannot change. Robbed of volition, natural men and women fall to the level of animals. They become members of a wild kingdom rather than autonomous citizens or even worthy adversaries. So long as the gender system considers femininity as dependent, feminizing men justifies excluding them and all women from power, since both groups lack autonomy.

267

Patriarchy, Masculinity, and Social Order

Revolutions, attendant wars, and social change generally disrupt ordinary life, leading to a sense of chaos that intensifies rhetoric about women needing protection. At the same time, during wars, even women accustomed to working at home begin to work for wages outside the home. With the goal of supporting their families, Mexican women inadvertently subverted patriarchal systems of authority and challenged masculinity during the Mexican Revolution on at least two counts. First, according to the ideals of patriarchy, men care for women and children in exchange for making all the decisions that affect them, thus turning them into dependents. Workers' associations also claim to protect the families of the men who formed the majority of their membership. In fact, many of the founding documents of early unions on three continents justified their organizations as protectors of helpless women and children. The union became a space where working men could contend with the government, man to man, while they attempted to earn a single male wage that would permit them to support a wife and children. Second, women workers supposedly undercut the possibility of higher wages precisely because men of all classes thought they would. Those women who worked for wages really needed unions to help them gain a living wage. Instead, the employers exploited them, and many male workers viewed them both as impediments to improving the relations between labor and capital and as "street women," rather than as respectable wives and mothers.[12]

The Catholic Church also intervened in revolutions and movements for social change, most notably by dealing with poor and working-class mothers and with workingwomen. In 1891 Pope Leo XIII issued the Rerum Novarum, dedicating the church to solving the world's social problems. An important element in the pope's plan to have the church help mute social conflict was for the church to create its own cooperatives, clinics, orphanages, food kitchens for pregnant and nursing women, and unions to vie for power with those that socialists and anarchists had launched. Whereas many of the socialist and anarchist groups envisioned a world in which women and children would be liberated from the workforce, the more conservative Catholic Church attempted to address the immediate needs of the poor while tying them to participation in church activities. Dubbed "yellow unions," the Catholic trade unions of Belgium, Italy, Spain, and Mexico—to name just a few—made great headway among large groups of women workers. Female textile workers in Milan, Italy, and seamstresses in Barcelona, Spain, who made linen cloths and cotton undergarments, joined Catholic workers' associations. Female factory workers found shelter in Catholic hostels for workingwomen.

Catholicism also provided justification for conflicts with the church hierarchy about strategies to protect poor, working-class women. When the wages of the linen and tablecloth seamstresses in Barcelona fell to substarvation rates in 1918, elite women who called themselves Catholic feminists organized a boycott of the work done by nuns in convents. The Catholic feminists argued that the nuns drove poor workingwomen to starvation because the nuns did not have to pay their own overhead given that the convents provided thread, candles, and rent.[13] Yet, faced with competing patriarchal institutions, workingwomen sometimes chose the Catholic institutions that offered immediate benefits over secular trade unions, which did not.

The Mexican revolutionary government was avowedly secular and regarded any attempt to promote organized religion as a challenge to the order it tried to impose. Kristina A. Boylan highlights Catholic women's attempts to compete for power against the government they thought injured them and their children in the guise of creating secular society. Presuming that the women she studies were rational within the confines of their immediate conditions, Boylan shows how they tried to impose their own vision of social order. She argues that when the women viciously attacked socialist schoolteachers, they did so as free agents, not as pawns of the church. Other right-wing women's groups also claimed to be overcoming chaos, as did Feminine Power (Poder Feminino) in their onslaught against the legally elected socialist government of Salvador Allende in Chile between 1970 and 1973.[14]

269

Even progressive movements of women could destabilize the existing social order embedded in gender. María Teresa Fernández-Aceves, Heather Fowler-Salamini, and Susan Gauss consider how wage-earning women inadvertently challenged patriarchy. According to Gauss, workingwomen frequently faced opprobrium as bad mothers, ignorant caretakers, and bad workers simply because reformers and revolutionaries did not want them in the workforce. But she, Fernández-Aceves, and Fowler-Salamini study women who confronted employers to win higher wages and dignity on the job. They grappled with the unions to gain equality as workers and tangled with fathers and husbands to get relief from domestic abuse. In a critique of well-meaning social critics, all three share the historian Heidi Tinsman's argument that, for better and worse, women who worked for wages were autonomous actors rather than dependent victims. Tinsman, in examining the lack of enthusiasm some rural women showed for Salvador Allende's land-reform programs in Chile in the 1970s, attributes their discomfort with the Popular Unity government to the way it disrupted their home lives by liberating men—but not women—to travel around, ignore domestic responsibilities, and sometimes beat wives who complained.[15] Feeling excluded from participation in the massive social change the Popular Unity government undertook, many rural women failed to identify its goals with their needs. On the other hand, Thomas Miller Klubock, in his study of the El Teniente mining community in Chile, explores how women used the desire of the mining administrators and the unions for social stability to win their own freedom from domestic abuse.[16] Many groups on the left might claim to be promoting the achievement of social order by fighting for more equitable distribution of resources and more democratic control of power, but Jocelyn Olcott highlights a less favorable example of how international influences affected Mexican political practices. She argues that the Popular Front policy of the Communist Third International, which urged leftist groups to overcome their differences in order to unite against fascists and neofascists, ultimately undermined the cause of women's suffrage in Mexico. Liberals and leftists in Catholic countries had long opposed votes for women for fear that women would vote for the Catholic parties. In fact, in Belgium, where socialists and laborites first fought for the principle of "One Man, One Vote" in 1902 in order to overcome a system in which voting rights accumulated with property, the conservatives countered by calling for "One Person, One Vote," presuming that they could count on support from women. Socialists such as the German leader Clara Zetkin fought at the beginning of the twentieth century to persuade her comrades that workingwomen needed the suffrage, but leftists continued to be ambivalent, especially after Spanish women, enfranchised in 1931, contributed to electing a right-wing government in Spain in 1933.

Calming Chaos in the Public Sphere

Without specific attention to breaking the link between masculinity, patriarchy, and social stability, revolutionary governments casually reinstate some form of patriarchal rule as a means by which to stabilize the country, but they face resistance all along the way. Revolutionary governments eager to overcome a sense of chaos call on self-abnegating mothers and their surrogates to buttress public life and patriarchal authority. Nurturing work that sustains everyday life—feeding, clothing, and caring for people—becomes a matter of public concern, and women of all races, classes, and ethnicities bear the greatest responsibility for providing these

TEMMA KAPLAN

necessary services. Occupying contradictory positions, simultaneously cast as dependents and nurturers, women of all classes join brigades, enter schools, and take their places in the public sphere.

Having women appear to nurture the public much as they did their families may have calmed the sense of chaos that frequently followed in the wake of social strife. As a public sector emerged in certain countries in the eighteenth and nineteenth centuries, the services women performed in private carried over to the public sphere, which became feminized. According to the historian Denise Riley, the whole notion of society was gendered female, a situation she claims developed in the nineteenth century in Europe and the United States. While society became that realm of public life that women were thought to dominate, politics and economics continued to be gendered as masculine.[17] Large numbers of women labored as public servants, as teachers, as caretakers of children in orphanages, and as social workers, performing in public tasks that mirrored their domestic activities. Civil society, which included religious organizations, families, schools, and public activities, thus reemerged in highly gendered ways. With other careers effectively blocked, women of all classes gravitated toward service work. But rather than enhance the sense of women as full participants in public life, their work in the service sector actually reenforced patriarchy and reinstated women's images as nurturing mothers.

Mexico women occupied various public realms in the 1920s, 1930s, and 1940s, but they had to fight continuously against masculine domination and patriarchal authority. Indigenous, poor, and rural women remained largely in their own public sphere, laboring, laundering, and selling goods at market, with very little contact with government authorities except when they collided around questions of divorce and adoption. Even before the revolution, the Mexican state had assumed control over registering marriages, divorces, and deaths. Rights of women to divorce abusive husbands stood at the center of nineteenth-century struggles for female emancipation in the United States and western Europe as well. When the North American feminist and communist Meridel Le Sueur was an infant, her mother left Iowa to escape her drunken, abusive husband. Her mother only gained her freedom when Le Sueur's father decided to divorce his wife "on the grounds of desertion and her interest in 'dangerous literature.'"[18]

Divorce plays an important role in preserving domestic and public order. Women need rights of divorce not only to escape abusive relationships but also to secure the resources necessary to support themselves. Under patriarchal governments, family stability serves as a metaphor for social order. Stephanie Smith, who writes so convincingly about later struggles over divorce, has also focused on indigenous Maya women's use of the short-lived popular revolutionary tribunals that General Salvador Alvarado established in Yucatán. These women went to court to win legal separations from husbands, many of whom had already abandoned them, and they attempted to win property rights over the land they tilled but their husbands continued to own.[19] Chinese women also craved access to resources as part of their revolutionary demands. In the 1930s, during the Long March, when the Chinese communists set up self-governing soviets in rural China, women gained collective rights to farm. In fact, the People's Republic of China, founded in October 1949, quickly set out to find ways to feed the population, win popular support, and destroy the patriarchal family system and the warlords' domination of rural life. Within a year, the communist government passed both the Agrarian Law and the Divorce (actually, the Marriage) Law of 1950, which granted equal rights to control land and equal rights of divorce to men and women.[20]

Much earlier in Mexico, rights of divorce had equally liberating and destabilizing effects on social order. If women were not assured the economic resources necessary to support their families, divorce could be disastrous for them and their children. Stephanie Smith argues that while women of all classes sought divorce in larger numbers than men during the first years of the Mexican Revolution, the situation later reversed itself. From the 1920s on, men divorced their wives at a greater rate, leaving many women without custody of their children or means of support. As in other places where the line between state and civil society became blurred, the divorce courts could cause the chaos they were designed to prevent.

The Mexican government was not alone in its willingness to trade patriarchal authority at the local level of the family for other political and social benefits, according to the sociologist Judith Stacey.[21] Although the Chinese revolutionary state attempted to break the power of the landlords by giving women access to property, the revolution may have intensified patriarchy. Writing about the dissolution of the peasants and women's associations after the victory of the revolution in China in 1949, Stacey claims that Chinese landlords, who had raped peasant women with impunity and turned them into concubines, lost their power. Chinese peasant men, who had gained power through independent peasant organizations, permitted their dissolution. In exchange, they gained individual patriarchal rights to control the sexuality of their wives and daughters. Patriarchy became "democratized" and privatized, and women again lost their autonomy.

Traditional views about the relationship between social order and stable families should favor adoption. But, despite patriarchal rhetoric presuming that all families are alike, families actually differed by class and race. Ann S. Blum's essay on adoption shows how even as the Mexican government attempted to place the abandoned children of the poor and to prevent adopted children from being turned into servants, they promoted class biases that intensified the patriarchal system governed by ruling-class men. After the revolution, with increasing concern about educating all children, the government tried to turn motherhood into a middle-class civil-service job. Not only was the mother to nurture the child, but she was also supposed to inculcate middle-class values in order to stave off the disorder posed by children outside the control of the government. Blum claims that fostering a child to promote his or her physical well-being only assured that that child would not become a ward of the state. Adoption increasingly required access to wealth and a support network of servants. Lacking that, the government required adopted mothers to remain at home, thus preventing women who had to do waged work from adopting children. The same women who ministered to children's physical needs as foster mothers and servants were denied rights to adopt the children whom they nurtured.

Motherhood itself became a means by which to assure social stability during and after the Mexican Revolution, though it could also be disruptive. By refusing adoption to working-class and indigenous women, the government established a two-tiered system of motherhood. Nevertheless, the government spoke of mothers as classless and raceless, an essentialized group of women who indirectly served the government and supported social order. The post-revolutionary state, whether in the hands of progressives or conservatives, established fixed boundaries for all social identities, especially that of motherhood. The various images of motherhood served diametrically opposed political interests. Lázaro Cárdenas and Manuel Avila Camacho both held big Mothers' Day rituals as a way to highlight mothers' connection to the state. Some governments tried to supplant the celebration of International Women's Day on 8 March with Mothers' Day celebrations in order to replace a militant, working-class women's holiday with one that celebrated benign motherhood. Whereas International Women's Day called for equal rights for workingwomen and commemorated the uprising of Russian women that launched the February 1917 Revolution (March 8 on the Western calendar) in Russia, Mothers' Day homogenized the class and racial differences among mothers.[22]

Other governments tried to win over working-class women as mothers by providing material support for them, as did the Mexican government. For instance, Avila Camacho gave away sewing machines, and both Lázaro

Cárdenas and Avila Camacho promoted housewives' and mothers' centers, just as the Chilean Christian Democrats did in the late 1940s.[23] Social workers in Mexico, as in Weimar Germany in the 1920s, frequently attempted to turn poor women into government dependents.[24] The women may have benefited from the largesse of the government, but they lacked the authority they sometimes gained from participation in trade unions or social movements to shape their own goals and administer the resources they themselves secured. Patience A. Schell describes how government control increased in vocational schools, which taught women the correct ways to work in the home. Schoolteachers ridiculed the instruction mothers and aunts could provide and even established government authority over domestic work. Although female relatives generally instructed young women about the rules of housekeeping in their culture and historical period, governments increasingly tried to regulate housework by teaching new immigrants new values through required courses in home economics in the United States and through vocational schools in revolutionary Mexico.

274

The Recent Revolution

One of the greatest threats to patriarchal social order and the authority of the Mexican government came at the end of the twentieth century when indigenous women joined the challenge to the existing rulers. The anthropologist Lynn Stephen has documented the activities of women in the Zapatista National Liberation Army (EZLN) to link demands as women for control over their own bodies to social campaigns for human rights.

Stephen points out the ways in which the poorest Mexican rural and urban women developed organizational skills and grew increasingly conscious of the price they had to pay for breaking with historical patterns of deference to men. Seeking to find the constituents of these new strategies that certain grassroots women adopted, Stephen examines the Agro-Industrial Units for Women (UAIM) and explains how they attempted to provide rural women with collective access to the means of production in land even if that meant challenging patriarchal authority. Although the UAIMs generally failed, they succeeded in training a cadre of women to engage in collective action. But just as Mexican women with bobbed hair enraged some of their male classmates, grassroots women in Mexico and the rest of the world faced violence from male relatives who opposed women's increasing activism outside their communities. In Mexico in the 1980s, the Women's Regional Council of the National Council of Urban Popular Movements (CONAMUP) collectively confronted domestic violence, attempting to gain full human rights in the family at the same time as they fought for increased control over state resources.

Stephen argues that, to some extent, women's ability to confront repression at the domestic, state, and global levels is apparent in the national debate opened up by the women of the EZLN. "The Revolutionary Law of Women," issued simultaneously with the first declarations the Zapatistas made on 1 January 1994, was a women's bill of rights within the movement. By linking broad social aspirations for healthcare, decent wages, education, reproductive rights, free choice of sexual partners, and community sanctions against rapists, the women challenged patriarchy and presented a new image of themselves as full human beings deserving of respect.

Mexican women challenged patriarchal systems of authority and created new local and regional organizations to pursue their goals. As they mobilized in pursuit of human rights and their collective religious, social, and economic interests, their image as activists replaced their image as dependents. Whether or not they succeeded in winning their immediate goals, they gradually assumed their rightful place in determining the system of authority that passes from the government through the region, the workplace, the union, and the family. In the course of their struggles, they fought against the constraints of patriarchy and masculinity, overcoming admonitions about the chaos they might cause in their efforts to achieve control over their everyday lives.

When working-class, indigenous, rural, and Catholic women confronted patriarchy, they generally did so from local bases in their factories, neighborhoods, or regions. Despite admonitions that they threatened social stability, the women discussed in this volume inadvertently promoted a social order rooted in community associations. By attacking hierarchical systems, they challenged patriarchy from a variety of political perspectives.

Reorienting authority, whether to the left or the right, has undermined the idea of fixed gender identities. Not only at the outset of revolutions but in periodic uprisings gender identities that buttress family structures and patriarchal political systems have come into question, and none more so than in the images of women as mothers. Like all fantasies, maternal imagery is inherently unstable. The same women who appear as symbols of the nation can challenge patriarchy and nationalism by extending their demands for social change from the public sphere into the household, as Chilean women did when they demanded "Democracy in the Country and in the Home" in their struggle against the dictatorship of Augusto Pinochet. Whether through participation in mixed groups such as the

EZLN or in women's unions, Mexican women have attacked patriarchy, calling for some form of collective control over the treatment of women. The essays in this volume contradict the idea that efforts to undermine gender stereotypes and to gain autonomy prevail only during the early days of revolutions. In fact, these essays show that the practices of challenging the government, the unions, fathers, husbands, and male leaders periodically erupted in Mexico and in other countries when authorities least expected it. These campaigns opened up possibilities for new and sustained social change by helping to create new institutions to guarantee more local control. Through these institutions, working-class and rural women have at times gained the kind of authority that they have used to enhance their everyday lives.

Notes

1. Massell 1974; Northrop 2004.
2. Douglas 1995.
3. San Francisco Lesbian and Gay History Project 1990.
4. Kingston 1976; D'Emilio and Freedman 1997.
5. D'Emilio 2003.
6. Stansell 1987.
7. Croll 1978, 146–47, 150–51.
8. Engel 2003.
9. Massell 1974; Northrop 2004.
10. Sinha 1995.
11. Ortner 1974.
12. See Fowler-Salamini in this volume.
13. Kaplan 1992
14. Kaplan 2004, 40–72; Power 2002; Baldez 2002.
15. Tinsman 2002.
16. Klubock 1998.
17. Riley 1988, 46–51.
18. Le Sueur 1984, 45.
19. Smith 2002.
20. Salaff and Merkle 1970, 165–66.
21. Stacey 1983.
22. Kaplan 1988.
23. Rosemblatt 2000.
24. Hong 1998.

TEMMA KAPLAN

Bibliography

Archives

AGEV/JCCA Archivo General del Estado de Veracruz, Junta Central de
           Conciliación y Arbitraje. Jalapa, Veracruz
AGEY   Archivo General del Estado de Yucatán. Mérida, Yucatán
FJ   Fondo Justicia
FM   Fondo Municipio
FPE   Fondo Poder Ejecutivo
FPJ   Fondo Poder Judicial
AGN   Archivo General de la Nación. Mexico City
AHAM   Archivo Histórico de la Arquidiócesis de México. Mexico City
AHDF   Archivo Histórico del Distrito Federal. Mexico City
AHJ   Archivo Histórico de Jalisco. Guadalajara, Jalisco
AHTF   Archivo Histórico de Testimonios de Familia, Instituto
           Nacional de Antropología e Historia. Mexico City
AHSDN   Archivo Histórico de la Secretaría de la Defensa Nacional.
           Mexico City
AHSEP   Archivo Histórico de la Secretaría de Educación Pública.
           Mexico City
AHSSA   Archivo Histórico de la Secretaría de Salubridad y Asistencia.
           Mexico City
AHUFCM   Archivo Histórico de la Unión Femenina Católica Mexicana,
           Acervo Histórico, Universidad Iberoamericana. Mexico City
AMC   Archivo Municipal de Córdoba. Córdoba, Veracruz
APGD   Archivo Personal Gertrude Duby, Centro Cultural Na Bolom. San
           Cristóbal de las Casas, Chiapas
ACREY   Archivo Registro Civil del Estado de Yucatán. Mérida, Yucatán

CEMOS   Centro de Estudios del Movimiento Obrero y Socialista. Mexico City

CIDOC   Centro Internacional de Documentación / International Documentation Center. Cuernavaca, Mexico / Leiden, The Netherlands (microfiche collection)

Cineteca Nacional   Cuadernos de la Cineteca Nacional. Mexico City

SSM   Secretariado Social Mexicano. Mexico City

USDOS   National Archives and Records Administration, United States Department of State, Record Group 59. Washington, D.C.

USMIL   National Archives and Records Administration, United States War Department, *Military Intelligence Reports: Mexico, 1919–1940* México. Washington, D.C.

Publications

"La Acción Católica y la Acción Política." 1931. *Informador de las Brigadas Femeninas de Santa Juana de Arco* 2, no. 5 (31 May): 4.

Adame Goddard, Jorge. 1981. *El pensamiento político y social de los católicos mexicanos, 1867–1914.* Mexico City: Universidad Nacional Autónoma de México.

"Agradecimiento." 1930. *Informador de las Brigadas Femeninas de Santa Juana de Arco* 1, no. 1 (26 January): 1.

Aguilar V., Rubén, and Guillermo Zermeño P. 1992. *Religión, política y sociedad: El sinarquismo y la Iglesia en México (nueve ensayos).* Mexico City: Universidad Iberoamericana.

Aldana Rendón, Mario Alfonso. 1988. *Jalisco desde la revolución.* Vol. 1, *Del reyismo al nuevo orden constitucional, 1901–1917.* Guadalajara: Universidad de Guadalajara and Gobierno del Estado de Jalisco.

Alonso, Ana María. 1995. *Thread of Blood: Colonialism, Revolution, and Gender on Mexico's Northern Frontier.* Tucson: University of Arizona Press.

Alonso, Enrique. 1987. *María Conesa.* Mexico City: Océano.

Alvarado, Salvador. 1980. *La reconstrucción de México: Un mensaje a los pueblos de América.* Vol. 2. 2d ed. Mérida, Yucatán: Ediciones del Gobierno de Yucatán.

Alvarez, Rodolfo. 1920. "Gimnasia especial para las damas." *Arte y Sport* 1, no. 32 (17 April): 6.

Amador, María Luisa, and Jorge Ayala Blanco. 1999. *Cartelera Cinematográfico, 1920—1929.* Mexico City: Centro Universitario de Estudios Cinematográficos de Universidad Nacional Autónoma de México.

Angel Zárraga: El anhelo por un mundo sin fronteras en la legación de México en Paris. 1990. Mexico City: Museo Nacional de Arte.

Arizpe, Lourdes, and Josefina Aranda. 1986. "Women Workers in the Strawberry Agribusiness in Mexico." In *Women's Work: Development and the Division of Labor by Gender,* edited by Eleanor Leacock and Helen Safa, 174–93. South Hadley, Mass.: Bergin and Garvey.

Arnold, Marigene. 1973. Mexican Women: The Anatomy of a Stereotype in a Mexican Village. PhD diss., University of Florida.

Arrom, Silvia M. 1985. *The Women of Mexico City, 1790–1857.* Stanford: Stanford University Press.

———. 1994. "Changes in Mexican Family Law in the Nineteenth Century." In *Confronting Change, Challenging Tradition,* edited by Gertrude M. Yeager, 87–102. Wilmington, Del.: Scholarly Resources.

Art Déco: Un país nacionalista, un México cosmopólita. 1997. Mexico City: Instituto Nacional de Bellas Artes.

Ayala Blanco, Jorge. 1968. *La aventura el cine mexicano.* Cine-Club Era Series. Mexico City: Editorial Era.

"Ayuda laica a la jerarquía." 1937. *Christus* 2, no. 20 (June): 750–55.

Azuela, Mariano. 2002. *The Underdogs: A Novel of the Mexican Revolution.* Translated by E. Munguía Jr. New York: Modern Library.

Baitenmann, Helga. 1997. Rural Agency and State Formation in Postrevolutionary Mexico: The Agrarian Reform in Central Veracruz (1915–1992). PhD diss., New School for Social Research.

———. 2000. Gender and Agrarian Rights in Twentieth-Century Mexico. Paper prepared for the meeting of the Latin American Studies Association, Miami, Florida, 16–20 March.

Baldez, Lisa. 2002. *Why Women Protest: Women's Movements in Chile.* New York: Cambridge University Press.

Bantjes, Adrian. 1998. *As If Jesus Walked on Earth: Cardenismo, Sonora, and the Mexican Revolution.* Wilmington, Del.: Scholarly Resources.

Barranco, V. Bernardo. 1996. "Posiciones políticas en la historia de la Acción Católica Mexicana." In *El pensamiento social de los católicos mexicanos,* edited by Roberto Blancarte, 39–70. Mexico City: Fondo de Cultura Económica.

Barre, Marie Chantal. 1983. *Ideologías, indigenismo y movimientos indios.* Mexico City: Siglo Veintiuno Editores.

Bartra, Armando. 1977. *Regeneración, 1900–1918: La corriente más radical de la revolución mexicana en 1910 a través de su periódico de combate.* Mexico City: Ediciones Era.

Bartra, Roger. 1987. *La jaula de la melancolía: Identidad y metamorfosis del mexicano.* Mexico City: Grijalbo, Colección Enlace.

Bauer, Arnold J. 1990. "Millers and Grinders: Technology and Household Economy in Meso-America." *Agricultural History* 64, no. 1: 1–17.

Beattie, Peter M. 2001. *The Tribute of Blood: Army, Honor, Race, and Nation in Brazil, 1864–1945.* Durham: Duke University Press.

Becker, Marjorie. 1995. *Setting the Virgin on Fire: Lázaro Cárdenas, Michoacán Peasants and the Redemption of the Mexican Revolution.* Berkeley: University of California Press.

Beezley, William. 1987. *Judas at the Jockey Club.* Lincoln: University of Nebraska Press.

Benjamin, Thomas. 2000. "Rebuilding the Nation." In *The Oxford History of Mexico,* edited by Michael C. Meyer and William H. Beezley, 467–502. New York: Oxford University Press.

Benjamin, Thomas, and Mark Wasserman, eds. 1990. *The Provinces of the Revolu-*

279

tion: Essays on Regional Mexican History, 1910–1929. Albuquerque: University of New Mexico Press.

Bergquist, Charles. 1986. *Labor in Latin America.* Palo Alto: Stanford University Press.

Besse, Susan K. 1996. *Restructuring Patriarchy: The Modernization of Gender Inequality in Brazil, 1914–1940.* Chapel Hill: University of North Carolina Press.

Blair, Fredika. 1987. *Isadora: Portrait of the Artist as a Woman.* Wellingborough: Equation Books.

Bliss, Katherine Elaine. 1997. "Theater of Operations: Feminist and Catholic Social Action in the Mexico City *Sifilicomio.*" Paper presented at the 20th Latin American Studies Association International Congress.

———. 1999. "The Science of Redemption: Syphilis, Sexual Promiscuity, and Reformism in Revolutionary Mexico City." *Hispanic American Historical Review* 79, no. 1: 1–40.

———. 2001. *Compromised Positions: Prostitution, Public Health, and Gender Politics in Revolutionary Mexico.* University Park: Pennsylvania State University Press.

Blum, Ann S. 1998a. Children without Parents: Law, Charity, and Social Practice, Mexico City, 1867–1940. PhD diss., University of California, Berkeley.

———. 1998b. "Public Welfare and Child Circulation, Mexico City, 1877 to 1925." *Family History* 23, no. 3 (July): 240–71.

———. 2003. "Dying of Sadness: Hospitalism and Child Welfare, Mexico City, 1920–1940." In *From Cholera to AIDS: History and Disease in Modern Latin America,* edited by Diego Armus, 209–36. Durham: Duke University Press.

———. 2004. "Cleaning the Revolutionary Household: Domestic Servants and Public Welfare in Mexico City, 1900–1935." *Journal of Women's History* 15, no. 4: 67–90.

Bonfil Batalla, Guillermo. 1990. *México profundo: Una civilización negada.* Mexico City: Grijalbo- Consejo Nacional para la Cultura y las Artes.

———. 1996. *México Profundo: Reclaiming a Civilization.* Translated by Philip A. Dennis. Austin: University of Texas Press.

Bortz, Jeffrey. 1995. "The Genesis of the Mexican Labor Relations System: Federal Labor Policy and the Textile Industry 1925–1940." *The Americas* 52 (July): 43–69.

Botey Estapé, Carlota. 1991. "La parcela ejidal es un patrimonio familiar." *Uno más uno,* suplemento, "El Ejido a Debate" (18 November): 3.

Boylan, Kristina A. 2000. Mexican Catholic Women's Activism, 1929–1940. PhD diss., Oxford University.

Brunk, Samuel. 1995. *Emilano Zapata: Revolution and Betrayal in México.* Alburquerque: University of New Mexico Press.

Buck, Sarah A. 2001. "El control de la natalidad y el día de la madre: Política feminista y reaccionaria en México, 1922–1923." *Signos históricos* 5 (January–June): 9–53.

———. 2002. "Mother's Day, the State, and Feminist Action: Maternalist Welfare Initiatives in 1940s Mexico." Paper presented at the 12th Berkshire Conference on the History of Women, University of Connecticut, June 2002.

Buffington, Robert M. 2000. *Criminal and Citizen in Modern Mexico.* Lincoln: University of Nebraska Press.

Butler, Judith. 1999. *Gender Trouble: Feminism and the Subversion of Identity.* New York: Routledge.

Calendario más antiguo de Galván. 2002. Mexico City: Editorial Murguía.

Campbell, Hugh G. 1976. *La derecha radical en México, 1929–1949.* Mexico City: Secretaría de Educación Pública.

Campobello, Nellie. 1931. *Cartucho: Relatos de la lucha en el norte de México.* Mexico City: Integrales.

Cano, Gabriela. 1988a. "El Coronel Robles: Una combatiente zapatista." *Fem.* (abril): 22–24.

———. 1991a. "Las femenistas en campaña: La primera mitad del siglo 20." *Debate Feminista* 2, no. 4 (September): 269–92.

———. 1991b. "Las mujeres en el proyecto educativo de José Vasconcelos." *Signos. Anuario de Humanidades 1991:* 265–75.

———. 1993. "Revolución, femenismo y ciudadanía en México (1915–1940)." In *Historia de la mujeres en Occidente,* edited by G. D. a. M. Perrot, 5:301–12. Madrid: Taurus.

———. 1997. "Soldaderas and Coronelas." In *Encyclopedia of Mexico: History, Society, & Culture,* edited by Michael S. Werner, 2:1357–60. Chicago: Fitzroy Dearborn.

———. 1998. "The Porfiriato and the Mexican Revolution: Constructions of Feminism and Nationalism." In *Nation, Empire, Colony: Historicizing Gender and Race,* edited by Ruth Roach Pierson and Nupur Chaudhuri, 106–20. Bloomington: Indiana University Press.

———. 1999. "La íntima felicidad del Coronel Robles." *Equis: Cultura y sociedad* (June): 25–34.

———. 2000. "Las mujeres como sujeto de la Revolución Mexicana. Una mirada historiográfica." In *El Siglo de la Revolución Mexicana,* edited by Jaime Bailón Corres, Carlos Martínez Assad, and Pablo Serrano Alvarez, 275–86. Mexico City: Instituto Nacional de Estudios Históricos de la Revolución Mexicana.

Cano, Gabriela, and Verena Radkau. 1989. *Ganando Espacios, Historias de vida: Guadalupe Zúñiga, Alura Flores y Josefina Vicens, 1920–1940.* Mexico City: Universidad Autónoma Metropolitana.

Cárdenas, Lázaro. 1978. *Palabras y documentos: Mensajes, discursos, declaraciones, entrevistas y otros documentos, 1928–1940.* Vol. 1. Mexico City: Siglo Veintiuno Editores.

Cárdenas, Olga. 2000. "Amelia Robles y la revolución zapatista en Guerrero." In *Estudios sobre zapatismo,* edited by Espejel López, 303–19. Mexico City: Instituto Nacional de Antropología e Historia.

Cardoso, Ruth C. L. 1984. "Creating Kinship: The Fostering of Children in *Favela* Families in Brazil." In *Kinship Ideology and Practice in Latin America,* edited by Raymond T. Smith, 196–203. Chapel Hill: University of North Carolina Press.

Carr, Barry. 1992. *Marxism and Communism in Twentieth-Century Mexico.* Lincoln: University of Nebraska Press.

———. 1994. "The Fate of the Vanguard under a Revolutionary State: Marxism's Contribution to the Construction of the Great Arch." In *Everyday Forms of*

State Formation: Revolution and Negotiation of Rule in Modern Mexico, edited by Gil Joseph and Daniel Nugent, 326–54. Durham: Duke University Press.

Carranza, Venustiano. 1964. *Ley sobre relaciones familiares: Expedida por el primer jefe del ejército constitucionalista, encargado del poder ejecutivo de la nación, el 9 de abril de 1917, publicada en el "Diario Oficial" de los días 14 de dicho mes, al 11 de mayo, fecha en que entró en vigor.* 2d ed. Mexico City: Editorial Andrade.

Carrillo, Teresa. 1990. "Women and Independent Unionism in the Garment Industry." In *Popular Movements and Political Change in Mexico*, edited by Joe Foweraker and Ann L. Craig, 213–33. Boulder: Lynne Reinner.

Casasola, Agustín V. n.d. *Historia gráfica de la Revolución Mexicana*, cuaderno 8. Mexico City: Editorial Trillas.

Castells, Manuel. 1999a. *The Power of Identity.* Oxford: Basil Blackwell.

——. 1999b. *The Rise of the Network Society.* Oxford: Basil Blackwell.

Caulfield, Sueann. 2000. *In Defense of Honor: Sexual Morality, Modernity, and Nation in Early-Twentieth-Century Brazil.* Durham: Duke University Press.

Ceballos Ramírez, Manuel. 1991. *El catolicismo social: Un tercero en discordia.* Mexico City: El Colegio de México.

Chassen-López, Francie R. 1994 " 'Cheaper than Machines': Women and Agriculture in Porfirian Oaxaca, 1880–1911." In *Women of the Mexican Countryside, 1850–1990*, edited by Heather Fowler-Salamini and Mary Kay Vaughan, 27–50. Tucson: University of Arizona Press.

Chesler, Ellen. 1992. *Woman of Valor: Margaret Sanger and the Birth Control Movement in America.* New York: Simon and Schuster.

"Circular No. 8, 2 Oct. 1936." 1937. *Christus* 2, no. 14 (January): 14.

Civardi, Luigi, Msgr. 1935. *A Manual of Catholic Action.* Translated by C. C. Martindale, S.J. London: Sheed and Ward.

Código Civil del Estado de Yucatán. 1918. Mérida, Yucatán: Gobierno del Estado.

"Conclusiones aprobadas en la Segunda Asamblea General de la UFCM." 1935. *Boletín Eclesiástico de la Arquidiócesis de Guadalajara* 4, no. 4 (1 April): 159–60.

Contreras, María Isabel. 1940. *La parroquia de zapotiltic y la congregación de la doctrina Cristiana.* Querétaro: Imprenta Paulín.

Cornelius, Wayne A., and David Myhre. 1998. Introduction. In *The Transformation of Rural Mexico: Reforming the Ejido Sector*, edited by Wayne Cornelius and David Myhre, 1–24. La Jolla: Center for U.S.-Mexican Studies, University of California, San Diego.

Craig, Ann. 1983. *The First Agraristas: An Oral History of a Mexican Agrarian Reform Movement.* Berkeley: University of California Press.

Crespo Oviedo, Luis Felipe, ed. 1988. *"Los días eran nuestros . . .": Vida y trabajo entre los obreros textiles de Atlixco.* Puebla, Mexico: Secretaría de Educación Pública, Universidad Autónoma de Puebla, Instituto Mexicano de Seguro Social.

Crider, Greg. 1996. Material Struggles: Workers' Strategies During the "Institutionalization of the Revolution" in Atlixco, Puebla, Mexico, 1930–1942. PhD diss., University of Wisconsin, Madison.

Croll, Elisabeth. 1978. *Feminism and Socialism in China.* New York: Schocken Books.

Cueva Tazzer, María Lourdes. n.d. Entre el nacionalismo cultural y el interna-
cionalismo proletario: Textos y prácticas de mujeres comunistas en México,
1924–1934. Unpublished paper, Universidad Autónoma Metropolitana
Iztapalapa.

Dávila Garibi, J. Ignacio. 1920. *Memoria histórica de las labores de la Asociación de
Damas Católicas de Guadalajara durante la ausencia de su Meritísimo Fundador,
Illmo y Rmo. Sr. Dr. y Mtro. D. Francisco Orozco y Jiménez, o sea del 19 de mayo
de 1914 que partió de la ciudad episcopal, al 14 de octubre de 1919 que volvió de su
destierro.* Guadalajara: J. M. Yguiniz.

"Decoración de la Sala de Conferencias en la antigua iglesia de San Pedro y San
Pablo." 1922. *Boletín de la Secretaría de Educación Pública* 1, no. 2: frontispiece.

De Grazia, Victoria. 1992. *How Fascism Ruled Women: Italy, 1922–1945.* Berkeley:
University of California Press.

——, ed., with Ellen Furlough. 1996. *The Sex of Things: Gender and Consumption
in Historical Perspective.* Berkeley: University of California Press.

de la Colina, José. 1985. "El canto bárbaro de Emilio Fernández." *Semanario Cultural de Novedades* 3, no. 149 (24 February): 1–2.

"De la excentricidad mundial." 1924. *Jueves de Excélsior*, no. 109 (10 July): 13.

de los Reyes, Aurelio. 1987. *Medio siglo de cine mexicano (1821–1880).* Mexico
City: Editorial Trillas.

D'Emilio, John. 2003. *Lost Prophet: The Life and Times of Bayard Rustin.* New
York: Free Press.

D'Emilio, John, and Estelle B. Freedman. 1997. *Intimate Matters: A History of
Sexuality in America.* 2d ed. Chicago: University of Chicago Press.

Deutsch, Sandra McGee. 1991. "Gender and Sociopolitical Change in Twentieth-
Century Latin America." *Hispanic American Historical Review* 71, no. 2: 259–
316.

Diario de los debates del Congreso constituyente de 1916–1917. 2 vols. 1922. Mexico
City: Cámara de Diputados.

Diario Oficial de la Federación. "Decreto que crea la Legión de Honor." 8 February 1949, 5. Mexico City: Talleres Gráficos de la Nación, 1949.

Dirección General de Estadísticas. 1934. *Quinto Censo de Población, 1930: Estado
de Veracruz.* Mexico City: Dirección General de Estadísticas.

Documentos del Movimiento Campesino. 1984. "Acuerdos y resoluciones del II
congreso nacional ordinario de la CNPA." *Textual* 5, no. 17: 115–27.

Domínguez Pérez, Olivia. 1986. *Política y movimientos sociales en el tejedismo.*
Jalapa: Universidad Veracruzana.

Dore, Elizabeth, and Maxine Molyneux, eds. 2000. *Hidden Histories of Gender
and the State in Latin America.* Durham: Duke University Press.

Douglas, Mary. 1995. *Purity and Danger: An Analysis of the Concepts of Pollution
and Taboo.* New York: Routledge.

Drogus, Carole Anne. 1997. *Women, Religion and Social Change in Brazil's Popular Church.* Notre Dame: University of Notre Dame Press.

Duby, Gertrude. 1942. "Bauerngeneral Zapata und das neue Russland." *Freies
Deutschland* (November–December): 27.

Dussel, Enrique. 1981. *A History of the Church in Latin America: Colonialism to*

Liberation (1492–1979). Translated and revised by Alan Neely. Grand Rapids, Mich.: William B. Eerdmans.

Eltit, Diamela. 1991. "Las batallas del Coronel Robles." *Debate Feminista* 4 (September): 171–77.

Engel, Barbara Alpern. 2003. *Women in Russia, 1700–2000.* Cambridge: Cambridge University Press.

Enríquez, Victoria. 1998. "Hija de la Revolución: El Coronel Amelia 'La Güera' Robles." *Fem* (October): 41–43.

Enstad, Nan. 1999. *Ladies of Labor, Girls of Adventure.* New York: Columbia University Press.

Episcopado Mexicano. 1935. "Carta Pastoral Colectiva . . . sobre la doctrina educativa de la Iglesia" [21 November 1935]. *Christus* 1, no. 1 (1 December): 26–41.

Equal Rights. Official Organ of the National Woman's Party. 15 July 1937. Washington, D.C.

Erauso, Catalina. 1996. *Lieutenant Nun: Memoir of a Basque Lieutenant Nun: Transvestite in the New World.* Translated by Michele Stepto and Gabriel Stepto. Boston: Beacon Press.

Escontrilla Valdez, Hugo Armando. 2000. El Secretariado Social Mexicano. Los orígenes de la autonomía, 1965–1973. Master's thesis, Instituto de Investigaciones Dr. José María Luis Mora.

"La Escuela Hogar 'Gabriela Mistral.' " 1922. *Boletín de la Secretaría de Educación Pública* 1, no. 1 (March): 244.

Estrada Urroz, Rosalina. 1980. "El poder de compra de la clase obrera en Puebla, de 1940–1960." In *Memorias del encuentro sobre historia del movimiento obrero,* 349–77. Puebla: Universidad Autónoma de Puebla.

———. 1997. *Del telar a la cadena de montaje: La condición obrera en Puebla, 1940–1976.* Puebla, Mexico: Benemérita Universidad Autónoma de Puebla.

Falcón, Romana, and Soledad García Morales. 1986. *La semilla en el surco: Adalberto Tejeda y el radicalismo en Veracruz, 1883–1960.* Mexico City: El Colegio de México and Universidad Veracruzana.

Farnsworth-Alvear, Ann. 2000. *Dulcinea in the Factory: Myths, Morals, Men, and Women in Colombia's Industrial Experiment, 1905–1960.* Durham: Duke University Press.

Fazio, Carlos. 1997. *Algunos aportes del Secretariado Social Mexicano en la transición a la democracia.* Mexico City: Academia Mexicana de Derechos Humanos.

Fernández, Adela. 1986. *El Indio Fernández: Vida y mito.* Mexico City: Panorama Editorial.

Fernández-Aceves, María Teresa. 1996. "El género, la diferencia sexual y la igualdad en los debates feministas: Entrevista a Joan Scott." *La Ventana* 4: 226–29.

———. 2000. The Political Mobilization of Women in Revolutionary Guadalajara, 1910–1940. PhD diss., University of Illinois, Chicago.

———. 2003. "Once We Were Corn Grinders: Women and Labor in the Tortilla Industry of Guadalajara, 1920–1940." *International Labor and Working-Class History* 63: 81–101.

Fernández-Aceves, María Teresa, and Hermelinda Orejel Salas. 1987. Sindicalismo Femenino en Jalisco, 1920–1940: Las trabajadoras en la industria de nixtamal. Unpublished licenciature thesis, University of Guadalajara.

Ferro, Marc. 1974. "El cine ¿un contraanálisis de la sociedad?" In *Hacer la historia*, edited by Jacques le Goff and Pierre Nora, 3:241–60. Barcelona: Ed Laia.

Field, Les W. 1999. "Complicities and Collaborations: Anthropologists and the 'Unacknowledged Tribes' of California." *Current Anthropology* 40, no. 2: 193–209.

Findlay, Eileen J. 1999. *Imposing Decency: The Politics of Sexuality and Race in Puerto Rico, 1870–1920*. Durham: Duke University Press.

Flores Arellano, Nélida, and América Wences Román. 1992. *Doña María de la O: Una mujer ejemplar*. Chilpancingo: Universidad Autónoma de Guerrero, Centro de Estudios Históricos del Agrarismo en México.

Flores Clair, Eduardo. 1991–1992. "Diversiones públicas en la ciudad de México, 1920–1940." *Historias* 27: 163–69.

Fowler-Salamini, Heather. 2002. "Women Coffee Sorters Confront the Mill Owners and the Veracruz Revolutionary State, 1915–1918." *Journal of Women's History* 14: 34–63.

———. 2003. "Gender, Work, and Working-Class Women's Culture in Veracruz Coffee Export Industry, 1920–1945." *International Labor and Working-Class History* 63: 102–21.

Fowler-Salamini, Heather, and Mary Kay Vaughan, eds. 1994. *Women of the Mexican Countryside, 1850–1990*. Tucson: University of Arizona Press.

Franco, Fernando. 1991. "Labor Law and the Labor Movement in Mexico." In *Unions, Workers, and the State in Mexico*, edited by Kevin J. Middlebrook, 105–20. San Diego: Center for U.S.-Mexican Studies, University of California, San Diego.

French, John D., and Daniel James, eds. 1997. *The Gendered Worlds of Latin American Women Workers*. Durham: Duke University Press.

Frías, José D. 1924. "Angel Zárraga y las corrientes de la pintura contemporánea." *Revista de Revistas* 15, no. 734 (1 June): 21–22.

Galán G., Emma. 1947. *Naturaleza y misión actual de la mujer*. Mexico City: Secretariado Social Mexicano.

Galeana, Benita. 1994. *Benita*. Translated by Amy Diane Prince. Pittsburgh: Latin American Literary Review Press.

Galindo Mendoza, Alfredo, M.Sp.S. 1945. *Apuntes geográficos y estadísticos de la Iglesia Católica en México*. Mexico City: Administración de la Revista La Cruz.

Gallo, Rubén. 2005. *Mexican Modernity. The Avant-Garde and the Technological Revolution*. Cambridge, Mass.: MIT Press.

Gamboa Ojeda, Leticia. 2001. *La urdimbre y la trama: Historia social de los obreros textiles de Atlixco, 1899–1924*. Mexico City: Benemérita Universidad Autónoma de Puebla, Fondo de Cultura Económica.

García, Brígida, and Orlandina de Oliveira. 1994. *Trabajo femenina y vida familiar en México*. Mexico City: El Colegio de México.

García Martí, V. n.d. *Normas para Actuar en la Vida Social y Mundana*. Mexico City: Biblioteca Para Ellas y Para Ellos.

García Quintanilla, Alejandra. 1986. *Los Tiempos en Yucatán: Los hombres, las mujeres y la naturaleza.* Mérida: Claves Latinoamericanas and Departamento de Estudios Económicos y Sociales del Centro de Investigaciones Regionales "Dr. Hidey Noguchi" de la Universidad Autónoma de Yucatán.

García Riera, Emilio. 1987. *Emilio Fernández, 1904–1986.* Guadalajara: Universidad de Guadalajara, Centro de Investigaciones y Estudios Cinematográficos.

———. 1992. *Historia documental del cine mexicano.* Vol. 3. Guadalajara: Universidad de Guadalajara, Consejo Nacional para la Cultura y las Artes, Instituto Mexicano de Cinematografía.

Garrido, Felipe, ed. 1997. *Luz y Sombra: Los inicios del cine en la prensa de la ciudad de México.* Mexico City: Consejo Nacional para la Cultura y las Artes.

Garro, Elena. 1969. *Recollections of Things to Come.* Austin: University of Texas Press.

Gauss, Susan. 2003. "Masculine Bonds and Modern Mothers: The Rationalization of Gender in the Textile Industry in Puebla, 1940–1952." *International Labor and Working-Class History* 63: 63–80.

Gil, Miguel. 1933. "Los neutros en la Penitenciaria hablan a *Dectectives* sobre el amor." *Detectives: El mejor semanario de México,* 4 April: 8, 9, 15.

———. 1938. *La tumba del Pacífico,* Mexico City: Ediciones La Prensa.

Gill, Mario. 1956. *El movimiento Escuderista de Acapulco.* Mexico City: Ediciones Mexico Libre.

Ginsburg, Faye, and Rayna Rapp. 1991. "The Politics of Reproduction." *Annual Review of Anthropology* 20: 311–43.

Gómez-Galvarriato Freer, Aurora. 1999. The Impact of Revolution: Business and Labor in the Mexican Textile Industry, Orizaba, Veracruz, 1900–1930. PhD diss., Harvard University.

Gonzalba Aizpuru, Pilar, ed. 1998. *Historia de la educación y enseñanza de la historia.* Mexico City: El Colegio de México.

González Navarro, Moisés. 1974. *Población y sociedad en México (1900–1970).* 2 vols. Mexico City: Universidad Nacional Autónoma de México, Facultad de Ciencias Políticas y Sociales.

Gordon, Linda. 1988. *Heroes in Their Own Lives: The Politics and History of Family Violence, Boston 1880–1960.* New York: Penguin.

———. 1999. *The Great Arizona Orphan Abduction.* Cambridge, Mass.: Harvard University Press.

Goribar de Cortina, R. 1937. "Balance del Año." *Acción Femenina* 3, no. 11 (December): 2.

Gotschall, Elwood R. 1970. Catholicism and Catholic Action in Mexico, 1929–1941: A Church's Response to a Revolutionary Society and the Politics of the Modern Age. PhD diss., University of Pittsburgh.

Goytortúa Sánchez, Jesús. 1969. *Pensativa.* Mexico City: Editorial Porrúa.

Gudorf, Christine E. 1983. "Renewal or Repatriarchalization? Responses of the Roman Catholic Church to the Feminization of Religion." *Horizons* 10, no. 2 (fall): 235–38.

Gutiérrez Álvarez, Coralia. 2003. "Las mujeres en las fábricas textiles de Puebla y Tlaxcala, siglo XIX." *Estudios del Hombre* 16: 67–92.

Gutiérrez del Olmo, José Félix Alonso. 1993. "De la caridad a la asistencia: Un enfoque de la pobreza y la marginación en México." In *La atención materno infantil: apuntes para su historia*, by Secretaría de Salud, 9–51. Mexico City: Secretaría de Salud.

Gutiérrez de Mendoza, Juana. 1936. *República femenina*. Mexico City: n.p.

Guy, Donna J. 2000. *White Slavery and Mothers Alive and Dead*. Lincoln: University of Nebraska Press.

Hall, Stuart. 1996. "Introduction: Who Needs 'Identity'?" In *Questions of Cultural Identity*, edited by Stuart Hall and Paul du Gay, 1–17. London: Sage.

Hanson, Randall S. 1994. "The Day of Ideals": Catholic Social Action in the Age of the Mexican Revolution, 1867–1929. PhD diss., Indiana University, Bloomington.

———. 1997. "Mujeres Militantes: Las Damas Católicas and the Mobilization of Women in Revolutionary Mexico, 1912–1929." Paper presented at the Conference on Latin American History Annual Meeting.

Harris, Alex, and Margaret Sartor, eds. 1984. *Gertrude Blom: Bearing Witness*. Durham: Duke University Press.

Hart, John. 1978. *Anarchism and the Mexican Working Class, 1860–1931*. Austin: University of Texas Press.

———. 2000. "The Mexican Revolution, 1910–1920." In *The Oxford History of Mexico*, edited by Michael C. Meyer and William H. Beezley, 435–66. New York: Oxford University Press.

Harvey, David. 1993. *The Condition of Postmodernity*. Oxford: Basil Blackwell.

Harvey, Neil. 1998. *The Chiapas Rebellion: The Struggle for Land and Democracy*. Durham: Duke University Press.

———. 1994. "Rebellion in Chiapas: Rural Reforms, Campesino Radicalism and the Limits to Salinismo." In *Rebellion in Chiapas*, Transformation of Rural Mexico Series, No. 5. La Jolla: Center for U.S.-Mexican Studies, University of California, San Diego.

Heredia, Carlos. 1996. "Downward Mobility: Mexican Workers after NAFTA." *NACLA Report on the Americas* 30, no. 3: 34–40.

Hernández Castillo, Aida, Shannon Speed, and Lynn Stephen, eds. 2006. *Dissident Women: Gender and Cultural Politics in Chiapas*. Austin: University of Texas Press.

Herrera, Celia. 1985. "La vida en Parral: tenebrosa pesadilla." In *Cuentistas de la Revolución Mexicana*, edited by Xorge de Campo, 85–86. Mexico City: Comisión Nacional para las Celebraciones del 175 Aniversario de la Independencia Nacional y 75 Aniversario de la Revolución Mexicana.

Herrera, Hayden, Julie Taymor, and Salma Hayek. 2002. *Frida: Bringing Frida Kahlo's Life and Art to Film*. New York: Simon and Schuster.

Herrera-Sobek, Maria. 1990. *The Mexican Corrido: A Feminist Analysis*. Bloomington: Indiana University Press.

Hershfield, Joanne. 1999. "Race and Ethnicity in the Classical Cinema." In *Mexico's Cinema: A Century of Film and Filmmakers*, edited by Joanne Hershfield and David Maciel, 81–100. Wilmington, Del.: SR Books.

287

Hong, Young-sun. 1998. *Welfare, Modernity, and the Weimar State, 1919–1933.* Princeton: Princeton University Press.

Hutchison, Elizabeth Quay. 2001. *Labors Appropriate to Their Sex: Gender and Labor Politics in Urban Chile, 1900–1930.* Durham: Duke University Press.

"Importantísimo." 1931. *Informador de las Brigadas Femeninas de Santa Juana de Arco* 2, no. 3 (29 March): 1.

Instituto Interamericano del Niño. 1961. *Legislación atinente a menores de las Américas.* 3 vols. Montevideo: Instituto Interamericano del Niño.

Irwin, Robert McKee, Eduard J. McCaughan, and Michelle Rocío Nasser. 2003. *The Famous 41: Sexuality and Social Control in Mexico, 1901.* New York: Palgrave Macmillan.

Jackson, Jean. 1999. "The Politics of Ethnographic Practice in the Colombian Vaupés." *Identities: Global Studies in Culture and Power* 6, nos. 2–3: 281–317.

Jacobs, Ian. 1982. *Ranchero Revolt: The Mexican Revolution in Guerrero.* Austin: University of Texas Press.

James, Daniel. 1981. "Rationalisation and Working Class Response: The Context and Limits of Factory Floor Activity in Argentina." *Journal of Latin American Studies* 13, no. 2 (1981): 375–402.

———. 2000. *Doña María's Story: Life, History, Memory, and Political Identity.* Durham: Duke University Press.

Jara Miranda, Jaime. 1968. *La legitimación adoptiva.* Santiago: Editoral Jurídica de Chile.

Jiménez, Blanca, and Samuel Villela. 1998. *Los Salmerón: Un siglo de fotografía en Guerrero.* Mexico City: Instituto Nacional de Antropología e Historia.

Joseph, Gilbert M., and Daniel Nugent. 1994a. "Popular Culture and State Formation in Revolutionary Mexico." In *Everyday Forms of State Formation: Revolution and Negotiation of Rule in Modern Mexico,* edited by Gilbert M. Joseph and Daniel Nugent, 3–23. Durham: Duke University Press.

Joseph, Gilbert M., and Daniel Nugent, eds. 1994b. *Everyday Forms of State Formation: Revolution and Negotiation of Rule in Modern Mexico.* Durham: Duke University Press.

Kaplan, Temma. 1988. "Commentary on the Socialist Origins of International Women's Day." In *Internationalism in the Labour Movement 1830–1940,* edited by Frits Van Holthoon and Marcel Van Der Linden, 188–94. Leiden, The Netherlands: E. J. Brill.

———. 1992. *Red City, Blue Period: Social Movements in Picasso's Barcelona.* Berkeley: University of California Press.

———. 2002. "The Disappearing Fathers under Global Capitalism." In *The Socialist Feminist Project: A Contemporary Reader in Theory and Politics,* edited by Nancy Holmstrom, 152–57. New York: Monthly Review.

———. 2004. *Taking Back the Streets: Women, Youth, and Direct Democracy.* Berkeley: University of California Press.

Kelley, Jane Holden. 1978. *Yaqui Women: Contemporary Life Histories.* Lincoln: University of Nebraska Press.

Keremetsis, Dawn. 1983. "Del metate al molino: La mujer mexicana de 1910–1940." *Historia mexicana* 33: 293.

———. 1984a. "La doble jornada de la mujer en Guadalajara, 1910–1940." *Encuentro* 1: 41–64.

———. 1984b. "Latin American Women Workers in Transition: Sexual Division of the Labor Force in Mexico and Colombia in the Textile Industry." *The Americas* 15 (April 1984): 491–50.

Kingston, Maxine Hong. 1976. *The Woman Warrior.* New York: Vintage.

Klubock, Thomas Miller. 1998. *Contested Communities: Class, Gender, and Politics in Chile's El Teniente Copper Mine, 1904–1951.* Durham: Duke University Press.

Knight, Alan S. 1985. "The Mexican Revolution: Bourgeois? Nationalist? Or Just a 'Great Rebellion'?" *Bulletin of Latin American Research* 4, no. 2: 1–37.

———. 1990. "Racism, Revolution and Indigenismo: Mexico, 1910–1920." In *The Idea of Race in Latin America, 1870–1940,* edited by Richard Graham, 71–114. Austin: University of Texas Press.

———. 1991. "The Rise and Fall of Cardenismo, c. 1930–c. 1946." In *Mexico since Independence,* edited by Leslie Bethell, 241–320. Cambridge: Cambridge University Press.

———. 1996. "Estado, revolución y cultura popular en los años treinta," In *Perspectivas sobre el cardenismo: Ensayos sobre economía, trabajo, política y cultura en los años treinta,* edited by Marcos Tonatiuh Aguila M. and Alberto Enríquez Perea, 297–324. Mexico City: Universidad Autónoma de México.

Kuri-Aldana, Mario, and Vicente Mendoza Martínez, eds. 1987. *Cancionero Popular Mexicana Volumen 1.* Mexico City: Secretaría de Educación Pública.

Lailson, Silvia. 1987. "El trabajo y las organizaciones laborales de mujeres en Jalisco: 1920–1940." *Encuentro* 15: 59–82.

Lalvani, Suren. 1996. *Photography, Vision and the Production of Modern Bodies.* Albany: State University of New York.

Lamas, Marta. 1998. "De la A a la Z: A Feminist Alliance Experience." In *Women's Participation in Mexican Political Life,* edited by Victoria Rodríguez, 103–15. Boulder: Westview Press.

Lamas, Marta, Alicia Martínez, María Luisa Tarrés, and Esperanza Tuñon. 1995. "Building Bridges: The Growth of Popular Feminism in Mexico." In *The Challenge of Local Feminisms: Women's Movements in Global Perspective,* edited by Amrita Basu and C. Elizabeth McGrory, 324–50. Boulder: Westview Press.

Lavrin, Asunción. 1995. *Women, Feminism, and Social Change in Argentina, Chile, and Uruguay, 1890–1940.* Lincoln: University of Nebraska Press.

Lear, John. 1998. "Mexico City: Popular Classes and Revolutionary Politics." In *Cities of Hope: People, Protests, and Progress in Urbanizing Latin America, 1870–1930,* edited by Ronn Pineo and James A. Baer, 75–78. Wilmington, Del.: Scholarly Resources.

———. 2001. *Workers, Neighbors, and Citizens: The Revolution in Mexico City.* Lincoln: University of Nebraska Press.

Legislación revoluciaria: Código del Registro Civil del Estado de Yucatán, edición del Diario Oficial. 1918. Mérida: Imprenta Constitucionalista.

Leñero Franco, Estela. 1984. *El huso y el sexo: La mujer obrera en dos industrias de Tlaxcala.* Mexico City: Cuadernos de la Casa Chata.

Lepidus, Henry. 1928. *The History of Mexican Journalism. The University of Mis-*

souri Bulletin. Vol. 29, no.4. Journalism Series, 49. Columbia: University of Missouri.

Lerner, Victoria. 1979. *Historia de la Revolución Mexicana, 1934–1940.* Vol. 17, *La educación socialista.* Mexico City: El Colegio de México.

Le Sueur, Meridel. 1982. *Ripening: Selected Works, 1927–1980.* Old Westbury, N.Y.: Feminist Press.

———. 1984. *Crusaders: The Radical Legacy of Marian and Arthur Le Sueur.* Reprint edition. St. Paul: Minnesota Historical Society Press.

Levenson-Estrada, Deborah. 1997. "The Loneliness of Working-Class Feminism: Women in the 'Male World' of Labor Unions, Guatemala City, 1970s." In *The Gendered Worlds of Latin American Women Workers,* edited by John D. French and Daniel James, 208–31. Durham: Duke University Press.

Ley de divorcio: Reformas al Código del Registro Civil y al Código Civil del Estado: Suplemento al numero 7,803 del "Diario Oficial" del Gobierno Socialista del Estado de Yucatán, Correspondiente al 3 de Abril de 1923. 1923. Mérida: Talleres Tipográficos del Gobierno del Estado.

Ley de relaciones familiares: Expedida por el C. Venustiano Carranza, primer jefe del ejército constitucionalista, encargado del poder ejecutivo de la nación. 1917. Mexico City: Edición Económica

"La ley revolucionaria de las mujeres." 1994. *Doble Jornada* (7 February): 8.

Ley sobre el divorcio: Reformas de diversos artículos del Código Civil del Estado de Yucatán. 1915. Mérida: Imp. de la Empresa Editora Yucatecan.

Lieuwen, Edward. 1968. *Mexican Militarism: The Rise and Fall of the Mexican Army, 1910–1940.* Albuquerque: University of New Mexico Press.

Lomnitz, Claudio. 2001. *Deep Mexico, Silent Mexico: An Anthropology of Mexican Nationalism.* Minneapolis: University of Minnesota Press.

Lomnitz, Larissa A., and Marisol Pérez-Lizaur. 1984. "Dynastic Growth and Survival Strategies of Mexican Grand Families." In *Kinship Ideology and Practice in Latin America,* edited by Raymond T. Smith, 183–95. Chapel Hill: University of North Carolina Press.

———. 1987. *A Mexican Elite Family, 1820–1980.* Princeton: Princeton University Press.

López de Nava Camarena, Rodolfo. 1995. *Mis hechos de campaña: Testimonios del General de División Rodolfo López de Nava Baltierra, 1911–1952.* Mexico City: Instituto Nacional de Estudios Históricos de la Revolución Mexicana.

Lorey, David. "Post-Revolutionary Contexts for Independence Day: The 'Problem' of Order and the Invention of Revolution Day, 1920s–1940s." In *Viva Mexico! Viva la Independencia! Celebrations of September 16,* edited by William H. Beezley and David Lorey, 233–48. Wilmington, Del.: Scholarly Resources.

Loyo, Engracio. 1997 [1988]. "La lectura en México, 1920—1940." In *Historia de la lectura en México,* 243–94. Mexico City: Colegio de México–El Ermitaño.

"M." 1937. "JCFM: Dirigentes-Como Formarlas." *Christus* 2, no. 20 (July): 643.

Macías, Anna. 1982. *Against All Odds: The Feminist Movement in Mexico to 1940.* Westport, Conn.: Greenwood Press.

Maier, Elizabeth. 1994. "Sex and Class as a Single Entity." In *Compañeras: Voices*

From the Latin American Women's Movement, edited by Gaby Kuppers, 40–45. London: Latin American Bureau.

Malpica Uribe, Samuel. 1984. "La Derrota de la FROC en Atlixco, 1931–1939." In *Memorias del Encuentro Sobre Historia del Movimiento Obrero*, 149–58. Puebla: Benemérita Universidad Autónoma de Puebla.

Maria Candelaria (Xochimilco). 1953. Director, Emilio Fernández. Mexico City: Films Mundiales.

Márquez Capert, S. J. 1958. *Las grandes encíclicas sociales*. Madrid: Editorial Apostolado de la Prensa.

Márquez Carrillo, Jesús. 1983. Los origenes de Avilacamachismo: Una arqueología de fuerzas en la constitución de un poder regional: El estado de Puebla, 1929–1941. Unpublished licenciature thesis, Universidad Autónoma de Puebla.

Martínez Vásquez, Victor Raul. 1994 *Historia de la Educación en Oaxaca (1825–1940)*. Oaxaca: Instituto de Investigaciones Sociológicas, Universidad Autónoma Benito Juárez de Oaxaca.

Massell, Gregory J. 1974. *The Surrogate Proletariat: Moslem Women and Revolutionary Strategies in Soviet Central Asia: 1919–1929*. Princeton: Princeton University Press.

Massey, Doreen. 1994. *Space, Place, and Gender*. Minneapolis: University of Minneapolis Press.

Mattiace, Shannon. 1998. Peasant and Indian: Political Identity and Indian Autonomy in Chiapas, Mexico, 1970–1990. PhD diss., University of Texas, Austin.

McSweeney, William. 1980. *Roman Catholicism: The Search for Relevance*. New York: St. Martin's Press.

Méndez, Margarita G. de. 1980. "Síntesis Histórica de la UFCM." *Acción Femenina*, special issue (September): 29.

Mendieta Alatorre, Angeles. 1961. *La mujer en la Revolución Mexicana*. Mexico City: Instituto Nacional de Estudios de la Revolución Mexicana.

Mexicana: Redstone Matchbox #3. 1998. San Francisco: Chronicle Books,

Mexicano: Esta es tu Constitución. 1968. Mexico City: Cámara de Diputados del 2d Congreso de la Unión 47 Legislatura.

Meyer, Eugenia, ed. 1976a. "Mauricio Magdaleno." *Testimonios para la historia del cine mexicano*. Vol. 3, 25–36. Mexico City: Cineteca Nacional.

———. 1976b. "Stella Inda." *Testimonios para la historia del cine mexicano*. Vol. 3, 115–32. Mexico City: Cineteca Nacional.

Meyer, Jean. 1973–1974. *La cristiada*. 3 vols. Mexico City: Siglo 21.

———. 1977. *Estado y sociedad con Calles. Historia de la Revolución Mexicana, 1924–8*. Mexico City: El Colegio de México.

———. 1979. *El sinarquismo: ¿Un fascismo mexicano? 1937–1947*. Mexico City: Editorial Joaquín Mortiz.

———. 2003. *El sinarquismo, el cardenismo y la iglesia (1937–1947)*. Mexico City: Tusquets Editores.

Meyer, Michael C., and William H. Beezley, eds. 2000. *The Oxford History of Mexico*. New York: Oxford University Press.

Meyerowitz, Joanne. 2002. *How Sex Changed: A History of Transsexuality in the United States.* Cambridge, Mass.: Harvard University Press.

Michel, Concha. 1938. *Dos antagonismos fundamentales.* Mexico City: Ediciones de la Izquierda de la Cámara de Diputados.

Middlebrook, Kevin. 1995. *The Paradox of Revolution, Labor, the State, and Authoritarianism in Mexico.* Baltimore: Johns Hopkins University Press.

Millan, Verna Carleton. 1939. *Mexico Reborn.* Boston: Houghton Mifflin.

Miller, Barbara Ann. 1981. The Role of Women in the Mexican Cristero Rebellion: A New Chapter. PhD diss., University of Notre Dame.

———. 1984. "The Role of Women in the Mexican Cristero Rebellion: *Las Señoras y Las Religiosas.*" *The Americas* 40: 303–23.

Mistral, Gabriela. 1967. *Lecturas para Mujeres.* Mexico City: Editorial Porrúa.

Mitchell, Stephanie. 2002. La Noble Mujer Organizada: The Women's Movement in 1930s Mexico. PhD diss., University of Oxford.

Mogrovejo Aquise, Norma. 1990. Feminismo popular en Mexico: Análisis del surgimiento, desarrollo y conflictos en la relación entre la tendencia feminista y la regional de mujeres de la CONAMUP. Master's thesis, Facultad Latino-americana de Ciencias Sociales, Seminario Movimientos Sociales Generación 88–90.

Molina, Isabel, ed. 1988. *Mujeres del Sur.* Chilpancingo: Gobierno del Estado de Guerrero.

Molloy, Sylvia. 1998. "The politics of posing." In *Hispanisms and Homosexualities*, edited by Silvia Molloy and Robert McKee Irwin, 141–60. Durham: Duke University Press.

Molyneux, Maxine. 1985. "Mobilization without Emancipation? Women's Interests, the State, and Revolution in Nicaragua." *Feminist Studies* 11, no. 2: 227–53.

Monsiváis, Carlos. 1977. "Notas sobre la cultura mexicana en el siglo XX." In *Historia general de México*, 4:303–476. Mexico City: El Colegio de México.

———. 1984. "La aparición del subsuelo: Sobre la cultura de la Revolución Mexicana." *Historias* 8–9 (January–June): 159–77.

———. 1997. *Mexican Postcards.* Translated by John Kraniauskas. London: Verso.

———. 1998. Prologue. In *La estatua de sal*, by Salvador Novo, 11–41. Mexico City: Consejo Nacional para la Cultura y las Artes.

———. 2002. "'Soy porque me parezco': El retrato en México en el siglo XX." In *Espejo mexicano*, edited by Enrique Florescano, 178–221. Mexico City: Consejo Nacional para la Cultura y las Artes / Fondo de Cultura Económica.

Montejo, Victor. 2002. "The Multiplicity of Maya Voices: Maya Leadership and the Politics of Self-Representation." In *Indigenous Movements: Self-Representation and the State in Latin America*, edited by Jean Jackson and Kay Warren, 123–48. Austin: University of Texas Press.

Moreno Ochoa, Angel. 1959. *Semblanzas revolucionarias: diez años de agitación política en Jalisco.* Guadalajara: Galería de Escritores Revolucionarios Jaliscienses.

Morton, Ward. 1962. *Woman Suffrage in Mexico.* Gainesville: University of Florida Press.

Nelson, Barbara J. 1990. "The Origins of the Two-Channel Welfare State: Workmen's Compensation and Mothers' Aid." In *Women, the State, and Welfare*, edited by Linda Gordon, 123–51. Madison: University of Wisconsin Press.

Nizza da Silva, María Beatriz. 1989. "Divorce in Colonial Brazil: The Case of São Brazil." In *Sexuality and Marriage in Colonial Latin America*, edited by Asunción Lavrin, 313–40. Lincoln: University of Nebraska Press.

Northrop, Douglass. 2004. *Veiled Empire: Gender and Power in Stalinist Central Asia*. Ithaca: Cornell University Press.

"Noticiero Films Mundiales." 1943a. *El cine gráfico*, no. 520 (July 25): 16.

———. 1943b. *El cine gráfico*, no. 520 (October 24): 16.

Novell, Elizabeth Jean. 1996. "Los ciudadanos sindicalistas: La Federación Local de Trabajadores del Puerto de Veracruz, 1919–1923." In *Actores sociales en un proceso de transformación: Veracruz en los años veinte*, edited by Manuel Reyna Muñoz, 55–75. Jalapa: Universidad Veracruzana.

Novo, Salvador. 1972. *Las locas, el sexo, los burdeles*. Mexico City: Organización Editorial Novaro.

Ochoa, Alfonso R. 1921. *El niño*. Mexico City: Departamento de Salubridad.

O'Dogherty Madrazo, Laura. 1991. "Restaurarlo Todo en Cristo: Unión de Damas Católicas Mejicanas, 1920–1926." *Estudios de Historia Moderna y Contemporánea de México* 14: 134–52.

Olcott, Jocelyn H. 2000. Las Hijas de la Malinche: Women's Organizing and State Formation in Revolutionary Mexico, 1934–1940. PhD diss., Yale University.

———. 2002. " 'Worthy Wives and Mothers': State-Sponsored Women's Organizing in Postrevolutionary Mexico." *Journal of Women's History* 13, no. 4: 106–31.

———. 2003. "Miracle Workers: Gender and State Mediation among Textile and Garment Workers in Mexico's Transition to Industrial Development." *International Labor and Working-Class History* 63: 45–62.

———. 2005. *Revolutionary Women in Postrevolutionary Mexico*. Durham: Duke University Press.

O'Malley, Ilene. 1986. *The Myth of Revolution: Hero Cults and the Institutionalization of Revolution*. New York: Greenwood Press.

"Orígenes de las Damas Católicas." 1937. *Acción Femenina* 3, no. 7 (1 September): 7, 16–17.

Orozco y Jiménez, F. 1930. Circular 15–30, "A los Sres. Sacerdotes del Arzobispado," 28 April 1930. *Boletín Eclesiástico de la Arquidiocesis de Guadalajara*, 1, no. 4 (1 June).

Ortner, Sherry B. 1974. "Is Female to Male as Nature Is to Culture?" In *Women, Culture, and Society*, edited by Michele Zimbalast Rosaldo and Louise Lamphere, 67–87. Stanford: Stanford University Press.

Padilla, Florencio. 1937. "Reformas legislativas para facilitar y hacer mas amplios los casos de adopción." In *Memoria del VII Congreso Panamericano del Niño*, 2:129–33. Mexico City: Talleres Gráficos de la Nación.

Pansters, Wil. 1990. *Politics and Power in Puebla: The Political History of a Mexican State, 1937–1987*. Amsterdam: Center for Latin American Research and Documentation.

Pappe, Sylvia. 1994. *Gertrude Duby-Blom: Königin des Regenwaldes*. Bern: Efef Verlag.

Paré, Luisa. 1990. "The Challenge of Rural Democratization in Mexico." *Development Studies* 26 (July): 79–96.

Paredes, B. A., S.C. 1937. "Rubricas." *Christus* 2, no. 18 (May): 438.

Parsons, Wilfrid. 1936. *Mexican Martyrdom*. New York: Macmillan.

Passet, Joanne E. 2003. *Sex Radicals and the Quest for Women's Equality*. Urbana: Univeristy of Illinois Press.

Peiss, Kathy. 1987. *Cheap Amusements: Working Women and Leisure in Turn of the Century New York*. Philadelphia: Temple University Press.

"Las Pelonas" (unsigned poem). 1924. *Revista de Revistas* 15, no. 733 (25 May): 6.

Peniche Rivero, Piedad. 1999. "La comunidad doméstica de la hacienda henequenera de Yucatán, México, 1870–1915." *Mexican Studies* 15 (winter): 1–33.

Pérez Rosales, Laura. 1992. "Las mujeres sinarquistas: Nuevas adelitas en la vida pública mexicana." In *Religión, política y sociedad: El sinarquismo y la Iglesia en Mexico (nueve ensayos)*, edited by Rubén Aguilar P. and Guillermo Zermeño P., 169–93. Mexico City: Universidad Iberoamericana.

Piccato, Pablo. 2001. *City of Suspects: Crime in Mexico City, 1900–1931*. Durham: Duke University Press.

Pilcher, Jeffrey M. 1998. *¡Qué vivan los tamales! Food and the Making of Mexican Identity*. Alburquerque: University of New Mexico Press.

Pineo, Ronn, and James A. Baer, eds. 1998. *Cities of Hope: People, Protests, and Progress in Urbanizing Latin America, 1870–1930*. Wilmington, Del.: Scholarly Resources.

Porter, Susie S. 2003. *Working Women of Mexico City: Public Discourses and Material Conditions, 1879–1931*. Tucson: University of Arizona Press.

Power, Margaret. 2002. *Right-Wing Women in Chile: Feminine Power and the Struggle against Allende, 1964–1973*. University Park: Pennsylvania State University Press.

Prewett, Virginia. 1941. *Reportage on Mexico*. New York: E. P. Dutton.

Primer Congreso Mexicano del Niño. 1921. *Memoria del Primer Congreso Mexicano del Niño*. Mexico City: El Universal.

Prosser, Jay. 1998. "Transsexuals and the Transsexologists: Inversion and the Inversion of Transsexual Subjectivity." In *Sexology in Culture: Labelling Bodies and Desires*, edited by Lucy Bland and Laura Doan, 116–31. Chicago: University of Chicago Press.

Quevedo y Zubieta, Salvador. 1927. *México manicomio: Novela histórica contemporánea, época de Venustiano Carranza*. Madrid: Espasa-Calpa.

Quintero Figueroa, Adelina. 1977. "La trayectoria política de Rafael Odriozola, primer liberal oaxaqueño." *Historia Mexicana* 26, no. 3: 456–81.

Raby, David L. 1974. *Educación y revolución social en Mexico, 1921–1940*. Mexico City: Sep-Setentas.

Radkau, Verena. 1984. *"La Fama" y la vida: Una fábrica y sus obreras*. Mexico City: Centro de Investigación y Estudios Superiores en Antropología Social.

Ramírez, Santiago. 1983 [1977]. *El mexicano: Psicología de sus motivaciones*. Mexico City: Colección Enlace.

Ramos Escandón, Carmen. 1987. *Presencia y transparencia: La mujer en la historia de México*. Mexico City: El Colegio de México.

———. 1988. *La Industria Textil y el Movimiento Obrero en México*. Mexico City: División de Ciencias Sociales y Humanidades, Departamento de Filosofía-Historia, Area de Cultura, Universidad Autónoma Metropolitana.

———. 1990. "Mujeres Trabajadoras en el México porfirano: Género e ideología del trabajo femenino, 1876–1911." *European Review of Latin American and Caribbean Studies* 48: 27–46.

———. 1998. "Gender, Labor, and Class Consciousness Among Mexican Factory Workers, 1880–1910." In *Borders Crossing: Mexican and Mexican-American Workers in Transition*, edited by John Mason Hart, 71–92. Wilmington, Del.: Scholarly Resources.

———. 2003. "Diferencias de género en el trabajo textil en México y Estados Unidos durante el siglo XIX." *Estudios del Hombre* 16: 41–65.

Rascón, María Antonieta. 1979. "La mujer y la lucha social." In *Imagen y realidad de la mujer*, edited by E. Urrutia, 139–74. Mexico City: Secretaría de Educación Pública / Editorial Diana.

Riley, Denise. 1988. *"Am I that Name?" Feminism and the Category of "Women" in History*. Minneapolis: University of Minneapolis Press.

Rivero Quijano, Jesús. [1930s.] "La Industria Textil del Algodón y el Maquinismo." Lecture delivered at the Escuela Nacional de Ingeniería, Palacio de Minería, 29 July and 1 August.

Robles, Rosario, Josefina Aranda, and Carlota Botey. 1993. "La mujer campesina en la época de la modernidad." *El Cotidiano* 52: 25–32.

Robles de Mendoza, Margarita. 1931. *La evolución de la mujer en México*. Mexico City: Imprenta Galas.

Rockwell, Elsie. 1994. "Schools of the Revolution." In *Everyday Forms of State Formation: Revolution and Negotiation of Rule in Modern Mexico*, edited by Joseph and Nugent, 170–208. Durham: Duke University Press.

Rodríguez Cabo, Matilde. 1937. *La mujer y la Revolución*. Mexico City: Frente Socialista de Abogados.

Rodríguez-Centeno, Mabel. 1993. "La producción cafetalera mexicana: El caso de Córdoba, Veracruz." *Historia Mexicana* 43: 81–115.

Rojina Villegas, Rafael. 1997. *Compendio de derecho civil: Introducción: Personas y familia*. Vol. 1. 7th ed. Mexico City: Editorial Porrúa.

Romero, Laura Patricia. 1988. *Jalisco desde la revolución*. Vol. 3. *La consolidación del estado y los conflictos políticos*. Guadalajara: Gobierno del Estado de Jalisco, Universidad de Guadalajara.

Rosemblatt, Karin Alejandra. 2000. *Gendered Compromises, Political Cultures and the State in Chile, 1920–1950*. Chapel Hill: University of North Carolina Press.

Rubenstein, Anne. 1998. "Raised Voices at the Cine Montecarlo: Sex Education, Mass Media, and Oppositional Politics in Mexico." *Family History* 23, no. 3 (July): 312–23.

Rubin, Jeffrey W. 1997. *Decentering the Regime: Ethnicity, Radicalism, and Democracy in Juchitán, Mexico*. Durham: Duke University Press.

Salaff, Janet Weitzner, and Judith Merkle. 1970. "Women and Revolution: The Lessons of the Soviet Union and China." In *Women in China*, Michigan

Papers in Chinese Studies 15, edited by Marilyn B. Young, 145–77. Ann Arbor: Center for Chinese Studies, University of Michigan.

Salas, Elizabeth. 1994. "The *Soldadera* in the Mexican Revolution: War and Men's Illusions." In *Women of the Mexican Countryside 1850–1990*, edited by Heather Fowler-Salamini and Mary Kay Vaughan, 93–105. Tucson: Arizona University Press.

Sanders, Nichole. 2003. Gender, Welfare and the "Mexican Miracle": The Politics of Modernization in Postrevolutionary Mexico, 1937–58. PHD diss., University of California, Irvine.

San Francisco Lesbian and Gay History Project. 1990. " 'She Even Chewed Tobacco': A Pictorial Narrative of Passing Women in America." In *Hidden from History: Reclaiming the Gay and Lesbian Past*, edited by Martin Duberman, Martha Vicinus, and George Chauncey, 184–94. New York: Meridian.

Santín de Fontoura, Margarita. 1924. "Los sports femeninos." *Revista de Revistas* 15, no. 736 (15 June): 38–39.

Sartorius, Carl Christian. 1961 [1858]. *Mexico about 1850*. Stuttgart: Brockhaus.

Schell, Patience A. 1998. "Training Loving Hands: Women's Vocational Education in 1920s Mexico City." *Anuario de espacios urbanos. Historia, cultura, diseño 1998*: 249–71.

——. 1999. "An Honorable Avocation for Ladies: The Work of the Mexico City Unión de Damas Católicas Mexicanas, 1912–1926." *Journal of Women's History* 10, no. 4 (winter): 78–103.

——. 2003. *Church and State Education in Revolutionary Mexico City*. Tucson: University of Arizona Press.

——. 2004. "Nationalizing Children through Schools and Hygiene: Porfirian and Revolutionary Mexico City." *The Americas* 60, no. 4: 559–87.

Scott, James C. 1990. *Domination and the Arts of Resistance: Hidden Transcripts*. New Haven: Yale University Press.

——. 1998. *Seeing Like a State: How Certain Schemes to Improve the Human Condition Have Failed*. New Haven: Yale University Press.

Scott, Joan. 1988. "Gender: A Useful Category of Historical Analysis." In *Gender and the Politics of History*, 28–60. New York: Columbia University Press.

——. 1996. *Only Paradoxes to Offer: French Feminists and the Rights of Man*. Cambridge, Mass.: Harvard University Press.

Secretaría de Educación Pública. 1924. *Escuelas del Departamento de Enseñanza Técnica, Industria y Comercial*. Mexico City: Secretaría de Educación Pública.

——. 1938. *Memoria de la Secretaría de Educación Pública, sept. 1937–ago. 1938, presentada al H. Congreso de la Unión por el Lic. Gonzalo Vázquez Vela, secretario del ramo*, Vol. 1, Part 2. Mexico City: Departamento Autónomo de Prensa y Publicidad.

Secretaría de la Asistencia Pública. 1940. *La asistencia social en México: Sexenio 1934–1940*. Mexico City: Secretaría de la Asistencia Pública.

——. 1942. *Informe de labores presentado al H. ejecutivo de la Unión, por el Dr. Gustavo Baz, Secretario del Ramo, 1941–1942*. Mexico City: Secretaría de la Asistencia Pública.

Secretaría de la Economía Nacional. 1933. *El café: Aspectos económicos de su pro-*

ducción y distribución en México y en el extranjero. Mexico City: Secretaría de la Economía Nacional.

——. 1936. *Segundo Censo Industrial, 1935: Hilados y Tejidos de Algodón.* Vol. 3. Mexico City: Secretaría de la Economía Nacional.

——. 1937. *Segundo Censo Industrial, 1935: Bonetería.* Vol. 3. Mexico City: Secretaría de la Economía Nacional.

Secretaría de Salud. 1993. *La atención materno infantil: Apuntes para su historia.* Mexico City: Secretaría de Salud.

Secretaría de Trabajo y Previsión Social. 1941. *Memoria de Labores* [September 1940–August 1941]. Mexico City: Secretaría de Trabajo y Previsión Social.

Sefchovich, Sara. 1999. *La Suerte de la Consorte.* Mexico City: Editorial Oceano.

Serrano, Carlos. 1924. "El reinado de las pelonas." *Revista de Revistas* 15, no. 733 (25 May): 9.

Sewell, William H., Jr. 1980. *Work and Revolution in France: The Language of Labor from the Old Regime to 1948.* Cambridge: Cambridge University Press.

Sexto Censo General de la Nación, 6 de marzo de 1940: Resumen General. 1942. Mexico City: Talleres Gráficos de la Nación.

Sheridan Prieto, Cecilia. 1983. *Mujer obrera y organización sindical: El sindicato de obreras desmanchadoras de café, Coatepec, Veracruz.* Mexico City: Casa Chata.

Sherman, John W. 1997. *The Mexican Right: The End of Revolutionary Reform.* Westport, Conn.: Praeger.

Sierra, Maria Teresa. 2002. "The Challenge to Diversity in Mexico: Human Rights, Gender, and Ethnicity." Working Paper No. 49. Max Planck Institute for Social Anthropology.

Silvester, Christopher, ed. 1997. *Las grandes entrevistas de la historia, 1859–1992.* Madrid: El País / Aguilar.

Sindicato Único de Trabajadores de la Enseñanza en Yucatán. 1937. *Estatutos del Sindicato Único de Trabajadores de la Enseñanza en Yucatán.* Mérida: Sindicato Único de Trabajadores de la Enseñanza en Yucatán.

Sinha, Mrinalini. 1995. *Colonial Masculinity: The "Manly Englishman" and the "Effeminate Bengali" in the Late 19th Century.* Manchester: Manchester University Press.

Sluis, Ageeth. 2005. City of Spectacles: Gender Performance, Revolutionary Reform, and the Creation of Public Space in Mexico City, 1915–1939. PhD diss., University of Arizona.

Smith, Stephanie J. 2002. Engendering the Revolution: Women and State Formation in Yucatán Mexico, 1872–1930. PhD diss., State University of New York, Stony Brook.

Snodgrass, Michael David. 1998. "The Birth and Consequences of Industrial Paternalism in Monterrey, Mexico, 1890–1940." *International Labor and Working-Class History* 53 (spring): 115–36.

Sorando, Xavier. 1924. "Las pelonas." *Revista de Revistas* 15, no. 743 (3 August): 5–6.

Soto, Shirlene. 1990. *Emergence of the Modern Mexican Woman: Her Participation in Revolution and Struggle for Equality 1910–1940.* Denver: Arden Press.

Soustelle, Jacques. 1976. *México, tierra india.* Mexico City: Secretaría de Educación Pública.

297

Speed, Shannon. 2006. "Rights at the Intersection: Gender and Ethnicity in Neoliberal Mexico." In *Dissident Women: Gender and Cultural Politics in Chiapas*, edited by Shannon Speed, R. Aida Castillo, and Lynn Stephen, 203–21. Austin: University of Texas Press.

Spivak, Gayatri C. 1989. "In a Word: An Interview." *Differences* 1: 124–56.

——. 1990. *Postcolonial Critic: Interviews, Strategies, Dialogues*. New York: Routledge.

——. 1993. *Inside the Teaching Machine*. New York: Routledge.

Stacey, Judith. 1983. *Patriarchy and Socialist Revolution in China*. Berkeley: University of California Press.

Stansell, Christine. 1987. *City of Women: Sex and Class in New York, 1789–1860*. Chicago: University of Illinois Press.

Stavenhagen, Rodolfo. 1979. "Clase, etnia y comunidad." In *Problemas étnicos y campesinos*, edited by Rodolfo Stavenhagen, 11–53. Mexico City: Instituto Nacional Indigenista.

Stellweg, Carla. 1992. *Frida Kahlo: La cámara seducida*. Mexico City: La Vaca Independiente.

Stepan, Nancy Leys. *"The Hour of Eugenics": Race, Gender, and Nation in Latin America*. Ithaca: Cornell University Press, 1991.

Stephen, Lynn. 1989. "Popular Feminism in Mexico." *Z Magazine* 2 (December): 102–6.

——. 1991. *Zapotec Women*. Austin: University of Texas Press.

——. 1997. *Women and Social Movements in Latin America: Power From Below*. Austin: University of Texas Press.

——. 2002. *Zapata Lives! Histories and Cultural Politics in Southern Mexico*. Berkeley: University of California Press.

Stern, Alexandra Minna. 1999. "Responsible Mothers and Normal Children: Eugenics and Nationalism in Post-Revolutionary Mexico City, 1920–1940." *Historical Sociology* 12, no. 4: 369–97.

Taibo, Paco Ignacio, I. 1986. *El Indio Fernández. El cine por mis pistolas*. Mexico City: Joaquín Mortiz / Planeta.

Talavera Aldana, Luis Fernando. 1976. "Organizaciones sindicales obreras de la rama textil: 1935–1970." *Revista Mexicana de Ciencias Políticas y Sociales* 21 (January–March): 227–99.

Tamayo, Jaime. 1985. "Movimiento obrero y lucha sindical." In *Guadalajara: La gran ciudad de la pequeña industria*, edited by Patricia Arias, 149–50. Zamora: El Colegio de Michoacán.

——. 1988a. *Jalisco desde la revolución*. Vol. 2, *La conformación del estado moderno y los conflictos políticos, 1917–1929*. Guadalajara: Universidad de Guadalajara and Gobierno del Estado de Jalisco.

——. 1988b. *Jalisco desde la revolución*. Vol. 4, *Los movimientos sociales, 1917–1929*. Guadalajara: Universidad de Guadalajara and Gobierno del Estado de Jalisco.

Tarrés, María Luisa. 1998. "The Role of Women's Nongovernmental Organizations in Mexican Public Life." In *Women's Participation in Mexican Political Life*, edited by Victoria Rodríguez, 131–45. Boulder: Westview Press.

Thompson, Paul. 1988. *The Voice of the Past: Oral History.* 2d ed. Oxford: Oxford University Press.

Tinsman, Heidi. 2002. *Partners in Conflict: The Politics of Gender, Sexuality, and Labor in the Chilean Agrarian Reform, 1950–1973.* Durham: Duke University Press.

Torres Septien, Valentina. 1992. "La UNPF: La lucha por la enseñanza de la religión en las escuelas particulares." In *La ciudad y el campo en la historia de México*, edited by Ricardo Sánchez et al., 2:927–35. México City: Universidad Nacional Autónoma de México / Instituto de Investigaciones Históricas.

Trejo Camara, Eliézer. 1923. "PRO-FEMINISMO: Sí el amor esclabiza . . . ¡Maldito sea el Amor!" *Tierra* 15 (5 August): 12.

Tromp, Sebastián, S.J. 1937. "Editorial: De los principios de la AC propuestos a los Obispos Mexicanos en la Encíclica 'Firmissiam Constantiam.'" *Christus* 2, no. 21 (August): 674.

Tuck, Jim. 1982. *The Holy War in Los Altos: A Regional Analysis of Mexico's Cristero Rebellion.* Tucson: University of Arizona Press.

Tuñón, Julia. 1987. *Mujeres en México. Recordando una historia.* Mexico City: Editorial Planeta.

———. 1988. *En su propio espejo: Entrevista con Emilio "Indio" Fernández.* Mexico City: Universidad Autónoma Metropolitana Iztapalapa.

———. 1992 (1995). "Emilio Fernández: A Look Behind the Bars." In *Mexican Cinema*, edited by Paulo Antonio Paranagua, 179–92. London: British Film Institute and Instituto Mexicano de Cinematografía.

———. 1998a. *Mujeres de luz y sombra en el cine mexicano: La construcción de una imagen, 1939–1952.* Mexico City: El Colegio de México, Instituto Mexicano de Cinematografía.

———. 1998b. "Una escuela en celuloide. El cine de Emilio 'Indio' Fernández o la obsesión por la educación." *Historia mexicana* 58, no. 190: 437–70.

———. 1999. *Women in Mexico: A Past Unveiled.* Translated by Alan Hynds. Austin: University of Texas Press.

———. 2000a. *Los rostros de un mito. personajes femeninos en las películas de Emilio "Indio" Fernández.* Mexico City: Consejo Nacional para la Cultura y las Artes / Instituto Mexicano de Cinematografía.

———. 2000b. "La Revolución Mexicana en el cine de Emilio Fernández: ¿Vuelta de tuerca o simple tropezón?" In *El siglo de la Revolución Mexicana*, edited by Jaime Bailón Corres et al., 2:215–23. Mexico: Instituto Nacional de Estudios Históricos de la Revolución Mexicana—Secretaría de Gobernación.

———. 2002. "Sergei Eisenstein y Emilio Fernández, constructores fílmicos de México: Los vínculos entre la mirada propia y la ajena." *Filmhistoria Online* 12, no. 3.

Tuñón Pablos, Esperanza. 1992. *Mujeres que se organizan: El Frente Único Pro-Derechos de la Mujer, 1935–1938.* Mexico City: Editorial Miguel Angel Porrúa.

Turok, Marta. 1988. "Amelia Robles." In *Mujeres del sur*, edited by Isabel Molina, 41–44. Chilpancingo: Gobierno del Estado de Guerrero.

Twinam, Ann. 1999. *Public Lives, Private Secrets: Gender, Honor, Sexuality, and Illegitimacy in Colonial Spanish America.* Stanford: Stanford University Press.

"UDCM en el 20 Aniversario de su Fundación, La." 1993. *Acción Femenina* I, no. I (I January): 3–4.

"UFCM en Ocotlán, La." 1940. *Acción Femenina* 5, no. 21 (I October): 12.

Vaca García, Agustín. 1998. *Los silencios de la historia: las cristeras* (Zapopan: El Colegio de Jalisco.

Valencia Castrejón, Sergio. 1996. *Poder regional y política nacional en México: El gobierno de Maximino Ávila Camacho en Puebla (1937–1941).* Mexico City: Instituto Nacional de Estudios Históricos de la Revolución Mexicana.

Valero Chávez, Aída. 1994. *El trabajo social en México: Desarrollo y perspectivas.* Mexico City: Universidad Nacional Autónoma de México, Escuela Nacional de Trabajo Social.

Varley, Ann. 2000. "Women and the Home in Mexican Law." In *Hidden Histories of Gender and the State in Latin America,* edited by Elizabeth Dore and Maxine Molyneux, 238–61. Durham: Duke University Press.

Vaughan, Mary Kay. 1977. "Women, Class, and Education in the Mexican Revolution." *Latin American Perspectives* 4:1–2: 63–80.

——. 1982. *The State, Education, and Social Class in Mexico, 1880–1928.* DeKalb: Northern Illinois University Press.

——. 1990. "Women School Teachers in the Mexican Revolution: The Story of Reyna's Braids." *Journal of Women's History* 2, no. 1: 143–68.

——. 1994. "Rural Women's Literacy and Education During the Mexican Revolution: Subverting a Patriarchal Event?" In *Women of the Mexican Countryside, 1850–1990,* edited by Heather Fowler-Salamini and Mary Kay Vaughan, 106–24. Tucson: University of Arizona Press.

——. 1997. *Cultural Politics in Revolution: Teachers, Peasants, and Schools in Mexico, 1930–1940.* Tucson: University of Arizona Press.

——. 1999. "Cultural Approaches to Peasant Politics in the Mexican Revolution." *Hispanic American Historical Review* 79, no. 2: 269–305.

——. 2000. "Modernizing Patriarchy, State Policies, Rural Households, and Women in Mexico, 1930–1940." In *Hidden Histories of Gender and the State in Latin America,* edited by Elizabeth Dore and Maxine Molyneux, 194–214. Durham: Duke University Press.

Vega, Patricia. 1999. "La casa-museo de Amelia Robles." *Equis: Cultura y sociedad* (June): 35.

Velázquez H., Manuel. 1978. *Pedro Velázquez H.: Apostol de la justicia, vida y pensamiento.* Mexico City: Secretariado Social Mexicano.

Ventura Rodríguez, María Teresa. 1984. "La FROC en Puebla, 1942–1952." In *Memorias del encuentro sobre historia del movimiento obrero,* 227–76. Puebla: Benemérita Universidad Autónoma de Puebla.

Vera, Rodrigo. 1998. "Derechos humanos y democracia, los futuros puntos del conflicto Iglesia-Estado." *Proceso* 1134 (26 July): 22–27.

Villarreal, Magdalena. 1994. Wielding and Yielding: Power, Subordination and Gender Identity in the Context of a Mexican Development Project. PhD diss., University of Wageningen, Koninklijke Bibliotheek, Den Haag.

Villoro, Luis. 1987 [1950]. *Los grandes momentos del indigenismo en méxico.* Mexico

City: Centro de Investigación y Estudios Superiores en Antropología Social-Secretaría de Educación Pública.

Vincent, Mary. 1990. "The Politicization of Catholic Women in Salamanca, 1931–1936." In *Elites and Power in Twentieth Century Spain*, edited by Frances Lannon and Paul Preston, 107–26. Oxford: Clarendon Press.

Vizcaíno, Rogelio, and Paco Ignacio Taibo II. 1983. *Socialismo en un solo puerto: Acapulco 1919–1923*. Mexico City: Editorial Extemporáneos.

Warren, Kay. 1998. *Indigenous Movements and Their Critics: Pan-Maya Activism in Guatemala*. Princeton: Princeton University Press.

Weiner, Myron. 1991. *The Child and the State in India: Child Labor and Education Policy in Comparative Perspective*. Princeton: Princeton University Press.

Weinstein, Barbara. 1997. "Unskilled Worker, Skilled Housewife: Constructing the Working-Class Woman in São Paulo, Brazil." In *The Gendered Worlds of Latin American Women Workers*, edited by John D. French and Daniel James, 71–99. Durham: Duke University Press.

Welter, Barbara. 1966. "The Cult of True Womanhood, 1820–1860." *American Quarterly* 18: 151–74.

Werth, Alvin, O.F.M Cap., A. M. Mihanovich, and Clement S. Mihanovich, eds. 1955. *Papal Pronouncements on Marriage and the Family*. Milwaukee: Bruce Publishing.

Wheelwright, Julie. 1990. *Amazons and Military Maids: Women Who Dressed as Men in the Pursuit of Life, Liberty and Happiness*. London: Pandora.

Wilson, Fiona. 1990. *De la casa al taller: Mujeres, trabajo y clase social en la industria textil y del vestido. Santiago Tangamandapop*. Zamora: El Colegio de Michoacán.

Womack, John, Jr. 1968. *Zapata and the Mexican Revolution*. New York: Vintage Books.

Wood, Andrew Grant. 1998. "Viva la Revolución Social! Postrevolutionary Tenant Protest and State Housing Reform in Veracruz, Mexico." In *Cities of Hope: People, Protests, and Progress in Urbanizing Latin America, 1870–1930*, edited by Ronn Pineo and James A. Baer, 102–6. Wilmington, Del.: Scholarly Resources.

——. 2000. *Revolution in the Street: Women, Workers, and Urban Protest*. Wilmington, Del.: Scholarly Resources.

Yáñez, Agustín. 1963. *The Edge of the Storm*. Translated by Ethel Brinton. Austin: University of Texas Press.

Young, Marilyn, ed. 1973. *Women in the Chinese Revolution*. Ann Arbor: Center for Chinese Studies, University of Michigan.

Zapata, Francisco. 1976. "Afiliación y Organización Sindical en México." In *Tres Estudios Sobre el Movimiento Obrero en México, Jornadas* 89. Mexico City: El Colegio de México.

Zeldin, Theodore. 1994. *An Intimate History of Humanity*. New York: Harper Collins.

Zelizer, Viviana A. 1994. *Pricing the Priceless Child: The Changing Social Value of Children*. Princeton: Princeton University Press.

Zolov, Eric. 1999. *Refried Elvis: The Rise of the Mexican Counterculture*. Berkeley: University of California Press.

Contributors

Ann S. Blum teaches at the University of Massachusetts, Boston. She has published her research on child abandonment, adoption, maternal-child health, and domestic service in *Journal of Family History*, *The Americas*, and *Journal of Women's History*, as well as in anthologies on gender and medicine in Latin America. She is currently completing a book titled *Domestic Economies*, which examines economically marginal families and domestic labor in Mexico City in the late nineteenth century and early twentieth.

Kristina A. Boylan is currently assistant professor of history at the State University of New York Institute of Technology. Her work focuses on gender and religion in revolutionary Mexico.

Gabriela Cano is professor of history at Universidad Autónoma Metropolitana-Iztapalapa in Mexico City. She is coeditor, with Isabel Morant, Asunción Lavrin, and Dora Barrancos, of the multivolume *Historia de las mujeres en España y América Latina* (2005–6). Her book project, *Colonel Robles's Intimate Joy: Gender Battles in the Mexican Revolution* received the Martin Duberman Award of the Center of Lesbian and Gay Studies of the City University of New York and will be published in English.

María Teresa Fernández-Aceves is a research professor at the Centro de Investigaciones y Estudios Superiores en Antropología Social-Occidente, Mexico, in the area of cultural and social history and gender studies. She is the author of several articles and book chapters on women's and gender history, including histories of the Mexican Revolution, women's mobilizations, and women's labor.

Heather Fowler-Salamini, a professor of history at Bradley University, is the author of *Agrarian Radicalism in Veracruz, 1920–1938* and coeditor, with Mary Kay

Vaughan, of *Women of the Mexican Countryside, 1850–1990*, both of which have been translated into Spanish.

Susan Gauss is an assistant professor in the Department of History and the Department of Latin American, Caribbean, and U.S. Latino Studies at the University at Albany.

Temma Kaplan, a feminist scholar and activist, is a professor of history at Rutgers University. She writes about human rights, art and politics, and women's social movements in Latin America, South Africa, Europe, and the United States. Her recent books include *Taking Back the Streets: Women, Youth, and Direct Democracy* (2004) and *Crazy for Democracy: Women in Grassroots Movements* (1997).

Carlos Monsiváis, a leading Latin American intellectual and cultural critic best known for his chronicles of Mexico City and popular culture, has published, edited, and introduced more than fifty books, and written hundreds of essays and articles, including *Mexican Postcards* (1997), the first English translation of his work. In addition to honorary doctorates from several universities and many prestigious literary prizes, he has also received the National Journalism Award, the Mazatlán Award, the Xavier Villaurrutia Award, and most recently, the National Award of Arts and Sciences.

Jocelyn Olcott is the Andrew W. Mellon Assistant Professor of History at Duke University and the author of *Revolutionary Women in Postrevolutionary Mexico* (Duke University Press, 2005). Her current research explores the labor, political, and conceptual history of motherhood in twentieth-century Mexico.

Anne Rubenstein is associate professor of history at York University in Toronto. In addition to many articles, she has written *Bad Language, Naked Ladies, and Other Threats to the Nation: A Political History of Comic Books in Mexico* and *Going to the Movies in Mexico: Cultural Politics in the Post-Revolutionary Era*. She has also coedited, with Gilbert Joseph and Eric Zolov, *Fragments of a Golden Age: Mexican Cultural Politics Since 1940* and, with Victor Macías, *Men's Rooms: Masculinity, Sexuality and Space in Modern Mexico*.

Patience Schell teaches history at the University of Manchester, England. She is the author of *Church and State Education in Revolutionary Mexico City*, as well as of a variety of articles on education and its consequences in Mexico. Her current work examines how male friendship fostered the development of the natural sciences in nineteenth-century Chile.

Stephanie Smith is an assistant professor of history at the Ohio State University. She is the author of several review articles and forthcoming book chapters examining women and gender in Latin America and is currently completing her book manuscript, *Sex in the Cities' Courts: Women during the Mexican Revolution in Yucatán, Mexico, 1872–1930*. Her research focuses on women's participation in shaping the Mexican Revolution, especially through their use of the judicial system.

Lynn Stephen, Distinguished Professor of Anthropology at the University of Oregon, has written extensively on the ways in which political identities articulate with ethnicity, gender, class, and nationalism in relation to local, regional, and national histories, cultural politics, and systems of governance in the Americas. Her three most recent books are *Zapotec Women: Gender, Class, and Ethnicity in Globalized Oaxaca* (2005), *Zapata Lives! Histories and Cultural Politics in Southern Mexico* (2002), and *Perspectives on Las Américas: A Reader in Culture, History, and Representation* (2003).

Julia Tuñón is a researcher at Dirección de Estudios Históricos of the Instituto Nacional de Antropología e Historia in México City. Among other books, she has authored *Women in Mexico: A Past Unveiled* (1999) and *Los rostros de un mito: Personajes femeninos en las películas de Emilio "Indio" Fernández* (2000, 2003).

Mary Kay Vaughan is professor of history at the University of Maryland. Her authored books include *Cultural Politics in Revolution: Teachers, Peasants, and Schools in Mexico, 1934–1940* (1997) and *The State, Education, and Social Class in Mexico, 1880–1928* (1982). Her edited works include, with Stephen E. Lewis, *The Eagle and the Virgin: Nation and Cultural Revolution in Mexico, 1920–1940* (Duke University Press, 2006) and, with Heather Fowler-Salamini, *Creating Spaces, Shaping Transitions: Women of the Mexican Countryside, 1850–1990* (1994).

Index

Ejército Zapatista de Liberación Nacional (EZLN), 32, 241–42, 250, 254, 256–58; Revolutionary Law of Women and, 255, 258, 275; women in, 254–57

ejidos, 200, 242–46, 248, 254; unions of, 249; women in, 245–46, 250

elections, 223–24, 270

Emiliano Zapata Peasant Organization. *See* Organización Campesina Emiliano Zapata

Equal Rights Amendment (U.S.), 223

Erauso, Catalina de, 54 n.11

Escuela Nocturna Doctor Balmis, 68

Estadio Nacional, 59, 72–74

Estrada, Esteban, 51

ethnicity, 83, 109 n.22, 260 n.28; "strategic essentialism" and, 259 n.1. See also *indigenismo*

eugenics, 115, 122

Europe, 50, 57, 59, 163, 203, 271

Excélsior, 47, 64

families: class entitlements to, 132; networks of, 133; public policy regarding, 128–30, 134–35, 141, 235, 271–72; "revolutionary family," 72, 128–29

fascism, 50, 214, 219 n.12, 227, 228, 231, 237, 270

Federación de Sindicatos de Trabajadores del Estado (FSTE), 17

Federación de Trabajadores de Jalisco, 160

Federación Internacional de Mujeres Demócraticas, 18

Federación Regional de Obreros y Campesinos (Puebla) (FROC), 182, 184–85, 188, 191

Federal Labor Law (1931), 158–59, 167, 179 n.30, 185

Federation of State Employees' Unions. *See* Federación de Sindicatos de Trabajadores del Estado

Félix, María, 18, 19, 93

femininity, 7, 10, 11, 15, 19, 266–67; alterity and, 88–89; beauty and, 58, 94; fashion and, 57–76, 120, 124; labor solidarity and, 29, 150; male, 88–89, 264–65, 267; middle-class norms of, 173, 176; working-class, 174–75, 177, 181–83, 193, 265. See also *chicas modernas;* New Women; *pelonas*

feminism, 10, 16, 28, 30, 32, 121, 122, 147; anticlericalism and, 3, 149; Catholic, 217, 269; *feminismo popular,* 251–52, 254, 258; movements linked to, 210 226, 228, 241; opposition to, 106, 202; scholars and, 49, 224; second-wave, 31, 242, 244, 251, 253, 255, 258; teachers and, 112–13, 123; transnational, 15, 53

Feminist Peasant Network, 251

Fernández, Emilio "El Indio," 18, 31, 32, 81–95, 267

Figueroa, Gabriel, 18

Filo del agua, Al, 11

First Red National Feminine League of Acapulco, 230

First Regional Peasant Convention, 243

Flaherty, Robert, 86

Flores, Vda. de Trujillo, 139. 140

Ford, John, 82

Fordism, 23

Fox, Vicente, 259

France, 62, 104, 227; revolution in, 262

Frauenrecht, 51

Frente Nacional para la Liberación y Derechos de la Mujer (FNALIDM), 251

Frente Único Pro-Derechos de la Mujer (FUPDM), 16, 17, 29, 49, 210, 223–38, 243–44, 247

Frías, Heriberto, 2

Froebel, Friedrich, 115

Gabriel Mistral Vocational School, 112–24, 265

Galán, Emma, 217

Galeana, Benita, 16, 252

García, Emilio Riera, 93

index

312

313

314

Ministry of Labor, 153
Ministry of National Defense. *See* Secretaría de Defensa Nacional
Ministry of Public Assistance. *See* Secretaría de Asistencia Pública
Ministry of Public Education. *See* Secretaría de Educación Pública
Mistral, Gabriela, 75, 112, 115, 121; vocational school of, 112–24, 265
modernism, 73
modernity, 22, 71–72, 83, 85; cinematic representations of, 87, 92, 95; cosmopolitanism and, 31, 35, 58; feminism and, 15; family formation and, 130; gender ideologies and, 20, 24, 26–28, 57, 61, 64, 67, 113, 123–24, 158; international, 61–62; technology and, 68
modernization, 83; of domesticity, 102, 104, 108, 113; of production, 163, 182–83, 188–90, 193
Modern Women. See Mujeres modernas
molino de nixtamal. See corn mills
Montenegro, Roberto, 45
Montezuma Seminary, 212
Mora y del Río, José, 204
morality, 118, 135–36, 175, 264; femininity and, 15; secular, 150; religious, 120, 202–5, 214
Morelos, 50, 60; Cuautla, 47
motherhood, 113, 273–74; access to public life through, 133; Catholicism and, 210; celebrations of, 18, 27, 29, 117–18, 121, 142; contestations over, 128, 215, 275; femininity and, 132, 162, 180 n.49; Mother's Day and, 15, 142, 201, 212–13, 273; status and, 132–33; wage labor and, 128, 135, 137–38, 141–42; working-class, 142, 181, 189–92, 269. *See also* maternalism
Mujer, La, 14
Mujer Católica Mexicana, La, 204
Mujer mexicana, La, 3
Mujeres modernas, 61, 63
Muñúzuri, José, 2

Muslim, 262, 267
Murnau, F. W., 86

National Action Party. *See* Partido de Acción Nacional
National Agrarian Commission, 69
National Coalition of Women. *See* Bloque Nacional de Mujeres
National Confederation of Catholic Labor. *See* Confederación Nacional Católica de Trabajo
National Confederation of Veterans of the Revolution. *See* Confederación Nacional de Veteranos de la Revolución
National Council for the Urban Popular Movements (CONAMUP). *See* Consejo Nacional de Movimientos Urbanos Populares
National Education Workers' Union. *See* Sindicato Nacional de Trabajadores de la Educación
National Ejidal Credit Bank, 235
National Feminine Alliance. *See* Alianza Nacional Femenina
National Feminine Committee. *See* Comité Nacional Femenino
National Feminine League, 230
National Front for Women's Rights and Liberation. *See* Frente Nacional para la Liberación y Derechos de la Mujer
nationalism, 40, 59, 75, 189, 241, 242, 264; gender and, 45, 62; motherhood and, 133, 141; national identity and, 84; popular culture and, 81–82, 90–91; revolutionary, 244, 248, 258; women and, 82, 87–88, 91
National League for Defense of Religious Freedom. *See* Liga Nacional Defensora de la Libertad Religiosa
National Parents' Union. *See* Unión Nacional de Padres de Familia
National Peasants' Confederation. *See* Confederación Nacional Campesina

〰️

319

Jocelyn Olcott is the Andrew W. Mellon Assistant Professor of History at Duke University. She is the author of *Revolutionary Women in Postrevolutionary Mexico* (Duke University Press, 2005).

Mary Kay Vaughan is professor of Latin American history at the University of Maryland. She writes and publishes about issues of education and culture, gender, and women in twentieth-century Mexico. With Steve Lewis, she recently edited *The Eagle and the Virgin: National Identity and Cultural Revolution in Mexico: 1920–1945* (Duke University Press, 2006).

Gabriela Cano is professor in the Departamento de Filosofía e Historia at the Universidad Autónoma Metropolitana, Mexico City. She is the author of *Cuatro estudios de género en el México urbano del siglo 19* (2001) and, with Verena Radkau, *Ganando espacios: Historias de vida: Guadalupe Zúñiga, Alura Flores y Josefina Vicens, 1920–1940* (1989).

Library of Congress Cataloging-in-Publication Data
Sex in revolution : gender, politics, and power in
modern Mexico / edited by Jocelyn Olcott,
Mary Kay Vaughan, and Gabriela Cano.
p. cm.   Papers originally presented at a conference
"Las Olvidadas: Gender and Women's History in
Postrevolutionary Mexico," held at Yale University in May 2001.
Includes bibliographical references and index.
ISBN-13: 978-0-8223-3884-0 (cloth : alk. paper)
ISBN-10: 0-8223-3884-x (cloth : alk. paper)
ISBN-13: 978-0-8223-3899-4 (pbk. : alk. paper)
ISBN-10: 0-8223-3899-8 (pbk. : alk. paper)
1. Women—Mexico—History—Congresses.
2. Women in politics—Mexico—History—Congresses.
3. Feminism—Mexico—History—Congresses.
4. Sex role—Mexico—History—Congresses.
I. Olcott, Jocelyn. II. Vaughan, Mary K.
III. Cano, Gabriela.   HQ1462.S49 2006
305.420972'0904—dc22
2006023687